D0435756

THE LIFE OF MARGARET LAURENCE

THE LIFE OF MARGARET LAURENCE

James King

ALFRED A. KNOPF CANADA

PUBLISHED BY ALFRED A. KNOPF CANADA

Published in Canada by Alfred A. Knopf Canada, Toronto, in 1997. Distributed by Random House of Canada Limited, Toronto.

Canadian Cataloguing in Publication Data

King, James
The life of Margaret Laurence

ISBN 0-676-97073-7

1. Laurence, Margaret, 1926–1987 - Biography.
2. Novelists, Canadian (English) - 20th century - Biography.*
I. Title.

PS8523.A86Z7 1997 C813'.54 C97-931058-X
PR9199.3.L38Z7 1997

Printed and bound in the United States of America
First Edition

For the friends of Margaret Laurence,

especially Mary Adachi, Gordon Elliott,
Joan Johnston, Alan Maclean, Jack McClelland,
Mona Meredith and Malcolm Ross

and for my wife, Christine Dalton,
who urged me to write this book

"Now I am rampant with memory.... Each day, so worthless really, has a rarity for me lately. I could put it in a vase and admire it, like the first dandelions, and we would forget their weediness and marvel that they were there at all."

The Stone Angel

Contents

List of Illustrations

Except where noted, these photographs are courtesy of Jocelyn and David Laurence.

Acknowledgments

THIS IS NOT an "official" or "authorized" biography, but I am deeply grateful to Jocelyn and David Laurence for the unqualified support they have given me in writing this book. My arrangement with the Laurences has been simple and straightforward: in exchange for the ability to see and use the unpublished material by their mother of which they hold copyright—particularly her letters to close friends, the unpublished journal and the other unpublished writings—they asked to read my typescript in order to correct any errors of fact. This arrangement has been adhered to strictly. In fact, the Laurences gave me information which supplanted factual errors on my part, but, at the same time, they provided me with further information which has been incorporated into this book. Jack Laurence spoke to me with great candour.

I am grateful to the friends of Margaret Laurence who opened their doors, their memories and, quite often, their hearts to me: Sheila Andrzejewski, Alexander and Delores Baron, Jan de Bruyn, Ian Cameron, Sandy Cameron, Stevie Cameron, Zella Clark, A.O.C. and Jean Murray Cole, Gordon Elliott, Charlotte Engel, Alice Dahlquist Hackett, Penny Jamieson, Peter A. Jordan, Judith Jones, Nadine Jones, Louise Kubik, Alan and Robin Maclean, Wes McAmmond, Jack McClelland, Mona Meredith, Catherine Milne, Catherine Munro, Ruth Parent, the late Olive Pennie, Ken Roberts, Florence and Mordecai Richler, Bill and Anne Ross, Malcolm Ross, Fred and June Schulhof, Dmitry Stone, René and Eva Temple, Leona Thwaites, Michelle Tisseyre, Robert Weaver, Pat Wemyss, Marjory Whitelaw, Alice Williams, and Lois and Roy Wilson. Margaret Laurence's friends in the writing community have been equally generous: Margaret Atwood, Don Bailey, Douglas Fetherling, Timothy Findley, Robert Fulford, Graeme Gibson, Dennis Lee, Alice Munro, Al Purdy, Jane Rule, Miriam Waddington and Budge Wilson. I am grateful to the following for facilitating my research: Bill Gusen, Austin Clarke, Elsa Daniels, Jonathan Lovat Dickson, Greg Gatenby, Ted Kotcheff, Peter D. Laurie, Fred Ofosu, John R. Schram, Shelley Sorin and Tamara Stone.

The following individuals have provided me with important research material: Paul Banfield and Pamela Thayer, Queen's University Archives; Dietrich Bertz, Research Collections, The University of Victoria; George Brandak, The University of British Columbia Library; Gene Bridwell, Simon Fraser University Library; Sarah Cooper, Assistant to Margaret Atwood; A. Denkabe, University of Ghana; Anne Goddard and Michael Stewart, National Archives, Ottawa; Edna Hajnal, Thomas Fisher Rare Book Library, University of Toronto; John Handford, Macmillan Archive; Kent Haworth, York University Archives; Dorothy Henderson, Margaret Laurence House, Neepawa; Chris Hives, The University of British Columbia Library; François Ricard, the Gabrielle Roy trustees; Josephine Sapper, Ghana News Agency; Margaret M. Sherry, Princeton University Library; Linda Simpson, Director of Records, The University of Winnipeg; Barbara Smith-Laborde, Harry Ransom Humanities Research Centre; Apollonia Lang Steele, Special Collections, The University of Calgary; G. Thomas Tanselle, the John Simon Guggenheim Memorial Foundation; Bruce Whiteman, McGill University Library; Douglas G. Worling, St. Andrew's College.

My debts to Margaret Laurence scholars are listed in the footnotes and endnotes. I should like to give special thanks, however, to Greta Coger, John Lennox, Fiona Sparrow, and Nora Stovel. I have learned much from my graduate students: Grazyna Antoszek, Jennifer DeAlwis, Rebecca Gagan, Valentina Gal, Karey Lucas-Hughes and Susan Woods. I should like to give special thanks to Charlotte Stewart and Carl Spadoni, Research Collections, McMaster University Library, and to my two research assistants, Brenda Gunn and Jane Clarke.

This book has benefited enormously from the penetrating but kind guidance of my publisher, Louise Dennys. I am also much indebted to Diane Martin for editing this book with extraordinary precision and tact. Mary Adachi's sensitive and diligent eye went far beyond the bounds of copy-editing.

THE LIFE OF MARGARET LAURENCE

Preface

During Thanksgiving weekend 1986, Margaret Laurence telephoned her friend Lois Wilson, the Moderator of the United Church of Canada, to announce that she was dying and to plan her funeral. A short time later, she sent Lois the following memorandum:

> SUGGESTIONS FOR M.L.'S FUNERAL AND BURIAL
> I would like the following incorporated into the service: 1. Readings: Old Testament: Ecclesiastes 3: 1-12 ("To everything there is a season"); New Testament: Corinthians 1: Ch. 13 ("Though I speak with the tongues of men and of angels"); 2. The Lord's Prayer; 3. Hymns: (a) No. 12 "All people that on earth do dwell", (b) No. 129: "Unto the hills", (c) "Guide me, O thou great Jehovah."

During their final visit together, Margaret was, Lois observed, "grieving, jubilating and raging. She loved life passionately. 'Life is for rejoicing—for dancing,' she said. With tears streaming down her face, out of a mixture of physical weakness and intense emotion, she cried out to me, 'And I've danced. I've danced.'"

Two months later on January 9, 1987—four days after her death at the age of sixty—an emotionally charged "service of worship" in memory of Margaret Laurence was held at a packed Bloor St. United Church in Toronto. (A private funeral was held the day before at Lakefield United Church.) As Lois Wilson put it, Margaret had planned the "place, the form, the hymns, the thrust" of a ceremony which emphasized "grief, memory and hope." Few who were in attendance at Lakefield or Toronto realized that Margaret Laurence had chosen to take her own life in the face of terminal cancer. She chose to die alone. Her recognition of herself as a loner had marked her life since early childhood, yet much of her life had been a battle against solitude.

She was one of the most famous and beloved of Canadians. Still, during the last decade of her life, she had also been reviled, someone accused of being a pornographer. A deeply sensitive and private person, she had been terribly hurt by these accusations since she knew herself to be a truly righteous person, a writer dedicated to exploring human nature in all its various complexities. Since Margaret Laurence had been subject to intense public scrutiny of all kinds, most Canadians felt they had a reasonably good idea of her. The simple fact is that she was an extremely secretive person. We never really knew her.

Margaret Laurence planned the contents and form of her memorial service, as if she realized that this was indeed the last time she would be able to use her gifts as a writer to impose form on the chaos of life and, in this instance, death. Just before she discovered she was dying from cancer, Margaret completed the first draft of her final book, *Dance on the Earth: A Memoir* (published in 1989, two years after her death), where she carefully crafted what she would reveal about herself. The result is much more apologia than autobiography. In it, she tells of some of the circumstances that formed her, but it is self-consciously fictional in that she relates her life history very much in the manner of a novelist telling her readers exactly what she wants them to know—and no more. The result is deliberately evasive. Nevertheless, Margaret's strong beliefs on a number of vital social issues (nuclear war, abortion, mothers and children) are clearly defined.

Dance on the Earth remains a shadowy book, one in which the complexities of the autobiographer's existence are scarcely hinted at. Readers who, before they read it, may have been puzzled by the circumstances of the famous writer's life, remained so. Knowing the limitations that she had imposed, Margaret began on her sixtieth birthday another substantial (as yet unpublished) journal in which she addressed some of the issues not answered in *Dance*:

> I have not published an adult novel since 1974, & although I have since published a book of essays & 3 books for children, the worried ones either are not aware of this fact or point out that the last book was published in 1980. What has happened to Margaret Laurence?

Margaret's reflections were interrupted by the discovery of cancer, her illness and death. In large part, this book deals with her own unanswered question and, of course, with many of my own: for example, who was the real Margaret Laurence and how did she become the most renowned writer in Canadian literary history?

My interest in Margaret Laurence—whom I never met—began with my awareness that there was a considerable gap between her public presentation of herself as a pleasant, ordinary, middle-aged woman and the extraordinary gallery of strong, self-willed women she created in her fiction. What was the link between Margaret Laurence and her heroines? For example, was Margaret Laurence at all like Hagar, the most formidable and yet most loved woman in all of Canadian fiction?

The more I investigated her life the more I became fascinated—and haunted—by a woman who changed dramatically through the course of her life: from the willowy beauty of Neepawa, to the young, wifely Peggy, to the determined writer, Margaret, and, finally, to the stout dowager of Lakefield, Margaret Laurence, the celebrity.

I discovered a woman of many complexities, of considerable elusiveness. There was the young writer who was convinced that readers would hate *The Stone Angel*: "No seductions. No rapes. No murders.... It is the work of a lunatic, I think. It has hardly anything to recommend it to the general public." There was the ground-breaking writer who led the way for other women—even though she was deeply troubled by the conflict between being female and a writer, between being a wife and a writer, and between being a mother and a writer. There was the older woman, who having sacrificed so much to become a writer, reluctantly accepted the fact after she completed *The Diviners* that she had nothing more to say. In a very real sense, Margaret Laurence refused to strike out, to produce inferior books. She tried to make the words come but to little avail. Painful though it was to wind up as a non-writing writer, she accepted her new status with both deep regret and considerable grace.

Margaret Laurence, who knew full well that she would someday be the subject of a biographer such as myself, once observed to the novelist Marian Engel: "I would rather have people read my *work* than be entertained by me in person or pore over the details of my life, which has actually been pretty sedate, but when I come to think of it, it has always seemed very very dramatic to me." To another close friend, Gordon Elliott, she once observed: "One's writing is not meant to be bound up with one's life, but only jerks believe this." The inner world of Margaret Laurence was intense and filled with drama, and her writings are intimately interconnected with her life. More than that, hers is the very human story of a woman's struggle to find—and define—herself in a male-centred world.

For me, researching and writing this extraordinary life became a journey filled with surprises. I assumed I would discover a powerful and strong person reminiscent of the enormous strength and vitality that is readily visible in Margaret's heroines. I did find that person. I assumed I would gain even further insight into her legendary generosity. I did. I assumed Margaret's grit and determination were strong elements in her character. I now know this to be true. What I was perhaps not prepared to discover—and look at—was the extent of Margaret's anguish and suffering, of her incredible insecurities, of the many ways in which she punished herself, of the loneliness and isolation in which she dwelt nearly all her life.

Margaret Laurence was a person of many secrets. Like most of us, she could be unreasonable, cruel and vindictive, but she carefully hid her dark side, in large part because she felt compelled to live up to the expectations of her many devoted admirers. After all, a person who becomes lionized sometimes feels compelled to fall in line with the resulting burdens of adulation. Margaret Laurence was in reality a much more gutsy, sensuous and self-willed person than her public image allowed. Indeed, she was very much like Hagar and Morag. The adversities she herself faced went into the making of all her heroines, each of whom is a mixture of great strengths and great weaknesses—a reflection of the powerful, vibrant and tormented woman who wrote the Manawaka novels.

Part One

PEGGY

"That house in Manawaka is the one which, more than any other, I carry with me."

A Bird in the House

I

Blood Child

(1926-1930)

The little girl's first memory was of the kitchen of her maternal grandparents' house. Cupboards loomed over her four-year-old head as she struggled to lug her tricycle up the back steps leading off the kitchen. An aunt helped her negotiate the trike along the hall at the landing. The youngster's goal was to pay a surprise visit to her mother, who was resting in a bedroom. The little girl wheeled her birthday present to her mother's side and told her how delighted she was with it. For Margaret Laurence, that incident in childhood's past remained forever bathed in a luminous present: "My mother, lying in the grey-painted double bed, smiled at me. Her face is white and her dark hair is spread out across the white pillowcase. She touches my face, my hair."

Verna, Margaret's mother, was the sixth of seven surviving children —Stuart, Ruby, John (Jack), Rod, Margaret (Marg), Verna and Velma (Vem)—born to John and Jane Simpson (an eighth died in infancy). John was a legendary figure in Neepawa, Manitoba, where he spent most of his life. The epitome of the self-made man, he was shrewd, enterprising and uncompromising. He was usually respected, sometimes admired and almost always disliked. He was not a person to bow to the bad opinion of others, however. His stern demeanour, accentuated by his steely blue eyes, thrived in opposition, due in large part to his sense of having succeeded in life against insuperable odds.

John Simpson.

Sometime in the 1870s, John, who was born in 1853 in Milton, Ontario, where he trained as a cabinet-maker, decided he might better prosper if he settled in Portage la Prairie, Manitoba, where a cousin sold men's clothing. The young man, virtually destitute, made his way by Red River steamer to Winnipeg but walked the rest of the fifty miles to Portage la Prairie. There, he worked with his cousin and met Jane Bailey. They married in 1886, and two children, Stuart and Ruby were born there. The small family lived in cramped quarters above the clothing store; after four years they decided to move to Neepawa.

The charter of the town had been granted only seven years before the arrival of the Simpsons in 1890. Six years before that, in July 1877, a group of thirty settlers from Listowel, Ontario, reached Palestine (now Gladstone), Manitoba. About half of the group decided to remain there, but the fourteen members of the Graham family continued on to what is now the town of Neepawa. The first homestead was on a high, well-drained plateau overlooking a valley where two creeks join to form the Whitemud River. Although this locale is relatively flat, the first settlers found the surrounding landscape pleasantly hilly. By 1883, the town was fully settled: it had seven grain elevators and was on the CP-CN line to Edmonton.

By the 1920s, the Neepawa John Simpson had helped to make had progressed from a mud-spattered prairie village of lumber buildings to a substantial town of tree-lined streets with magnificent municipal buildings, such as the sandy-coloured brick Beautiful Plains County Court Building—a monument of High Victorian architecture, the two-storey Empire Block, the Opera House and the Land Titles Office. All of these buildings on Hamilton Street, Neepawa's main street, gave the town an imposing grandeur. In the thirties, the Opera House was renamed the Roxy, and its exterior was stuccoed to give it an Art Decoish appearance. Intersecting Hamilton Street was Mountain Avenue with more office buildings and shops; this street was also home to some magnificent houses as well as St. James Anglican Church and Neepawa United Church.

Mountain Avenue, Neepawa. 1906.

Mountain Avenue divided the town into north and south and into rival commercial groups, with the possession of the rail line giving a decided edge to the north side. The houses on the north side, the domain of the business and professional classes, were certainly more spacious and bountiful. Surrounding the town were a variety of farms, some bestowing great wealth on their owners, others allowing their inhabitants only a subsistence existence.

From the start, Margaret was aware of the distinction between the "right" (north) and "wrong" (south) sides of Neepawa: "I ... walk past the quiet dark brick houses, too big for their remaining occupants, built by somebody's grandfathers who did well long ago out of a brickworks.... The timber houses age fast, and even the brick looks worn down after fifty years of blizzard winters and blistering summers.... This is known as the good part of town. Not like the other side of the tracks, where the shacks are and where the weeds are let grow knee-high and not dutifully mown, and where a few bootleggers drive new Chevrolets on the strength of home-made red biddy."

The cemetery above the town and its stone angel are Margaret's most celebrated re-creations of her birthplace, as in this eerily beautiful sentence: "In summer the cemetery was rich and thick as syrup with the funeral-parlour perfume of the planted poppies." For Margaret Laurence, her childhood world was lushly beautiful, but it was infused with the menacing presence of death.

In Neepawa, John Simpson built and ran both a furniture store and a hardware store. His skills as a carpenter led this enterprising man to establish a third business: casket-maker and, as a consequence, funeral director. When, about ten years later in 1903, his family had increased in size and his various enterprises had flourished, the family moved from a flat above one of the stores to the north side of

"The Brick House," 312 First Avenue, Neepawa. Now the Margaret Laurence Home.

town: 312 First Avenue, a solid two-and-a-half-storey buff brick house incorporating many of the features of Italian villa architecture. This was the "Big House" or the "Brick House": "plain as the winter turnips in its root cellar ... part dwelling place and part massive monument." Whether writing about her grandfather in fictional guise or in autobiography, Margaret depicts him as a wounded bully, imprisoned within his own narcissistic vulnerability; and the house as the epitome of its owner: large, imposing, forbidding.

She was deeply fond of her grandmother Jane, whose Empire Loyalist family had abandoned the United States for Amherstburg, Ontario. Later, a branch of the Baileys moved to Portage la Prairie, where Jane met and married John Simpson. If her grandfather was all sharp edges, Jane was for her granddaughter a gentle, unassuming woman with a distinctly artistic sensibility, which she bestowed on the interior of the Big House: "The works of her art were all around us in the Simpson house, and remained so long after she died."

In Margaret's judgment, John was the harsh, acerbic patriarch who imposed his will upon his wife and family. Another granddaughter, Catherine Simpson Milne (fourteen years older than Margaret), flatly contradicted her cousin's memories. To her, John had been a courtly, indulgent, only occasionally petulant grandparent. Her grandmother, she also observed, was a far shrewder, more manipulative person than Margaret ever allowed. Jane Simpson, she recalled, developed a number of subterfuges (albeit silent ones) to get around her husband's grumpy attempts to control her (according to one account, he curbed any tendency for her to purchase on impulse by not allowing her to carry any money on her person when she went shopping alone).

Margaret's uncle Stuart, the eldest child, felt obliged to go into business with his father, a decision which caused him great unhappiness, especially when he had to take on the duties of undertaker, a profession he loathed. Catherine Milne, his daughter, recalled that he was an especially sensitive man, very different in temperament from "wicked" Uncle Jack who served in both world wars, moved to Hollywood where he was a horseman in *Lives of a Bengal Lancer* (1934), and married, according to family lore, three or four times. Another uncle, Rod, the third son, was not rebellious: he served in the Great War, became a pharmacist and eventually settled in Oregon.

Olive Pennie, Verna's closest friend, insisted there were two generations of daughters in the Simpson family. Yet, Margaret Laurence in her autobiography never emphasized the disparity in age between Ruby (b. 1888) and Margaret (usually called Marg; b. 1890) on the one hand and, on the other, Verna (b. 1896) and Velma (known as Vem; b. 1902). According to Olive, the older two had the sober, haughty temperament of their father, whereas Verna and Vem were fun-loving and playful, more like their mother in personality.

In fact, Ruby and Marg treated Verna and Vem more like daughters than sisters. Of John Simpson's seven children, only his two older daughters were prepared to battle him openly. In fact, as very young women, Ruby and Marg had determined to become professionals, and they expected—and received—their father's (sometimes limited) support in their endeavours. Even a patriarch as unremitting as John Simpson knew when he had met his match. Margaret Laurence, who was subjected to Ruby's acid tongue on many occasions, truthfully characterized her Aunt Ruby as bossy and interfering, very much her father's daughter. Once, offended by the sexuality of some of her niece's characters, Ruby, as her father no doubt would have, asked her niece: "Why do you write such stuff?"

Once, Verna was forced by Ruby and Marg, who had invited some friends from Winnipeg to lunch, to dress as a maid and to serve the meal to the most exacting standards of etiquette. There was a strong sisterly alliance between Verna and Vem, as Margaret Laurence was well aware: "I have a picture of Verna taken with her younger sister. She must be about ten and Vem was about four. Vem is standing on an upholstered armchair, clad in a frilly ruffled dress. Verna stands beside her, one arm protectively around the youngster." In photographs, Verna sometimes looks a bit dour, but in this instance the camera is lying. Everyone who knew Verna was entranced by her sprightliness, especially her sparkling laugh.

John Simpson understood the practicalities of life, and he had no real objection to Ruby leaving home in order to train as a nurse. Although Marg was an outstanding student in high school, her father saw no reason for her to take a general arts course at university. A bit more compliant and silent than Ruby, she settled for teacher training and then took a post in Calgary. Her independent spirit can be seen in her decision, at the age of thirty, to go to Bermuda. This turn of events was later described with gleeful and malicious pleasure by Margaret Laurence: "That year away must have been a great adventure, and an unusual step for a young woman from a small Canadian town. Her father undoubtedly ranted and stormed over her departure. I can just hear my grandmother saying in the placating way that I remember so well, 'Now, John, now John,' her hands fluttering in distress."

Earlier, in 1914-5, eighteen-year-old Verna enrolled in the Domestic Science course at Manitoba Agricultural College, south of Winnipeg. She could only attend for a year because her father complained he "did not feel like paying good money so that his daughter could learn to cook." The following year, in opposition to their father's harsh behaviour, Ruby and Marg insisted on moving their mother, together with Verna and Vem, to Winnipeg so that Verna could pursue her real interest—the piano. There, she took lessons, but Verna, whose health was delicate (she had missed Grade 8 with scarlet fever), had appendicitis at the end of the school year, at which point Jane and her two youngest daughters returned to Neepawa.

Verna lived at home and taught piano. In 1922, she became engaged to a lawyer, Robert Wemyss, who was a year and a half older than she and was an almost compulsively friendly man, the complete opposite of Verna's father. Upon their engagement they composed a letter together to his sister. It began: "Verna is sitting on my knee so please excuse the scrawl. I should have told you 'Nous sommes engagé,' if you can guess what that means." Verna is teasingly demure: "You've got a nut of a brother, haven't you? But nevertheless am forced to admit am most awfully *keen* on him. Am not really sitting where he said I was." According to Bob, she was telling a white lie: "She is! We are both broke but happy. For the love of pete, don't show this letter to the neighbours." Margaret Laurence took great joy in this letter, as it showed the gleeful love that existed between her parents.

Bob's grandfather had been a tea merchant in Edinburgh in the 1870s. According to family lore, when his partner cheated him, he headed for Canada, settling in Raeburn, Manitoba, with his wife and all their children except one. The eldest, John, stayed on at Glasgow Academy and was supposed to serve as an apprentice lawyer with his uncle, Sir John Wemyss, in India. When Sir John died unexpectedly, John abandoned Scotland for Canada in 1881, articled in Winnipeg, and then settled in Neepawa, where he became the town's first lawyer (he incorporated the town in 1883). Although he died two weeks after she was born, Margaret was deeply proud of her paternal grandfather: "He was the only person in Neepawa at that time, and possibly at any other time, who could read the Greek tragedies and comedies in the original ancient Greek." John's wife, Margaret, the daughter of a physician, was the great-granddaughter of Dr. David Harrison who came to Manitoba from Ontario by Red River cart. He entered politics, became Manitoba's minister of agriculture in 1886 and even premier for a few weeks in 1887-8 when his predecessor resigned. Grandmother Wemyss was renowned for her icy, acerbic behaviour.

Margaret Laurence was deeply proud of her Scots ancestry, to which she attributed her love of life and the accompanying Celtic gloom. However, her sense of being Scots was not a central part of her early consciousness; it was something she came deeply into touch with in early middle age: "No one could ever tell me whether my family had been Lowlanders or Highlanders because no one in the prairie town where I grew up seemed very certain exactly where that important dividing line came on the map of Scotland. I decided, therefore, that my people had come from the Highlands. In fact, they had not, but Highlanders seemed more interesting and more noble to me in every way ... I do not remember at what age the disenchantment set in, but gradually I began to perceive that I was no more Scots than I was Siamese. Whatever of the Old Country had filtered down to me could roughly be described as Mock Scots. The Scotland I had envisaged as a child had been a fantasy, appealing because it seemed so much more bold and high-hearted than the prairie town where I really lived."

Late in life, Margaret was often said to have the appearance or look of a native person. Although she would have been proud to claim such ancestry, there is no evidence to link her to such a genealogy. In 1980 or thereabouts, Margaret encountered a drunken couple on the bus from Toronto to Lakefield. She cast the encounter in the form of a mini-play which she sent to Adele Wiseman.

> *Lady*: (scrutinizing me closely; I have high cheekbones and slightly slanted eyes inherited from my long ago Pictish and Celtic ancestors.) I know what you are! You are one of those damn people from Vietnam or Taiwan! That's what you are. Boat people! One of them. [Margaret explains that she is from Manitoba.]
> *Lady*: Manitoba! Jeez! Well, now I know what you are. I shoulda' known. Yer a half-breed, one of those goddamn half-breeds. Admit it! You are!
> *Me*: Madam, if I were a Métis, I would certainly not deny it. I would be proud.

In a letter to Adele Wiseman of May 17, 1981, Margaret made this comment when speaking of a white person who had costumed herself as a native: "But I am not an Indian and have this strong feeling that it is a kind of insult to *them* to be a make-believe one—I have known a number of whites who have tried to become make-believe Indians or Africans. Trying to understand and respect is one thing; trying to change one's own background is quite another."

Bob's family's professional background was markedly different from Verna's. The Wemysses were members of the Senior Bridge Club whereas Simpsons played at the Junior Bridge Club, an important class distinction in a small town such as Neepawa. (The imposing Wemyss house was on the north side of Neepawa, one street away from the Simpson residence.) Bob evidently became a lawyer by default, not choice; he was

Wemyss house, 483 Second Avenue, Neepawa.

destined from birth to follow in his father's footsteps. Other, crucial decisions were apparently made for him. His father had no faith in prairie schooling for his eldest son and enrolled him in St. Andrew's College, Toronto. However, there is some evidence he was sent to boarding school because he was a rebel; his daughter nurtured the fond wish that this piece of gossip had a basis in fact: "One family legend, perhaps apocryphal, had it that Bob was something of a hellion and was sent to St. Andrew's because the local teachers couldn't handle him. I always hoped myself that was the real reason." After St. Andrew's, Bob became a lawyer, but the Great War intervened while he was articling.

An exceptionally sensitive person, Bob felt a great deal of shame about a childhood accident when he fired a BB gun which deprived his brother Jack, three years younger, of the sight of one eye. He remained deeply protective of his younger brother, with whom he enlisted in the Canadian Field Artillery in Winnipeg in 1916. In the surviving photograph from that time the brothers, aged twenty-one and eighteen, look like enterprising, slightly bashful young men about to go off on a big adventure. For Margaret Laurence, another photograph of the two, who stayed together during their time in the army, taken two years later in France, told a completely different story: "The only traces of a uniform are the clumsy puttees on their legs and their tin hats.... Around their necks they each carry a small battered bag containing a gas-mask. But it is in their faces and their eyes that the greatest contrast with the other picture is evident. Their expressions are wary, bitter.... Back home in Canada they will regain some of the appearances of youth, but these will be appearances only." After the war, Bob completed articling with his father, who then took him in as a partner.

Verna and Bob did not marry until July 25, 1924, probably because they felt under pressure to save money and buy a house. When they did so, they purchased on the south—wrong—side of town. Not much is known about the emotional life of this young couple. Without doubt, Bob, who enjoyed manual labour, would have preferred the life of a

"The Little House," 265 Vivian Street, Neepawa.

carpenter to that of a lawyer. And, certainly, his daughter believed he had been badly shaken by his war experience. In contrast, Verna had high spirits, which even John Simpson had not been able to break. The Wemyss's marriage was a love match, although one of opposites. Verna's spontaneity offset her husband's melancholia—perhaps getting him back in touch with the "hellion" side of his nature, whereas Bob's gentleness must have been a welcome relief to Verna from her father's harsh intrusiveness. It was to these two people that Margaret Laurence was born on July 18, 1926 at Neepawa General Hospital at 7:30 on a Sunday evening.

Verna Simpson Wemyss.

"My mother's idealization of her perfect child, me, is amusing and touching." This was Margaret Laurence's response to Verna's entries in *Mother's Record of Baby from birth to five years of age*, a gift from great-grandmother Harrison to the baby, who was named Jean Margaret in honour of her two grandmothers.

Verna was the kind of mother who was attuned to every aspect of her only child. One day she was so engrossed in playing with Peggy—as the baby soon became known—she forgot to make dinner. On August 23, she was particularly gratified that her daughter's first conscious "notice" was of music; the baby laughed on October 14 and took her first step at fifteen months. Beyond her careful attention to the baby was the mother's obvious pride in everything her child did:

> At ten months, saying Mama, Dada, "bow-wow," pretty.
> At thirteen months trying to say practically every thing.
> At sixteen months talking well, & putting 3 or 4 words together.
> At two years telling us "she was crazy about beet greens." ...
> Informed us she had "a bad little twinkle in her eye."
> Said to her mother in speaking of a bad night she had had, "Don't let's mention it, mummy." (2-1/2 yrs)

> A great imagination. Speaks a lot of her "funny house," where "paper slim, & Mr. & Mrs. Slim live, also sister "Polly," of whom she speaks, play "Three Bears" a lot, with herself as "Tiny," her mummy as "Mammy Muff," & her daddy, "Father Bruin."
> Starts her stories always "once upon a time."

Entries under "First Confessions of Wrong-Doing" and "First Punishment" are left blank. In fact, Verna's entries, like the ones cited above, emphasize the baby's lively response to words and the verse and stories that can be created from them: "Very fond of listening to little rhymes at 1-1/2 yrs. At twenty-two months knew several herself. Loves looking at picture books. At 2-1/2 exceptionally fond of being read to." Verna did not record her worry about Peggy's constant sucking of her thumb and fingers (she was concerned about the resulting shape of her mouth). She sewed up the sleeves on her sleepers, but the toddler always found a way around this barrier. To all who encountered them, the young mother's joy in her happy, exceptionally intelligent and talkative baby was obvious. The reader of Verna's entries would not gather that Peggy had her sober side, but photographs taken when she was two and four show a slightly sad, certainly reflective little girl.

Peggy Wemyss and Mona Spratt, both aged two, Neepawa. 1928.

Margaret Laurence's memory of taking the tricycle to her mother's bedroom was her first and last of Verna, who died at the age of thirty-four of an acute kidney infection two days after her daughter's fourth birthday. Her single remembrance of her mother was linked to the tragedy of her death. Although Peggy was never told directly by her father or aunts that her mother was gravely ill and, later, that she had died, she had from the first intuited something was drastically wrong. As soon as her mother became ill, she went to stay with her uncle Stuart, his wife, Bertha, and their daughter, Catherine. One night, Bertha put Peggy to bed, but the little girl would not settle because "Peggy Noni," a flannelette rag to which she was attached, could not be located. Without success, Bertha tried to find a substitute. Peggy would not calm down and, finally, Uncle Stuart walked the mile to the Wemyss house to fetch it.

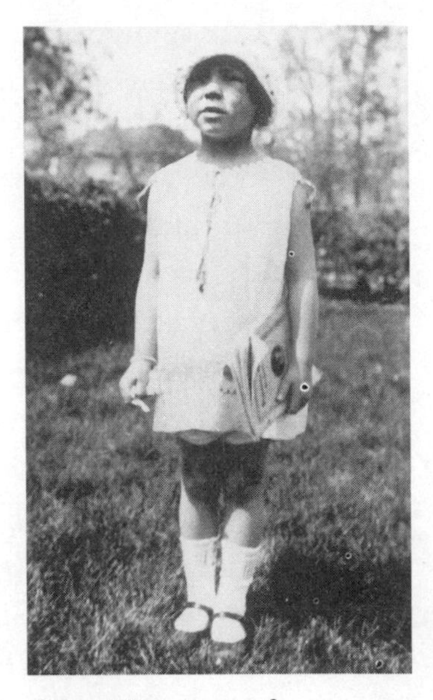

Peggy Wemyss, age four, Neepawa. 1930.

Catherine Simpson, then eighteen, looked after Peggy during the days immediately following Verna's death. To her surprise, the four-year-old showed almost no emotion, except when a five-year-old friend confronted her with the news. Of this event, Margaret Laurence had a clear recollection:

> I am back home at the Little House and I am playing outside with my friend from across the road. We are tramping around in our rubber-boots, in a ditch that contains a few inches of rain-water. The muddy, weed-filled water is a sea. Neither of us has ever seen a sea.... My friend is a year older than I, and so of course much smarter. I follow her lead gladly, proud that she will play with a

little kid like me. Suddenly she looks at me strangely, almost with a frightened expression.

"Your mother's dead," she says.

She has undoubtedly been told not to say this to me. She is five years old, and not at an age for keeping secrets.

I stare at her. Then I get very angry.

"She is not! You're telling a lie! Liar! Liar!"

I run inside the house...

Once, over breakfast, Margaret Laurence's friend, the writer Sylvia Fraser, having read that children who lose a parent at an early age are "'blood' children because that shocking severance of the blood tie creates a psychic wound that time never heals," related this theory to Margaret, "who remained enigmatically silent in the face of one more crude attempt to pigeonhole her." Yet, Sylvia Fraser noticed, she would frequently burst into tears when told of tragedy and injustice: "I wondered if the tears she so generously shed for strangers were a kind of stigmata of the soul." Crude theory or not, she was deeply wounded by the death of her mother. Towards the end of her own life, she once again mourned the loss of that delicate young woman: "I am so much older now than she ever became. Sometimes I think of her as my long-lost child."

About a year after Verna's death, Peggy accompanied Uncle Stuart, Aunt Bertha and Catherine to their cottage at Clear Lake, a wild, rustic place sixty miles north of Neepawa. As they approached the Simpson cottage, the rain beat down mercilessly, making the road impassable. Stuart and Bertha told the children they would have to walk the remaining half-mile. Peggy took the news calmly, got out of the car, but then quickly removed her new raincoat and placed it on her doll. Outraged, Bertha ordered her to place the coat back on herself. Defiantly, the little girl refused. Howling her rage at such an unjust request, she cradled the doll and ran away into the wood.

2

Snapshots

(1930–1935)

The next five years of Peggy's life passed by in a blur, but there were intense moments etched forever in her memory. The first was of Aunt Marg's new role in her life. After Verna's death, Marg, who had been home from Calgary for the summer holidays, decided to remain behind in Neepawa in order to look after her motherless niece. Mona Spratt, Peggy's closest childhood friend, remembered that she heard her parents saying that the Simpson family had decided only a woman from the Simpson family could raise Peggy. For about a year, Marg lived in the little back bedroom, Bob in the bedroom he had once shared with Verna, and the little girl in her attic room. This arrangement, which hinted of scandal in a small town, lasted just over a year, at which time Marg and Bob were married in a civil ceremony. He was thirty-seven, she forty-one. Later, in her wry, detached way, Marg told Peggy she had worn a green dress and "that some of the good ladies of Neepawa had kindly informed her that green was an unlucky colour to be married in." There was also a common belief in the town that "a man was not supposed to marry his deceased wife's sister." Years later, Margaret Laurence, who realized her father's second marriage was not one of youthful ardour, did not envision it simply as one of convenience: "They joined in a marriage that was marked both by mutual need and by mutual respect and deep affection.... They married not just to look after me but to look after each other."

Margaret Simpson Wemyss, age sixteen.

In Margaret Laurence's recollection, "Mum was never my stepmother. She was just my Mum." This is undoubtedly true, but the stepdaughter's memory fails to capture some of the intricacies of the past. As *Dance on the Earth* reveals, there were many silences—never broken—between Peggy and her new mother. For example, the girl never felt comfortable expressing any strong feeling, such as anger, to Marg. Years later, Margaret Laurence put it this way: "I can only guess at how she felt." At about the age of five, however, Peggy, without prompting, began to call Marg "Mum": "She told me when I was older that she and my dad were so pleased and relieved, not to say grateful" at this turn of events.

Catherine Milne remembered when Peggy began to call Marg "Mum," but she also noticed the word "Mother" was reserved exclusively for Verna. In Catherine's opinion, there was a world of difference between her two aunts. She herself venerated Marg but adored Verna. She was also of the opinion that Marg was a much more demanding mother than Verna would have been. For example, excellence in school was important to her whereas Verna, she was certain, would have paid more attention to her daughter's feelings. Put simply and realistically, Marg was a much more reserved, withdrawn person than Verna. In surviving photographs of the two sisters, Marg has a demure, poignant and reflective countenance, whereas Verna's face is charged with feeling. Emotionally, Peggy was—and remained—Verna's daughter.

Marriage had never been a real option for Marg before her younger sister's death, but she was a woman for whom responsibility was *the* core issue. Without doubt, Marg's gentle presence brought genuine comfort to Peggy. Later, Margaret Laurence commented that she appears "small and sad" in photographs taken after her mother died, whereas she is joyful in those taken after Marg had married Bob: "In those pictures, I am a perfect little poser but I'm always grinning quite self-consciously."

In the "Baby Book," Margaret Laurence could plainly see the differences in her two mothers: "The entries (except for [the] fourth birthday ... and the fifth birthday, when the book stops, babyhood over) are in my mother's handwriting, so much like my own sprawling penmanship and so unlike the even and beautifully formed handwriting of her sister, my aunt and stepmother." In this passage, written near the end of her life, she perhaps unconsciously highlights her affinity with her birth mother.

One of the early photographs is of Peggy's first day of school. She stands outside the Little House, shy and a bit withdrawn. She clutches a notebook to one arm, her straight hair held in by a barrette, one leg placed tentatively in front of the other. According to family memory, she had been ill the day before, having eaten some green tomatoes. Her own recollection of that day was a bit different: "I was pretty annoyed I didn't learn how to read after one whole day."

Although she was—and remained—an excellent student, Margaret Laurence's own memories of her past centred on her precociousness in reading, writing and observing. First, there was the "Blue Sky" and "Funny House" of Peggy's imagination, the latter filled with all manner of playmates and dishes. Later, she staged her dramas in an actual playhouse built by her father. "It wasn't a tiny little Peter-Pan-and-Wendy effort. This was the real thing. It had a sloped roof and was about the size of a largish woodshed, big enough for an adult to stand up straight in. Dad had even equipped it with windows that opened and window boxes planted with various perennials." By Grade 3, Peggy the writer came into being, when she began writing stories down; by Grade 5 she had scribblers filled with both prose and verse. At about this time, Marg made an important suggestion to her daughter: she advised her to write of what she knew and observed rather than concocting tales of medieval lords and ladies.

In her own recollections of her youthful coming into being as a writer, Margaret never highlighted her inquisitiveness. As a young child, she became famous for asking difficult, embarrassing questions, of defying the conventions of what could be asked and, in turn, told, especially in a small town. Somewhat obscured in her autobiography—both as girl and woman—was also her incredible sense of herself as strong and reliant, and most significantly, of being from childhood a person of ruthless determination. Margaret Laurence liked to skip over—and, if she could get away with it, hide—this side of herself, perhaps because she imagined, despite the example of Marg and Ruby, that ambition was perceived as a male attribute.

One persistent memory of Peggy's childhood was of her father as photographer. She was particularly fond of one photograph showing her and Marg, in about 1932, beside a barnstormer plane: "Mum is holding her hair against the wind with one hand. I'm next to her, a little kid in a short dress and coat, white socks and black-buttoned shoes, who's just had her first ride." In another photograph from this time, a sad, shy and apprehensive Peggy seeks refuge in her genial father's comforting arms.

Robert and Peggy Wemyss.

She also remembered how adept her father was with his hands. One Christmas gift was her first, tiny desk: "He had found it in the attic and had repaired and painted it turquoise-blue for me. It was possibly the most beloved desk I have ever owned. It had chains on either side that let down the writing side and pigeon-holes to hold important stuff." In a writer's life, this is a crucial moment, but in her memories of her father she stresses, quite accurately, the great pleasure he took in manual activities. Those who knew Bob well are certain carpentry was his real vocation. His qualities of mind did not make him happy in the profession of law, and in 1930 he had to endure the death of a dearly beloved wife.

If he was a disappointed man, Bob made a good job of hiding it. Mona Spratt recalled how indulgent he was when she and Peggy visited his office. He actively participated in—as well as encouraged—their shenanigans, as the two little girls climbed on his desk and, in general, left his office a mess. And Bob had an instinctive way of dealing with Peggy, as when he taught her to swim: "He had taken me into the shallow water in Clear Lake, supported me with his hands for a minute or so, then removed his hands and said, 'Okay, now swim.'"

From May 1933, another face, that of a baby boy, makes its appearance in the family album. In *Dance on the Earth*, Margaret Laurence mentions her new brother was named Robert Morrison Wemyss "after our dad. I had been an only child for seven years. A baby brother! I was overjoyed. Overjoyed, that is, until I realized that a baby is a demanding creature, and that your mum has to spend a lot of time looking after this kid.... Mum might have

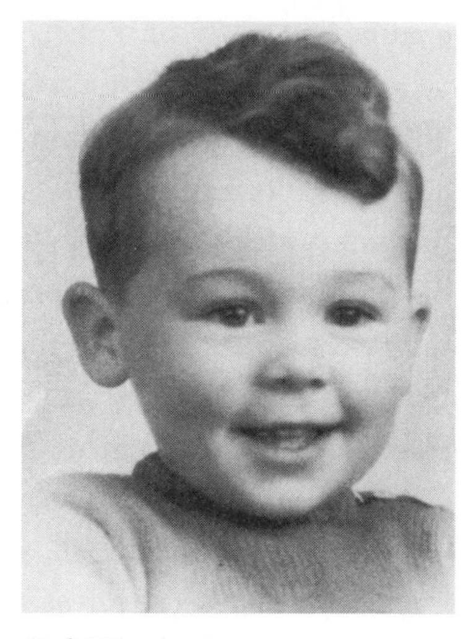

Bob Wemyss.

been more nervous ... than she would have been if she had been a younger mother. She was in her early forties when he was born, after all." These sentences give the reader the totally incorrect impression Bob was born to Bob and Marg. The reality is that he was born in Winnipeg on May 21, 1933 and adopted by the Wemysses shortly thereafter. Mona's parents told her the baby boy was adopted so Peggy would not be an only child; he was to keep his elder sister company. Although Margaret knew he was adopted, she felt Bob was as much a brother as if he were a blood brother.

Sibling rivalry seems to have been minimal, although Peggy once remembered giving him a hard pinch. Marg came running out of the house. "'What's the matter, is Bobby all right? Peggy, what's happened?' I leaned nonchalantly against the wicker baby carriage. 'Gee, I don't know.' She never questioned me." In "To Set Our House in Order," the birth of a baby boy causes disruption in the life of his sister, but he is described benignly. When the reader meets him, the "small creature" is lying in his cot, "with his tightly closed fists and his feathery black hair."

In 1934, the Little House, which had become too small, was abandoned in favour of the Wemyss house at 483 Second Avenue. (After her husband's death, Grandmother Wemyss moved to Winnipeg to live with her daughter, Norma.) Before that, the Wemyss home had become for Peggy a mausoleum, a grim monument to past glory and her grandmother, its custodian, a crusty matriarch, who besides having unreasonable expectations of her elder son, was tetchy to everyone she encountered. Margaret Wemyss's bedroom, as described in her granddaughter's story "To Set Our House in Order" was filled with "stale and old-smelling air, the dim reek of medicines and lavender sachets." The living room "was another alien territory where I had to tread warily, for many valuable objects sat just-so on tables and mantelpiece, and dirt must not be tracked in upon the blue Chinese carpet with its birds in eternal motionless flight." Moreover, the exterior of this big red-brick house, built in the late 1800s and in a bad state of repair, was large and imposing to the little girl. The Virginia creeper, which covered its front, added to the house's sinister appearance. This was relieved somewhat by a round, rose-coloured window on the second storey; the front door had set into it a pane of glass with colours which also appealed to Peggy.

The large kitchen, built to be staffed by servants, was cumbersome to use. The little girl, eyeing enviously the delicious sandwiches and cakes distributed at her mother's afternoon teas, was a bit annoyed at being excluded from such largesse when town ladies gathered in the living room. The room of the Wemyss house she adored was her father's study, which had bookshelves holding all of his copies of *National Geographic* magazine. There were some additional comforts. The family had two dogs, Jerry and Jock. Bob, a dedicated gardener, was renowned for his gladioli. For Peggy, nevertheless, the Wemyss residence remained her grandparents' house; it never became her real home.

One childhood friend, Phyllis Ralph, recalled happy memories of being with Peggy in the attic in the Wemyss house and, especially, in the backyard playhouse built by Bob. However, she also remembered how fraught her friend could become: "We would play in [the backyard] by the hour. I remember one day ... there was a terrible thunderstorm. It was wicked. She started to scream. I can see her screaming yet. She was scared skinny. I can see her dad coming out with his coat over his head to rescue her and carry her in. Me, I walked along behind him. Peggy was very hyper." Phyllis and some other children took her to the nearby fairgrounds: "We used to take Peggy up there because she'd scream so. Terrible! There were always bats flying around. I don't think there were electric lights in there. It was dark. We'd tell spook stories." This was likely the same group that gave her the nickname "Piggy" until "she smacked one of the kids across the face." At the end of her life, Margaret Laurence, perhaps recalling such incidents of youthful insensitivity—and the fact she was perceived as "different" by her childhood playmates, said: "I really am an aberration. I was always a lonely child."

More than anything else, Neepawa was primarily for Peggy a place of death. In January 1935, Robert Wemyss came down with pneumonia. Shortly after the onset of his illness, Marg moved to the guest bedroom:

"My father had been sick for only a few days when I asked Mum one evening if I could sleep with her. I was uneasy.... She agreed. Dad was in his and Mum's room, attended by two of our local doctors. When I woke up in the middle of the night, my mother was crying, and I knew my father was dead." She felt helpless. She also wanted to protect her mother, but she was not sure against what. When Verna had died five years before, Peggy had felt abandoned in the face of death, and this time she responded in a similar way when her father died on January 13.

> I remember being angry at the minister who came to give his condolences and support.... All I knew when I was nine was that my dad had died, my Mum was bereft, and my brother was still just a baby, too young, really, to understand. It was difficult to return to school and be stared at by the other kids, and hard to accept my teacher's expression of sympathy. I was desperately afraid of crying and so must have seemed merely sullen and withdrawn.... That surly, often angry mask was my only defence. I could not, would not break up. I and Mum had to carry on somehow.

Here, although the strength of the little girl is plainly visible, her vulnerability is also apparent. She assumed an angry face to greet the world, afraid of letting others know how frightened she really was—and perhaps making herself even more subject to the cruel whims of fate.

Peggy the child used anger creatively to keep despair at bay. As an adult, Margaret Laurence often kept such feelings in check. She was remarkably similar to her father in her kindness, generosity and warmth, but, like him, she tried to hide her fears from others. Her jovial exterior was genuine, but it concealed the tormented inner little girl who had suffered the trauma of the loss of both birth parents.

In "A Bird in the House," Margaret Laurence fused the worlds of fiction and autobiography in these simple, beautiful words, the final snapshot in her childhood album of loss and abandonment: "After a while the first mourning stopped, too, as everything does sooner or later, for when the limits of endurance have been reached, then people must sleep."

3

Horses of the Night (1935-1939)

> We didn't stay in the big red-brick house for long [after the death of Bob Wemyss], but we were still there when the polio epidemic happened. Perhaps I make this sound as though my childhood years were rife with medieval plague, death right, left, and centre. It wasn't like that at all, of course. I remember a lot of very happy things.

Peggy's young heart had been scarred by cruel wounds, her early existence filled with tragedy, but, like many children in similar circumstances, she had to get on with the business of life. "Sometimes," she realized, as she contemplated her youthful self, "your pain is so great, although possibly unacknowledged, that you have nothing to lose; you are fearless because you don't care what anyone says or does to you." At the age of nine, nevertheless, the volatile side of Peggy began to disappear. In part this was because Marg did not like displays of temper. She once told Peggy she had a "carrying voice," even though, the daughter remembered, "She could summon up a pretty good carrying voice herself. Even deadlier were her quiet sermons when things became so rough that yelling wouldn't cut any ice."

Another memory of this time was of the two menacing boys who lived next door. Her "burning fury" sometimes scared these two off when they attempted to invade her garden, and Marg encouraged her daughter not to act as a victim. Then, one of the boys, Gavin, came down with polio and died: "I had been afraid of those kids and managed to drive them off, but I wouldn't have wished or imagined either of them dead. Kids like me didn't die. But they did. They do. I had scared Gavin away and he had died." One can imagine how Peggy felt, wondering if doing battle with Gavin had somehow led to his death.

Peggy resented the fact that Marg made her visit the graves of her parents at the Neepawa cemetery, where the Wemyss plot, in spring, was surrounded by peonies. For the remainder of her life, she hated those flowers.

The little girl was relieved when Marg sold the Wemyss residence and moved her two children back to the Little House, where Peggy was delighted to have her attic room restored to her. She returned her blue desk to the "corner where it had always belonged." Still, she realized, "[t]hings could never be the same." A doctor and his family purchased the Wemyss house and covered it with yellow stucco. This angered her, even though she hated the place. "I hadn't actually loved that house at all.... But I vented my bewilderment and rage at fate by refusing ever to walk down that street in Neepawa again."

Although Peggy's "bewilderment and rage" at the injustices she endured in her young life were driven inward, her resiliency soon surfaced, in large part because she wanted to help and comfort Marg. Sometimes, as she observed, the sleep of oblivion is a much-needed comfort.

There were happy times, as Margaret Laurence insisted. Radio serials provided much enjoyment to Peggy and her friends. "We all had Little Orphan Annie secret codes and badges and rings and other enchanting junk." They also had "Big Little Books" in which they inscribed their own secret codes. Of course, there were secret hiding places and buried treasures. A friend of Marg, Gertrude Johnson, the superintendent of the Neepawa hospital, made Peggy a child's first-aid kit, fitted into a wooden cigar box: "She'd painted the box with a white cross on the top. It held real stuff from the hospital: rolls of bandages, absorbent cotton, scissors, a thermometer, Mercurochrome ... Mona and I and our friends made great use of this kit in our games. At this point, my ambition was to be a nurse, and naturally I needed no persuasion to treat the slightest scratch on my young brother or my friends." Miss Johnson also persuaded a local carpenter to make Peggy a tool bench, complete with a vice. "Girls," she recalled, "were supposed to be strictly interested in dolls, but I wasn't alone in my love of carpentry." She constructed a number of bread boards in the "shape of a portly and simplified pig and made gaily painted scenes from what I imagined to be life in other countries—a Dutch windmill, a Chinese pagoda." Peggy did not neglect the scribblers she carried everywhere with her: "I was writing, too, all the time. Clumsy, sentimental poetry, funny verses, stories, and once a highly uninformed but jubilantly imaginative journal of Captain John Ball and his voyages to exotic lands, complete with maps made by me of strange, mythical places."

At the age of eleven, Peggy bought her first bicycle from Bert Batchelor, the milkman. She walked out the several miles to his farm to pick it up, and he also provided her with her first and only lesson in using it. She wobbled it around the farmyard a few times. Then Bert pointed her in the direction of town and gave her a little shove. "I was off. No one has ever learned to ride a bike more quickly. By the time I had reached home, I had pretty well mastered the art. What I had forgotten, though, was how to stop, but a ditch near our house solved the problem."

At about the same time, Peggy made her first long train trip to Toronto to visit Aunt Norma, who had moved to Newmarket. Ruby Simpson, who was attending a conference in Quebec, accompanied her niece part way. The little girl was enchanted with the glamour of the event: meals in dining cars, porters, ladders to upper berths. During her stay in Ontario, she was taken with her aunt's warmth and her funny stories, her uncle Mord's tales of his exploits as a bush pilot in northern Manitoba and her cousin Terry's eager friendliness. As before, Grandmother Wemyss's austere behaviour, very much in the mode of John Simpson, frightened the little girl. So perhaps did the two car accidents she witnessed on the car ride from Toronto to Newmarket. Norma was "terrified" that the blood and bodies on the road would scar Terry and Peggy. The car sped on, and Peggy didn't think she took it all in. To her, "only deaths in the family seemed real."

The deaths of her sister and, later, her husband also left indelible marks on Marg Wemyss, who, in the midst of the Depression, had to cope on her own with two young children. If, as is probable, she had in part become a teacher in order to evade the net of Neepawa, her life from 1930 changed markedly. Before the death of her sister, Marg had spent a great deal of money dressing stylishly. She had also been noted for her keen intellect, which could sometimes wander into a sharp turn of phrase. Marriage and children softened her, bringing to the surface her warm and compassionate side. Independence, once a much cherished ideal, was further removed from her in 1935 by another death, this time her mother's. Now, she also had to worry about the management of an increasingly pernickety father.

For three years, Marg maintained a semblance of autonomy at the Little House, but, in 1938, she was forced by financial constraints to move her small family to the Big House. For her, this was a particularly grim and ironical turn of events, as she now had to minister to her father without benefit of the consoling presence of her mother. In turn, Peggy was compelled to live in the house associated with the bitter memory of her mother's death. Moreover, for the first time, the young girl was exposed on a daily basis to the domestic tyranny of John Simpson.

Neepawa is in most ways a typical Prairie town. The winters can be desperately cold and long, the summers exceedingly hot and humid. The civic buildings are suitably impressive, the residential streets wide and lined with handsome trees. The very ordinariness of Neepawa is sedate, even comforting. Alice Munro, who visited Neepawa for the first time in the summer of 1996, was astonished not by the physical differences between it and her hometown of Wingham, in southwestern Ontario, but by the sheer luxury of the Simpson house (now the Margaret Laurence Home) as compared to the shabby house in which she grew up. But that is not how Peggy Wemyss saw things. Compared to others, she lived in a relatively spacious home, but to her it was a cage. And the Manawaka she later ripped from the flesh of Neepawa is a hothouse of stifled feelings.

Even as a child, Peggy was a keen observer of her native town, noting the incredible discrepancies between appearances and realities. She had the eye of the artist, who understands that existence is an uneasy mixture of pleasure and pain. In Neepawa resided a heart of darkness, which the young girl knew intimately.

In the fiction of Margaret Laurence, there is no greater villain than Grandfather Timothy Connor in *A Bird in the House*, a portrait based on her grandfather Simpson. In many ways, he is a Canadian King Lear, a man whose weaknesses, transmogrified into vindictive, wilful cruelty against his family, are the stuff of tragedy. He was also a powerful character, a man of steadfast determination and will. In her entire life, the contradictory strains in no other person ever fascinated Margaret Laurence quite as much. From her grandfather came many of her own strengths, both as a person and as a writer. Margaret Laurence, who created so many strong-minded heroines, never really liked to envision herself as similarly empowered, in large part because she would have had to acknowledge she shared some traits with John Simpson. In 1938, she began to be drawn into a relentless war with this demagogue.

In "The Mask of the Bear," from *A Bird in the House,* Vanessa MacLeod sometimes—to herself—called her grandfather, "The Great Bear": "The name had many associations.... It was the way he would stalk around the Brick House as though it were a cage, on Sundays, impatient for the new week's beginning that would release him into the only freedom he knew, the acts of work." The young girl is also repulsed by any sign of affection or need by the old man, as when he tells her that his wife has died: "Then, as I gazed at him, unable to take in the significance of what he had said, he did a horrifying thing. He gathered me into the relentless grip of his arms. He bent low over me, and sobbed against the cold skin of my face."

"Suppressed unhappiness." This was Peggy's catch-phrase for the first year in the Simpson house. She began to sleepwalk. For the remainder of her life, she never forgot the feeling of panic that invaded her when she awoke from such episodes, accompanied as they were by the feeling she was going mad. The girl, knowing the horrible situation confronting her mother, tried to be stoic, but this was a demanding chore, especially when she overheard Marg, in despair, saying to her friends, "He'll outlive me."

Peggy Wemyss, about age fourteen.

In addition, like many teenagers, Peggy felt awkward. In a photograph taken when she was about fourteen, she clings to her pet dog, her face scowling a bit at the intrusive photographer. She looks slightly apprehensive, as if afraid of any new turn of event.

In her mind and heart, there was a bitter contrast between her dead young father and her immortal-seeming grandfather. In *Dance*, she mentions that her beloved, messy playhouse was moved to the back of John Simpson's property, where it resided near "the huge and lengthy woodpile, Grandfather's pride, that stood in three straight, military-like ranks." So invasive was her grandfather that Peggy needed physical and psychic space apart from him.

At the age of twelve, she recalled, the Playhouse "changed its function. It became my study, my refuge, my own private place."

Under the huge branches of the enormous spruces that bent over the playhouse's gently sloping roof, she found an ideal retreat, where she could read and write for many uninterrupted hours. She was drawn to adventure stories, which allowed her to imagine herself in a variety of foreign lands and dangerous situations: Conan Doyle's *The White Company*, Kipling's *Kim*, Stevenson's *Kidnapped* and *Treasure Island*, Twain's *Huckleberry Finn*. She did not spurn books about girls, even though they were not as plentiful. Lucy Maud Montgomery's *Anne of Green Gables* gave her great pleasure as did Gene Stratton-Porter's *A Girl of the Limberlost* and *Laddie*, a book which reduced her to tears. Nellie McClung's Pearl Watson novels—set in Manitoba—appealed to her: "The indomitable Pearl, holding the family together against vast difficulties, must have been to me what people now call a role model. Pearlie was young but she was brave and strong. She had humour and wit, and she put up with no nonsense from snobs." As a youngster, she was also taken with Montgomery's *Emily of New Moon*: "Both Anne and Emily were rebels—intelligent, talented girls who were not about to be put down. Emily had the added appeal of wanting to become a writer—*no*, of actually *being* a writer, as I myself was."

Sometimes, Peggy, the would-be writer, was more compliant than Anne, Emily and Pearl. Under duress, she took music lessons. She declared a preference for the guitar, but Marg considered that instrument vulgar. So she had to suffer the embarrassment of being the only student learning to play the violin in the cavernous Oddfellows' Hall. She did her best, even to quivering her left wrist to achieve a semblance of vibrato. Her vision was poor, and she had to squint to see the music; the resulting sounds were "ear-boggling." "I hated that damned violin," she recalled, "but what kept me from saying so was that my Mum put such stock in my learning how to play." Marg felt an obligation to expose Verna's daughter to music, but she desisted when Peggy—in her first year of high school—finally confessed her desire to quit. "She had done her best by her dead sister. I had shown I was not musically inclined."

In order to evade violin practice, she found a new refuge, this time the loft above the garage that housed her grandfather's Buick. "There was an outside staircase to this loft, and I had discovered that I could hide away better there than in the playhouse. It was more inaccessible to the adult eye." Inspired by the apothecary in Willa Cather's *Shadows on the Rock*, she grew herbs there and, under John Simpson's watchful, approving eye, marketed them. As Mona Spratt, Peggy's closest friend, recalled, he was delighted she and Peggy were finding a way to make money; he was not aware that the two girls had also become nefarious thieves of the local crab apples. However, Peggy soon fell afoul of him when she lit candles in the dark, spooky loft. Fearful of a fire in such a potential powder keg, he had cautioned her against doing so. "We naturally ignored this order and regularly lit candles until one day my grandfather invaded the sanctuary and discovered the candle stubs. He raged for days."

Peggy's bedroom in the Big House had once been her grandmother's, although it had been redecorated for Peggy by Marg. Off this was a small dressing room, where, one day, Mona and Peggy combined firecrackers with the ingredients of a chemistry set. The resulting "Gunpowder Explosion"—as the fracas became known—blew glass all over the small room and brought an enraged John Simpson up the stairs. Peggy was often quick to take revenge, as on the day she was preparing her grandfather's dinner. She told the friend assisting her: "He likes the meat well done. Burn it!"

In her little dressing room, there were some old books, including, unbeknownst to the adults, *What Every Young Married Man Should Know* and *What Every Young Married Woman Should Know*. From these texts, Peggy gained her first "scientific" knowledge of sex, although she immediately realized—"even at [my] tender age"—that the one sentence she could recall, written by a man, had to be wrong: "Fortunately for the survival of the race and of civilized society, women do not need to feel any physical interest in sex." At the age of twelve, in 1938, she longed, in the wake of Frank Sinatra's popularity, to faint and swoon, as did some of her friends, at the mere mention of his name. She was "too proud and shy" to do this and, a bit reluctantly, was captivated by the more childlike romance of Disney's *Snow White and the Seven Dwarfs.* She even constructed her own miniature dwarfs' house out of a wooden apple box.

For Peggy, her childhood "could be said," she claimed, to have ended that summer and autumn. Her account of the events leading up to that turning point is cryptic:

> That summer I visited a much loved-cousin and his family on their farm, north of Riding Mountain. It was a sad visit in many ways. I was dreadfully homesick. I knew my cousin well because he had gone to high school in Neepawa, but I didn't know his brothers and sisters or his mother. Although they were all very kind, I felt shy and lonely except when Bud and I went to the hayfields beside the vast lake. He would talk to me there when his work was finished, and tell me of his dreams for the future. He had originally wanted to go to university, but this was the Depression and he'd been forced to return to the farm. He still hoped, somehow, sometime, to get out of his present situation. I didn't know what to say. We both knew there was no money and no likelihood of any. I felt inadequate, too young to say anything to help or even comfort him, yet old enough to understand his tragedy.... His eventual release was only another enslavement. He joined the army.

Lorne "Bud" Bailey. c. 1935-36.

Lorne—always known as Bud—was the son of William Bailey, the brother of Jane Bailey Simpson, Peggy's grandmother, and Frances, née

Porter, who had emigrated to Canada from the United States. Bud (b. 1915), one of seven children, wanted, as a young man, to find his destiny away from Bluff Creek, the family farm north of Riding Mountain.

In her story "Horses of the Night" Margaret Laurence provided a harrowing depiction of Bud's stay at the Big House, where his ambition to make something of himself was cruelly undermined by John Simpson, who had reluctantly taken his wife's nephew into his house. When Chris, as he is called in the story, first arrives, Mrs. Connor prepares a special meal. An incensed Grandfather Connor says, within Chris's hearing, "Potato salad would've been plenty good enough. He'd have been lucky to get it.... Wilf's family hasn't got two cents to rub together. It's me that's paying for the boy's keep." During subsequent encounters with Grandfather Connor, Chris is determined not to hear, and thus react, to his insulting behaviour.

> The method proved to be the one Chris always used in any dealings with my grandfather. When the bludgeoning words came, which was often, Chris never seemed, like myself, to be holding back with a terrible strained force for fear of letting go and speaking out and having the known world unimaginably fall to pieces. He would not argue or defend himself, but he did not apologise, either. He simply appeared to be absent, elsewhere. Fortunately there was very little need for response, for when Grandfather Connor pointed out your shortcomings, you were not expected to reply.

Behind his angular, thin, handsome face Chris never betrays anger. Not only is Vanessa taken with his cheerful stoicism in the wake of Grandfather Connor's bad manners, she also responds to her cousin's imagination when he tells her of the wonders of his childhood home at Shallow Creek.

Chris's ambitions do not lead him very far in Manawaka. He abruptly leaves the town but drops in occasionally over the following years. At various times, before returning home, he peddles vacuum cleaners and magazines. After her father's death, Vanessa visits Shallow

Creek, where the reality of the farm is far different from Chris's lyrical descriptions of years before. Vanessa, who wants to form a close bond of some sort with Chris, realizes the ten-year difference in their ages has created an insuperable barrier: "I could not speak even the things I knew. As for the other things, the things I did not know, I resented Chris's facing me with them." Later, in the concluding portion of the narrative, Vanessa learns that Chris, who has joined the army and been stationed in England, had been discharged because of a mental breakdown and, later, ensconced in a provincial mental hospital: "He had been violent, before, but now he was not violent. He was, the doctors had told his mother, passive."

Vanessa cherishes Chris's hopefulness, and his genuinely creative imagination in which he transforms the dross of his life into something enchanting and magical. His desire to become an engineer reflects his wish to escape from desperate circumstances: "Have you ever seen a really big bridge, Vanessa? Well, I haven't either, but I've seen pictures. You take the Golden Gate Bridge in San Francisco, now. Terrifically high—all those thin ribs of steel, joined together to go across this very wide stretch of water. It doesn't seem possible, but it's there. That's what engineers do. Imagine doing something like that, eh?" Chris's old nags at the farm are transformed by him into sleek race horses, but, as the story concludes, Vanessa's mind dwells on another image, that of the horses of the night, wild beings whose irrational wills lead them to self-destruction.

Vanessa MacLeod does not state that she is physically drawn to her cousin, but the story is suffused with her ripening sensuality. Her cousin's kindness and goodness, in marked contrast to Grandfather Connor, remind her of her gentle father, who is dead when the story comes to a conclusion. In 1976, Margaret Laurence, at the age of fifty, wrote an elegiac poem, "For Lorne," included in the small collection of verse at the end of *Dance on the Earth*. Here, where she was much more direct about the passionate side of her attraction to her second cousin, she also revealed her awareness of his tragic life.

After Grade 12, Bud, always known as a "snappy" dresser, was apprenticed to a jeweller, but he could not make a go of it. As early as 1936—when Peggy was ten—he had shown signs of schizophrenia. He would be taking part in an ordinary conversation and would then start speaking of something else. Sometimes, he became violent. At Bluff Creek, there were several episodes—at least one involving pitchforks—when he "scared everybody." He, like the fictional Chris, joined the army, was discharged and confined to a mental institution in Brandon. Later, he took up farming, but his subsequent life was one spent in various mental institutions. He died in 1996.

As a young woman, Peggy was a hapless witness to Bud's fate; as an older woman she imagined the possibility of helping Bud. She romantically envisioned that the two of them "could have loved/wed" almost as if she could have enabled Bud to put aside his mental afflictions. He was the first man to whom she was sexually attracted, but, in the process, she learned of love's complexities. He was a gentle, optimistic person, but there was also within him a psychic wildness which could not be tamed. Through him, she became aware of the soft, compassionate side of love, but, she became gradually aware that his imagination and his escape were part of his mental illness. She would have liked to have had within herself the power to cure and redeem him, but, as girl and woman, she sadly knew this was not possible. In 1939, at the age of thirteen, her innocence slipped away when she came to the realization she could not destroy the barriers between herself and Bud, when it first dawned on her that the redeeming power of love is limited.

4

A Prairie Flower

(1939-1944)

Once upon a time, long ago in 1940, there was a prairie flower named Peggy Wemyss. She was fourteen years old and she had just acquired two things—her first boyfriend and a knowledge of touch-typing at the Neepawa College Institute. The first proved not to be of lasting value in her young life. The second proved to be one of the smartest things she ever did. Why? Because she was a writer.

WITH SOME CONSIDERABLE affection, Peggy is commenting on her young, somewhat gauche self. The boyfriend was Donald Strath, who like Bud Bailey, was an outsider to Neepawa. His family lived some distance away on a farm, and he stayed—six miles from the town—with his aunt and uncle while attending Neepawa Collegiate. Peggy thought he was "heroic because he had a black stallion that he used to ride to school, day after day, month after month, in all seasons. He was a couple of years older than I was." According to her friends, she was fascinated by Donald because he was an outsider.

A year later, in 1941, she was attracted to "young Johnnie" Simpson, born and raised in California, who came to Neepawa determined to join the RCAF, for which he was technically not qualified since he was an American citizen. Captivated, Peggy cherished him as "My American Cousin." Marg was flustered by Peggy's interest, "Johnnie being the son of her charming & much loved & sort of black-sheep brother. Grandfather was churlish, as usual."

Outwardly, Peggy had changed a great deal. Although more serious about schoolwork and more concerned about the war in Europe than most of her girlfriends, she wanted to "fit in" and she did. Her close friendship with Mona remained constant, but her group of friends expanded to include Louise Alguire, Margery Crawford, Alice Dahlquist and Anna Rowe, Donald's cousin. She joined the Babushka Club, named for the headgear worn by the Ukrainian women in town, but their babushkas were brightly coloured, not the traditional black. At Margery's home, Peggy and her friends would drink freely from Mr. Crawford's booze and then fill up the missing portions with water. At the ages of sixteen and seventeen, Peggy was known for her placid exterior, although one night, when she was playing bridge at Mona's, she suddenly—for apparently no reason—threw her cards on the table and left.

Like many of her friends, Peggy felt stymied by Neepawa, especially by the rituals of small-town prairie life in the forties—rituals that had changed little over the decades. Every Saturday night, inhabitants of the town and surrounding farms congregated on Hamilton Street. Men would drop into public houses to drink, teenagers would fill the soda parlours, and a wide assortment of people attended the movie at the Roxy. Along the street, Peggy and her friends would sit in Mona's father's darkened car, watching the various processions—illuminated by the lights emanating from the various establishments—come and go on their appointed rounds. The trouble with this was the relentless sameness in these sightings week after week. These young women feared their lives would never begin, that they would be stuck forever in Neepawa.

At the very same time Peggy assimilated herself comfortably into a circle of friends, her desire to write became more focused and determined. Her first typewriter, a small Remington portable nicknamed Victoria, was purchased for fourteen dollars. Peggy had saved seven dollars from her Saturday afternoon job at Leckie's Ladies' Wear, Marg had provided the rest. At this time, Peggy submitted a piece called "The Land of Our Fathers" to a *Winnipeg Free Press* competition—in which the name "Manawaka" makes its first appearance. Years later, she retained a sketchy memory of this piece of juvenilia: "The only part of the story I recall was a sensational scene in which the young pioneer wife delicately communicates to her husband that she is pregnant by the tactful device of allowing him to arrive home and witness her making a birch-bark cradle." Her typing skills were not yet up to par: "My aunt's secretary very kindly performed this service for me and only once, when I entered the office unexpectedly, did I catch her and my aunt mildly chortling."

A few months later, a story of hers called "The Case of the Blond Butcher" was printed in the young people's section of the Saturday edition of the *Winnipeg Free Press*. It was a murder story in which it turned out that no murder had been committed. She also received her first fan letter. "It was written in purple ink and it was from a boy in Winnipeg. I was so embarrassed I didn't know what to do, so I threw it in the kitchen woodstove before Mum could see it and I never told a living soul."

The aspiring writer was not always so modest, but she was often silent. In class, she hardly ever spoke, although Mildred Musgrove's memory contradicts the impressions of the other teachers. In Mildred's English and typing classes, Peggy was outspoken, determinedly so. Alice Dahlquist—Peggy's only serious rival for top grades (Peggy was the superior student in English, history and French, whereas Alice topped her in mathematics and science)—recalled the strong glimmer in her rival's eyes when she raised her hand to speak in English class.

Mildred Musgrove was renowned for her no-nonsense approach to teaching (Alice Dahlquist never saw her smile in class and was once flabbergasted to see her laugh at a tea party), but her enthusiasm for English literature—especially poetry—was contagious. Peggy felt "as though a whole series of doors were opening in my mind." The two became close, "fighting the old Gestetner together" to put out the school newspaper, *The Black and Gold*. They would get covered "with pungent and gooey black ink in the process." Peggy recalled: "For the last couple of years of high school, I edited that paper. I don't think anyone else wanted to and I certainly needed no urging. Mildred Musgrove was the guiding spirit."

Peggy was never put off by the acerbic persona Mildred assumed for teaching purposes. For one thing, her manner bore a superficial resemblance to character traits of Aunt Ruby and Grandfather Simpson. However, Peggy could see beyond this to a woman who had a passionate love of writing, someone who felt women had the right to be ambitious. In addition, Mildred assured Peggy that the literary calling was not only a wonderful way to enact ambition but also a suitable profession for a woman, sentiments shared by Marg Wemyss who was actively involved with the Neepawa Library, particularly the selection of titles.

English literature and the school newspaper were the chief joys of Peggy's high-school experience. "I remember practically nothing that I learned in other courses. Mathematics, geometry, algebra were my nemeses and I barely scraped through." Later, she resented how history was taught only from the anglophone point of view, one that presented Louis Riel, Gabriel Dumont and Big Bear as villainous outsiders.

> I studied the Manitoba School Act of the late 1800s without having the faintest idea of what it actually meant, namely that in my own native province, some of my ancestors had been responsible, directly or indirectly, for depriving the quite large French-speaking populace, both whites and Métis, of their language rights, not only in provincially supported schools but also in the provincial legislature and the courts.

Margaret Laurence became aware of the serious flaws in her early education in history; Peggy Wemyss did not know of these deprivations. Yet, even as a teenager, she felt an instinctive identity with history's outcasts.

She also became aware—almost at a subliminal level—of her own destiny as a writer, when she read Sinclair Ross's novel of prairie desolation, *As For Me and My House* (1941): "I would have been 16 years old. I saw, reading it, that a writer *could* write out of a background similar to my own. You didn't need to live in London or New York."

Her column for *The Black and Gold* was called "I am Nosy" and there is no question that her journalistic inclinations meant she was, to a degree, the outsider looking on and judging the activities of others. She was also aware of the fact she dressed and looked like the other girls but somehow incorporated different standards. "I was," she recalled, "excruciatingly shy and tried to conceal it under a somewhat loud-mouthed exterior. I had a thirty-two inch bust at a time when Betty Grable had made it a shame, if not a downright disgrace, for girls not to have breasts like overripe cantaloupes." Peggy also resented the so-called rules that governed female existence: "Girls were supposed to flirt, to play hard to get, while all the time wangling the chosen male into their perfumed clutches."

From Marg and Mildred, she had learnt a different system of female values, but, nevertheless, she was a teenager caught up in the need for the approval of her peers. "All of us girls who didn't look exactly like one of the glamorous Hollywood movie stars (and who ever truly did?) would try desperately to fix our hair in fashionable, stiff, sausage-roll curls, getting sore scalps in the process from the nightly application of tightly rolled tin curlers." Conformity extended to the skating rink, one of the principal arenas of social activity.

> If you were a girl, and lucky, boys would ask you to skate with them and hold hands. If a boy liked you a lot, or even some, he might ask you to go for coffee or a Coke afterwards ... and then walk you home. After the second or third time, unless he was fresh and tried the first time, he might kiss you. After the fifth or sixth time, you would stand on the doorstep, the pair of you, doing such necking as was physically possible, given a temperature of 30 to 40 below, Fahrenheit, and the vast amounts of heavy clothing you both wore. No one's virginity was seriously threatened on those winter evenings, but we were a hardy lot and managed slightly more proximity than anyone hailing from softer climes would have believed possible.

Peggy was an adept skater, but found ballroom dancing, which she was taught by a refined lady who offered classes to the children of the genteel—if impoverished—middle class, an impossible skill to master. She also resented the gowns, borrowed via Aunt Ruby from a wealthy Neepawa family, that she was forced to wear to dances when she was fourteen and fifteen. Her first high-school dance was a particularly "grim experience" at which only the president of the school council—out of a sense of duty—asked her to dance. Before going to that event, she and Marg had a tiff when the teenager wanted to wear powder and lipstick. "My mother thought otherwise. Her daughter was going to succeed socially, was going to look like a million bucks, but by heaven, she sure wasn't going to look cheap."

Temperamentally, Peggy was different from even her closest friends. Her loss of her birth parents marked her apart from most of them. Her growing awareness of herself as a writer—as an observer of the lives of others and thus as someone who searches those lives for fodder—(an occupation she never tried to conceal) was a further demarcation. Much of the dissatisfaction she felt at the time had to do with her grandfather. She never really stood up to him—perhaps did not know how to do so—and was later angry at herself for never having openly confronted him regarding his atrocious behaviour. For her—rightly or wrongly—strait-laced John Simpson epitomized Neepawa and so, naturally, she vented much of her anger on the town. Sometimes, she ignored the influence of the town; for example, in *Dance*, she downplayed the valuable journalistic experience she gained at the *Neepawa Press* during the summer of 1943, when she was seventeen years old.

One other, curious aspect of *Dance on the Earth* is that Margaret, in re-creating her adolescence, does not emphasize her attendance at the United Church, a crucial part, she later claimed, of her ancestry. As young women, Louise Alguire and Mona Spratt were very conscious of the different denominations to which they belonged: Louise and Mona Anglican, Margie Street Presbyterian, Peggy Wemyss United. Since, in the young woman's mind, the United Church and John Simpson may have been synonymous, she could only separate the two from each other many years later.

Peggy was also keenly aware of almost invisible class distinctions within her circle. The Depression had reduced the value of the various Simpson businesses, and Bob Wemyss's premature death left Marg strapped for money. Not surprisingly, John Simpson was a tightwad who offered almost no financial support to his beleaguered daughter and her two children. The Alguires were a wealthy family whose fortunes were not unduly affected by the fluctuations in the economy. Mona's father was a successful commercial traveller, a pharmaceutical representative. Although the Spratts did not have a house (they lived in a flat on Mountain Avenue in the centre of Neepawa), they had a large disposable income. Mona had beautiful clothes to compliment her film-star looks, whereas Peggy's clothes often barely passed muster.

Her early womanhood was spent under yet a further shadow. The war in faraway Europe sucked up into its vortex all the young men of Neepawa, and many never returned. The horrors of Dunkirk and Pearl Harbor were very real to her and all her friends: "When I was in Grade Eleven, there were only two boys in our class. By Grade Twelve, there were none. They were all at war." More than most of her contemporaries, Peggy was heavily involved in the war effort, actively espousing the sale of war stamps in her editorials and becoming an ardent saleswoman of them in the town. She even knitted three socks, wondering later if some unfortunate soldier had to settle for a single sock since she had never completed its mate.

From her slight income working at Leckie's, she began to spend almost every cent she earned on satin underwear "never to be seen by anyone other than [her]self" and on dresses to wear at the dances at the local dance hall—which Marg permitted her to attend only in the company of girlfriends.

There is a lingering sadness in these recollections and in Peggy's meories of the further financial deprivations brought by the war. Marg, who took in a boarder—the much-loathed "man from Miramichi"—in order to make ends meet, gave up her bedroom and moved into Bobby's.

In the shuffle, Peggy had to give up her little dressing room to her brother. Not surprisingly, John Simpson was rude to the outsider.

Peggy Wemyss and Derek Armstrong. January 1944.

Another person to whom John Simpson was unfailingly unpleasant was Derek Armstrong, or, as he styled himself, "Benjamin Britten." In the middle of the war, an RAF training base was built just outside Neepawa. Soon, a frenzy of anglophilia swept the town, and Peggy was soon caught up in it: "I fell in love with an RAF man when I was seventeen years old. He was not only handsome and ten years older, he was also well read." For a teen-age girl with romantic and literary inclinations, this new outsider was hard to resist; like Bud, he was significantly older than herself. In the one surviving photograph of Derek and Peggy, she looks flushed with happiness as she chats with the dashing airman.

Peggy met Derek at a Saturday-night dance, occasions detested by Marg because she considered them rowdy. Of course, she was "absolutely right," but this made these events even more enticing. According to Peggy, two types of women attended, the "brash" and the uninitiated high-school girls. Each dance that a girl did not dance became a personal failure. And the music—big band and boogie—helped to release a lot of pent-up feeling. "I had at last learned to dance very well. In those days, though, dancing with someone who also loved to dance was not just a sexual experience; it almost went beyond the sexual. The uncertainties of war meant we danced with a heightened tribal sense of being together. Dancing became a passionate affirmation of life and the desire to go on living." Derek's own interests, largely centred on classical music, met with Marg's approval. She encouraged Peggy to attend the RAF camp's musical evenings to which Derek invited her, perhaps feeling guilty about Peggy's lack of musical education. In her turn, her daughter preferred the sound of bagpipes. "In love though I was, I was at least smart enough to realize that no Englishman would understand the Scots part of me. I dutifully sat and listened to classical music on the gritty old 78 records at the camp, pretending a warm response."

Perhaps it was on one of these evenings that Derek revealed to Peggy his "real" name was Benjamin Britten and that he was a composer. Correctly, Derek assumed Peggy would not know of the existence of the real-life composer of that name. If he had attempted to impress a naive seventeen-year-old, he succeeded. In the autobiographical story "Jericho's Brick Battlements" in *A Bird in the House*, Margaret Laurence describes how Vanessa falls in love with an airman from British Columbia.

> Like me, Michael wrote stories and poems, a fact which he did not divulge to his Air Force friends. When we were together, there was never enough time, for we had everything to talk about and discover.

> I tried not to remember that in a few months he would be going away. I had never met anyone before who was interested in the same things as I was.

Ever xenophobic, Grandfather Connor, who despises Michael, tells his granddaughter: "You ought to know better than run around with a fellow like this ... I'll bet a nickel to a doughnut hole he's married. That's the sort of fellow you've picked up."

One evening, John Simpson came upon the couple in the living room. He wound his watch with considerable gusto, obviously to indicate it was late and Derek should be leaving. When the hint was not taken, he ordered Peggy to bed. He did not know Derek was married, but made the accusation in order to insult and confuse. On this score, he was, as usual, remarkably successful. Peggy received only a few letters from Derek after he returned to England; ten years later she learned that her airman had been married.

Peggy was sorely tempted, but she did not go to bed with Derek. Young women of Peggy's class did not sleep with their boyfriends. Also, they did not know much about sex, as she later recalled:

> When I married, I was a *technical* virgin. I had, however, wanted to have sex long before, at about the ages of 14, 15, 16 and 17 and so on, but did not do so. Not because I was so moral, but because the young women of my generation were absolutely terrified of getting pregnant. And we really had no idea how to prevent it. There were many unwilling virgins in those days.

However, Derek did awaken in Peggy the considerable capacity she had for the pleasures of the body. He made her aware that sexual fulfilment—when she could finally take advantage of it—would be one of the great blessings of her life.

In the story—the last in *A Bird in the House*—although her mother comforts her, Vanessa hates her grandfather more than ever before: "What I could not forgive was that he had been right, unwittingly right." The next paragraph begins: "I was frantic to get away from Manawaka and from the Brick House."

Although the war was obviously drawing to a close, Peggy was determined to join one of the services. She wanted out of Neepawa, her mother had no financial resources, and John Simpson adamantly refused to pay a cent towards his granddaughter's further education. Therefore, for her, the WRENS (Women's Royal Canadian Naval Service) had a glamorous ring to it, especially for someone from the prairies. After she submitted her application, she had to deal with a distraught Marg. "Since I was of an age to join up, Mum could only worry. She had just finished panicking about a seventeen-year-old daughter who might at any moment declare her intention to wed an RAF man ten years her senior. Now this. Mum and I used to quote poetry to each other while we did the dishes, taking turns line by line, but with all these tensions, Browning's 'My Last Duchess' no longer tripped from our lips as we performed our after-dinner tasks."

When the WRENS called to accept Peggy, she was not at home. She was secretly pleased when a letter from the navy arrived, telling her they had tried unsuccessfully a few days before to call and that they had not kept the place open. Very relieved, Peggy, who really wanted to go to university, turned her attention to fulfilling that goal: she applied for a Manitoba Scholarship and admission to United College in Winnipeg. She obtained both and thus, with a combination of bravado and fear, could leave her birthplace. Since Grade 12 in Manitoba counted as the first year of an arts degree, she would have to spend only three years working towards her bachelor's degree.

Later in life, Margaret Laurence had a very different perspective on her departure from Neepawa:

> When I left my home town Neepawa at the age of eighteen, I guess, I couldn't wait to get out of that town. I thought, "I *never ever* want to live in a small town again." At that age, a small community

> becomes—rather stifling. Little did I know that out of that community, most of my writing would be done. I think that by the time I got around to writing about a small prairie town, I could see it with a much better perspective, and I could see it with a great deal more compassion and understanding than I had had as a kid.

Part of that last summer in Neepawa was spent at Clear Lake with Mona, Louise Alguire and other friends. Clear Lake was a wonderful escape from Neepawa. There, the young women could stay up late into the night without worrying about parental rules, or they could walk along the edge of the immense lake, or they could venture into the majestic, forbidding woods. Years later, looking at a photograph of herself with Mona and Louise, Margaret told Louise:

> That pic of the three of us has always touched me, somehow, and continues to do so when I get out all the albums to show to someone. There we are ... slender beautiful teenagers, not knowing of course that we were beautiful (at that age, one thinks everyone *except* oneself is beautiful!) I always think of that pic as "Three Smart Girls" ... remember the old Deanna Durbin film? Looking so hopefully into the camera, not at all aware of what our lives would be like.

Louise Alguire, Mona Simpson and Peggy Wemyss. July 1944.

5

Halls of Sion

(1944-1947)

> Winter, and snow of many textures. Hard-packed snow on Portage Avenue and the downtown streets, dirty from the trampling boots. Deep, dry snow, creaking underfoot.... And on lawns and little-used roadsides, the drifts are three feet high, crusted and white like royal icing, and when you break through the crust, the snow underneath is light and powdery as icing sugar. Snow everywhere. Black bare tree boughs are transformed overnight into white glittering traceries, candelabra, chandeliers of trees, the sun lighting them as though from within.

In this lyrical passage from *The Diviners,* Margaret Laurence provides a description of Winnipeg in winter emphasizing the beauty of the snow-clad city. She was not always so upbeat: "Oh many are the memories I have—frozen knees, in the days when I was young and too proud to wear 'overstockings,' a peculiarly unattractive type of heavy hose worn over the nylons in order to prevent freezing of the lower limbs. My ma used to say 'Your pride will keep you warm,' but unfortunately it didn't—I froze my knees with great regularity every winter." Despite bad weather, both Winnipeg and United College provided much-needed refuges from Neepawa to Peggy Wemyss.

The General Strike of 1919 had left the indelible mark of class struggle on Winnipeg. The intervening Depression had helped to underscore the differences between rich and poor. Twenty-five years later, when Peggy arrived there, it was still a city torn apart by class differences. By nature, she was inclined to sympathize with the underdog. In Neepawa, all of her friends had come from families that had taken knocks in the thirties. Some—like Mona Spratt's—had more money and could dress a bit better than others. In general, the middle-class of Neepawa lived in severely reduced circumstances, real poverty being peripherally visible only in some of the farms at the edge of town. In 1944, Peggy witnessed urban squalor. Her immediate reaction is not recorded, perhaps because it took a while for the grimness of the situation to sink in.

Her first priority in September 1944 was to settle into Sparling Hall, the women's dormitory at United College. At this time, university students in Winnipeg had a choice between science-oriented University of Manitoba and its affiliate, United College, which had a stronger programme in arts. The college had been formed in 1938 by an amalgamation of Methodist Wesley College and Presbyterian Manitoba College. In the mid-forties, United had a faculty of twenty and a student body of about five hundred, consisting of two distinct groups, those straight out of high school and soldiers returning to civilian life. Peggy was not completely isolated in Winnipeg because Mona and other Neepawa friends were at the University of Manitoba, a half-hour bus ride away.

Sparling Hall had been sober Mildred Musgrove's home when she attended Wesley College, but in 1944, as Peggy's friend and classmate Lois Freeman recollected, there was a different atmosphere: "I remember one occasion when several of us, Margaret included, wended our way to the windows of the third floor of the building, secreting under our arms paper bags filled with water. Our juvenile stunt was to drop the bag on some luckless individual entering the halls of learning. Water bombing it was called." Peggy was paid back one evening when, standing on the fire escape outside one of the classrooms, she began to declaim some lines from Shelley "only to receive a water-bomb treatment from the occupants of the floor above. It cured me of public oratory."

Residence food—often bulked up by large chunks of turnip—lingered precariously on the edge of inedibility, and the students sometimes wandered over to a "nearby hamburger joint called the Salisbury House, where," Peggy recalled, "we spent an inordinate amount of our slender allowances." Before arriving at Sparling, Peggy—who had been used to having her own room—was apprehensive about acquiring a roommate, but she and Helen Warkentin quickly became friends and shared a room for two years. They drew a mural of dinosaurs and jungles, working their way up, they planned, to Adam and Eve. Her wardrobe consisted of two sweaters, two skirts, two blouses, one good dress, one pair of sensible shoes and one pair of high heels. Some girls from well-off families had angora sweaters and necklaces of artificial pearls. Peggy practised reverse snobbery in condemning such girls, but, she really knew, "they were as happy as larks and furthermore, they averaged more dates."

Peggy, who had been seeing an "older" man in Neepawa, was now in a different environment, where soldiers were less plentiful and girls thus tended to date boys their own age. But one thing remained constant: "You hoped and prayed that some guy, however gauche or buck-toothed, would ask you to one of the dances or to a film." In her recollection of these years, Margaret Laurence referred to her glamorous friends, especially the stunningly beautiful Patricia Blondal, also an aspiring writer. "It must have upset them at times," she reflects, "to be valued, as they were, primarily for their physical beauty." However, she puts herself down in the next sentence: "They had to cope with things that I didn't know about." Peggy Wemyss may have had a subtle beauty, but it was one readily visible in her almond eyes, delicate lips and willowy figure.

She was also a young woman of independent views. Although she wanted to be an active participant in the social life of the college, she decided against joining a sorority, which would have given her instant access to a network of friends. She refused, partially because she could not afford to join, partially because of her strong—but still largely unformed—egalitarian beliefs. She told herself sorority girls were dim-witted. Then and later, she realized that her "principles, although relatively laudatory, were also a crude mask for my own uncertainties."

At first, Peggy was at a loss. United College was a lot larger than Neepawa Collegiate, and the students from Winnipeg tended to be snobbish about those from small-town Manitoba: "Kids from the farms were lowest on the scale; kids from the very small towns, whistle stops, were next; kids from slightly larger towns were next; kids from small cities, like Brandon, were next; the city kids (and Winnipeg was the only proper city) ranked as overlords." In this particular caste system, she fitted into the uncomfortable middle. Soon, however, those in residence formed a close-knit group. At Tony's, the college's cramped lunchroom and coffee shop in the basement of the main building, Peggy became embroiled in long discussions about politics, religion and writing. During rousing conversations and heated arguments at Tony's, Peggy first imbibed the doctrines of the "Winnipeg Old Left," of J.S. Woodsworth, Stanley Knowles and Tommy Douglas, the founders of the Co-operative Commonwealth Federation (CCF).

Margaret Laurence admits that, although she was an excellent student in English, her marks in other courses were "either mediocre or fairly abysmal." In fact she was a gifted student in philosophy, but her grades in other subjects—especially history—were not exceptional. "Obviously," she observed, "I had a one-track talent." Her classmates agreed. Her entry in the 1947 yearbook reads: "When Peggy was a little girl, her mother inadvertently dropped onto her a volume of Robinson Jeffers on the floor. She has been writing poetry ever since."

In class, she was extremely reserved, never speaking unless addressed by the professor. English classes were different, as Lois Freeman recalled: "Right from the start, it was obvious that she was fascinated with words and ideas, and frequently the class evolved into a dialogue between her and Professor Carl Halstead or Professor Meredith Thompson." The pursuit of English literature brought out the intrepid, daring side of Peggy. In second year, she asked one of her professors, Arthur Phelps, how to join the English Club. Unbeknownst to her, membership in this group was by invitation only and second-year students were seldom accorded this privilege. He did not inform her of this when he invited her to the next meeting, at which she was received cordially by the members of the club. Only thirty years later did she learn that, prior to her first appearance, Phelps had warned the members: "You are expected to show courtesy and no surprise at her presence in your midst."

Phelps—a friend of Frederick Philip Grove and also of Morley Callaghan, who attended a meeting of the Club—encouraged the group to read Canadian fiction. As Peggy recalled, "we couldn't afford to buy them, and they weren't even greatly in evidence at the Public Library, but we read Gabrielle Roy, Hugh MacLennan, Morley Callaghan, and others, in the book department of the Hudson's Bay Company, just across the road from the college, a chapter at a time, hoping the sales clerks wouldn't notice us standing there, turning pages."

The one course she took at the University of Manitoba—in Milton and seventeenth-century thought taught by Malcolm Ross—"profoundly affected" her life. The sometimes gruff but always tenderhearted Ross, a Renaissance specialist who later became one of the first advocates of Canadian literature as a university subject, remembered that Peggy hardly ever spoke in his class, a small one conducted as a seminar. She would make the requisite contributions but otherwise had nothing to say. When he met with her in his office, she was articulate, open and friendly. In the 1980s, Margaret Laurence had very different memories, as can be seen in snippets from two letters to Ross:

> Who would have thought it, when I was a young hesitant student (well, sometimes hesitant and sometime strident in my arguments in classes, I think!) at the U of M?!

> Frankly, I can't remember whether I ever felt "intimidated" by you, all those years ago at the U of M, or not. I don't think so. I was so shy personally but so brash and enthusiastic in terms of the courses in English at university, that I think probably my enthusiasm overcame my personal shyness in that kind of situation. What I recall

most is sitting around (or along) a huge table and discussing and arguing, and you challenging all of us to support our views.

Ross saw two sides of Peggy Wemyss, and he was never able to completely reconcile them. In his view, Margaret reinvented herself in *Dance*—and in letters to him—to the extent she presents herself as far more daring and sophisticated than she in fact was during those years. She had, nevertheless, he recalled, an "eager awareness" of the possibilities life might present to her, particularly the literary life.

Like many women writers before her, Peggy Wemyss was certain she would receive a fairer reading if she assumed male guise: "...when I first submitted poems to the University of Manitoba student paper, *The Manitoban*, I sent them in under the name of Steve Lancaster. After the Lancaster bomber, and I had always liked the name Steve. I cringe with shame to recall it now. Later, I dared to use my own name, but it was J. M. Wemyss, I think, not Jean Margaret. In one of my early stories, published in the United College magazine, *Vox*, I actually used a first-person narrative, but my narrator was a man."

Her first efforts were confined to poetry because she did not have the time to tackle prose. Also, as she sagely observed, "As a short, intense form, it often appeals to young writers as being in more accord with youthfully intense, and usually intensely subjective, feelings." She was thrilled when one of the "Steve Lancaster" poems was published, but she was also apprehensive she might overhear someone trashing it. This never happened and, gradually, her courage increased. Not only did she publish poems under her own name but she also composed a poem, memorized it and then appeared at the *Manitoban* office where she "proceeded to type out [the] poem from memory."

In addition to poems and an essay on Robinson Jeffers' poetry, she published two short stories in *Vox*. "Calliope" appeared in 1945, after she had spent part of the summer visiting a friend in Carman, Manitoba, where the two of them had helped to run a hot-dog stand at the town fair. Fascinated by the "carnies" and their strange style of life, she told the story of "German Joe," a souvenir vendor. At the beginning of the story, he is lost in a reverie about his bleak financial prospects. He is interrupted by rain leaking through a hole in his roof and the plaintive cry of a small lost boy. "German Joe looked at the kid thoughtfully.... A man should have sons." Far from his homeland, he identifies with the lost boy and experiences a moment of happiness so piercing with its vivid associations of his own past that when he is left alone again, he is plunged into deeper desolation than before. He copes with the reality of his bleak existence through alcohol and the creation of a mythological past. The fairground, a garish place that "screams" colours of purple, red and green like "an aging slut without makeup," is his world.

The second story, "Tal des Walde," had a more complicated genesis. As a child, Peggy had heard of an Austrian nobleman who built a medieval estate near Riding Mountain, Manitoba. At a small dark watchmaker's shop where time seems to have stood still, a traveller stops to have his watch repaired and, while working, the watchmaker tells the story of an Austrian noble, Count Zbrueckner. He traces the fortunes of the Count from one of shameless frivolity and financial ruin to his immigration to Canada where he begins a new life as a feudal overlord, whose life is forever altered by the death of his wife and child. The house is never completed, and he abandons his land to settlers. As the story concludes, the traveller realizes the watchmaker is the former Count: "Yes, even after all the humbling years, the bearing, the manner, the very inflection of the voice were unmistakably aristocratic."

Years afterwards, Margaret Laurence was harshly self-critical about these two apprentice pieces. The first was "overwhelmingly sentimental" and the other markedly deficient because the traveller is male, as if she herself had not thought a female character of sufficient interest to have a tale told to her. However, she did see connections between "Tal" and her later narratives in that the Count attempts, in an overbearing way, to control life: "The most interesting thing to me now about the story is that it does connect with all my subsequent writing in one way—a basic life-view that could say, even then, '...a man is never God, even in his own domain' and '...one should not mould the lives of others.'" Even in her earliest stories, she was already subtly criticizing John Simpson's view of the world. And both stories, dealing with displacement and irrevocable loss, have central characters who are outsiders, one German, the other Austrian.

Often, Peggy Wemyss seemed a very ordinary young woman:

> When I was in third year university, I had a boarding house in the North End, about a mile past the end of the Selkirk Avenue streetcar line. Whenever I had a date that winter, and the guy discovered where I lived and in those days it was considered necessary for a man to pick up the girl and take her home later, I rarely had a date with the same boy twice. Flounder-flounder-flounder through a mile of snowdrifts, and at the end of it, a chilly necking session on the *front porch*, at 30 below zero. It would have cooled the hottest ardour, believe you me. Finally my girlfriend and I moved from this northerly accommodation and got a small flat on Broadway, after which our social life improved considerably.

Yet there was always another side to her in her almost instant identification with those who are in any way disbarred from the mainstream. For her, the Canadian experience was one wherein a multiplicity of outsiders were joined together.

Part of her attraction to Adele Wiseman, who also had literary aspirations and later became Peggy's closest friend, was rooted in her Jewishness as well as her passionate commitment to the life of writing. According to Adele (who attended the University of Manitoba), their friendship did not begin until about 1947-8: "Margaret was a year or two ahead of me and at United College, so that I didn't know her during my university years." This is not correct: the two did not become close friends immediately, but they knew each other as students. Margaret

Laurence was vague on this issue, but in *The Diviners* Morag meets Ella Gerson—"short rather stocky girl with auburn hair"—at the *Veritas* office, a publication similar to *The Manitoban.* Both are outsiders to the "in-group" that runs the magazine, both are shy and have concealed their submissions within a book. They decide to forget about *Veritas* and go off to a coffee shop where they soon are reading—and criticizing—each other's work. There, Morag realizes, quite simply, that Ella is a "friend for life." This passage from *The Diviners* is not literally accurate, but it is close to the truth: three women who became novelists—Margaret Laurence, Adele Wiseman and Patricia Blondal—were members at the same time of Malcolm Ross's seventeenth-century seminar. Peggy was withdrawn in class, Patricia spoke occasionally, and—as was her wont—Adele was outspoken and argumentative. (The letters from Margaret Laurence to Adele Wiseman are extensive and are the most revealing she ever wrote. In fact, some periods in Margaret's life—particularly the years in Ghana—can only be reconstructed from that correspondence. Adele kept almost every letter Margaret wrote to her, whereas Margaret was not in the habit of keeping letters she received.)

Adele Wiseman. 1978.

Adele Wiseman was a life force, a person imbued with a seemingly endless list of questions about existence and with an equal amount of energy to answer those queries. Adele's own inclination from early childhood was to dedicate herself to writing: "I always knew I was going to write from the time I first knew it was possible to write, from the time I knew what a story was, and certainly from the first moment I started to read. I can remember watching my brother and sister at the kitchen table, sitting there, staring down intently at the table; I couldn't figure out what it was they were doing and why I couldn't talk to them, why they kept shushing me. Then my next memory is doing the same thing, when I first realized that these books were teaching me something while I was reading."

Adele's conviction of her destiny as a writer came in large part from her parents, Chaika and Pesach, who had emigrated to Canada from the Ukraine. By the time he was seven, Pesach dreamed of becoming a cantor and was eagerly studying the Torah. Two years later, he was apprenticed to a tailor. This did not impede his ambition, but his father's death three years later meant he was the sole support of his mother and several younger sisters. Later, his singing voice was ruined in the trenches of World War I. Reading was the great solace of his subsequent existence. Against her parents' wishes, Chaika became a dressmaker. Her fascination with the textures and colours of fabric remained with her, leading her as an older woman to create dolls, puppets and figurines.

Adele was convinced she had inherited her love of literature from her parents and that by becoming a writer she was doing something that had been closed off from them. Her destiny was to fulfil theirs. Another legacy from her parents was her sense that life was turbulent, messy and shockingly beautiful. The Wisemans, who had first arrived in Montreal and then went to Winnipeg, were always at the edge of destitution during their time in North End Winnipeg, where Pesach worked as a tailor and Chaika as a dressmaker. They had to take in boarders, but they always had room in their small house in Burrows Avenue for others.

> There was one winter [Adele recalled] when the three-bedroom house had roomers in at least two and sometimes all three of those bedrooms. To sleep, we [Pesach, Chaika, Adele, her two brothers and sister] were moved around in the living room and in the dining room, just wherever we could sort out places. My dad was in Vancouver looking for work, and a down-and-outer came to the

> door. He was either Ukrainian or Polish—to my mother all people in trouble were the same—and he had been turned away from one of the shelters because he didn't have the necessary two bits. Mom told him that if he looked after the furnace he could sleep downstairs. He put up some boards on four logs, Mom gave him bedding and he slept down there for a whole winter.

When Peggy met the Wisemans, she was overwhelmed by their generosity and by their palpable passion for life in spite of their financial difficulties.

To her, this was in startling contrast to Neepawa, where Marg had been forced to sell the Brick House and move herself, her son and her increasingly difficult father to the Little House, where, Peggy recalled, "my brother inherited my old attic room. It remained his until he, too, grew up and left home. Grandfather had the back bedroom that had once been my brother's. As the boy grew into young manhood, so the old man relapsed into a sour second childhood. I was spared those years and I was too self-absorbed to want to look closely at what Mum went through when Grandfather, in his last years, would rant and rave, going out into the night streets of the town looking for his long-dead wife."

Peggy, who did not feel bound to return to Neepawa, graduated from United College in the spring of 1947. She was twenty-one, imbued with a wonderful optimism, certain, at long last, she was entering her "adult, hopeful" life. She also was in love, "seriously and deeply and, for the first time, realistically."

6

Uncertain Flowering (1947-1950)

At the beginning of 1947, Peggy and her roommate, Mary Turnbull, moved to a boarding house at 139 Roslyn Avenue. There, Peggy met Jack Laurence, also a lodger. Once, she referred to him as a "handsome devil" in tribute to the fact that he embodied another, closely related set of clichés: tall, dark and handsome. For her, it was love at first sight: "One day I came into the house and on the stairs stood a young man. I thought that his face not only was handsome but also had qualities of understanding. I said to myself, 'That's the man I'd like to marry.'" Behind the good looks of a leading man was a sensitive person of considerable, genuine charm, someone who shared many of

Jack Laurence. c. 1942.

her attributes and interests. Not only was his mother a novelist, he himself was a would-be writer.

Jack, thirty-one when he met Peggy and thus ten years older, was the eldest child of Elsie Fry Laurence, the youngest child of a Church of England minister from Waterfield, Sussex, and John Laurence, a Highland Scot from the Shetland Islands. Elsie's adventurous spirit was linked to her writing, a fact that gave her daughter-in-law special pleasure: "When she was eighteen, Elsie went to pre-revolutionary Russia and worked in Moscow as a governess for a Jewish family. While she was there, she wrote a novel under the pen name of Christine Field. The novel, titled *Half a Gypsy*, concerned a young Englishwoman who went to Russia as a rebellious young person ... taught as a governess, and ultimately met and married a young man who turned out to be an English titled gentleman."

Elsie Fry Laurence.

After she completed the novel in Moscow, Elsie returned to England, at which point the recently widowed Mrs. Fry determined to take herself, Elsie and another daughter to Canada, where her two sons had emigrated. The three women settled in South Fort George, British Columbia. There, Elsie met and married John Laurence in August 1915 and gave birth to John Fergus Laurence a year later. Before the marriage, John Laurence had joined the army, and he was away when Jack was born. In the midst of all the changes in her life, Elsie was amazed to learn in 1917 that the English firm Andrew Melrose Ltd., to whom she had submitted her manuscript, had published the book in 1916, after trying unsuccessfully to contact her. (Her second novel—*Bright Wings*—did not appear until 1964; her other books are *The Band Plays a March and Other Poems* [1936], *Rearguard and Other Poems* [1944], and *Affirmations: An Anthology, 1929-1978* [1978].)

When the war ended in 1918, John Laurence returned to Canada. The experience of war had left an indelible black mark on his soul. Soon after his homecoming, he and his family moved to Edson, Alberta, where he was employed as a CNR linesman. Elsie, whose family grew to seven children, pursued her writing career in the few spare moments that were given to her. She was, as Margaret Laurence proclaimed her, "a woman with a vocation."

Like his mother, Jack was filled with wanderlust, combined with a strong sense of responsibility. Very much his mother's son, he wanted as a young man to become a writer. This aspiration, which lasted well into his forties, was readily evident to all his close friends. Also obvious was his incredible ability to build and mend all manner of mechanical devices. "I remember, as a kid," he once recalled, "taking an old Model-T apart and putting it together again." In Edson, he became an apprentice printer. Then, in 1939, at the outset of the war, he bought with his sparse savings a one-way boat trip to England so that he could join the RAF. This was his escape, a way in which his adventurous spirit and sense of duty could find outlets. He was a sergeant and mechanic in the RAF, before being seconded to the RCAF towards the end of the war. As Margaret Laurence recalled: "He served some years in [India], where he was called 'Driver' Laurence for the way in which he drove himself—and those under his orders—to extremes of work and perseverance."

After he was demobbed, Jack, still in the RAF, lived for a time in Carberry, Manitoba. From there, he would travel into Winnipeg, where, through his mother, he met Watson Thomson, a writer and guru who had formed a group called the Prairie School for Social Advancement. This organization, which was committed to Third World development, was also devoted to communal living and had set up its headquarters at 139 Roslyn Road in such an experimental fashion. Jack began to spend all his weekends there. (He became a bit disillusioned with communal living when someone stole his typewriter.) When Thomson and the Prairie School vacated 139 Roslyn Road it became a boarding house, and Jack, who had left the army and enrolled at the University of Manitoba, moved in.

Jack's magnetic appeal was overwhelming to Peggy, who was delighted to throw over small-town trappings. At 139 Roslyn Road, she and Jack lived together openly, causing one friend—Alice Dahlquist, who was visiting from the States—some considerable shock and dismay. Her friend Mona took an instant dislike to Jack. One day in the winter of 1947, she paid a surprise visit to Peggy, who was not at home. She ran into another resident, a man, who offered to take a message. A few days later, Mona telephoned and told her old chum how much she was appalled by the "military manner" of the chap she had met. When Peggy informed her that the man was her lover, Jack, Mona was especially upset at how much older he was than Peggy. Mona cautioned her: "He is way too much like Derek." Mona was put off by what she considered to be Jack's condescending manner; she was also spooked by the remarkable physical resemblance between him and the Englishman. Although Peggy did not tell Mona that she was deeply offended, she broke with her for several years and did not invite her to her wedding which took place at the United Church in Neepawa on September 13, 1947.

Peggy realized Marg "must have thought I was rather young to get married" but nothing was said. Although Marg did not leave her daughter completely in the dark about sex, she found the topic a difficult one. Her solution to the problem was not successful: "Just before I was married, she and one of her friends gave me a story. It was called 'Here We Are,' by Dorothy Parker, about a young couple on their honeymoon who are very embarrassed about sex. I didn't know if Mum thought this amusing, but I was upset and offended, although I never told her so."

Marg acted under the misguided assumption that Peggy was completely inexperienced sexually. It would have been surprising if they had talked about sex openly. What Peggy is really complaining about is the hamfisted, indirect and insensitive way her mother chose to broach the topic. Even at that time, when mothers and daughters would never think of openly discussing many intimate issues, the oppressive, characteristic silences between this mother and daughter were excessive. Although Marg was particularly concerned about birth control, that was another topic she did not wish to discuss:

> Why was she so frightened? I have no notion. It was a subject then, I guess, that was not to be talked about, except secretly, among women. The doctors were all male doctors, and they were certainly not sympathetic to young married women who did not want children. Mum did the best she could for me. She gave me the advice, not of the local doctor, but of *his wife*. There was a name of a birth control cream that I could buy without a prescription. Before Jack and I were married, I went into a drug store in Winnipeg and bought this stuff. I feel so embarrassed now, for my much younger self. I did not even know how to pronounce "vaginal."

The wedding was a joyous event—but one into which the character of the town crept: "Mum was not a teetotaller, but she knew the community in which she had spent most of her life. For a reception of roughly thirty people, she'd bought one bottle of sherry."

Margaret Laurence on her wedding day.

Peggy was "incredibly happy" and thought she looked "quite beautiful" on her wedding day. However, she allowed a little bit of sly humour to escape when describing the outfit she wore when she and Jack departed for their honeymoon at Clear Lake: "a navy-blue suit with a tight skirt down nearly to my ankles and a cumbersome gold-braided puff-sleeved jacket that must have made my slender twenty-one-year-old body look like a dirigible. High-heeled shoes, of course. A natty little navy-blue felt hat, tri-cornered, with a huge pink ribbon bow, fashioned by Miss Phipps, the local ladies' milliner in my home town. I thought it was just wonderful."

Up to the time of their honeymoon, Peggy and Jack had not had sexual intercourse, even though they had lived together. Her remembrances of that time were rapturous: "Sex was never a problem for us.... Not only did we *love* one another, we *wanted* one another.... our love and our love-making were marvellous, amazing." Throughout their entire marriage, their sex life remained on an even keel. However, like Marg, Peggy did not feel comfortable discussing birth control—even with Jack: "I don't think my husband knew, partly because I did not tell him, of my rage and bewilderment about the whole birth control matter. We used 'safes' for a whole year because for that time I was scared to go ... to a doctor."

Even after her marriage, the intangible but nevertheless long reach of Neepawa haunted Peggy, who determined to rid herself of the resulting desolation. One way to do this was to avoid the place, but such a course of action was not always possible. Her response to the town is best captured in a letter written to Adele Wiseman when, after her marriage, Peggy was visiting Marg (Jack was at St. Norbert working as a surveyor): "Stranded. Neepawa, as usual, is very much like itself. Nausea, real not mental, as usual, has set in. The uncomfortable accompaniment of great mental stress and strain. However, your voyageur is making valiant attempts to control the digestive system, and so far I haven't thrown up on anyone's oriental rugs." Her attempt at cheerfulness is half-hearted at best because the town cast such a long shadow on her existence. Neepawa would always remain a grim interior landscape for her, one which would only be partly purged in the creation of Manawaka.

When the Laurences returned to Winnipeg after their honeymoon, they moved to 515 Burrows Avenue, a duplex, where they rented the upstairs from Anne and Bill Ross. Peggy had heard that these rooms were available through Adele, whose family lived across the street. During the years on Burrows Avenue, Peggy and Adele's friendship ripened. They talked at length about their desire to become writers, conversations which even extended to speculations as to which of them would first win the Governor General's Award for fiction. At the time, these seemed to be unrealizable desires, although each woman saw in the other the drive necessary to transform fantasy into reality.

One way for Peggy to practise her skills as a writer was to become a journalist. Her first job was with *The Westerner*, a Communist newspaper, although at the time she started there she was not aware of its party allegiance. In 1947, she and Jack shared the same attitudes towards social and political change. Jack, deeply influenced both by the ravages of war he had seen in the Far East and by Watson Thomson's teachings, wanted to use the practical skills he was acquiring in his engineering course to further advancement in the Third World. Very much in the manner of a teacher, he tutored Peggy in his philosophy, she being an ardent disciple.

Anne and Bill Ross noticed Peggy eagerly followed where Jack led. In her, Anne discovered a vibrant, sweet but naive friend; she did not like Jack, whom she found cold and austere. There was, however, a complicated agenda at work. Bill Ross, born Cecil Zuken in the Ukraine, had a different idea of social change from the Laurences. At the outset of the war, he had been the Secretary of the Young Communist League and a school trustee. When the Communist Party was declared illegal, he went underground, living in twenty-four different places between June 1940 and October 1942. The political beliefs of Bill and Jack were at odds, accounting in part for the disdain Bill and Anne felt for Jack.

Peggy, who may have heard of the job at *The Westerner* through Bill, had little or no idea of the weekly's political agenda—"when I began I didn't even know enough to know it was a Party paper—thought it was left-wing vaguely; why they hired me I cannot think; I did book reviews and reporting—and did I learn a lot in that year! My big break with the editor (whom I still feel enormous affection towards) was when I reviewed some novel or other and said 'this novel stinks', and he said, you can't say it stinks, it's on the right side, and I said I thought otherwise." The offending piece was a review of a book of poems by Joe Wallace. The editor informed her: "You can't write that kind of review about Joe's poems. He's a hero of the left." She refused to budge, "They're not good poems. That's all I care about." She was eventually fired—not for insubordination but for lack of funds. Years later, she realized that her then nascent political beliefs were not very different from those of her employers: "Those old-time Communists in the forties in Winnipeg were not proposing violent revolution. They were proclaiming a need for social justice in terms of our land."

She then worked for *The Winnipeg Citizen*, "the only co-operative daily ever to come into existence in Canada. It lasted a year. I wrote a radio column, did book reviews, and covered the labour beat, about which, at twenty-one, I knew absolutely nothing." After a year there, she resigned when the managing editor summoned her to his office, having been informed she was a communist. The rumour, probably generated by her association with Bill and Anne, offended her, not so much because someone accused her of being a Communist (she wasn't) but because the editor assumed it was his right to invade her privacy.

Her next job was as the registrar at the YWCA, a hectic bustling job especially when swimming and gym classes were being enrolled. When the Japanese Canadians who had been released from the internment camps in British Columbia began to arrive in Winnipeg, the Y started a teen group. In Peggy's opinion, this was very much a band-aid solution to the horrors that had been inflicted by the Canadian government, but at least the Y was trying to do something to rectify a tragic situation.

"North Winnipeg in the 1940s decided a lot of my life." There, she began to become more and more aware of the possibilities life offered her. Two interests predominated: she wanted to be involved in work which bettered the conditions of others and she was certain of her destiny as a writer. She closed Neepawa off and saw Marg at increasingly long intervals. She dealt with her guilt by writing to her mother on a regular basis, often weekly. At this time, Peggy saw no connection between her past and the future that seemed to be unfolding in a potentially golden way.

By 1949, Jack, who had completed his engineering degree, wanted to put into practice the ideals he had imbibed from Watson Thomson. At one point, he considered taking a job building a railway in Bulgaria. This prospect alarmed Marg, and she may have been equally dismayed when Peggy informed her that she and Jack had decided to settle in England for a short stay, in preparation for a much longer sojourn elsewhere. At this time, London, which was the gateway for all engineering jobs in the Third World, was an ideal stopover practically and emotionally.

Peggy, who landed office work with a small employment agency (Suit-All) shortly after arriving in England in July 1949, had an exhilarating stay in London, despite the fact she and Jack were always broke. He had an engineering job, but they could only afford a bedsitter on Finchley Road. Years later, she wrote a short account of that room:

> It had a gas-fire, and gas-ring on which we did all our cooking in a pressure cooker. Whatever we put in it, it came out tasting like stew. Rationing was still on, and we had to queue for our minuscule bit of beef each week. I got very friendly with a lady at the greengrocer's who liked me because I was Canadian and she was the aunt of Abe Yanovsky, a Canadian and world chess champion. She used to give me extra oranges. Our room had a gas-meter. We used to run out of sixpences in the cold weather, and Jack would pick the lock on the meter and we would take out some sixpences. Being honest, we would mark down how many we borrowed, and return them. Cigarettes were in short supply. We used to save the butts and re-roll them. On weekends, to keep warm cheaply, we used to ride the underground.

Peggy's ambition to write was not forestalled—she even managed to get something published, as she excitedly wrote to Adele Wiseman in January 1950:

> The long-awaited day has arrived at last ... the Canadian Tribune has published one of my poems ... it was in the January 9 issue ... In their letter they said they had just received another poem which I had sent them, but didn't say whether or not they would print it ... I rather hope they do, as it is a better poem, on the whole, and is about the revolt of the Italian peasants which began in earnest last fall.
>
> Another stroke of luck ... we have recently won £64 in the Football Pools! By the old rate of exchange, that is about $250!!!... Half of it will go towards our holiday, which we fervently hope to spend in France and Italy. The rest is being spent on concerts, theatres, ballet, clothes and books ... With our Pool money, also, we are in the process of buying a few more clothes to combat the English weather.

Gleefully, the Laurences then squandered their entire take on a trip to Paris.

Peggy's letters to Adele capture the excitement the newly married Laurences found in each other and in life. The tone is of domestic comedy, of two young people, very much in love and without much money, facing life together. Their love had the power to remove all manner of impediments, and their imaginations, as Peggy later recalled, led them in some zany directions: "We were going to make a million by writing a book on the country homes of England, or the time we were (in our minds, anyway) nearly on easy-street through writing a series of children's books dealing with visits to the doctor and dentist (which would remove fear from the kids' minds ... the books to be distributed by the big chemical and medical companies)." There was another project, as Peggy later remembered: "When Jack and I were first in England in 1949, there was a contest for a toothpaste called 'Gordon Moore's Cosmetic Toothpaste', which tinted the gums crimson. You were supposed to send in a little verse, & Jack did: 'Cosmetic Toothpaste by Gordon Moore/ Has made many a virgin look like a whore.'"

Postwar London recovered slowly from the war, and evidence of the blitz confronted the Laurences every day. Despite murky weather and poor living conditions, Peggy was entranced. But she was not deceived. This can be seen in her ten-page unpublished account, "England by Me," which she divided into five sections: "1. Scenery, History and Old Junk in General, in the Land of the Shilling Guidebook; 2. Food; 3. Manners and Morals; 4. Vultures for Culture; 5. Us." She included a two-page advertising supplement she had come across, in which large lettering—under the photo of a young attractive woman reads—"I'D MARRY HIM AGAIN BUT…"; the quotation then continues in a much smaller typeface, "I *do* wish they'd teach bridegrooms about rationing!" Her commentary: "makes you gasp, until you read that last word 'rationing'!"

Peggy's diary-letter (augmented by Jack's pencil sketches) is very much tongue-in-cheek: "Windsor Castle, now. There's the place. It's terrific. It's colossal. It's super-stupendous. But, having learned to be restrained (so as not to be confused with the Americans) you murmur softly, 'Rather nice, what?'"

> Hampton Court is another Palace. There are so many palaces you soon lose count. The interesting thing about Hampton Court is that Henry VIII lived there, and the old boy had … (dare I say it?) … baroque tastes. Not to mention Late Renaissance, with a soupçon of just plain old ordinary vulgar. Nude women (pictures, i.e.) romp around the walls.… It is a dead place, filled with memories of brawls and lovemaking and the hypocrisy common to courts, but now its day is done, and it is almost with a sense of relief that you hear a little boy running down the great hallway, and shouting "mummy, come and see the picture of the man with the funny-looking feather in his hat!"

Peggy comments on a wide variety of topics: the horribleness of English puddings (more interesting as a concept than a reality), the wealthy ("In the employment agency where I work I see a lot of rich-bitches, who can't run a house without six servants, and who tell you that they won't hire 'foreigners'."), contemporary English painting ("they still return to haunt me in dreams. Those knock-out shades of pink. That green flesh."), and the state of the Laurence marriage ("insofar as it's possible to be happy in this kind of a world at the present time, we're happy here").

"England by Me" was a Christmas gift to Adele and her family back in Winnipeg—she would never have sent such a letter to Marg, who would not have seen the humour in it. And Peggy Laurence was growing bolder. She no longer had to show just her "nice" side. Despite the privations, England was liberating her, allowing her to speak frankly and racily when she felt like it. However, her marriage was the real source of her new-found freedom. Her closeness to Jack pervaded every aspect of her being, allowing her to experience life intensely and joyously.

Money-making schemes and the daily rigours of English life aside, her ambition to write had been recharged, as she wrote to the Wisemans back in Winnipeg after Adele arrived in London later that year: "was over at Adele's the other afternoon, and we read each other's scripts and told each other that we were going to write the two great novels of the century! In actual fact, however, if she gets this novel of hers finished the way she wants it to be, it will be infinitely better than anything I shall ever write."

Finally, the break Jack had been looking for surfaced in a newspaper advertisement placed by the British Colonial Service, which was in search of a civil engineer to supervise the building of thirty dams (*ballehs*—huge water catchments) in the Somaliland Protectorate: "The average maximum capacity of each dam will be 10 million gallons. The Engineer will be required to carry out all reconnaissance and detailed survey [under the supervision of the Director of Public Works], to do all calculations and designs, to be responsible for expenditure and the supervision of staff and plant." Jack felt, as Peggy later recalled, "a need to work for once on a job that plainly needed doing.... a job in which the results of an individual's work could be clearly perceived, as they rarely could in Europe and North America." She also wanted to put into action many of the ideas about social action she had formed in

Winnipeg. And her imagination, like Jack's, was fuelled by the prospect of escaping the grey skies of England.

Jack was offered the job, but the Colonial Service regretted they had no accommodation for married couples and informed him Mrs. Laurence would have to remain behind. That obstacle was removed when Jack assured his employers that his wife was a "typical" Canadian girl ("an accomplished woodswoman, a kind of female Daniel Boone"), one habitually used to living in tents and wielding an axe. The ploy worked, and the Laurences were on their way to a new challenge. Peggy's high spirits are evident in a letter that November:

> We went on a shopping spree last week, and bought a lot of clothes for both of us. Jack is highly annoyed at having to get an evening suit, for the first time in his life, but I keep telling him he won't put on any weight so he'll be able to wear it forever.... We got a lovely formal for me. I had to get a washable one, as there is no dry-cleaning in Somaliland.... It is in glazed chintz.... Boned top so I can wear it strapless if I want, and very full skirt. White background, with a pattern of huge butterflies all over it, in shades of mauve, yellow and dark brown.

She was filled with the most wonderful sense of expectancy. At last, she was going to escape to a truly foreign land. Although extremely shy, she was eager to take on new experiences, taking pleasure in the brightly coloured dress which showed off her slim body. Like the colourful butterflies, she was in full sail, ready for a great adventure.

7

Water for a Dry Land (1950-1952)

A little bit of Peggy's élan in the Somalia adventure was punctured by the sea voyage to Africa. Before that, she had to put up with the confusion generated by the Colonial Office's muddled notions of life in Somaliland. First, the Laurences were given a pamphlet which stated they must carry with them a year's supply of tinned food and a portable bath. This injunction proved to be out of date. Then they were warned of the omnipresent danger of "woolly-bears," cloth-eating insects. Juxtaposed in her mind were such practicalities and the images she had retained from her reading of Sir Richard Burton's adventures, from her recollection of the legend of Prester John, and from her knowledge that "Somaliland was the end of a bitter journey and the beginning of a lifetime of bondage, for there the Arab slave routes had emerged at the sea, and from there the dhow-loads of slaves had once been shipped across the Gulf of Aden to be sold in the flesh markets of Arabia."

The Laurences booked passage from Rotterdam to the Red Sea on the *Tigre*, a Norwegian passenger-cargo vessel. Unfortunately, the *Tigre* was delayed by a week, and the almost penniless couple had to find a way to survive until the ship reached the Netherlands. Restaurants in which

English was spoken were beyond their means, so they were reduced to eating *wiener schnitzel* and *slagroomwafel* (waffle with whipped cream) and walking the slippery streets of chilly Rotterdam. Jack spent much of his time reading *War and Peace*, which he had the foresight to bring. Peggy paced the room until she discovered the Gideon Bible, whereupon she read the five books of Moses for the first time. When their ship finally arrived, the tired and disgruntled couple "tramped on board dully, expecting nothing." There, they were the only passengers and were ensconced in the owner's outrageously opulent suite. "We mustn't act surprised," a grinning Jack instructed his wife, as he sprawled on a velour sofa. "The idea is that we take it all completely for granted." The crew's friendliness extended to sharing their Christmas celebrations with the young couple. Jack was given a bottle of whisky, Peggy a marzipan pig. Genoa was their first extended stop. Later, they passed by Sicily. One night they even saw Mount Etna, "a far-off red glow in the black sky."

On board the *Tigre*, Peggy kept herself busy working on a novel, as she rather matter-of-factly informed Adele on December 27: "I've been going ahead with my story not too badly, having finished Chapter III (rough draft!) yesterday. I've done 25 shorthand pages since leaving London, and now must transcribe them.... I'm reading 'The Brothers Karamazov' now.... I've never read a book that impressed me so much with its sharpness of perception, vividness of dialogue, and a way of catching the full complexity of its characters."

Peggy's first view of the mysterious east was a Coca-Cola sign in Arabic at Port Said, a sure sign of imperialist presence. "But," as she pointed out, "the dhows were there, too, with their curved prows and triangular sails." Some of these—the smaller ones—were "shabby," and in her recollections of Port Said—and later of Somaliland—there is a contrast between first impressions, such as a town or village's beautiful appearance, and the often grim realities of what they were really like. Like most travellers, Peggy was always having to adjust her sights in order to meld reality with fantasy: "We went ashore and walked the crowded and intricate streets where stained mud buildings stood side by side with slick stuccoed apartment blocks in florid pinks and greens.

Rows of ragged palms fringed the roads where horse-drawn carriages unbelievably rattled along like old engravings come to life. And the people—merchants waddling slow and easy in long striped robes and maroon fezzes, nimble limping beggars who trailed the tourists, girl children with precociously knowing eyes...."

The passage through the Suez Canal was cold. Wrapped in sweaters and coats, they saw villages of square clay houses slip past them, "tattered children, and black cattle and women in *purdah*." At Aden, they switched to a smaller ship, the Bombay-owned *Velho*, which was to take them across the Gulf of Aden to Berbera on the northern coast of the Somaliland Protectorate. The new vessel was inhabited by those like the Laurences, who were arriving, and those returning from leave in England, who could hardly wait to get back to the "exile that had become beloved." One of the passengers, an Army sergeant, gloomily warned them: "This your first time out? You'll hate it. Nothing there but a bloody great chunk of desert. It's got the highest European suicide rate of any colony—know that? Good few blokes living very solitary there in outstations, that's the reason. They go round the bend."

Peggy was drawn to the Somalis crowding the third-class section, whom she saw from her matchbox-size first-class room.

> They were tall gaunt men, most of them, their features a cross between negroid and Arabian. They wore tunic-like robes called *lunghis*, knotted around their waists and reaching just below their knees. The cotton materials of their robes were of every shade and variety—splendid plaids, striped or plain, green and magenta and mauve. Around their heads were loosely constructed turbans, pink, white, blue. The few Somali women on board seemed a contrast to the brash, assertive men.

At a glance, these women seemed "meek and gentle," an impression that would be modified in the next two years. At first, Peggy was also content to accept Jack's injunction: "In this part of the world, you have to learn that if you can't change something, you might as well not worry about it."

However, a dispute between her and Jack arose just as they arrived at Berbera, when Peggy did not wish to make use of the services of Mohamed, a Somali, who was to act as their servant. Jack informed her: "'This isn't Winnipeg or London. You don't tote your own luggage here. It just isn't done. Maybe we don't agree with the system, but there it is. Another thing—he'll be useful in the shops. If you buy anything by yourself, before you know what's what, you'll likely get cheated by the local merchants.'" The advice was good and obviously well intentioned, but from the very start she rebelled at being the "Memsahib"—or being called or treated as one.

Peggy identified with the "other." She had a natural affinity for placing herself in the shoes of the outsider. Jack Laurence did not believe in the imperialist way of life, but he attempted to work within its constraints. For example, he obviously felt the technology of the West should be used to help the Somalis. Sometimes, Peggy could steel herself to see things from this vantage point, but her real position—as she became more and more aware—was in fact radically different from her husband's. Not only did she loathe the racist attitudes of the colonizers, but she came to see that any attempt to help was ultimately misleading and condescending. Instead, she searched for ways of understanding which emphasized similarities while still recognizing differences. Even in such instances she worried about her possible misappropriation of an alien culture.

Somalia in 1950 was a country that had been tossed back and forth by various European powers. After the opening of the Suez Canal in 1869, the French, Italian and English considered it to be of strategic importance. In 1887, Britain established the British Somaliland Protectorate there and, a year later, reached an agreement with France defining their Somali possessions. (The British Somaliland Protectorate is referred to hereafter as Somaliland.) In 1889, Italy created a small protectorate there. After Britain conquered Italian Somaliland during the Second World War, it became a UN trusteeship territory. Despite the fragmentation of

Somalian territory, the inhabitants shared one religion, Islam and one oral language, Somali. In 1951, the English were attempting to remedy the perennial problem of water supply in the Haud, the interior plateau region of 25,000 square miles. For this they had sent for young Jack Laurence.

The only written record of Peggy's stay in Somaliland is contained in *The Prophet's Camel Bell*, which was based on the diary she destroyed after that book was published. *The Prophet's Camel Bell* was written in the early 1960s, during which time her marriage was beginning to unravel. In that book can be glimpsed—in a subdued and submerged way—some of the differences between the Laurences, but since it was written almost ten years after the event, it may not be a completely accurate account of the emotional life of the couple at the time it is set.

There are two distinct areas to northern Somaliland, where Jack and Peggy lived. There is coastal Guban ("burnt") and Haud ("south"), separated by a high escarpment where the mountain town of Sheikh and the

Hargeisa.

capital, Hargeisa, obtain some relief from the rigours of the desert. The fertility of the Haud was of enormous concern because its population—the Somali Bedouin—are dependent on the summer grazing of flocks there. The building of *ballehs* was an attempt to overcome the privations of the desert during the dry season, to bring water to a dry land.

On their second day in Somaliland, the Laurences were driven to Hargeisa. During that trip Peggy faced the hazards of the desert for the first time: "The light brown sand glistened with mica and slid down into long ribbed dunes. It seemed to be no place for any living thing. Even the thorny bushes, digging their roots in and finding nourishment in that inhospitable soil, appeared to have a precarious hold on life, as though at any moment they might relax their grip, dry up entirely and be blown clean away." Later that day, she learned firsthand what an oasis was when she was confronted with the sudden sight of greenery and human dwellings. However, she did not receive any other nourishment there since, for her and Jack, Hargeisa was closely tied to the English Club, a low rambling structure surrounded by pepper trees and acacias: "It stood, like the European bungalows, at a considerable distance from the *magala* or Somali town."

That distance extended to every aspect of colonial existence, as she soon learned at the morning tea party, where the ladies present offered her conflicting advice:

> Always lock the storeroom door, or you will be robbed blind by your servants.
>
> Never lock the storeroom door, or your resentful servants will find other ways to pilfer food.

The common thread in these adages is the distrust of the servants. Peggy was not inclined to be overly sympathetic to the English women: she saw the barriers they put between themselves and the Somali, and she also reacted negatively to their attempt to establish a "little England" in the desert. She created a scandal when she went with Mohamed into Hargeisa. Her conduct was unusual enough for two Somali policeman to trail her unobtrusively. When she returned to the Club, she learned that "European women did not go to the Somali town alone, and no European ever went on foot. It simply wasn't done." She made this entry in her (now destroyed) diary: "Perhaps it is the sight of poverty that the memsahibs shrink from." Of course, she was not yet sensitive to the fact she might be transgressing the customs of the natives. Somehow, Peggy felt, she would be "immune from their bitterness."

From Hargeisa, the Laurences went to Sheikh, where they lived in a small dark-green house on a ridge away from the main settlement. So windy was their location that sandbags were placed on the roof to prevent it from blowing away. The house had some attractive features, such as a stone fireplace. At first, Peggy, in a frenzy to settle in, rearranged furniture, made curtains and cushions, and, in general, did everything to tame the house to her ways. Then, "I stopped my buzzing after a while and looked around, and then I noticed that everything was calm. The land was not aware of me. I might enter its quietness or not, just as I chose. Hesitantly at first, because it had been my pride to be as perpetually busy as an escalator, I entered. Then I realized how much I needed Sheikh, how I had been moving towards it through years of pavements, of doom-shrieking newspapers, and the jittery voices of radios." The moment was transformative, for she began a slow but steady process wherein she accepted Somaliland and its people as they were, not as she would have them be.

There were many wonderful things to explore, such as the early morning clouds that swept so low one could walk through them. There were always new customs to be aware of, as when Peggy received three elders. Protocol dictated a woman did not receive such guests by herself, and the elders decided to return at a time when Jack was at home. They discussed the *ballehs* with him, even confronted him with their fear that the English, having provided themselves with a continual supply of water, might attempt to push the Somalis out and live there themselves. Peggy also became aware of the outcast tribes among the Somali, the Midgans who did menial work, the Yibir who were magicians and sorcerers, and the Tomal, the workers in metal. She also learned that the wearing of slacks by women brought protests from passers-by: "Look, Dahab! Is it a man or a woman? Allah knows. Some strange beast—."

Jack's life was divided between Sheikh and the camp in the Haud where the *ballehs* were being constructed. When Peggy accompanied him to the camp, she saw a vivid contrast between the desert in the dry season—the *jilal*—

> No green anywhere, none, not a leaf, not a blade of grass. In stretches where the wind-flattened grass remained, it had been bleached to bone-white. The earth was red, a dark burning red that stung the eyes. The sun was everywhere; there was no escaping its piercing light. The termite mounds, some of them three times the height of a man, rose like grotesque towers, making part of the plain seem like a vast city of insects....

and the flowering paradise it became after the rain—

> On that portion of the plain where once only the red termite-mounds stood, now the grass grew several feet tall, ruffled by the wind and swaying gently. The thorn trees were thick with new leaves and the country seemed to have filled in, the grey skeleton no longer visible. The whole was laced with flowers. White blossoms like clover were sprinkled through the short grass under the acacias.

Unfortunately, this change often brought about a strange tragedy whereby men and animals who were dying of thirst would be swept away when the rivers overflowed. As Peggy said, "This must be the ultimate irony, surely—to drown in the desert."

This fate almost befell her. Soon after she and Jack had settled at Sheikh, Peggy had been surprised to learn of the tribulations of the desert. At that point her imagination of those grim events was "depressingly limited." Her baptism was exactly that when she, Jack and Abdi, their driver, were caught in the flooding at the onset of the rainy season. "We were forced to follow the path pointed by this swift torrent of water, for it became impossible for us to see anything. There could be no darkness anywhere to compare with this darkness, unless in caverns under the sea where the light never reaches." Finally, after many hesitant starts and quick stops, the car bogged down completely. After an hour, the rain stopped. The three slept and, in the morning, they awoke to find the flooding had abated.

> I glanced at myself in the Land Rover mirror and immediately looked away again. I was covered with clay and grime, my clothes filthy and dishevelled. I had never felt more demoralized and miserable in my life. Last night we were keyed up, tense, ready for anything, but now that feeling was gone. We were depressed, wondering how long it would take us to get back to Hargeisa, or if we would get back at all. The thought of slogging through the mud again filled us with weariness.

Although her mouth was filled with bile and her stomach empty with the nausea of emptiness, she, Jack and Abdi finally made it back safely to Hargeisa.

There were more tranquil moments. In her account of the Haud, Peggy evoked the wildlife in language of incredible vivacity. The hyenas emerged, "long shadows sneaking from bush to bush ... They were scavengers, not fighters, these giant bastard dogs with massive shoulders and jaws that could have broken a man's neck in a single snap. They had strength but no heart." Perhaps the strongest passage is that dealing with the approach of the "yellow canaries": "The dozen pairs of wings became two and three dozen, a multitude, and I saw that the creatures were not little yellow canaries but large yellow locusts. They were in the middle stage of their growth. When they were fully mature, their wings would be scarlet, with a span as wide as a man's hand. Soon we were driving through a swarm of them. They fluttered blindly in through the Land Rover windows, and launched themselves like bullets at our heads."

The most painful incident involved a cheetah shot by Abdi. It was illegal to torture these beautiful but dangerous creatures, but the Somalis ignored this and proceeded to torment the cat as it clung to life. Since Jack was away at the *balleh*-site, Peggy was alone in camp and had to deal with the situation on her own. She ordered the men to kill the animal, but they ignored her. Suddenly, the animal roused itself and tore a labourer's leg from knee to ankle. At this point, Jack arrived back and shot the beast. "Why," she later asked, "should they have any mercy for the cheetah, who killed their sheep when it could? Life was too hard, here, for any such sentimentality. I knew this very well, but I could not help admiring the desperate courage of the animal. The Somalis thought I was foolish to want the cheetah put out of its pain at once, and I thought they were cruel to want to prolong its agony. Neither of us would alter our viewpoints."

In many ways, Peggy was a hapless—but far from detached—observer of the gulfs between herself and the Somalis. She became particularly concerned with the plight of women, especially when she could do little or nothing to remedy a difficult situation. By dint of circumstance and determination, she taught herself to nurse. After word of her expertise spread, a group of women called on her for help with menstrual pains, pains made unbearable because of the removal of the clitoris or a sewing together of the labia: "I did not know what to say to these women. They were explaining, almost apologetically, their reasons for asking.... What should I do? Give them a couple of five-grain aspirin?... 'I have nothing to give you. Nothing.' This was the only undeceptive reply I could make. They nodded their heads unprotestingly. They had not really believed I could give them anything."

Her helplessness in this situation was mirrored in her confrontation with a parched Somali woman and her dying child:

> She must have possessed, once, a tenderly beautiful face. Now her face was drawn and pinched. In her hands she held an empty tin cup. She did not move at all, or ask for water. Despair keeps its own silence.... We had a little water left in our spare tank, and so we

> stopped. She did not say a word, but she did something then which I have never been able to forget.
>
> She held the cup for the child to drink first.
>
> ...To her, I must have seemed meaningless, totally unrelated to herself. How could it be otherwise ... What we could do here was only slightly more than nothing. Maybe she would reach the wells. Maybe she would not. She might with good reason have looked at us with hatred as we began to speed easily away, but she did not. She was past all such emotions. She knew only that she must keep on or she would perish, and her child with her.

This quintessential Madonna image, redolent of every essence of motherhood and seared into her memory, haunted her for the remainder of her life. Margaret Laurence, who would later in her fiction create a gallery of strong women, obviously received some of her inspiration from these encounters.

Cosmopolitan Djibouti in French Somaliland proved a welcome distraction when Jack and Peggy travelled there to supervise the unloading of the huge tractors and scrapers that could not be accommodated at the smaller port of Berbera. In Djibouti, no one went to bed before two or three in the morning; they frequented nightclubs on the sea front. There were all manners of exiles at the club—middle-aged prostitutes, various kinds of remittance men, colonial service officials in their immaculate whites—and they all co-existed peacefully, if resignedly. "Life was an existing from one whisky-and-soda to the next, and home was a place you would never see again." She found refuge from the daytime heat by spending a large part of each day in the huge bathroom of the British Consul's residence, where they were staying: "Each morning I filled the tub with cold water and perfume, and spent most of the day there, emerging at intervals to re-fill my pint glass of orange squash."

At English-held Zeilah, on the coast near Djibouti, the Laurences stayed at the Residency, reputed to be the only three-storey dwelling in

Somaliland. Built of coral-coloured stone blocks, its middle tier was surrounded by grey wooden verandas. In the 1950s, this absurd but magnificent building no longer had any official status. During their stay, the Laurences had the eerie feeling that an invisible presence surrounded them. Later, they learned there was a legend that a Somali policeman had been murdered there. According to the locals, the Laurences had obviously encountered his ghost.

When he went back by himself to Zeilah, Jack, not someone usually susceptible to ghost stories, refused the comforts of the Residency in favour of an airless shack. Only years later did he and Peggy learn the truth: a British administrative officer—not a Somali policeman—had killed his wife there and then shot himself. "I cannot entirely dismiss" the story, she later said; "Nor [could I] deny the overwhelming sense of occupation we felt in the tall grey house at the edge of the leaden sea, where the locusts flew with the silken wings of destruction, while out on the shore the whorled and fluted sea-shells, pearl white or gaudy as paints, inhabited by living claws, scuttled across the wet sands like creatures of fantasy which only in that one place could exist."

A similar ghostly presence could be felt at the ruins of Amoud ("sand"), near Borama. Peggy could imagine a once-prosperous settlement, but what she saw was one of time's sad relics: "The walls were falling away, and the mosque was desecrated by birds and small wild animals. The candelabra trees had grown inside the houses, their bright green tapers looking as though they had been here always."

Gradually, Jack became known to the Somalis as *odei-gi rer-ki*, the old man of the tribe. The nickname signifies their acceptance of his special role in assisting them to overcome the hardships imposed by their unfriendly landscape. When the Caterpillar D-4 tractors and D-4 bulldozers were being uncrated at Zeilah, they could not be moved because they were jammed solidly behind a pillar in the ship's hold. Further confusion ensued because Jack's principal assistant was an Italian with no English. When Jack wanted to give him a message, he gave the message to Hersi, one of the Somalis, who translated it into Somali for a colleague, who then translated it into Italian. "I know now," Jack exclaimed, "exactly what the tower of Babel must have been like."

Relentless in his dedication, he was sometimes incautious. One day, the sun blazed even more fiercely than normal as Jack worked on the docks. When he arrived home, he hesitated at the doorway and called out, "Peg—give me a hand, will you? I can't seem to see." His blindness was accompanied by a splitting headache. Peggy became frantic, but the consul, who happened to be there, nonchalantly assured them it was sunstroke: "Bound to happen sooner or later, working out in the sun all day. It'll probably pass off after an hour or so." A few hours later, Jack was fine, and he returned to work the next day.

Jack was long-suffering. On one occasion, he had made a crucial point in painstaking detail to some of his workers, who merely nodded their heads in agreement although they had no idea what he was saying. "I was explaining," he told Peggy, "the fact that the wing halls will have to jut out in a straight line, and I realized from that what they said that they didn't have any concept of what a straight line is. Why should they? There aren't any straight lines here. There isn't a tree that doesn't grow crookedly."

Small problems were often of unsurmountable complexity—one such difficulty was the presence of a child prostitute, Asha, who was part of a *jes*, a Somali family following the camp, who sold tea and sweets to the workers. Asha, who was about eight years old, was accompanied by a disreputable-looking man, an old woman and an attractive girl of sixteen. Asha and Peggy hardly ever spoke, except when Asha, who was unusually unkempt for a Somali child, asked to borrow a comb. She was happy to comply, but she and Jack did not know how to deal with the horrendous circumstances of the child's existence. If they interfered, Asha would be forced to leave and might face even more unpleasant circumstances. They did nothing. Then, during the *jilal* of 1952, Asha and her *jes* vanished. But the little girl never disappeared from Peggy's imagination: "Asha's half-wild, half-timid face with its ancient eyes will remain with me always, a reproach and a question."

Peggy felt silenced. She had not yet found a voice to deal with such agonies. The very form of *The Prophet's Camel Bell* reveals her hesitancy. Only after she has described her slow acclimatization to Somaliland does she attempt to give the reader a series of vivid portraits of some of the people she met there: the Italians Umberto and Gino, Hersi the interpreter and language teacher, Mohamed the cook, Arabetto the truck-driver, and another driver, Abdi, "The Old Warrior," whose canny behaviour had saved the lives of the Laurences when they were overtaken by the flood. Peggy felt she could not venture to describe these persons until she had provided a context for them in the reader's mind, almost as if she cannot attempt to explain another person until she has come to some solid understanding of his life. Almost painfully, however, these portraits—in form very much like short stories—show how even the strongest will to understand can be defeated because of cultural differences.

The saddest gap between intention and reality is contained in the story of the disintegration of the Laurences' friendship with Abdi, who had become increasingly jealous of their generosity to Mohamed.

> We were caught between the two. All we wanted to do was keep the peace. We could not see why either of them should be making so much fuss about so little. We came to see something of Mohamed's outlook, but Abdi's was more difficult to see, for it was more deeply hidden. To us, the old warrior appeared to be two men. One was gentle, compassionate, courageous, the man who stopped the car rather than run over a bird, the man who sorrowed for his destitute people, the man who would walk calmly up to a poisonous snake. The other was fierce, violent, raging, the man whose anger had to run its course before it faded.

Abdi also disapproved of what he considered Arabetto's influence over the Laurences, but the situation was modified by the favours dispensed by Jack, who intervened on his behalf to have his wages increased. Then, Jack fired a labourer, who turned out to be a relative of Abdi. "We will take that man back," Abdi informed Jack, who retorted: "Oh no, we damn well won't." A series of minor incidents followed. When Abdi went to visit his family (using Jack's Land Rover), Jack was willing to provide half a drum of water. Abdi wanted a full one and told anyone that would listen that the sahib was a *shaitan*, a devil, and a miser. Increasingly, Abdi became more withdrawn and sullen in the presence of the Laurences. Then, when his animosity turned against Hersi, Jack had to fire him.

At first, Peggy—as she told her diary—was inclined to believe "Abdi's sweet talk to us was in the main a method of achieving favours. I think he has always hated us, simply because we are *Ingrese*, and that he could never feel any differently." This was her suspicion at the time of Abdi's apparent paranoia. Only years later did she realize this was not only too simple an explanation—one that distorted the truth whatever that was—but also a form of misguided, cultural appropriation. If she tried to understand the meaning of the break in Western terms, the reality of the situation would completely evade her. Ultimately, her way of dealing with the situation was to make it open-ended: "Abdi was a man of integrity, but in his own terms, not ours." Her final conclusion was that Abdi's "truest and most terrible battle, like all men's, was with himself."

Towards the end of *The Prophet's Camel Bell*, Peggy provides another, extended portrait of "The Imperialists." The opening of this chapter is given over to a description of "the English monarch's official birthday celebrated in the outposts of empire with pomp and with tumult." Her rendition of the event is laced with heavy sarcasm: "Every last one of these people purported to hate Africa, and yet they all clung to an exile that was infinitely preferable to its alternative—nonentity in England." So angry did the trappings of empire make her that she "imagined that if I ever wrote a book about Somaliland, it would give me tremendous joy to deliver a withering blast of invective in their direction." Her sense of fair play was such that she adds to this chapter a long gallery of small portraits of the foreigners who, despite their dubious status, tried to find ways of coming into accord with the Somalis.

As can be seen in a letter from November 1952, she kept important revelations about the English out of the book.

> We were so glad to get away from Hargeisa, with all its constant and unvarying drink-parties, its bed-hoppers, and its gossip! Wait till I tell you about it! I never used to realize what Hargeisa was really like, but now that we've seen a bit more of it, we see that it's no different from any other colony (at least Jack says it's the same as India in that way) in its petty intrigues and all that. However, most of the Hargeisa population is discreet enough to keep their private lives reasonably private.

This code of silence had been broken by the outrageous behaviour of one couple. Peggy provided no details concerning the exact nature of their conduct in her letter. Later, at the time of the publication of *The Prophet's Camel Bell*, she felt her book was much too sanitized, almost as if she had airbrushed essential—earthy—things out of the book. She held herself back in this book, as if she did not wish to reveal anything of her own thoughts or feelings about sex. In those days, Peggy could be easily shocked. When this was not the case, later on, she did not wish to betray her youthful naivety.

Fiction was safer. Indeed, "Uncertain Flowering," Margaret Laurence's only surviving short story set in Somaliland, contains a very unflattering portrayal of the sexual mores of the English. That story, a sombre one of initiation in which sixteen-year-old Karen Aynsley learns in a particularly painful way about the discrepancies between reality and appearance, is Margaret Laurence's most powerful indictment of the world of white mischief airbrushed out of *A Prophet's Camel Bell.* When Karen, on holiday from boarding school in England, visits with her parents at Bor Mado (obviously Hargeisa), she becomes aware her mother and father are both having love affairs, a situation they attempt to conceal in half-hearted ways. A shocked and confused Karen pretends to a knowledge of the world well beyond her years. She convinces a young officer, obviously infatuated with her mother, that she takes such matters in stride and, indeed, is herself a woman of the world, one recovering from a broken affair. This revelation lessens Howard's reserve: "not thinking now, [he] pulled her closer to him, and let all his young longing for a woman take her as its object." After they have sex, realizing that she lied to him, he is angry and repulsed: "You might at least have the decency to cover yourself." He leaves the room:

> "You think I should be glad," she whispered. "You really think I should be glad..."
>
> She lay there on the bed, still as stone, her body rigid. Her eyes were open, but they saw only the wall.

Young Peggy Laurence's reaction to the expatriate world in which she was an unwilling participant can be glimpsed here. In Somaliland, she was forced to see how the world says it is governed by one set of rules, whereas, of course, another set prevails.

Somaliland provided yet another initiation to Peggy Laurence. Just as her husband was attempting to help in the fertilization of the Haud, she tried to find a parallel way of making a contribution to this strange desert land. Jack's work was one of enlightened assistance, whereas Peggy's was a fundamentally different one in which she searched for a way to make Somali culture accessible to the English.

Shortly after arriving in Somaliland, Peggy, who had long had an abiding interest in the magic of words, found a kindred spirit in Bogomil Andrzejewski, always known as Guś (pronounced "Goosh"). He was a tall, thin, angular Pole, who having escaped his native country during World War II, joined the Free Polish Forces in England and subsequently attended Oxford University. A linguist specializing in the Somali language and its phonetics, he spoke Somali better than any other European there. In Poland, he was a published poet, which immediately established a bond with Peggy. Sheila, Guś's English wife, was also a kindred spirit, a link clearly established on the day she informed her: "I don't really think I was cut out to be a memsahib." Peggy was not as attuned to Musa, Guś's Somali assistant, a well-known poet.

One evening, while she and Sheila had been listening like "acolytes" to Musa speaking of some of the intricacies of his language, Peggy, in her impulsive way, blurted out, "Could some of the Somali poems be rendered into English?" "Absolutely not," rejoined Musa derisively. Guś was intrigued, and a somewhat chastened Musa said he would have to ponder the possibility. Later, after the other two had left, Jack advised his wife: "Take it easy. It may not work out." But even that evening, Peggy was convinced it would. During the following months, she and Musa even became close friends.

Her first step was to learn to speak Somali, a frustrating experience because she was often misunderstood and condescended to by those with whom she was trying to communicate. Eventually, she, Guś and Musa devised a working relationship:

> Musa knew a great many *gabei* [a long, elevated poem] and *belwo* [a short, lyric love poem], and had a wide knowledge of the background and style of Somali poetry, but while his command of English was fluent, he had to discuss the subtler connotations of the words with Guś in Somali. Guś and I then discussed the lines in English, and I took notes on the literal meanings, the implications of words, the references to Somali traditions or customs. I would then be able to work on this material later, and attempt to put it into some form approximating a poem, while preserving as much as possible of the meaning and spirit of the original.

In her introduction to the published translations, she makes her motives clear: "In a country as barren as this, where the population is almost entirely nomadic and where the actual process of salvation demands so much effort and tenacity from each tribesman, it seems remarkable that there should be such a large body of unwritten literature, containing such a high degree of dramatic sense, vivid imagination and wit." She did not want to undertake a useful writing task as much as she wanted to preserve something which might otherwise be lost.

Throughout her entire writing career, she would be obsessed with the idea that through her creativity—the often painful act of writing—she was rescuing something that otherwise might be destroyed or never come into its rightful existence.

Peggy's introduction to *A Tree for Poverty* is a beautiful, crisp and concise explication of an oral literature that has, through her, found its way on to the printed page. In the text that follows, she translates thirty poems and paraphrases thirty-six tales, either Arabic or Somali in origin. In addition, she provides explanatory notes on the customs and traditions informing these texts. For her, this was a literature which dealt in a fundamental way with strong, basic feelings: "Love was one of the two great subjects of Somali poetry, the other being war. Love between men and women did not here contain the dichotomy long ago imposed upon it in the Western world by the church, that of separating it, as though it were oil and water, into elements labelled 'spiritual' and 'physical.'" In fact, the essence of this literature was the free expression of passion:

> Love was an intense and highly emotional state—it was not expected to endure. Indeed, so much was it at variance with the starkness of usual life that no wonder love in this sense did not survive for long after marriage.
>
> Love was a serious matter, a delight which could turn to disaster. But no Englishman ever died of love—of this fact the Somalis were quite positive. It seemed doubtful to them that the *Ingrese* had much need of love at all.

In her later career as a writer, Margaret Laurence was intrepid in her exploration of the intense—often dark—impulses of the human heart. Part of her inspiration was her first-hand knowledge of the "primitive" oral literature which she rendered into written words.

For her, the rejection of the "primitive" spoke volumes about the corruption of Western culture, one which often rejected the true language of feeling. As in this excerpt from a *belwo*, the expression of loss can be a central theme in literature:

I long for you, as one
Whose dhow in summer winds
Is blown adrift and lost,
Longs for land, and finds—
Again the compass tells—
A grey and empty sea.

Somali literature extends to the grotesque, as in the story of Deg-Der, the cannibal mother, who is murdered by her daughters. In this tale, the sin of the mother reasserts itself when the third daughter confronts her husband at their locked threshold:

"Suppose I kill a fat camel," the husband pleaded, "the best of my herd, and you may cook the meat for your meal. Will you open the door then?"

But still his wife refused.

Then the husband's face grew wan with fear.

"And if I kill you a fat ... boy?" he asked.

But the wife would still not unbar the door.

Then the husband's brow grew tight with anxiety.

"And if I kill you a fat ... girl?" he asked.

But the door remained closed.

Then the husband's heart grew chill with dread

"If you want none of these things for your meal," he said, "perhaps the one you hunger for is ... myself?"

And then the third daughter of Deg-Der opened the door and met him.

The last portrait in "The Imperialists" (in *The Prophet's Camel Bell*) is of a District Commissioner, Michael Wilson, called "Matthew" in the book, who had a wonderful appreciation of the Somalis, although he was their polar opposite: "They were emotional and dramatic. He was restrained. They spoke with a thousand intricacies and embroideries.

He spoke with a plain lucidity. They were capable of guile." Wilson could appear cold—a trait he shared with Jack Laurence—but he was also, like Jack, a man capable of deep passion. One day, Peggy showed her translations to him. His response was immediate: they must be published, if only because of one passage. That "was a description of the Somali tribesmen's harrowing and precarious life in the dry *jilal.* I realized then how deep was his attachment to this land and these people, and how carefully he must keep his own feelings in check, if he was to do his work at all."

Through the efforts of another sympathetic Englishman, Philip Shirley, the Administrator of Somaliland, *A Tree for Poverty* was published for the Protectorate at Nairobi in 1954. When working on the translations, she had no certainty they would ever be published: "Still," she told Adele, "it was interesting work and I'm not sorry I did it." Years later, Margaret Laurence would rightly claim her African books could not be regarded as "separate entities" from her Canadian ones, "for it really was Africa which taught me to look at myself."

Peggy had several other literary irons in the fire during her two years in Somaliland, as she informed Adele that September:

> I've been terribly busy all these past months. First of all, I've been keeping a diary, or rather a series of descriptions and interesting bits of information, with an eye to a possible series of articles or something in a year or so. Secondly, I've begun a new phase in writing. I must admit I haven't worked on my novel for a hell of a time, and now feel that the whole thing will have to be completely re-written. What set this off was the beginning of some writing about this country ... about 2 months ago I wrote a short story, and a few weeks ago, I wrote another 2 stories, about Somaliland, or rather, set in an East African colony, without mentioning any names. Listen Adele, they're good! Pardon this unpardonable attitude of pride, but really, I honestly think they are. I think, as a matter of fact, they're the only good

> things I've every written in prose, except for odd passages here and there. But I mean as a whole. Jack thinks so, too. Adele, it really is the first time I've every written anything that he thought was good, as a whole. There have been odd bits in the novel that he liked, and his criticism was always very helpful, but this time it was a bit different. I think this is for 2 reasons: a) for the first time in my life I really tried to write as I thought my characters would think, and not as I thought myself ... i.e. both stories are without propaganda entirely; b) they are both written mainly in conversation. I am beginning to feel that this may be the start of a new way of doing things. I'm unsure of the method, of course, but I do feel it's the most hopeful thing that's happened. Because, on reading over the novel, I find that a good deal of the conversation seems quite good, but the descriptive passages, especially those describing people's reactions and feelings, are really pretty bloody. It seems that when I go much beyond conversation, I get pompous and rather unsubtle. I seem to do better sticking to what people actually say, and letting the reactions and feelings and any deeper significance show up between the lines, rather than actually stating it. I don't know if this will lead to anything, but I feel quite hopeful at the moment.

Two months later, on November 5, Peggy sent the typescript of "Uncertain Flowering" to New York City to Whit Burnett, the editor of *Story: The Magazine of the Short Story in Book Form.* Five days later, she had abandoned the novel. "The reason," she informed Adele, "is simple. It stinks." Still, she remained confident about her short stories, although she lamented the fact she was not "a Steinbeck or a Hemingway or even ... now I come to think of it ... a Kipling!"

Somaliland unleashed Margaret Laurence the fiction writer, although only one surviving story is set there. In a letter to Sheila and Guś of November 1951, she says: "I have been writing a number of stories set in 'an East African colony' (guess where?). Did I tell you all this before? If so, please forgive me. I've done four so far, not counting the first story, which I wrote long ago (the one about the houseboy and the English woman ... you read it, Sheila). It was very badly written, and I've tried to re-write it, but I can't make it sound convincing, so I'll leave it for awhile. The other four seem to me to be the best things I've ever written ... I've sent them to various publications, but I am not being very hopeful about it yet." ("Uncertain Flowering" was one of these.) In January 1952 she provided Adele with additional information about her fiction writing: "I've been trying for 2 weeks to settle a plot of a short story. It is a good story, about an eastern Jew in Africa, and is based to some extent on fact ... i.e. the character of the man, not the plot itself. I know exactly what I want, but when I try to plan it out it gets absurdly tangled up, and I find myself in a confusion of the Jewish and Muslim religions, ineffectually leafing through the Old Testament and the Koran! From time to time I wonder if I shall become a permanent vegetable, but perhaps this isn't likely. All my stories so far have come back like homing pigeons, blast them." She was mildly pleased when the *Atlantic Monthly* sent her a real letter instead of a printed rejection slip. At times, she felt dealing with publishers was like squeezing "bread from a stone, or blood from a turnip or whatever it is! I have sent them all out again. It takes so long to hear. Also, I have discovered that most magazines send the scripts back all covered with coffee stains etc., which is most annoying as you have to type the offending pages all over again and then they don't look the same as the rest."

At the beginning of 1952, it was clear the Laurences would soon be leaving Somaliland, since as Peggy told Adele at the time of the completion of the third *balleh*: "it would be a waste of Jack's time to stay on a job where there is so little experience to be gained ... a good foreman can carry it on." She had been working at the Secretariat, as confidential secretary to Philip Shirley, but had to give this up temporarily when she became pregnant with her first child, Jocelyn. For at least two years, Peggy had tried without success to get pregnant. She miscarried at least twice. When she seemed to be miscarrying once again, she became frantic. Only years after the event did she provide Adele with a history of those dark days.

> I nearly lost her, did I ever tell you? I was only 26, and healthy as a horse, but had been going around the desert over no roads in a Land Rover and could hardly believe I was pregnant anyway because I wanted a kid so much and couldn't believe it would happen. Anyway, the bleeding began and I went to the doctor, and he said it would probably be okay and to take it easy for a few days. Then, a woman put her feet up and stayed that way for several weeks and at the first sign of bleeding, did the same again instantly and called for the doctor. So I did that. After the first three months were over, I was able even to return to the office.

At the time of the completion of the first *balleh*, Ahmed Abdillahi, a young Eidagalla chieftain, presented Jack with a large camel bell which he had made of *galol* (acacia) wood. He did this to symbolize his acceptance of the huge containers which would provide life-sustaining water. Just before they were leaving, husband and wife revisited this *balleh*, which had quickly become so assimilated into the life of the desert that even Jack Laurence, who had helped to build it, was seen as an intruder. This was a bit disturbing, but they were also moved by how the technology of the West could be so gracefully incorporated.

At the end of *The Prophet's Camel Bell,* Peggy joined together her Somalian experience with that of her husband: "Whenever we think of Somaliland, we think of the line of watering places that stretches out across the Haud, and we think of the songs and tales that have been for generations a shelter to nomads on the dry red plateau and on the burnt plains of the coast, for these were the things through which we briefly touched the country and it, too, touched our lives, altering them in some way forever."

The "we" did not survive. The transformation of Peggy would be far-reaching. At the edges of *The Prophet's Camel Bell* can be seen the varying views husband and wife had of colonial existence. These differences were indicators of what were, in fact, profound dissimilarities in their personalities which would later destroy their marriage. However, their two years in Somaliland were a shared adventure and an extended honeymoon, a time in which their marriage flourished. But, beyond that, Peggy Laurence experienced Somaliland as both an unknown and unknowable entity, something she could not fully penetrate. What is more, she did not want to do so. She came to see herself in the same way, as carrying within herself an essential loneliness or separateness. Painful though it would be, the seeds of this knowledge would eventually bear fruit.

8

Crossing Jordan

(1952-1957)

In the summer of 1952, Peggy was preoccupied with the forthcoming birth of her first child and planning, en route to London, a stopover in Rome, where Adele was living. In England, the Laurences would spend their leave and also meet up with Marg. Their ground-floor flat in a large brick house in Hampstead soon became "excessively African" and they were comfortably settled there by early July. Six weeks later, on August 18, "the whole problem," as Peggy wearily and impatiently revealed to Adele, "is that the wretched baby hasn't arrived yet, altho nearly a week overdue ... I wish the little so-and-so would decide to get itself born."

Ten days later, on August 28, "a lovely little girl," Barbara Jocelyn, was born at the Elizabeth Garrett Anderson Maternity Hospital at Belsize Park. During the pregnancy, Peggy had been confident she would have an easy delivery, but this did not prove to be the case. A relieved Peggy—not released from hospital until September 10—told Adele on September 6: "I was in labour for 36 hours, which was rather unfortunate, since by the time she came to be born, I was too tired to manage her by myself. Finally, they had to give me an anaesthetic and finished the delivery with forceps." Just before using the anaesthetic, one of the doctors sympathetically reminded her that in this instance, "The spirit is willing, but the flesh is weak." The baby's collarbone was cracked during delivery, but this healed quickly. The new mother's first question concerned the baby's health. Then, she asked the nurse: "Did I have to be cut?" When the answer was yes, she was a bit dismayed: "Oh my God, I won't be able to sleep with my husband for months." The nurse burst into laughter: "Take lots of salt baths."

She was not allowed to hold or nurse the baby until she was three days old because of the cracked bone but she quickly found herself transformed into a doting mother, much to her surprise: "She is so sturdy and well built, and has none of that puckered, newborn look." Jack had wanted a boy but soon pronounced himself delighted with his daughter. Overall, she had not been prepared for the mysterious, strong feelings that overwhelmed her: "...holding this miracle in my arms, seeing her quiet contented breathing, her latching onto my breast for nourishment, taught me something I had never begun to guess at." Part of this she articulated when she stated that the bearing and caring for children brought her into touch with the realization she could love someone else more than she loved herself. Another, corresponding portion of this feeling—more difficult for her to voice—was the feeling of vulnerability she experienced, a vulnerability linked to the fact she had been as a youngster deprived of her own parents, of those who could have loved her more than they had loved themselves.

In order to visit with the Laurences, Marg had to find a housekeeper to stay with her difficult father. Unfortunately, the visit was not a complete success. For one thing, Marg was supposed to stay for several weeks after the baby was born. As it turned out, the late delivery meant she did not have as long a visit as anticipated with her granddaughter. For another, Peggy was filled with an incredible sense of optimism about her writing: "I was ecstatic. I also knew that I would go on and write books." Marg's habitual way of being was reserved. With hindsight, Peggy came to this conclusion: "I thought I could do everything. Mum knew, as I did not, that there would be a price."

During this visit, she also came to the realization that Marg, now sixty-two, was getting old. The clash between the two came to a head one day when, before Jocelyn's birth, Peggy was fussing with her hair. Marg exploded: "A lady gets dressed and makes up her appearance and then forgets about it." Peggy was hurt, but she "later saw that what she was trying to say was about herself, not about me at all." Her explanation is accurate, but only to a point. Although she was reluctant to admit it, an invisible barrier of silence remained between mother and daughter, a barrier which was never torn down.

Two months later, in the midst of the Laurences' preparations to return to Africa, Jocelyn reacted badly to her injections for smallpox and yellow fever. She was in her crib, when suddenly her tiny body went into convulsions. The Laurences took her to Lawn Road Fever Hospital, where a doctor accused the young mother of having caused the problem because she had continued breast-feeding even after the baby had become ill. The nurses were sympathetic, the doctor "wished I would go away." She held firm, walking nearly two miles, four times a day, to feed the baby. When she returned to the flat, the young mother would burst into tears. Jack was heroic, and Peggy confronted the doctor again, who treated her like a kind of "lesser species." Very much lacking in any kind of bedside manner, he informed the anxious parent the baby might have a "tendency to convulsions, which she might or might not get over by the time she was sixteen, or else she had spinal meningitis.... The fact was that he didn't know what was wrong so he tossed out those two facile and brutal answers." After a week, the convulsions miraculously ceased and the "blossoming" baby, who had gained two pounds, was able to leave hospital. Only years after the event did Margaret Laurence come to some sort of understanding of that crisis: "...when it is someone you love, you feel an overwhelming sense of rage and panic and helplessness—a kind of protest against fate, I guess, or at least that is how I felt when my daughter had convulsions when she was [two months] old."

On December 1, three months later, Peggy was still haunted by the nightmarish existence into which she had been plunged by Jocelyn's illness: "After the first week, when her temperature still wasn't down, the doctor said they'd have to take off some spinal fluid to do the tests for meningitis." That month, the Laurences had just begun to settle into life in Accra in the Gold Coast, where Jack had taken a job as second-in-command of building the new port of Tema, ten miles to the north. The first three weeks after their arrival had been miserable. Before their housing was ready, the Laurences stayed with Jack's boss and his wife, a childless couple. Jocelyn was not settling easily so Peggy walked the floor with her, hoping the baby would not make too much noise.

Their "architect-designed" house, which "had no screens in a land of bugs," was in a complex of modernistic bungalows originally built for the Volta River Project on the fringes of Accra. Peggy felt utility had been sacrificed to beauty: "The living room and dining room had louvers, as did the bedrooms. You took your choice. Either you opened the windows and took the chance of thieves, or you closed the windows and opened the lower-level louvers, inviting in scorpions or snakes.... When we went to bed, we chose to close the louvers in the bedrooms and open the windows, preferring the chance of marauders to the chance of snakes and scorpions." Peggy's greatest fear, however, was of bats, creatures which occasionally got into the living room. Such invasions reduced her to paralysis, infuriating Jack who needed assistance in order to rid the place of the intruders: "How the hell do you expect me to get this damn bat out unless you help me?"

Despite drawbacks, Peggy's first impressions were extremely positive, although she found the dry heat of Somaliland preferable to the humidity of the Gold Coast.

> The country is ... midway between being under the Colonial Office and ruling itself. Nationalism is very strong, and in particular among the young educated men one sees a real enthusiasm for the future of the country as an independent nation. We have not as yet met any of the educated Africans, but hope to do so soon through the university here at Achimota, not far from Accra. But the newspapers are always printing articles dealing with various aspects of the country's future and its problems. There seems to be an admirable tendency

> among many educated people here now to emphasize the importance of keeping many features of the old African culture ... literature, music, dancing, the arts in general, as well as certain features of the tribal system, and adapting these to the modern world rather than imitating slavishly the European modes of culture. It is a fascinating place to be, really, as one feels it is typical of both the old and the new Africa. In the interior, the tribal system still holds good; the chief religions are still the old idol ones; witch-doctors and magic are still prevalent. And yet here in Accra you find people at the other extreme ... African doctors, lawyers, writers, judges, etc. From the little we have seen of the country, I think we are going to enjoy being here.

Later, her optimism would be considerably modified. For the previous two years, she had found a way of relating to the Somali; the inhabitants of the Gold Coast, on the verge of becoming citizens of Ghana, were hostile to any overtures, however well intentioned, from the whites, who, nominally, still ruled over them.

Ghana, lushly greenly beautiful in contrast to the harsh yellows and browns of Somaliland, takes its name from a medieval African empire, which was disintegrated by the thirteenth century. In precolonial times, the region known as the Gold Coast had been divided into a number of independent kingdoms, including the Ashanti confederation in the interior and the Fanti states on the coast. The British, allying themselves with the Fanti, defeated the Ashanti in 1874. The Gold Coast went through many changes during the next eighty years, but in 1951, in the face of nationalist activity, Britain allowed the colony to proclaim a new constitution and to hold general elections. At that time, Kwame Nkrumah became premier and the way was paved for Ghana to become an independent republic within the Commonwealth of Nations in 1957.

In Somaliland, Peggy and Jack had led a semi-nomadic existence. On the Gold Coast, the Laurences—and the other foreigners employed by the engineering firm of Sir William Halcrow & Partners—lived together in the same complexes, whether in Accra or Tema. The change was a difficult one. The Laurences also had to be concerned with the practical realities of living with a young baby:

> We have been lucky with neighbours [she told Adele].The people on one side of us are extremely nice ... she was in the Army for a long time, and is a highly intelligent and practical girl ... just my age, which is nice. On the other side, the people have a three-year-old girl, so we are working a mutual baby-sitting arrangement, which is nice for all of us. However, I'm afraid Lois (the mother of the little girl), while pleasant and friendly, will never be much of a bosom pal. She was brought up in a wealthy family in England; never worked; didn't want her child when it came along and therefore left it to the care of her mother largely; and can't seem to cope out here at all. She said to me the other day that she hated roughing it. I stared at her in amazement as I thought of these luxurious bungalows, complete with electricity, running water, and servants! Jack and I couldn't help wondering what she would have thought of our home in the back of a Bedford three ton truck in S'land. However, I know the tropics don't suit all people, so I suppose I ought to be more sympathetic. I hope to god she doesn't go home ... there will be our baby-sitting arrangement finished. I sound like a selfish brute, don't I? Well, I am. So there.

Even with the help of a cook and manservant, Peggy found the good-natured baby took up a great deal of each day, leaving her only a few free hours. There were pleasant diversions in Accra, however. She particularly liked the nightclubs filled with the exuberant sounds of West African high-life music with its counterpoint rhythms of drums. And she was still a good dancer: "When young African men asked me to dance, I was honoured—they didn't ask just anyone."

Peggy was pleased to drop the title of "memsahib," but the corresponding Ghanaian title of "madam" made her sound, she observed, like the "proprietress of a low-class brothel." She was glad to be able to get to the beach, but driving lessons made her feel exceedingly old and awkward: "I lose all semblance of poise and become like Stephen Leacock in a bank." She never learned to drive, so Jack drove their small second-hand standard when they went on outings. The Laurences first lived near Accra and then, in the autumn of 1954, moved to Tema to a set of bungalows and apartment buildings.

The Laurence bungalow at Tema. 1955.

At the end of 1952, she congratulated Adele on placing a piece of writing and, as she informed her friend, Jack had recently had a similar success in having several poems published in English magazines: "You and Jack now rank in the class who have sold something, and I am going to start collecting autographs!" As it turned out, Peggy had to wait only a month for similar good news.

Well before she left Somaliland, Peggy had sent the typescript of "Uncertain Flowering" to Whit Burnett at *Story* magazine on November 5, 1951. Nine months later, on July 19, 1952, he accepted the story. His letter, arriving after the Laurences had left for Europe, did not reach her until January 1953.

Story had been started in Vienna in 1931 but was moved to New York in 1933. The contribution of Whit Burnett and his wife, Hallie, to

American writing would be hard to overestimate. The first accepted short fiction of Norman Mailer, Joseph Heller, J.D. Salinger and Truman Capote appeared in *Story*. The black writer Richard Wright was also discovered by the Burnetts. Peggy, obviously knowing of the magazine's penchant for selecting the work of young unknowns, was setting her sights high and must have been particularly gratified by Burnett's remark: "You have a fine fictional and character sense, and we wonder if you have a novel we could consider for book publication under the Story Press imprint."

On January 29, the somewhat startled young writer responded to Burnett:

> You asked if I had a novel which you might consider. Up to this point, I have not thought of writing a novel, but I have a number of other short stories set in Somaliland. Some of these are in finished form and others I am working on at the present time. Is it a policy of The Story Press to publish books of short stories by a single writer, and if so, would you by any chance be interested in seeing these stories when they are all completed? This would be in about a year's time. If not, might I send you now the scripts of a few of them for consideration, with a view to possible future publication in Story magazine?

Eight days later, Burnett advised her: "Books of short stories are very hard selling in this country as they certainly are also in England and we would much rather see you work on a novel. However, let us see, from time to time, your best short stories and scripts and believe us that we do not want to lose touch with you for we think you are a very good writer and should have a valuable writing future."

More than willing to take the advice of an experienced professional, she told him in February: "I had not realized that books of short stories were so difficult to sell. Since this is the case, I might be well advised to attempt a novel with an East African setting instead of working entirely on short stories." Spurred on by Burnett's request, she abandoned a novel (begun in 1951), which she felt was top-heavy and filled with far too many sub-plots and major characters. That April, she informed Burnett she had begun work on a novel set in Somaliland, although she was careful not to mention it was her second attempt at a full-length narrative set in that country. Six months later, she had scrapped that book in favour of a third, with the same locale. She was discouraged but remained persistent: "I keep telling myself that one learns with experience, but sometimes I wonder."

The experience of Ghana could be frightening. In January 1953, six-month-old Jocelyn almost drowned when she and her mother were swimming at the beach near Tema. Peggy turned her back on the waves and the baby "naked and slippery as a little eel" almost slipped away when a giant breaker swept her mother off her feet. "I clutched my daughter desperately; if I had loosened my grip on her for a second, she would have been gone forever. Breakers came in and swept out. Jack ran down and instantly hauled both of us onto the beach." Six months later, the Laurences' house was broken into by way of the windows in Jocelyn's room. "Fortunately," she told Adele, "we woke up when they had just gone into the living room, and they fled." The most harrowing event of that year was the sudden death of the little boy next door following an attack of cerebral malaria. "It happened so suddenly," she recalled. "He got sick in the morning and was dead by noon.... The hearse was a government Land Rover, and the tiny coffin jolted around in it. The flowers, picked that morning, were all dead." Peggy, who doted on Jocelyn—writing often with great enthusiasm and with considerable detail about her daughter's milestones to Adele—was badly shaken by this death.

The death of John Simpson on April 29 that year, one month before his ninety-seventh birthday, does not seem to have touched Peggy deeply. In *Dance on the Earth*, she laconically states: "When Mum went back to Canada, she had to look after the old man for another eight

Peggy and Jocelyn, Ghana. c. 1955.

Peggy and Jocelyn, Ghana. c. 1955.

months, until his death." Of much more concern to her was the delight she and her husband took in their daughter. Jack's role in Peggy's writing career was also crucial at this time. Her third attempt at an African novel, centred on the relationship between a District Commissioner and a Somali woman, caused her great distress, which could only be relieved by her husband's approval since he proved to be a demanding critic.

> You are the only person [she told Adele] I feel like writing to since Jack is at the moment going through Episode #4 of my story, and I am sitting here trying not to chew my nails. If he says it stinks, then it does in fact stink. The first two times he read this episode, he tore it to bits (it had then been re-written about five times already) so I hope he thinks it stands up better this time. I am fed up with it. I wish I could disagree with J's criticisms—but they are so damned logical & sound—I always wonder why I didn't see it myself. If I ever write anything with any merit, it will be largely due to him—

> he's always getting me to rework things until they're at least the best I can do—I sometimes think that I myself would never operate at full strength otherwise.

Peggy's trust in her husband's literary judgment—harsh though it could be—indicates the strength of their marriage in the early 1950s.

She was still working on her Somali stories, some of which were sent to the CBC—and may have been broadcast by them. She submitted "Amiina" to the *Queen's Quarterly*, but the editor, Malcolm Ross, her old teacher, rejected it. She had begun short narratives set in the Gold Coast, of which the first was "The Drummer of All the World." The novel she was working on was written from two perspectives, as can be discerned in a letter to Adele Wiseman:

> I am doing the story mainly from the European woman's point of view. In the (necessary) places where the Somali world is the setting it is mainly seen through the Somali girl's eyes—this combination is risky, obviously, but better I think than my original idea of writing it from the man's (D.C.'s) point of view. I have not got the necessary scope of talent to write from a man's point of view. I feel more relaxed about it now that I am not struggling against my own nature.

Later that year, Malcolm Ross accepted a Somali story, but "The Drummer" was later substituted for it.

The big event of 1954 was a visit to Canada. Jack, Jocelyn and Peggy flew to Montreal and then crossed by train to Vancouver, from where they took the ferry to Victoria, where they visited Marg, and Jack's parents who had also settled there. Jocelyn was talking "non-stop," to the delight of her grandparents. The weather on Vancouver Island was a welcome relief from the moist heat of Ghana. Marg was keen to hear about Peggy's writing, and Peggy was happy to be able to show her the typescript of "The Drummer": "Yet there was a weariness in her. I sensed that she missed having her own home [she lived with Ruby]. All those harrowing years with Grandfather had also taken their toll. She was tired. No longer did she hate the thought of growing old. She felt old." Of course, as Peggy somewhat guiltily realized, Marg missed her.

At the end of the year, Peggy was pregnant again. The information about this in a letter of December 11 to Adele contains conflicting pieces of information:

> Now for the big news item—we're expecting another child—around the end of July, I think. To save you counting up—that makes me not quite 3 months pregnant now. We'd been hoping to start one this tour but had just given up hope—we don't want another one born while we are on leave so were going to stop trying soon. However, it seems we've been lucky after all—although if we'd managed it a few months sooner it would really have been more convenient—but I suppose one cannot be too fussy about these things. We only want 2 kids, so if all goes well, this will be our last, barring unforeseen accidents....
>
> Jack, if not as thrilled as Jocelyn and myself, is at least philosophical about the whole thing and admits he will probably be crazy about this one, too, when it is actually here—it is difficult for a man to feel very enthusiastic before the event, I think, especially as 9 months is a long time.

In the first paragraph, the pregnancy seems to be the result of a shared decision whereas the second hints at a difference between husband and wife. Jack Laurence did not want a second child, a wish he communicated clearly to his wife. When she became pregnant, he was furious. For him, this was the first serious disruption in his marriage. On her side, Peggy seems to have attempted to paste over the resulting discord by resorting to clichéd expressions—"not as thrilled" and "it is difficult for a man to feel very enthusiastic before the event."

Peggy may have had the capacity to blind herself to reality, but she also had a corresponding ability to know what was right for her. For her, the birth of books and the birth of babies were the central events in her life, even though she was well aware of the binds to which she might be subjected. In March 1954, she reflected on this very conjunction: "I suppose having a novel is similar to having a baby—when you're carrying it you think everything is going to be wonderful as soon as it's born, only to find that you enter then a new phase of existence that carries with it its own special problems."

This time round, the Laurences decided to have the baby in the Accra hospital—a first-class facility where the patients were a mix of Europeans, African civil servants and professionals, and members of the East Indian merchant class—and then to travel to England for their leave. Meanwhile, Peggy stayed at home to work on her novel: "Sometimes," she reflected, "I feel quite sure it is all a stupendous waste of time, but even if it is, I must finish it now." Jocelyn's bossy behaviour provided amusing distractions, such as the time she told her parents they could each have a sweet if they ate a good lunch. She also instructed her mother: "Don't bother me, I'm a busy woman." The parents laughed about the child's tough-minded bossiness: "By the time she is 18, we won't dare go out without her permission."

Peggy's second pregnancy provided some amusing moments. She was relieved when her doctor, an alcoholic, was away and, she saw a young African doctor to determine if she was pregnant. In those days, the urine of the woman was injected into a female frog. If it laid an egg, the woman was expecting a baby. Peggy's frog did not lay an egg. The doctor informed her she was not pregnant and asked if she was upset at the bad news. No, she assured him, but she felt very pregnant, whereupon the doctor responded: "Well, sometimes European women in the tropics do—um—they can develop neurotic symptoms." Nine months later, she would have liked the opportunity to show him her "little neurosis." The pregnancy was uneventful, although she was worried about the enormous weight gain. "I thought," she told Adele, "if I did my own housework, I wouldn't get so enormous, but I guess I just have a tendency that way."

Twice she went into false labour. The second occasion was complicated by the fact there was a spitting cobra in their garage that evening.

In the midst of contractions, Peggy had to worry about Jack being bitten and thus blinded for life. When she finally was ready to give birth on August 9, she was admitted to hospital. During labour, she was assisted by "an African midwife, a vast woman named Salome."

> When the final stage started, I suddenly could feel the child pushing into life. Ten minutes and there he was. Salome said calmly, "A fine boy." She placed him on my belly to make up for all the weight that was no longer inside me and to alleviate any cramps from this abrupt change. Because he was still curled up, they placed him with his back towards me, so what I saw was his tiny backside, his shoulders and the back of his head. I saw my son at the moment of his birth, before the cord was severed. I felt as though I were looking over God's shoulder at the moment of the creation of life.

The baby did not cry out at first, so Salome removed him to a nearby table in order to suck out the mucus preventing him from doing so.

Peggy with David, Ghana. c. 1955.

Then, Salome wanted to take the baby away in order to clean him up. Peggy became distraught: "No, I want to see him right now. What if you get him mixed up with somebody else's baby? I want to see his face. Bring him over or I'll get up off this table and go to him myself."

Jack finally arrived at the hospital at about four in the afternoon, looking really upset: "What's happening?" he asked. Then she realized he did not know that David (his given name is Robert David Wemyss) had been born. Jack had been phoning the hospital all day, but had been unable to locate anyone who could give him any information about his wife.

After another week's stay in hospital, she was able to go home. "I began writing the first draft of my first completed novel shortly after. I looked after the children myself, but I had a great deal of help with domestic chores. I accepted this with enormous guilt." In this instance, Margaret Laurence's memory was faulty. She did not begin the novel which became *This Side Jordan* until March 1956, eight months later. However, the birth of David did spur her on to work on the draft of her third (never completed) try at a full-length work of fiction set in Somaliland.

Three months later, in November, the four Laurences went to London, where they were joined by Marg and Ruby. This was not an easy time for Peggy. She and Jack could not find suitable accommodation within their budget, and she had to cope with two young children while he went out in search of a place to live. The Laurences, who were staying with Marg and Ruby in their small, expensive service flat, began to feel stir-crazy. Another complication was that Marg, several days after their arrival in London, slipped and broke her wrist. Finally, the six moved to a "dark, dusty, gloomy" third-floor flat in Knightsbridge. The occupant of the flat below them, a prostitute, did not like the fact Peggy left David's pram outside her door. There were further problems. David could not adjust to English time, the flat—supposedly centrally heated —was excessively cold and damp, and one day Jocelyn fell out of her chair and hurt herself. A very harassed, guilt-filled Peggy also had to deal with Ruby, who "couldn't understand why I kept the window slightly open in the children's room. She frequently told me that if the cold didn't kill them, the fog certainly would. Mum, who never gave unasked advice on how to raise my children, nevertheless didn't request that her elder sister refrain from doing so either. She twittered unhappily, torn between us." Peggy must have felt transplanted back to Neepawa, to the domain of tyrannical John Simpson.

Marg was thrilled to attend David's christening. Not surprisingly, however, she and her daughter were not able to talk to each other about anything that really mattered to them. However, Peggy did try to find a way to voice her deep feelings: "Just before the taxi arrived, I gave Mum a long letter I had written to her and asked her not to open it until they got aboard the ship.... I simply wanted to tell her (and for me, this was more possible on the page than in speech) how much I loved her, how much she meant to me, and how much her encouragement of my writing had strengthened me.... I also wanted to tell her that she could not have been more my mother if she had actually borne me." She may not have been able to tell Marg face to face how much she meant to her, but she could now use her form of communication—the written word—to express it. She was able to do so because as she became more and more aware of her calling as a writer, she realized how vital Marg had been in nurturing and mothering that destiny.

The Laurences remained in London for two months after Marg and Ruby left. When they returned to Ghana, Peggy was even more determined to become a professional writer. For her, this meant writing from about ten-thirty at night (when Jack went to bed) until two or three in the morning three times a week. In *Dance,* Margaret Laurence wrote that the writing of the first draft of *This Side Jordan* was exhilarating: "I scribbled on and on, as though a voice were telling me what to write down. It was the easiest novel I ever wrote because I knew absolutely nothing about writing a novel. The pages poured out." This is true, but she had worked on and abandoned three novels set in Somaliland before beginning her first published novel, which takes place on the Gold Coast.

By February 1956, a story [which formed the basis for *This Side Jordan*] had taken over her imagination: "An odd thing has happened. I'd had an idea for a short story for a long time—over a year, I guess—and I thought I'd take a break from the novel and do this story. That was about a month ago. It is now over 80 pages and not even half finished—quite impossible for a short story, obviously, and I don't know what to do with the damn thing. It probably won't be any use for anything, but parts of it are good. It's mainly about an African schoolteacher who's lost the old life and not yet firmly grasped the new."

Her ability to harness herself enthusiastically to her writing was done at considerable cost. Jack was very supportive, but she felt stranded in the company of the other Europeans working for Halcrow. Her existence was in an "intellectual desert," where she was afraid of boring her fellow residents. Peggy, who a few years before, had been excessively shy about expressing her feelings in public, now voiced them: "There were times when old colonials walked out of a cocktail party partly on account of remarks I had made. I *was* tactless. I was tactless, though, because I believed profoundly in what I was saying."

Her new sentiments arose in part from her friendship with Ofosu (called "Mensah" in her essay "The Best of Intentions"), a teacher at Achimsta College, later folded into what became the University of Ghana. In part, he was the model for Nathaniel, the African schoolteacher, in *This Side Jordan.* However, he was a much more resilient, strong-minded person than his fictional counterpart. The Laurences met Ofosu in 1952, shortly after they arrived in the Gold Coast. Since they had London friends in common, the newcomers, anxious to meet Africans, got in touch with him.

From the outset, Ofosu and Peggy fought. She was in her "militant liberal" phase, anxious to express her sympathy for African nationalism and culture. He rejected her well-meaning efforts. Once, she showed him an ebony head she had bought from a Hausa trader. "Look," she eagerly proclaimed, "Isn't this terrific? It's wonderful to see that carving is still flourishing in West Africa." His reply—perhaps because he felt she was being in part condescending—was harsh: "That? It's trash. They grind them out by the thousands. Europeans like that sort of thing, I suppose." Another time, she extolled African drumming. His response was predictable: "I am not such an admirer of these things as you are. Listen—shall I tell you something? My grandfather decorated his drums with human skulls. You see?" To Ofosu, parts of the past were easily forgotten, other portions of it were so bitter that he did not wish to be reminded of it. "African history?" he once sarcastically questioned her. "Africans have no history.... We are a simple people, you see. We have sprung directly from the loins of earth. History is too complicated a concept for us."

In retrospect, Peggy saw her love-hate relationship with Ofosu as part of a historical continuum in which, unfortunately, they were on different sides.

> Our mistrust of one another, and perhaps of ourselves as well, must have gone deep. For a long time I did not trust Mensah enough to disagree with him, for fear of damaging what I hoped was his impression of me—which was actually only my own impression of myself: sympathetic, humanitarian, enlightened. For his part, he did not trust me enough to permit himself ever to agree with me on any issue at all. Yet the force which made us seek each other's company must have been the sense we both had of being somehow out of tune with the respective societies in which we lived.

Cultural differences of an even more basic sort sometimes got in the way. The Laurences would always arrive promptly when Ofosu invited them to dinner, which put him in a temper because he regarded it as rude to arrive anywhere near the announced time. In her turn, she would be furious when he arrived late, usually by two hours.

Despite its difficulties, the association with Ofosu helped to unleash her creativity. Her first published West African story, "The Drummer of All the World," is a re-enactment of the gulfs between them. In that narrative, Matthew, the white minister's son who tells the story, and Kwabena have a close friendship as youths, but cultural discord separates them—despite the best of intentions—as adults. In *This Side Jordan*, inquisitive Miranda pursues a friendship with Nathaniel, a friendship which Nathaniel neither understands nor wants. There was another change in perspective. In Somaliland, Peggy had thought some sort of assimilation between colonials and colonized could be reached. Her experience in the Gold Coast destroyed that naive assumption.

Peggy's ability to vent her feelings publicly was also due in part to the excessive drinking that began to become a part of her daily life. In Somaliland, she had been a social drinker, one whose intake of alcohol was perfectly in accord with the behaviour of most of the whites residing there. Things changed dramatically in the Gold Coast, certainly by her last year there. Cay Munro, who during 1956-7 lived in the same complex as the Laurences, remembered Peggy would drink a whole bottle of sherry at dinner parties; then she would consume lots of wine during a meal. When drunk, she would become very repetitive, talking incessantly about her family, particularly her grandfather's horrible behaviour.

A party at the Tema complex, Ghana. c. 1956.

Heavy drinking was an inescapable fact of life in white colonial societies, especially English ones. But even for this hard-drinking group, Peggy drank a lot, certainly more than any other woman in the Halcrow compound. In Somaliland, the Laurences had wandered afield at the drop of a hat. They could no longer do so. She was certainly restricted in whom she met. On the other hand, she had the opportunity—because of servants—to devote her time to two things, her children and her writing. In the process, she liberated the writing self so vital to her; at the very same time, the often indolent life at Tema, where much time was spent at the Halcrow Beach Club, seems to have led to excessive drinking, to a search for oblivion.

The daily routine was simple and straightforward. She and the children would be at home until lunch-time, when they would be driven by a neighbour to the Club, a thatched ramshackle affair on the ocean.

Peggy with Jocelyn and David, Tema. 1956.

They would lunch, swim and then be driven home late in the afternoon. In the photographs taken at the Club, she seems extraordinarily happy and carefree, taking special delight in her two beautiful children. But there was a downside to this life. For example, she was not particularly fond of the other women in the complex. She preferred to spend her time writing and was thus seen as "different."

Why did she start to drink so much, particularly at a time when her writing career was getting off the ground? At long last, she was exploring the powerful creative urges in her being. If the raw material of one's early life has been dominated by sadness, a corresponding sorrow is perhaps activated when one begins to use that experience in one's writing. When she became poignantly aware of childhood's scars, she sought forgetfulness in alcohol.

Disagreements between husband and wife occurred more frequently and were more intensely bitter. Although Jack supported his wife's desire to write, he began to feel writing was the only thing that really mattered to her. It made him both angry and resentful. Peggy defended herself as best she could, often by yelling abuse at him. Jack conceived of marriage as a union of equals in which each partner is the most important person in the other's life. He was jealous of Peggy's writing because he felt it was now more central to her existence than he was. He was correct.

As a young woman, Peggy had been attracted to men significantly older than herself. Later, she herself was well aware that her husband—ten years older—was in part a father figure, someone who guided and protected her. At twenty-one, she found much comfort in that portion of her marriage. Jack was—and remained—a man to whom Peggy was deeply attracted sexually. The Laurence marriage started to unravel when a slightly older Peggy's sense of self was no longer dependant on Jack's fatherly approval and when she wanted to be independent of him in a new way, a way which fundamentally contradicted the terms on which their traditional marriage had begun.

Peggy had become more certain of her vocation as writer—and less reliant on her role as wife. In a photograph of 1956, a new Margaret Laurence poses for the camera. She looks a bit defiant as she allows a slight smile to escape her lips. This slim, beautiful woman imposes her point of view on the viewer—our approval seems quite unnecessary to her. More than ever before, she has come into her own as a person. She looks independent and, furthermore, she is beginning to think she can tolerate the loneliness that accompanies such freedom. This is the first photograph of Margaret Laurence the writer.

Margaret Laurence. c. 1956-57.

Cay, the Laurences' neighbour, also remembered Peggy as being "fairly intense" with little or no sense of humour. She also recalled instances when Peggy mentioned to her that a rejected story had just been returned in the post. Elsa, a friend of Cay's who lived next door to the Laurences, was incensed by the noise of the typewriter which would waft through the hot tropical nights when she was attempting to get to sleep. At the time, Peggy, well aware she was seen as strange and eccentric by the other Europeans, still clung to her husband as a bastion of support: "except for Jack—who is always a very helpful critic—I never talk to anyone about writing—in fact, most people here don't know how I spend all my time, and probably think I'm lazy as hell." Although Cay may have been one of the women Peggy felt no deep affinity with, she was sufficiently friendly with her to bake a cake—a pink one—to celebrate her friend's first wedding anniversary on June 4, 1956.

Friends of Peggy in Neepawa, Winnipeg and Somaliland had known someone who was sometimes shy and retiring, often overly anxious to please. In Ghana, her public manner changed to a remarkable degree. There, she was unhesitating in voicing opinions that would not meet with popular approval. This unabashed Peggy used cigarettes and alcohol excessively. Without doubt, she was a person who became easily attached to both as social props. Especially, she found relief in liquor from the intense self-scrutiny that accompanied her writing life. The sad irony is that she found her speaking and writing voices at the very same time she became heavily dependent on tobacco and liquor.

A certain hard edge enters her work when she begins to write a series of short stories and a novel which are deeply pessimistic about the possibility of ever really being able to cross over the river Jordan to the Promised Land. The setting may be the Gold Coast and, later, Ghana, but a change of name does not necessarily mean any kind of real transformation has occurred. "Freedom" is a word repeated numerous times in these narratives, but it has a deeply ambiguous meaning. To some of the Ghanaians, it signifies the possibility of incredible change; to the whites, it is a word replete with irony since it really connotes the switch of one kind of oppression (white colonial power) for another (black power). (All of Margaret Laurence's writing is about power and the acquisition of it. In her early writings, she concentrates on political power whereas the Manawaka novels are about the procurement of power by women.)

In July 1956, Peggy knew she had reached some kind of turning point in her life, but the meaning of what she experienced not only eluded her but also could not be put into words. She told Adele:

> I can't talk about it to anyone except Jack, and altho' he is wonderful about it, and has an excellent critical mind, he hasn't actually done this kind of work himself. I often feel I am leading a double life—do you? It seems a kind of irony to me that the thing in life which is most important to me, next to my husband and kids, is something I can never talk about, never let anyone know about, even. But it seems sometimes strange to me that [during] this past tour something important has happened to me, and Jack is the only one who knows anything about it. One feels sometimes it must show, but it doesn't. I am mother and housewife. Full stop. Thank god, at least Jack has followed it every step of the way—it would be unbearable if there wasn't anyone.

Her "double life" is the discrepancy between her perceived role as wife and mother on the one hand and writer on the other. She is asking herself all kinds of difficult questions. Do I have a right to pursue my vocation as writer? If I do follow my instinct to become a writer, will I be able to fulfil my other obligations? These are dilemmas men may never have to face, but they are problems confronted by many women writers, often on a daily basis. She was filled with such conflicts. And yet the portrait photograph of 1956–7 does give a glimpse of the new Peggy, the woman who was waging bitter fights with her husband, who—despite his own sense of hurt and frustration—was trying to understand the importance of the writing life in his wife's existence.

By the end of 1955, Peggy had accumulated a store of incidents and persons to translate into fiction. Ayehsa, the child prostitute in "The Rain Child," is obviously based on Asha, whose sorry existence is described in *The Prophet's Camel Bell.* The conduct of Sunday, the major-domo in "A Fetish for Love," is reminiscent of the Laurences' experience with their cook Mohamed in Somaliland. At the conclusion of *This Side Jordan,* Nathaniel's wife, Aya, gives birth to a son at about the same time as Miranda gives birth to her daughter. In "The Very Best Intentions," she mentions that Mensah's wife, Honour, gave birth to a son at about the same time David was born.

Despite its author's trepidations, the first draft of *This Side Jordan* was written quickly and decisively. By the middle of May 1956, she had reached the halfway point in her novel.

> I've finished the first half of my story, in the first draft, and have begun on the second half. It's not being done in any chronological order as the various parts will have to be inter-leaved in some miraculous fashion, if possible. But the second half deals with the situation from the point of view of a European woman. I'm finding it much more difficult than the part about Africans, mainly, I suppose, because I tend to be rather fed up at this point with the European community here and that is no attitude to have for writing. I don't want to condemn even them—I only want to understand them.

Less than two months later, although the end was in sight, she felt a gut-wrenching revulsion at the entire project:

> Did you feel discouraged when you were nearing the end? [she asked Adele]. I feel awful. I think the story is terrible. It is probably the worst piece of prose in history. Also, who am I to write about Africa? I don't know a damn thing about it, relatively speaking. I've had the nerve to write half the thing from an African's point of view. The Europeans will hate the European parts and the Africans will hate the African parts. Never mind—it has a good title. "This Side Jordan."

In the stories and one novel which have a West African setting, careful attention is given to the interior voices of the Africans—usually men. Peggy had a great deal of misgiving about such appropriation but for her it was an exercise similar to the translations in *A Tree for Poverty*: she was fascinated by the possibility of finding in words the equivalent of the African experience. The tenuous, never really established relationship between Miranda Kestoe, the wife of Johnnie, the chief accountant at Allkirk, Moore & Bright, and Nathaniel Amegbe, a teacher at the ironically named Futura Academy, holds the two plot strands of *This Side Jordan* together. The Gold Coast is about to become Ghana, and Allkirk reluctantly introduces an Africanization programme in its management division. Through Miranda's agency, Nathaniel places two unsuitable students in the firm, leading to a fight between Johnny and Nathaniel. At the end of *This Side Jordan*, differences between Europeans and Africans are pasted over: Johnnie and Miranda will remain in Africa; Nathaniel decides to return to his village. In doing so, he realizes he will never cross the river Jordan and will thus have nothing to do with the formation of the new Africa, that task being reserved for his newborn son.

> —Oh, River, you are not Jordan for me. Not for me. And you, Forest of a thousand gods, a thousand eyes, I am coming back. I will offer red "eto" to the gods, and scatter the sacred "summe" leaves. And some day I may forget this pain.

There may have been a touch of arrogance in daring to use an African voice. However, there was a corresponding portion of humility on the writer's part to cast herself as Miranda, the white executive's wife who asks many questions. She is sympathetic to the blacks, but is eventually shown to be hamfisted and ineffectual.

The strength of *This Side Jordan* resides in its use of two voices in the presentation of Nathaniel. Outwardly, he attempts to conform to the new nation and freedom that will be established by the republic of Ghana. Inwardly, he is torn between the claims of his African past and his adopted Christian faith. At the end of the book, he is a person caught in the contradictory webs of history, someone who cannot adapt to present turmoil. A glimmer of hope surrounds the conclusion to that narrative whereas the short stories are much more about the impossibility of any significant understanding between black and white.

In *Dance on the Earth*, mention is made of the Laurences' decision to return to Canada at the end of Jack's contract in Ghana. In that memoir, she also states: "Just before Christmas in 1956, Jack received a telegram from Aunt Ruby. She had sent it to him so he could give me the message and help me cope with it. Mum was dying of inoperable cancer of the pancreas. The doctors had, I learned later, tried to operate but realized when they did so that it was hopeless. They hadn't told her the operation hadn't been a success. It was the wrong strategy. Of course she knew, but she handled the knowledge, as she had always handled her problems, by herself." Margaret Laurence sometimes had a faulty, unreliable memory. In this instance, her letter to Adele of November 26, 1956, in which she mentions leaving Accra with the children on January 8, is not quite so dramatic: "My aunt wrote several weeks ago to say that my mother had had to have an operation for cancer—which was totally unsuspected up to that time—and that the doctor thought she might not live more than a year at most."

When she had left Somaliland five years before, Peggy had written a handful of stories and completed the typescript of *A Tree for Poverty* (published in 1954). Her five years in the Gold Coast had unleashed her creativity in a remarkable way: she had published two short stories and finally completed the draft of a first novel. Yet, her renewed sense of creativity—and of freedom—was onerous. She had begun to glimpse the heavy personal demands that the writing life would impose on her. In a sense, she did not really wish to comprehend those burdens because she knew at some level such knowledge would irrevocably alter the course of her life.

9

Part Fear, Part Eagerness

(1957-1961)

When Peggy and the children left the Gold Coast in January 1957, Jack stayed behind for the few months remaining to complete his tour of duty. The Laurences—principally because they were concerned with the children's education—had already decided to leave Africa at the end of that tour, but Marg's illness obviously precipitated Peggy's early departure. On one of the legs of the twenty-hour flight, a stewardess gave the anxious mother a magazine to read, the lead article in which was titled "Great Air Disasters of the Past Decade."

Peggy and the children first flew to London, where they stayed with Adele; then they went to Montreal and then Vancouver, where Mona, with whom Peggy had been reconciled about five years earlier, met their plane. A few days later, the three flew to Victoria. When Ruby met that flight, she was quite straightforward in expressing her relief: "You're young and strong. You'll take over. You'll manage things."

Marg was home from hospital but extremely weak, requiring huge doses of painkillers. She spent most of each day on the chesterfield. Quickly, Peggy found herself in a three-way conflict. She tried to keep the children busy and cheerful, obviously not wanting to make them aware of the precarious state of their grandmother's health. She sought to spend time with Marg but found Ruby's twitchy behaviour intrusive.

"I often felt," she recalled, "like blowing up at her, but knew I absolutely must not. There was a lot of John Simpson in us all, his impatience, his quick anger, but also endurance and strength." Soon, niece and aunt were snapping at each other. All of this came to a head over the living arrangements in Ruby's small, one-storey house with only two bedrooms, hers and Marg's. The children were to sleep in the basement and Peggy in a folding cot in Ruby's room.

Not only the lack of privacy but also Ruby's insensitivity bothered Peggy. One day, while Ruby and a slightly better Marg were out to tea at a friend's home, she made a pre-emptive strike: she created her own makeshift bedroom in the basement, next to the children's (this was Bob Wemyss's bedroom but he was working in Nanaimo). When Ruby returned home, she became angry at the *fait accompli.* "She not only couldn't conceive of a decent bedroom in the basement, she couldn't understand my need for privacy or my need to be close to my children. Under great strain, she lashed out at me. I became angry myself. 'You don't understand, you just don't. You've never had children. I'm not going to have them sleeping away down there if I'm not near them. And I'm not a child! I can't sleep in your bedroom!'" This was how Margaret Laurence remembered it towards the end of her life. A letter to Adele from the time gives a slightly different spin on the turn of events, emphasizing lack of privacy as the predominant issue:

> I have a room fixed for myself in the basement, here I can type at night and not disturb anyone. There is one bedroom down here, where the kids sleep, and I sleep in my den. The walls are only blankets pinned up, but I have made a wonderful desk from an old door set on two trunks, and I am quite happy down here. My aunt put us in her room, to begin with, and I had no privacy at all—I couldn't work at all, I couldn't even read in bed without waking the kids. She was very much against my moving down here—I don't know why, as it is so much better for everyone. I can't bear not to have some place I can call my own. I just cannot stand being with people all the time, even my own kids.

Not unexpectedly, Marg became deeply upset about the quarrelling between her sister and daughter. Years later, Peggy, after relating the bitter fight she had with Ruby, took back some of her negative statements, almost as if she could not tolerate the fact she had felt—and, more importantly, expressed—such enmity: "Every day, despite our occasional disagreements, I marvelled at her determined cheerfulness."

As before, Peggy did not have the words with which to speak to Marg. This time, she avoided the topic of death: "I decided at the time that if she wanted to, she herself would bring up the subject. I didn't feel I could." The closest the two came to such a conversation occurred on the day Peggy was sitting with Marg in her bedroom. Suddenly, she revealed to her daughter she had long admired a stanza from Walter Savage Landor's "On His Seventy-Fifth Birthday":

> I strove with none, for none was worth my strife
> Nature I loved, and next to nature, art
> I warmed both hands before the fire of life
> It sinks, and I am ready to depart.

These lines reflect a stoic—but isolated—grandeur, a quality admired by and embedded in mother and daughter. Peggy's eyes welled up with tears, she reached for her mother's hand, and both sat in a warm silence. Then Marg changed the subject. "I think," Peggy recalled, "she wanted it that way." Since they had always shared a love of literature, Peggy felt Marg had chosen this apt way to take her leave.

Hesitantly but eagerly, Peggy wanted to show Marg the typescript of *This Side Jordan.* When Ruby learned of the novel, she asked her startled niece if she could read it. Her only comment, not unexpected and very much in the John Simpson mould, was: "Dear, I think it's rather *gross.*" Somewhat improbably, Peggy later claimed a surge of affection for Ruby suffused her on that occasion. To complicate matters, Ruby and the children came down with "Asian flu": "Honestly ... for a few weeks I thought I would go out of my mind. I guess I hit the bottle pretty hard, and I swear that's the only way I got through those weeks."

Marg was a sympathetic but discerning reader, one who offered substantial criticisms of the narrative. She understood the energy and sympathy that had gone into the creation of the African characters but felt the Europeans had been slighted in the process: "Despite the fact that by then, she was usually not able to concentrate properly for more than short periods of time, I sat beside her bed and she went through the manuscript, section by section. We were back, suddenly, to her critic-teacher, love-of-literature self, and I, to my young self. It was her final gift to me." The literary collaboration of mother and daughter had another curious twist when, that March, Peggy had the first intimation of the novel which would evolve into *The Stone Angel*: "I picture [she told Adele] a very old woman who knows she is dying, and who despises her family's sympathy and solicitude and also pities it, because she knows they think her mind has partly gone—and they will never realize that she is moving with tremendous excitement—part fear and part eagerness—towards a great and inevitable happening, just as years before she experienced birth."

In 1957, a somewhat self-conscious Peggy confessed to Adele this "picture"—so odd did the subject matter seem—might lead her friend to think she was off her rocker. Significantly, she could tell Adele of her vision "because you are the only person, apart from Jack, to whom I can spout these vague and half-formed ideas." Later, *The Stone Angel* would play a part in the breakup of the Laurence marriage.

By the middle of March 1957, Peggy was eager to settle down. She also experienced "an overpowering urge to make up to my family (i.e. husband and kids) for all the neglect they have endured over the past year. Not really neglect, you know, but half my mind was elsewhere. I wonder what I shall want to write about next?" Jack felt neglected, and the children often felt their mother saw them as a nuisance. Under the circumstances, she found it arduous to resume work on her half-finished Somaliland novel.

During their first six months in Vancouver, the Laurences rented a ground-floor flat at 1540 St. George Avenue in North Vancouver, moving on March 3, 1958 to a small house they purchased at 3556 West 21st Avenue. Jack obtained work dealing with the highway being built between Vancouver and the little fishing town of Squamish. At first, Peggy had been eager to return to Canada, but then the "happiness pill" mentality of North American life began to bug her. This was in startling contrast to Africa: "it was a stinking place I suppose, but I loved it and felt at home there as I never did in my whole life here. I'd still go back like a shot ... and live all my life there."

That spring, Marg was well enough travel to the mainland to visit with the Laurences, although she was often exhausted and in pain. A few months later, she was confined to a hospital room. The injections of morphine made her mind wander, but she insisted on seeing her two grandchildren.

> The nurses tied her white hair with a blue ribbon, put on her lacy nightgown and a new soft, woolen jacket, installed her in a wheelchair, and brought her down to the lobby in the hospital, where Aunt Ruby and I were waiting with the children. The kids were very quiet, but they both said hello to Granny. By this time I had told them that she was dying, trying to explain it as best I could. After a few moments, the nurses took her back to her room, but not before she had looked carefully at the children, storing up a picture of them in her memory, memory that was soon to be lost.

Peggy and the children returned to Vancouver. Then, in September, not long after that visit, Ruby called to tell her Marg was in the final stages of her illness. Brother and sister travelled to Victoria, where they stayed with Ruby, Peggy sleeping in Bob's room and Bob, who worked as a town administrator, on the chesterfield. By this time, Marg's skin "had turned very dark, almost an olive black ... There was even a strange beauty about it."

Peggy and Bob, who had grown much closer in their mother's final days, had to return to their daily lives. Vem and Ruby were with Marg when she died. Peggy later reflected: "I've never liked people seeing me off at airports. Mum never liked people seeing her off on trips either. No one can tell about that last voyage—the one truly solitary one, but in a sense, not solitary at all—in which the baggage of an entire lifetime is finally lightened." What Margaret Laurence did not reveal in *Dance* was the full extent of her own painful reaction to the dementia that overcame Marg as her life came to an end on September 25, 1957 at the age of sixty-eight. At the time she herself was dying, she scribbled in her journal: "God, please don't let my mind go until I do. My mum's did. It broke my heart."

Earlier that autumn, Jack became severely ill with kidney stones, which had to be removed by surgery. At that time, Jack had been supplementing his income by working as a marking assistant to Gordon Elliott of the English department at the University of British Columbia, who taught a compulsory course for engineering students. Peggy took over her husband's responsibilities. Since the Laurences had been hit badly by lack of money following Jack's illness, she was glad of the work. More importantly, she became a close friend of the occasionally irascible, usually outspoken but always warm-hearted man who would remain one of her closest friends. Tall, thin and angular Gordon, six years older than Peggy, had attended the University of British Columbia and Harvard. Although he taught in the English departments at UBC and, later, Simon Fraser, he was equally interested in history. At the time he first met the Laurences, he was working as a research assistant on two projects, Margaret Ormsby's *British Columbia: A History* and R.E. Watters' *British Columbia: A Centennial Anthology.*

Peggy soldiered on with her Somaliland novel, submitted the typescript of *This Side Jordan* to the *Atlantic Monthly* contest, continued work on short stories set in West Africa and started to type out her Somaliland diary, an occupation "good for laughs." She didn't think she had "a hope in hell" of winning the contest but the reaction of the *Atlantic Monthly* was not as negative as she had feared: they pinpointed the weakness in the depiction of the European characters. If she rewrote those portions of the book, the editors expressed interest in reconsidering it.

In June 1957, Peggy wrote a warm letter of congratulation to Adele when she won the Governor General's Award for *The Sacrifice*, her powerful depiction of the hardships of immigrant experience: "When I saw the writeup ... I just felt like showing it to everybody and saying 'I know her!'" Although she could be rivalrous with other writers, such sentiments never entered into her friendship with Adele.

In the midst of financial struggles and resettling in Canada, Peggy was working frantically on a number of literary projects, each requiring a lot of attention. Sometimes, she was at the edge of despair, understanding for the first time why medieval man made it the paramount sin. Her writing touch seemed to be the reverse of Midas's—everything she touched turned to dust. She also found it impossible to give her writing the attention it needed and to deal with her housework, marriage and children. Often, she was crippled with guilt as well as despair, as she confided to Adele in February 1958:

> When you have two kids you'll probably wonder why you didn't keep a free mind! So much of one's thought, time and emotions are drained away from work, with a family. However, I guess it amounts to one's definition of "free"—I know I could never be truly free unless chained (in a manner of speaking) to these people I love, my man and my kids.
>
> I sometimes think "why can't I get away from all these screaming brats just for 2 months and finish my story!" No doubt there is much to be said for and against each way of life.
>
> I constantly lose my temper with the children, mainly out of a frantic desire to get all the housework done so I can get to work and a sort of impotent fury when they create more and yet more domestic work to be done before I can do any writing!

She was being invaded by guilt that she was not living up to her role as mother and housewife. The resulting conflicts made her difficult to live with. If she could not succeed as a writer, she knew her life was meaningless. Helpless in the wake of her strong wish to write and of her equally strong sense of her responsibilities to husband and children, she sometimes lambasted herself for "lack of guts," even though the problem, most simply put, was that there were not enough hours in *any* day to allow her to accomplish what she felt needed doing. In an attempt to distract herself, she even took to finishing furniture as a form of therapy. "Now, Adele, honest to God, I would *hate* to be thought 'artsy craftsy'—I simply *loathe* that kind of woman." But Peggy was often the model of a dutiful wife and mother, even though adherence to the con-

Peggy with Jocelyn and friend, Victoria. 1954.

Peggy arranging Jocelyn's hair, Vancouver. c. 1959.

ventional caused her anguish. In one photograph from 1954 during a visit to Canada, Peggy—dressed in her Sunday finery—poses with her daughter and another child; in another, she is the meticulous mother helping Jocelyn with her hair.

3556 West 21st Avenue, Vancouver.

The tiny Laurence home on West 21st Avenue contrasted drastically to the family car, a white Jaguar with red leather upholstery and walnut dashboard. The second-hand automobile was Jack's pride and joy. For him, the treasured Jag provided compensation for his new, humdrum life back in Canada. Peggy found no such exotic touch: she was confined to a small house and repetitive, hectic domesticity. Her minute ground-floor writing room—the walls of which were decorated with spears and shields—doubled as the family den. There were some diversions. She and Zella Clark, her neighbour from across the street, attended sessions called "Living Room Learning: Great Religions of the World," where tapes about various cultures were played, but Peggy seldom partook in the resulting discussions. She never became a part of the wifely culture of the street because—as in Ghana—she used all her spare time to write. She took comfort in visiting another housewife, Jan Bhatti, an immigrant from India. Peggy liked to drop in on this woman because she found in her home a serenity increasingly absent from her own.

She wanted to be a more than competent suburban housewife, but the mundane chores that constitute domestic life frustrated her. Sometimes, she could be ruthlessly practical. Never much interested in gardening, she turned half of her backyard over to David, who filled the space with canals, dams, roads and bridges. At other times, she used her storytelling gifts to intrigue the neighbourhood children with the tale of the Invisible Cats. This narrative—a serial in many parts—was so gripping that Jocelyn and her friends would race home from school for the next instalment.

In the summer of 1958, Jack worked as resident engineer on the dismantling of the old Peace River Bridge at Fort St. John. For the first time since returning to Canada, the Laurences felt at peace. Both she and Jack sensed they were "country people at heart," who did not much care for cities: "Farming, however, is out. We know nothing about it, and I would drop dead if I had to approach a chicken at close quarters." Nevertheless, the old problems continued to haunt her. She did not like Adele's suggestion that she spend some time in a writers' retreat: "I am not much on 'groups' of any kind having always preferred to be by myself when it came to work, but perhaps my work suffers from insufficient communication with other writers ... Apart from you, I don't really like writers very well."

Peggy also remained deeply sceptical of the state of existence in North America, even wondering if the Beat Generation—especially the fascination Jack Kerouac and his circle had with non-mainstream experience such as Zen Buddhism, progressive jazz and mystical experience—had it right in their rejection of the Western world and its values: "I really don't care for North America, but if you happen to be born a woman when the empire is falling, where else can you go?... Anyway, one can't go on being a stranger in a strange land, as we were in Africa ... One cannot identify oneself with another culture, because everyone carries his own culture with him, like his blood-group."

Not yet ready to write about her own culture, she revised *This Side Jordan* to the *Atlantic Monthly*'s specifications, but they refused it again, a decision to which she herself nodded in agreement: "...however you cut it, it's still salami.... I have begun to sharpen the red pencils and I'm going to go through and edit ruthlessly." She felt a "veritable babe in the woods" but decided that she would bring her typescript into a publishable state; she also worked on stories set in West Africa. In the midst of her struggles to find her own voice as a writer, she was bowled over by *Lolita* and *Doctor Zhivago*:

> Both, in their widely different ways, are tremendous books. "Lolita," I think for sheer brilliance of style; for subtlety and incredible perception, cannot be beaten. But the odd thing is that "Doctor Zhivago," with its much simpler style, a style that is almost prosaic in places, still manages to make almost everything else written in this century look like the work of grade school children. I felt that it was possibly the greatest contemporary novel I had ever read. One is led very quietly into its tragedy—there are no fireworks. And yet, by the end of the book, the characters have become more real than most real people one knows.

Peggy may have been a "babe" in the literary woods, but, in Pasternak's great novel, she glimpsed, in an even more forceful way than before, the simple truth that one's own experience must be the basis for any convincing piece of writing.

Meanwhile, wily Gordon Elliott, who had volunteered to type the latest draft of *This Side Jordan* and who was well aware of Peggy's disappointment with the *Atlantic Monthly* rejection, wrote secretly to Jack McClelland, the energetic, brash head of McClelland and Stewart, with whom he had a passing acquaintance:

> I have been hearing a good deal about an unpublished novel which is being passed around here in certain circles. The novel concerns the independence issue in Ghana and was written by a Mrs. Margaret Laurence, a Canadian, who was with her husband in Africa for six or eight years.
>
> I have not read the novel myself but others I know have and report that it is good. She has not as yet attempted to have it published, I understand, but I thought that you might be interested.

> I write this letter only to keep something reported to be good out of American hands because I have been told that some of her friends are trying to persuade her to send the manuscript to the States or to England first.

Gordon's letter provided the perfect bait for Canada's greatest publisher, himself a master—when necessary—of setting the perfect trap. His response was immediate: "I very much appreciate the tip re Mrs. Laurence and I have written to her asking her to let us have a look at the manuscript."

In 1946, at the age of twenty-four, Jack McClelland had joined the firm co-founded by his father, John, in 1906. Toronto-born and educated, Jack served during World War II as a commissioned officer in the Royal Canadian Navy, volunteering for active duty on torpedo boats in the English channel. Early on, Jack insisted McClelland & Stewart initiate a policy of seeking out and publishing Canadian authors. Before that, the company had concentrated on agency publishing (distributing books published by English and American houses). When he became general manager in 1952, he even more actively pursued this tactic, becoming in the process the most important and creative publisher in Canada. McClelland's manner, always genial and charming, sometimes concealed the enormous drive that fuelled his determination to make a place in the world for Canadian literature.

Jack McClelland.

Gordon Elliott, understanding McClelland's competitive spirit, wrote a letter calculated to force Jack to contact Peggy. The scheme worked perfectly, for it began an association between an ambitious publisher and the woman who would become one of Canada's most successful writers. Jack was an enabler, a publisher perfectly attuned to an author's needs, certainly to Peggy Laurence's in 1959—and in the years ahead.

By May 15, she had submitted the typescript to McClelland, although she was certain he would not take the book. Four months later, he told her he would publish *This Side Jordan* if he could find an American or English publisher to bring it out simultaneously (and thus make the project financially viable). By the end of November, Macmillan in England had accepted the book. (St. Martin's Press was the American publisher. Years later, she could look back with a smile at the report of one of that firm's readers: "The purple prose and overdone oratory of the last chapter left me only reasonably nauseated.") The nervous author was at last triumphant: "Hurrah! Hurrah! Hurrah! (They want 10,000 words deleted. A mere bagatelle! And it is too long—they're right.)"

Immediately, she telephoned Zella Clark to announce that she was dropping out of the Spanish course in which they were enrolled. Then a note of elation crept into her voice when she added that her African novel had been accepted but she had to work on revisions. New, exciting demands were being made on her time.

While waiting for word from Toronto on the fate of *This Side Jordan*, she was filled with apprehension about her future as a writer: "Without periodic encouragement, how can one possibly know if one's standards are any good or not?" She also did not know if she was placing too much emphasis on her career as a writer: "The main point is—if one is writing and more or less gambling one's whole existence on it and cheating family of one's time and care and putting into it very nearly the whole of identity and it turns out to be no good—what will you say then?" This was a frightening prospect, but, she was certain, the private world of the novelist must become public: "If it remains private, it is shrivelled as a stillborn child." Writing was the only thing in her life, "apart from sex and one's children," that gave her pleasure. So divided were her feelings she wished "to heaven I could drop the whole sorry business and become a Good Housekeeping Mom, complete with home-baked bread and glamour, but I can't."

Two days later, she asked Adele to ignore the "puerile outpourings" expressed above: "I am going to turn over a new leaf. This always happens in the Spring—both the discouragement and the new resolutions. I'm going to: a) be cheerful; b) be sensible; c) lose ten pounds; d) stop being obsessed with writing.... Talking of weight, I have been losing this same 10 lbs every spring. Why wasn't I born the slim sylph-type?" In the late 1950s and early 1960s, Peggy, although she was slim, was obsessed with her weight as another barometer of self-esteem. During these years, her drinking lessened considerably from her final days in the Gold Coast. She was a social drinker, who only occasionally over-indulged. She and Jack took up wine-making as a hobby and even had their own label printed. Throughout 1960, she continued to feel her writing was stolen time, but she came to the realization that perhaps "if we did not have these constant tensions we wouldn't write at all."

The children provided amusing and touching moments. In May 1960, the Laurences watched Princess Margaret's marriage on television. Peggy "bawled like the Missouri all through the ceremony." This led David to ask her: "Why on earth are you dripping?" Apologetically, she explained to him she cried at all weddings, whereupon he "asked me if I'd cried at my own."

Based on the evidence before his eyes, David had come to a remarkable conclusion. "Whoever heard of a book written by a *man*?" he incredulously asked his mother one day. As she informed Adele, "He had believed only mothers wrote books, and that writing was something in the same category as cooking or washing dishes."

In the summer of 1960, Peggy became ill with severe stomach pains, leading to the removal of her gall bladder. (This experience—although she did not dwell on it—would eventually be of tremendous assistance to her when she began work on her next novel.) A more pleasant distraction was the acquisition of a dilapidated cottage at Point Roberts, Washington, just over the border from British Columbia. Despite their precarious financial position, their summer home was cheap and, what was even more crucial, isolated. "It was fairly primitive, with no plumbing, and only partial dividers between the rooms. I recall many weekends when I scribbled by the light of a candle in the kitchen while the others slept." In family snapshots from this time, she looks relaxed, almost carefree. Her photograph of Jack and the children has a similar idealized look. Family life held many pleasures for her.

All in all, Peggy wondered if she groaned too much. In particular, the den on the ground floor was supposedly her room of one's own—her workspace, but "everybody and his dog tramples through it from morning to night, bringing with them bubble gum, hurt knees, and complaints about the nefarious behaviour of others." Did she have a right to complain? Like many women of her generation, she was not sure.

Margaret Laurence. c. 1959.

Margaret Laurence. c. 1959.

Jack, Jocelyn and David. c. 1959.

Throughout 1959 and 1960, Peggy continued "bashing away at short stories." She was both intensely restless and extremely disciplined. After "The Merchant of Heaven," which recounts the unsuccessful attempt of Brother Amory Lemon to proselytize his Evangelical Christianity in Accra, appeared in the first issue of the Vancouver-based *Prism International*, she encountered her first opposition on religious grounds to her writing: "...quite a number of people wrote to the newspapers here, regarding 'Prism', and some of them were very concerned about the publication of irreligious material (i.e., my story). Very peculiar. I thought of it as quite religious." She was correct: the story emphasizes cultural differences between Western and African sensibilities and does not attack religious belief. In any event, she no longer liked the story, which she now felt was too fancy: "my usual style is plainer, but in this case the character of the evangelist was rather flamboyant in a way, so I suppose that is the reason for some of the extravagance of style."

She was delighted when "Godman's Master," "about a dwarf who was an oracle," was accepted by the same magazine. In October 1959, she completed "The Perfume Sea"—perhaps the most accomplished of her short stories and the one that is most optimistic about the possibility people from the West can adapt to the new Africa: it is "about an Italian-American hairdresser ... Maybe nobody else will be interested in Mr. Archipelago, but I have been." As she struggled to impose her vision in these stories, she was often discouraged about the discrepancy between what she wanted to say and what she was able to put into words. At such moments, she received consolation from Browning: "'...a man's reach should exceed his grasp.'"

The most wonderful by-product of her short-story writing was the enthusiastic letter of praise for "The Merchant of Heaven" which she received from Ethel Wilson, Vancouver's premier writer and one of Canada's first great woman writers. The ensuing friendship was not a close one, but it gave Peggy a sense of what she herself could accomplish. Two years later, in 1962, she tried to find the right words to describe Mrs. Wilson:

> She is so terrific I don't know how to describe her. She not only writes like an angel (in my opinion) but is, herself, a truly great lady—again, that probably sounds corny, but I don't know how else to express it. Her husband is a doctor (retired) and they live in an apartment overlooking English Bay. She is very badly crippled with arthritis, but she never mentions her health. She is poised in the true way—she never makes other people feel gauche. And she is absolutely straight in her speech—she has no pretensions, nor does she ever say anything she doesn't mean, and yet she has a kind of sympathetic tact.

Later, when she herself became the grande dame of Canadian letters, Peggy's generosity to younger writers bears more than a superficial resemblance to the maternal warmth Ethel Wilson bestowed on her.

During the last six months of 1959, Peggy pruned *This Side Jordan.* Most of the cuts were made to those portions of the book dealing with Miranda, leaving Peggy open to the (justifiable) complaint that those sections of the book are much weaker than those devoted to Nathaniel. In order to find a way of dealing more effectively with the conflicts between blacks and whites in *This Side Jordan* and in her West African short stories, she turned to Joyce Cary's *Mister Johnson* (1939), his humorous novel about a native clerk in Africa: "I could have wept in rage and frustration—and admiration because he had done it. How?"

If a satisfactory way of dealing with colonial Africa eluded her, she nevertheless pursued her literary career with a vengeance. In addition to her other activities, she agreed to review books for the *Vancouver Sun.* At home, things seemed finally to be slipping into place. In July 1960, Jack, who had been working on an unsatisfactory job at Revelstoke, obtained the post of Plant Engineer at Wright's Canadian Ropes, a position he had very much wanted. When she was in hospital with the gall bladder operation, she had a chance to put everything into perspective: "I reviewed my life like a drowning man is said to do, and could see how stupid I've been to get myself in the position of having no reserves of energy or calm."

Shortly after Peggy made this resolve, events conspired against her. Jack McClelland—as a first step in the professionalization of Margaret Laurence the writer—undertook the task of obtaining an agent to represent her. On October 18, 1960, he approached Willis Wing, a New York agent who represented, among others, Brian Moore and Pierre Berton. "I presume you do handle women (don't we all?) even though yours seems to be a predominantly male list." Having insinuated Wing might be a bit of a chauvinist, he told him:

> This particular writer, if considerably less spectacular, may be even more promising than Jack Ludwig. I suspect that she could turn into the bread-and-butter type of client. I will give you a brief account of our association with her.... Her name is Margaret Laurence. She is a housewife. I would guess she is in her late thirties.... I heard about her through a mutual acquaintance and received a copy of her script hot off the typewriter. We thought it extremely good. She has a somewhat unique style, powerful, virile, vigorous—when I read it I found it hard to believe that the novel had been written by a woman. I'm not suggesting that she is the greatest literary discovery of the last ten years, but she is a serious writer, a writer of quality, and she tells a very good story.... She is, Willis, a gal who is serious about her writing and intends to continue.

Promptly, Wing accepted Peggy as a client. McClelland's acumen always worked overtime. He knew full well that, eventually, he would have to pay higher advances to an agented author, but he also realized Wing could help him to promote Margaret Laurence and thus provide the kind of broad base necessary to gain her recognition internationally.

In November 1960, she met Jack McClelland at a launch party held in Vancouver to celebrate the publication of *This Side Jordan.* As he told a fellow publisher, Jack was more impressed than he had anticipated:

> I have just returned from a trip to Western Canada, during which I had the opportunity to meet Margaret Laurence for the first time. I

> thought you might like to know that I found her to be a thoroughly charming woman, much younger and much less severe than her pictures make her out to be. She is determined to have a full writing career, will have another novel under way shortly, and I think we can both be confident that we have on our hands a writer who will produce many good books for us in the years to come.

Peggy, transported with joy that her writing career had begun in earnest, did not even mind mixed or bad reviews, she herself having come to the conclusion her first published novel was "amateurish," as she informed Adele:

> I've had quite a number of reviews now, mostly from England, and on the whole they are kind. *The London Times* [*Times Literary Supplement*] pans the book, saying that the relationships of white and black are of limited psychological interest, but they do certainly pick out the novel's weakest points very neatly which none of the other reviews have done—it is the only review to point out the flaws of construction which seem so glaring to me that I thought every review would mention them. I remember your saying how you wished that someone would read your book as carefully as you wrote it—few do, it seems. *The Statesman* gave it a very good review (hallelujah!) but said the ending was "suspiciously sunny". Richard Church, in the *Bookman*, on the other hand also gave it a very good review but said the ending was despairing and showed the impossibility of understanding between blacks and whites. This disparity of opinion can only be regarded as encouraging and at least so far no one has called the book "dull"—the only really damning word in my vocabulary. I thought I would be a nervous wreck when the reviews came out, but I do not find that I am really much affected one way or another.

Later, in September 1961, she was similarly unfazed by Kildare Dobbs's characterization of her book as boring: "I enclose Kildare Dobbs's review [in the Spring 1961 issue of *Canadian Literature*] of my novel. At first I wondered why it was so relatively loaded with smart cracks, but I learned that he spent a year or so in East Africa, so I guess he knows all about the soul of Africa. He had a poem in *Tamarack Review* a short time ago called 'African Poem', which was quite good poetry, I think, but its general outlook was that of the European who dislikes much of his own civilization and who finds in so-called primitive cultures the bloody splendour lacking in ours, almost the 'noble savage' outlook."

When Jack McClelland met Peggy that first time in Vancouver, he had glimpsed at firsthand the extremely ambitious person who was determined to carve out a career as a writer. She herself realized she had merely taken one more step in a ever widening gyre: "I always felt that if I could ever get this novel published, that would be all I would expect out of life, but of course it is not the end but the beginning."

Earlier, McClelland's enlightened self-interest had extended in another direction, when in July 1960 he sent Peggy *A Candle to Light the Sun*, by the recently deceased Patricia Blondal, who died of breast cancer. This was probably not a serendipitous move. In all likelihood, he was nudging her towards Canadian subject matter. However, he may not have realized she had never really liked the glamorous Blondal, when they were students together in Winnipeg. In fact, Peggy had been jealous of her classmate's magnetic sex appeal. Nevertheless, McClelland's ploy was to pay enormous dividends, as can be gleaned in Peggy's letter to Adele of July 21, 1960:

> Jack McC (obviously totally unaware that I had known Pat) asked me to read it & said he would like my opinion of it.... It would have been better to have been cut in places, but even as it stands, it is quite an achievement. She attempts such a lot—an over-all picture of a small prairie town & all its people; an historical picture of the late 30s & the war & the post-war years & our generation, a wonderfully complex analysis & picture of a man's search for his own

> identity & meaning.... Am I being influenced too much by her death?... I think her novel is really one of the best things on a prairie town that I've ever read, & it is much more as well.... if she had lived to work more on it, it would have been truly excellent, but even as it stands it is a remarkable job. I wish I could have told her so.

Three months later, Peggy was working up the courage to begin a new novel. In her mind's eye, it was "planned in rough, but what I fear more than anything else is that the theme will be too explicit and will overshadow the characters." Three months after that, she was able to focus in a much more precise way on her new project:

> Right now I think I'd like to come back home. This, of course, coincides with my own state of mind. I feel I'm here to stay, for better or worse, and that I don't need to go away any more, in fact can't go away. It's here, and in me, and I can't run forever to countries (real or imaginary) which I like because they didn't know me when I was young. If that makes any sense to you. I hated being here, for several years, you know. But now, for the first time, I feel the urge to write about the only people I can possibly know about from the inside. I don't want to write a "Canadian novel". It's just that I feel I might at last be able to look at people here without blinking. Having hated my own country most of my life, I am now beginning to see why. It's the mirror in which one's own face appears, and like Queen Elizabeth the First, you smash the mirrors but that doesn't change yourself after all. Very strange. I am glad I did not write anything out of this country, before, because it would have been done untruthfully, with bitterness, but perhaps not any more.

Realizing she was contemplating a completely new step, she relinquished her African writings and expectantly looked forward to what the future might bring: the past was "over, and I have a strange sense of release and relief."

She felt transformed, leading her to a new, heightened sense of identity, one which can be clearly seen in the postscript of her letter to Adele of January 22, 1961: "I've changed my name to Margaret ... it was Peggy I hated, so I have killed her off." In parenthesis, she added wistfully: "I hope."

Part Two

MARGARET

"I will be different. I will remain the same.... I will be afraid. Sometimes I will feel light-hearted, sometimes light-headed. I may sing aloud, even in the dark. I will ask myself if I am going mad, but if I do, I won't know it."

A Jest of God

10

Terrible Complexities (1961-1962)

Why did Margaret "kill off" Peggy? In part, because Peggy was her young, idealistic self, a person with whom she could no longer identify. By using the name Margaret, she also signified that she had changed from a person with a passionate interest in writing into someone who was a professional writer—and thus did not wish to be known by a nickname from childhood. But other psychic forces were at work. Peggy was the girl she had been, whereas Margaret was the woman she aspired to be. This transition was sudden and violent, almost as if a change in personality would follow a change in name. The metamorphosis had its positive side—her creativity was unleashed in a remarkable, new way. But dark forces were also at work. She became restless, discontented, filled with anguish over the direction her life should take—and whether she wished to be part of a family or live alone. The question could be rephrased: what had to be killed off for the new Margaret Laurence to survive?

Her future as a writer was not as clear-cut as she would have liked it to be. Nevertheless, she had a strong inkling her writing career was moving in a new direction, perhaps towards Canada. Although she was "sick of Africa," she had written—by January 1961—ten short stories set in the Gold Coast, and she did not yet "know enough" to write her Canadian novel. When she first met Jack McClelland in the autumn of 1960, she had pressed him to publish a collection of her African short stories. Correctly, he pointed out such books were hard to sell and suggested such a collection be released only after she had published her second novel. Margaret, who always had a keen sense of when others were stalling or putting her off, pressed McClelland again in January 1961: "Re: your suggestion that the sale of short stories might discourage me from attempting another book, might I suggest a solution? I have ten short stories on Africa done now, and by spring I will have perhaps fifteen ... You will recognize this as one of my long-standing hopes, and will probably think I have a one-track mind, which is perfectly true." Margaret may have been stubborn but so was McClelland: "My view hasn't changed—and Willis Wing concurs on this one—that it would be far better from the standpoint of your total career to leave the short story volume until after you have published at least one more novel."

That February she was filled with a pervading sense of emptiness. A month later, she informed Adele that she had torn up two previous letters to her because they "were so permeated with pessimism of a personal nature that it did not seem well-omened to send them." Her sense of malaise was owing in part "to my persistent feelings of doubt about the novel which I had begun." That novel, set in Africa, did not trigger her imagination, as she later recalled: "After I finished writing the stories later collected as *The Tomorrow-Tamer*, I had an entire novel planned, set in Africa. A beautiful plan it was, too. But I could not write it. I had really said everything about Africa that I had to say." In fact, another set of characters had begun to hover at the edge of her imagination: "They kept creeping in, as it were, to disturb my thoughts, and they were (and are) all people here, in this country. God knows I have no desire to write a 'Canadian' novel in that horrible nationalistic stilted sense, but if they happen to live here, that's another thing. One of these days something may take shape in that direction." The transition from Africa to Canada was arduous, in part because she usually wrote best about places she had left.

Further discouragement ensued when the *Vancouver Sun* abruptly discontinued its book page, and that outlet for reviewing disappeared. Her lack of self-confidence led her to consider the possibility of "spontaneous writing" in the manner of Jack Kerouac and the Beat Generation. But Jack McClelland's attitudes towards publishing provided a beacon of hope: "he is one of the very few who believe a Canadian book has to be judged like any other book—in other words, it doesn't automatically stink because it is Canadian, nor is it automatically marvellous."

Six months later, the characters gathered on the horizon of her imagination had, somewhat spontaneously, come to life in a book, the working title of which was *Hagar*:

> Probably the publishers won't like it. And even worse, if it ever gets published, a great many old ladies of whom I am extremely fond will never speak to me again. It is not a sensational novel. No seductions. No rapes. No murders. It's not "timely"—i.e. it is not about Africa or any other "newsworthy" place. It is not the novel I intended to write. It is the work of a lunatic, I think. It has hardly anything to recommend it to the general public.
>
> I made two false starts on 2 separate novels that I'd had in mind for some time and found I could not write either one. Very nicely plotted, they were, but dead as doornails. Then this daft old lady came along, and [all] I will say about her is that she is one hell of an old lady, a real tartar. She's crabby, snobbish, difficult, proud as Lucifer for no reason, a trial to her family, etc. She's also—I forgot to mention—dying.

Hagar came into being during an increasingly difficult time for Margaret. Her previous dislike of Canada had largely been in response to John Simpson's Neepawa. She had eagerly abandoned her country for England and then Africa. Vancouver in the late fifties and early sixties may have had a certain California look in lifestyle—one quite different from both Neepawa and Winnipeg—but it certainly was not a sufficiently literary city for her. In fact, she found the local cultural scene deeply wanting: "What amuses me is how many people in Vancouver now claim to have been bosom buddies with [the reclusive, alcoholic English-born writer] Malcolm Lowry—you can bet your bottom dollar they didn't feel that way when he was a drunk at [his shack at] Dollarton, but now he's been discovered by the literary reviews in Paris, and so the picture has changed, and also he is safely dead, which is such a comfort, as he can now be translated into whatever legend is most pleasing." In addition to Ethel Wilson, Margaret knew the poet Earle Birney and the novelist and short-story writer Jane Rule on a casual basis. (Later, Margaret wrote a series of important letters to Jane Rule, but Rule explains that she and Margaret met only a few times and that they never became close friends.)

Margaret also found it difficult to make friends on the west coast, at least that is what she implied in a letter to Adele of October 1960: "We don't seem to know very many congenial people, but in general, quite enough for the limited time we have to spend with friends." This claim belies the evidence of her good friends, Gordon Elliott, June and Fred Schulhof, and Eva and René Temple. In her, these people found a close, warm companion.

The Schulhofs lived a block away from the Laurences on West 20th Street, but the couples met when they were enrolled in Living Room Learning. June, Fred, Jack, Gordon and Margaret often had stirring, heated arguments on a wide variety of topics. The two women became close enough for Margaret to exclaim one day: "You're the first woman I ever trusted!" She also told June she hated housework (although the house was always spotless when June visited), particularly ironing. Her new friend also observed Margaret's hunger to write, which led her to rise at five in the morning several days a week. Although she was very conscious of the women's liberation movement, she told June she was certain Jack's intellect was superior to her own. Margaret also observed that Vancouver was a wretched, isolated place for a would-be writer to be stranded. June did have a significant influence on Margaret, for it was she who told her that her name was a beautiful one and urged her to discard "Peg" and "Peggy."

Margaret Hutchinson, Jocelyn's teacher and herself a writer, introduced the Temples to the Laurences. Eva was particularly struck by the fact that Margaret seemed to be more interested in being admired than being loved. She also remembered going to see *La dolce vita* (1960) with Margaret, who was deeply upset by the film's intimation of the coming of nuclear war. The Cold War gave her a pervasive sense of uneasiness. She was certain it would eventually unleash a terrible holocaust. Margaret was not politically active in Vancouver, but she retained the left-wing allegiances which had been a part of her since United College days in Winnipeg.

One image from the time recalled by all her friends in Vancouver was of an exceedingly slim Margaret pacing a room, cigarette in hand, and offering her thoughts on a variety of subjects in a staccato manner. Gordon Elliott recalled her temper. Once, he refused to buy Girl Guide cookies when Jocelyn proffered them on the phone. A few minutes later, an irate mother was on the line, telling him what a lousy bastard he was to upset her little girl. The next time he saw Margaret, she acted as if she had not made the call.

Another witness, albeit from a different perspective, to Margaret's life in Vancouver was a young man, Lino Magagna, a student in Gordon Elliott's English for Engineers class for which she acted as a marker. She took great pains over Lino's assignments and provided him with many encouraging remarks at the end of his essays; in particular, she made useful suggestions regarding the structure of his papers and the development of his arguments. From his perspective, Lino remembered Margaret as warm, whereas, when he met Jack, the young man felt Jack was cold and that the age difference between husband and wife seemed much greater than ten years. His accompanying impression—that Jack was very stiff and excessively strait-laced—was not one shared by Gordon, the Schulhofs and the Temples, who were equally fond of husband and wife.

Mona Spratt, now Mona Meredith, never liked Jack. From her perspective, a profound change in the Laurence marriage took place when they settled in Vancouver: Margaret was on the way up, whereas Jack, who had been in a position of great authority in Africa, was on the way down. There is obviously some truth in this observation. Jack had trouble finding work and the jobs he obtained did not carry the same level of responsibility as those in Somaliland and the Gold Coast. With the publication of *This Side Jordan*, she had made a real breakthrough in her career as a writer.

Nadine Jones, had similar views, although she encountered Jack only on a few occasions and had a positive impression of him. She met Margaret in a Vancouver bookstore, the Book Nook, where she was signing copies of *This Side Jordan*. Shortly thereafter, she phoned to ask for advice. She was on the verge of marrying a Ghanaian and needed her acquaintance's advice on embarking on such a venture. Margaret agreed, and this was the beginning of their friendship. (*The Tomorrow-Tamer* carries this dedication: "For Nadine and Kwadwo" [Assante].) Outspoken, headstrong and flamboyant, Nadine was the polar opposite of Margaret's other women friends. The hidden portions of Margaret—her increasing dissatisfaction with her marriage and the plight of women in general—could be voiced openly to Nadine, who did not think women should be silent about the oppressions they faced. For a long time, Nadine was Margaret's safety valve, the person to whom she could express the explosive feelings that were beginning to overwhelm her.

To Nadine, whom Margaret saw without Jack, she confided many of the conflicts and doubts which can also be seen in the letters to Adele, but these ruminations were more personal: she could not live up to her own image of herself and, she was certain, she could not measure up to Jack's expectations. Nadine observed a basic dichotomy in Margaret's nature: she wanted to be the opposite of what she *seemed* to be. Always very much on edge when they were together, Margaret once accompanied Nadine to a Unitarian Church, where, in the midst of the service, she burst into hysterical tears.

Increasingly, as she confessed to Nadine, she felt confined by her marriage in every conceivable way. Later, she would claim that Jack, during the years of their marriage, had placed his hands uncomfortably close to her face and neck when they were going to sleep. Her fantasy was that he might strangle or suffocate her. (In *The Fire-Dwellers* Mac, Stacey's husband, pretends to strangle her while demanding she say it doesn't hurt.)

Certainly, the tension level at the Laurence household heated up considerably in 1961. Margaret had a fierce temper and, when she became very angry, hurled things at Jack. In his turn, Jack would smoulder in a rage. Jocelyn, now nine, would act as the family peacemaker, a particularly thankless task for a young girl. She was her father's favourite child and when Jack became overwhelmed, he often found fault with David. As a result, Margaret often interceded on behalf of her son. Nevertheless, she could be harsh with him. Years afterward, Peggy still regretted "the fact that I once ... hit my son on the face so hard that his nose bled." She once washed Jocelyn's mouth out with soap and if she became angry at her daughter when brushing her hair, she sometimes tugged too hard. To the children, their mother often seemed in a fury; they saw her perform many routine domestic actions hurriedly and haphazardly. She could be both brusque and impatient. The children would see their parents drive out in the car some evenings in order to quarrel away from them. One major source of bickering was money. Margaret was not a spendthrift, but she was not as careful with money as her husband would have liked. Whatever their arguments were about was secondary to their underlying differences: Jacked wanted a traditional wife and Margaret no longer fitted—or wanted to fit—such a mould. Jack expected Margaret to be a homemaker and a writer, whereas she increasingly felt that she needed time away from him and the responsibilities of running a house in order to write.

From outsiders and even some close friends, the strains within the Laurence household were hidden. The two seemed to make an ideal couple, but they now had obviously vastly different notions of what constituted a good marriage. A few years later, in 1965, Margaret told Gordon of the high level of conflict between her private and public selves during the Vancouver years:

> You said that it seemed terrible to you that two people, both of whom you liked and had felt close to, could have been having internal stress without their friends knowing about it. But really, how could anyone else know about it? Wherever we went, we went together—to whom were either of us going to talk, as everyone we knew was a friend of both? I was on the verge of speaking to you, many times, probably many more times than you ever realized, but I did not, and I am glad I did not, as you were a friend of us both, and I think that to speak of one's difficulties would be some kind of disloyalty much worse than any definite and open separation, which must in the end be a private decision, done without explanation, and accepted by one's friends as such. I needed terribly to be able to speak with someone, but until I met Nadine I never could, and this holding-in, which was a matter of 15 years, was not a very good thing, I now see.

In an awful twist of fate, Margaret's success as a writer likely made things worse between herself and Jack. In June 1961, she was in Toronto to collect the Beta Sigma Phi award for *This Side Jordan*, which was named the best first novel published in Canada in the previous year. She also received the President's Medal from the University of Western Ontario for "A Gourdful of Glory," published the previous year in *The Tamarack Review.*

A casual witness to the Laurence marriage was Alice Munro, who also lived in Vancouver. The two women talked about children and the particular problems besetting married women writers with children and other domestic responsibilities. Alice recalled: "I remember her telling me she ironed all her husband's shirts. And I said, 'You mustn't do that. You must find some other way.' I have the impression of someone who was trying terribly hard to do everything."

Margaret tried to keep the appearance of normality. The Laurences spent part of the summer at their recently built cottage at Point Roberts. She wrote book reviews (for *Canadian Literature,* founded in 1959 by George Woodcock), marked essays and even taught Sunday school at the local Unitarian church. She was justifiably angry when she found out that a writer by the name of Jack Buchholzer had lifted paragraphs directly out of *A Tree for Poverty,* even presenting her insights and conclusions as his own, in a book called *The Horn of Africa*: "I didn't so much mind," she told Adele, "that he had taken my translations of poems and stories, because folk literature belongs to everyone, although I rather resented the fact that he implied he had simply gone out into the desert and sat around campfires and then taken down all these glorious songs and stories directly from the Somali." In 1962, in a letter to Rache Lovat Dickson, her publisher at Macmillan, she added: "I wrote to Mr. Buchholzer's publishers, pointing out that I did not in any sense attach any blame either to them or to the translator, but that I was somewhat disturbed by Mr. Buchholzer's unacknowledged borrowing of numerous paragraphs, because I intended to use portions of *A Tree for Poverty* in a book of my own [*The Prophet's Camel Bell*] and would not care to be suspected of plagiarism when in fact I was quoting myself. I received very courteous letters both from the publishers and from Mr. Buchholzer's agent, who apologized on his behalf and said my letter had been forwarded to Mr. Buchholzer, who might take some considerable time to reply as he was now residing in the wilds of Tierra del Fuego."

Work on *The Stone Angel* brought her to extremes of joy and frustration. She feared she might yet become manic-depressive. Adele pressed her to believe in herself and to trust to the unconscious processes which were always a part of creating a work of art. Margaret was not so sure.

> I wrote it in a kind of single-minded burst of activities, letting the thing go where it seemed to want to go and at the time I was (and still am, basically) completely convinced by the main character. But I'm beginning to anticipate the pitfalls—for one thing, it is written very simply and directly, for the simple reason that I am not clever enough to write it any other way, and in any event I still have a

> strong feeling for direct and simple writing; even though this style is perhaps almost archaic now. For another thing, it is by no means a new theme—but what is?

Hagar drained her creator's energy, leaving her completely unsure of her judgment. So, she "simply put down the story of the old lady as the old lady told it to me." Would another person find any meaning in the resulting story or see it as only as an "excessively simple and far-fetched tale?" She could not answer the question: "I can't know but I'm trying very hard to follow your example in this way, and take the thing on faith; for the moment, anyway I am terrified at the thought of submitting the manuscript, ultimately, somewhere. I never felt so hesitant about the first novel. Strange, isn't it?"

An odd combination of factors came together for Margaret during the writing of *The Stone Angel.* For one thing, even her stay in hospital became fodder for her imagination, as she told her journal in 1986: "I wrote *The Stone Angel* in the first draft in 1961. Twenty-five years ago.... It drew on some experience in hospital then, when I had my gall-bladder out, & there was indeed a very old woman (*not* Hagar) in the 4-bed ward where I was."

The original impetus for *The Stone Angel* came at the time Marg Wemyss was dying. The actual character of Hagar bears more likeness to Ruby than to Marg, however. Years later, Margaret admitted to Budge Wilson that Grandfather Simpson was the real model for Hagar, although it seems obvious that many of Hagar's external qualities are also derived from Margaret's almost equally abrasive Grandmother Wemyss. The courage to write about a small prairie town owes a great deal to Sinclair Ross's *As for Me and My House*, but Margaret was also inspired in part by Patricia Blondal's *A Candle to Light the Sun* and Ernest Buckler's *The Mountain and the Valley.* Another curious factor found expression and crystallization in Margaret's new book.

In Margaret's childhood and young adulthood, she had been subjected to the harsh cruelty of her grandfather, who was nevertheless a genuinely powerful person. She began to associate power with oppression and, obviously, distanced herself from negative displays of power. But, as she grew older and knew herself better, she correctly perceived herself as a strong person. As she got in touch with this very real side of her character, she no longer saw the assumption or use of power in a negative light (and something essentially male), even though she was well aware it could be a destructive force. By creating in Hagar a powerful but tormented woman, she was allowing herself to look at central issues that haunted her. Was she in fact very much like Grandfather Simpson? If she was temperamentally his offspring, how as a woman could she deal with that? What kind of role model had her grandfather been to her? Being a powerful person and a woman was not necessarily a bad mix, even though she had obviously feared they might be. Could she survive as an independent person? Do women have the right to seize personal power?

Margaret was attempting to find her writing self while fighting the conventional mores of the time. For her, the underlying fear was that she did not have a right to do this. These kinds of questions were especially tormenting because they led her to question the assumptions on which her marriage was based. This was particularly painful because she craved her husband's support and understanding in order to become an independent person and yet realized he was both uncomprehending of and hostile to those needs. So their bitter quarrels continued and so did the work on the book that vexed her deeply.

A person such as Hagar is not only born but made: deprived of her mother at birth and subjected to her father's harshness, she imitates his behaviour. From an early age, Hagar's identity is shaped by her father, not her dead mother who exists only as a portrait in a frame. She can only conceive of her mother as the antithesis of herself. Since her mother died while giving birth to her, Hagar has no real knowledge of her or her personality: "I used to wonder," she reflects, "what she'd been like, that docile woman and wonder at her weakness and my awful strength." When her brother Matt is dying, Hagar, who is well aware that he is like their mother and not their father, cannot bring herself to "mother" him: "I can't. Oh Matt, I'm sorry, but I can't, I can't. I'm not a bit like her." Children whose parents die sometimes unconsciously assume guilt for something which is obviously out of their control; at some level, Hagar feels guilt because her mother died giving her life, and her understandable aversion to such an uncomfortable feeling might explain her revulsion towards Matt, who is so much like the dead mother. Of course, Margaret Laurence herself may have also have felt responsible at an unconscious level for the deaths of her parents.

Despite many drawbacks, Hagar has many admirable qualities, which eventually prepare her for self-redemption towards the end of the novel. That salvation begins when she tells the story of her life to Murray Lees and bursts into tears. At that moment, she allows her thwarted femininity egress and in the process rescues herself from the constraints that have dominated her life.

Years later, when asked about the genesis of *The Stone Angel*, Margaret Laurence provided this explanation:

> My feeling about it was that I had written three books out of Africa, out of those experiences, and I really knew that I didn't want to go on writing about Africa, because otherwise my writing would become that of a tourist. I had written everything I could out of that particular experience, and I very *much* wanted to return home in a kind of spiritual way. I think that my experience when I wrote *The Stone Angel* was remarkable, because I kept feeling that I *knew* I was getting the speech *exactly right*! It was *mine*! It was the speech of my grandparents', my parents' generation, and so on. Whereas when I had been writing about Africa I could never be sure. It was not my culture, and of course we *know* things about our own culture, and about our own people that we don't even know we *know*. When I wrote *The Stone Angel*, it was really rather marvellous, because phrases, bits of

> idiom, would come back to me that I had forgotten, that I didn't know I even remembered, from my grandparents' speech.... And also that I do have, both in my own life and in my life view, a sense of the wheel coming full circle, that kind of journey, where we end up in the place where we began, but with a different perspective.

In her reply, Margaret Laurence recalls in vivid detail certain aspects of the joy that filled her as she worked on her first novel set in Canada, but she does not communicate the sense of unease which she also faced.

In March 1962, the book was a "terrible mess. It will have to be completely re-written." Three months later, she resumed work on "the old-lady novel" but in August she abandoned work on it, feeling the book was boring. Also, she was certain that writing a novel about an old woman was a form of evasion:

> I often feel that anything I write about people here will be naive or perhaps merely corny, and for this reason I have gone to any lengths to avoid writing about the situations which really concerned and moved me. I have the feeling that the novel about the old lady represented such an evasion. Perhaps in the long run there is no way other than to look inwardly and personally, and take the risk. I think the important thing is to go on doing something, and not to be paralysed by one's doubts and uncertainties, but of course this is easier said than done.

Her entire writing career, she became certain, was a "kind of screen ... so that one need never make oneself vulnerable."

The Stone Angel is many things, but it is not a work of art which is evasive. Margaret could not work on the book in any consistent fashion because she was getting in touch with painful memories and conflicted feelings. Like Hagar, she had suffered cruel losses at an early age, losses which were difficult for her to come to terms with except in writing. But the process of writing made her vulnerable because she was opening herself up to those forces which had earlier torn her apart.

As a respite from work on her second novel, she turned her attention to converting her Somaliland diaries into a travel book. Even this proved to be a more difficult task than she had at first envisioned: "I always had the feeling that all I would need to do would be to put together large chunks of my diaries, and that would be that. But no. I have changed so much, and I failed to see so much at the time, that the whole thing has to be done from scratch." Honesty was another issue that haunted her in the writing of *The Prophet's Camel Bell*: "How much of yourself do you reveal? in revealing this or that, are you being honest or merely showing off?" Despite such obstacles, the Somaliland typescript was completed by the middle of April 1962 and on its way to Willis Wing in New York. Three months later arrived the joyful news that Macmillan in London had accepted the book.

As Margaret was well aware, *The Prophet's Camel Bell* was a memento to her younger self and to the early days of her marriage. It was written at a time the Laurence marriage had reached a deep state of crisis. The full extent of the conflicts cannot be gauged in any extant letter from Margaret, but it can be seen in Adele's letter to her of April 20, 1962. Adele, just as fiery as her close friend—and perhaps even more committed to the writing life—was still single and could offer a detached, non-judgmental view of a fraught situation.

> I have far too much respect and fondness for both you and Jack to mistake this for anything but the kind of readjustment that takes place periodically between intelligent, loving people who need to be honest with each other. I guess you've let this pile up for a long time, Peg, so that now that it's come into the open it's done so with the force of a lot of repression released behind it,—what I'm trying to say is that you're still probably awash with various waves of emotion, guilt, relief, love, etc., etc., which haven't relaxed to their proper proportions yet ... I know how much you've always dreaded Jack's disapproval, and what this rebellion must have cost you,—at least I

> imagine it must seem like a rebellion in terms of what you've conceived your relationship with Jack to be. And yet, who knows, maybe complete submission isn't what Jack's wanted from you all along? Perhaps asking him to pass judgment on your "private area"—in this case your writing, is a kind of imposition on him too? It shifts your own responsibility for your private self onto him too, something which, ultimately, you've found impossible to bear because it reduces yourself to less than a whole person in your own mind, and something which I'm sure Jack doesn't need. Jack is far too big a guy and too capable in his own right to need the reassurance that you're not competing with him. So what has happened is a kind of habit pattern's been set up in which you both have been trapped. You rebel against what you've invited, Jack's views on work which you haven't allowed yourself to develop completely in what should be airtight—the crucible of your own imagination—and Jack, since he does have a marked literary turn of mind, [is] allowing himself to do what you seem to demand. What you really want is reassurance from him. What he gives you is what you say you want,—critical appraisal, at a time when you're too unsure of the thread to be able really to bear it.

In this extraordinary, passionate letter, Adele, with incredible dexterity, put the Laurence marriage into a perspective that eluded the unhappy couple.

Adele was pointing out to Margaret her inconsistencies in her dealings with her husband. Perhaps Jack should not be asked to pass judgment on his wife's "private area," perhaps to ask him to do so was a kind of set-up. Jack had read a draft of *The Stone Angel* during the winter or early spring of 1962. In *Dance on the Earth*, Margaret provided her own analysis of the situation:

> When I wrote the first draft of *The Stone Angel*, Jack wanted to read it. I didn't want him to. I think I knew his response would be pivotal in our marriage. I didn't want anybody except a publisher to

> read it. I allowed him to read it in the end and he didn't like it much, but for me it was the most important book I had written, a book on which I had to stake the rest of my life. Strange reason for breaking up a marriage: a novel. I had to go with the old lady, I really did, but at the same time I felt terrible about hurting him.

Jack obviously disliked the book, but he had been used to offering his wife frank criticism of her work. In addition, she was furious when he informed her she was really a short-story writer—not a novelist. Margaret could not accept his remarks because so much of herself had gone into her new book—the characterization of Miranda in *This Side Jordan* had been Margaret but in a superficial way, whereas many aspects in her character were nakedly revealed in *The Stone Angel.* Jack glimpsed the new Margaret in that draft, and he obviously did not like what he saw. His rejection of the book was essentially a rejection of the person she was in the process of becoming.

During the early part of 1962, Margaret was concerned with another image problem, this one involving her health. She experienced constant, pounding headaches and became convinced she had a brain tumour. This incident was transformed into fiction in *The Fire-Dwellers* when Stacey—filled with anxiety and unable to communicate with her husband—goes to her doctor halfway convinced and perhaps even hoping she has a brain tumour. Stacey's thoughts about her frustration at trying to explain herself are probably a reflection of Margaret's feelings in 1962: "How can I say anything else, without making it sound foolish? I can't put my finger on it, anyway. Too many threads. I can't say it, and who would believe me if I did? It's like being inside a balloon made out of some kind of glue, and when you try to get out, you only get tangled and stuck." Margaret's doctor told her she was suffering from hypertension.

Then, her attention was focused on her inability to control her weight, a new problem. In June, she confided in Adele: "I am taking diet pills, so I am either in a manic or depressive condition." She had shed fifteen pounds and had set her goal for another ten. In a letter to Gordon of June 1962, she tried to put her conflicts into perspective:

> I am back on my diet pills again, and am hence in either a manic or a depressive state most of the time. In my manic phase, I concentrate on that great Canadian novel which I am writing, convinced that it will ultimately turn out to be deathless prose. In my depressive phase, I know the novel is no good, and cannot feel it is even worthwhile to sit down and write to a friend, as I am suffering from both lung cancer and T.B. and will probably not survive the night. Only another few weeks of this, however, and I hope to have shed the final 10 lbs which is my goal. I went downtown today and was so heartened by the way I looked in a sheath dress that I bought not one but two!

In January 1962, the Laurences attempted to find a solution to their marriage by escaping Canada once again. They were planning to go "abroad again, if Jack can find the right kind of job," she informed Adele. Eight months later, when Jack received the offer of a post in East Pakistan, this solution was in the process of being abandoned: "Jack and I have been trying to sort out what it was that each of us really wants to do in this life, and this appears a more complex thing than we thought it might be—he may be going abroad again, and I know that is right for him, but I wonder if I can become a memsahib once more? Anyway, we shall see. I may stay with the kids in England for a year, I don't know." Uncertainty had given way to certainty twelve days later:

> It is still not quite certain about Jack's job, but it appears there will be little doubt that he will get it and will be going to Pakistan. However, we do not want to count any chickens yet. But we have discussed the whole thing, and we now feel that this will be the opportunity I have long needed, to stand on my own feet for awhile and learn to trust my own judgement. If he goes to Pakistan, he may have to go fairly quickly. I will remain here for the moment, and will go to England later this fall, probably November.... The main thing now is that I believe I can do it all right, although it will certainly not be without many qualms when the time comes.... But I feel free, or reasonably so, from the sense of despair that has been with me for

> some years now, so I don't really mind the slowness of growth. As far as I am concerned, this will be the opportunity to terminate a kind of delayed adolescence, at the advanced age of 36, and it is really now or never. I feel now that it will work out both to my advantage and Jack's, if things go as we hope and trust.

Even to Adele, Margaret was not completely honest for the reasons behind her decision to leave Canada for England and to separate from her husband. However, her letter to Adele of August 5 provides a clue: "I met the other day George Lamming, the West Indian writer ... who is here at the moment on a Canada Council something-or-other. He was unfortunately very drunk that night, so was lucid only in spells, but I thought he was terrific. Not only a very talented writer, but the kind of personality that hits you like the spirit of God between the eyes.... If he stops off in Winnipeg and you have the chance to talk with him, try to do so." The letter carefully avoids revealing she had embarked on an affair with Lamming.

Only years later was Margaret able to sort out the turmoil into which she was thrown: "When I first found out it was possible to love more than one person at a time, I mean sexually as well as other ways ... I was so profoundly shocked it was really traumatic. I went through a lot of torment, but of course at that time I was about to split up with my husband anyway, even tho I did love him.... Life is sure as hell full of terrible complexities." Shortly before her death, she tried to put this matter into an even fuller perspective: Lamming "was a crucial, if brief, part of my life. He was (is) a writer, too. I was simply one woman among dozens (hundreds probably) to him. But I am glad I made love with him those few times." Even in this moving passage, however, Margaret does not dwell on the mire of confusion into which she was plunged.

A year younger than Margaret, Lamming was born and raised in Carrington Village near Bridgetown, Barbados. At the age of nineteen in 1946, he went to live in Trinidad and, four years later, emigrated to England. At the time Margaret met him he had published four novels, including *In the Castle of My Skin*, and a work of non-fiction, *The*

Pleasures of Exile. During the fifties, he supported himself by working on overseas programming for the BBC, visited the USA in 1955 when he held a Guggenheim Fellowship and was awarded a fellowship by the Canada Council in 1962. Most of that year was spent in Toronto, although his home was in London.

In addition to being a writer of distinction, Lamming was a fervent critic of the colonial environment into which he had been born in the British West Indies. This would have immediately forged a strong bond with Margaret. So did the fact that he was black. A person who habitually identified with outsiders, she was drawn to someone who because of his race was rendered a member of a visible minority in North American society. Margaret, it must be remembered, hated certain aspects of that society; a love affair with a black man was a way of making a rebellious —if covert—statement in opposition to prevailing norms. Part of Margaret's fantasy was that Lamming would be sensitive to the needs of a fellow writer.

George Lamming. c. 1951.

Margaret Laurence, never simply attracted to the exotic, wanted to live and breathe it. For her, the ruggedly handsome Lamming was "very revolutionary in outlook, and with the strength of his convictions, but not in any sense liable to write merely propaganda." In the very same letter in which she tells Adele of Lamming's willingness to listen to her, she reveals that she finds it increasingly difficult to talk about her concerns with anyone in Vancouver, "although Jack, God knows, is sympathetic and would always listen. I feel he is quite patient enough about my writing and the withdrawn times which it involves, without listening to a constant spate of my uncertainties."

Five days later, she was on the verge of making the decision to split from Jack; twelve days after that, she had reached that turning point. What she does not reveal in any letter is that she had decided to follow Lamming to London, where she hoped to rekindle their brief affair.

When Margaret finally decided to make her move, she was painfully aware Jack was convinced—with some justification—she was abandoning him. She also realized she was uprooting Jocelyn and David precipitously, even though the publicly stated reason for her not accompanying Jack to East Pakistan was her concern about the education of the children. Also, Margaret, who sometimes had an inordinate capacity to blind herself to reality, was certain she would find in London a close-knit community of writers into which she could easily fit.

In many passages in *Dance on the Earth*, although Margaret tells the truth, she fails to provide the full context of crucial situations and events. This is especially true of the separation from Jack. This is her brief—reluctant—account in *Dance on the Earth*: "I suppose I should say something about Jack and myself. We both had a strong sense of our own vocations but they led us into different areas. It was hard for him, when I had one novel published and another book, *The Prophet's Camel Bell*, accepted, to understand that this was my vocation and I had to do it. It was hard for me, too." She then mentions the dispute regarding *The Stone Angel*.

Margaret may not have been fully aware of her motivations. She was struggling to stay alive as a writer. Slowly but very surely, her marriage seemed to be smothering that ambition, which had become the cornerstone of her identity. In part, Margaret had also become ruthless, very much in the manner of Hagar. As a child, she had lost both birth parents. In 1962, she could not tolerate another major loss, this time of her writing self. She could only create, she now felt, in isolation. In retrospect, she would later question the momentous decision she made in 1962, but "made" might be the wrong word—she was driven by inner forces so intense that she felt powerless to disobey them.

11

The Necessary Condition of Life

(1962-1963)

> My real concern is if I can write anything worth publishing, also how to get down at least some slight suggestion of the complexities which did not bother me at one time because I did not see they were there. Please write and tell me I am not really going off my rocker, and that this kind of split personality (the public self and the other) is quite normal, really.

THIS EXCERPT FROM a letter to Adele of August 1962 shows the kind of turmoil into which Margaret was thrown. Since, previously, she had never betrayed any sign of conflict, most of her friends and relatives were astounded by the turn of events in the Laurence marriage. The Schulhofs and the Temples were taken completely by surprise when she told them she and Jack were going separate ways. Fred Schulhof was particularly astonished because he, under the impression that all four Laurences were immigrating to the same place, had been the intermediary who had helped Jack obtain the job in Pakistan with Sandwell. The Laurences were so unsure of what they were doing and what was happening to them that they tended to give varying accounts of their future to their friends and relatives. To some, they claimed the children's education was the predominant issue: Jack had to work overseas, where Jocelyn and David would be subjected to poor teaching. Overlooked in this scenario were the emotional needs of the children. For a long time, the children had been painfully aware their parents' marriage was in disarray. Now, they were being uprooted, about to set off to a new place without their father. They were understandably upset and confused.

Since Jack had not initiated the break, he was especially uncertain of the future. He knew of his wife's relationship with Lamming, although little was ever said on the subject. To some people, such as Adele, Margaret claimed the separation was a temporary one to assist her in achieving independence as a writer and as a woman; to others, such as Nadine, she intimated that her marriage was over. So uncertain was Margaret of what she was doing that she asked for Mona's approval of the affair with Lamming.

On their way to London on October 12, Margaret and the children stayed briefly in Winnipeg. During that short visit, she was able to give Adele details about her somewhat precipitous behaviour. She also stopped over in Toronto—in hopes of meeting up with Lamming. The following, cryptic sentences—in a letter to Adele—refer to her disappointment in not seeing him: "Well, to begin where I left off, kid, the next round went to the Presbyterians, but more by accident than design, at least on my part, the man had already left the country, as I discovered by chance when I had lunch with Bob [Weaver]. Just as well, one might reasonably say. Of course, of course. I *do* say it but find it harder to believe. However, of all this no more probably need be said, now or ever." However, she was en route to England, to where Lamming had returned.

The Laurences had made an arrangement whereby Jack would provide support for the children and an allowance for his wife until she was able to be financially independent. Nevertheless, as she recalled seven years later, she had taken quite a risk: "When I first came to England, I needed help desperately and I had exactly 100 pounds of my own money and I was scared as hell, as I had never been on my own before in my life and was then 36 years old and with 2 kids."

So quickly had Margaret resolved her course of action that she had packed the draft of *The Stone Angel* into a large cardboard box containing, among other things, smelly tennis and running shoes, old books and David's treasured Meccano set. Since her luggage was over the weight limit, she decided when she arrived in Winnipeg to send the box to friends in England by sea mail, a voyage which took three months. "I almost seemed to be trying to lose it," she later reflected. "Guilt and fear can do strange things to the mind and the body. I questioned my right to write, even though I knew I had to do it."

In *Dance*, there is not the slightest evidence of Lamming's importance in Margaret's existence. But she does emphasize the support she received from her "third mother," Elsie Laurence, Jack's mother, who was also a writer. "She told me in a letter that at the end of the First World War, when Jack was two and her husband had just returned from the war, she seriously considered taking her young child and leaving her husband so she could concentrate on her writing. She stayed, of course." Elsie may not have been as sympathetic to her daughter-in-law, with whom she obviously strongly identified, if she had been told the full circumstances surrounding Margaret's departure for England that autumn. In a curious way, Margaret, by citing Elsie as an example of a woman who stays put and then has regrets, uses Elsie against her own son.

A friend, Nancy Collier, helped Margaret find a flat on Heath Hurst Road, close to Keats Grove, in a leafy, ramshackle part of Hampstead. At the end of October, she provided Adele with an account of her new home:

> We have landed on our feet so far in London. It hardly seems possible but I have found a flat for precisely the rent I had in mind (which is *not* cheap, but rents are so damn high here these days) and it is in the area I wanted, and I am really so pleased with it. I have a living room, my own bedroom, kitchen (rather antiquated equipment, but so what?) and the kids both have a small bedroom. Their

> rooms are up a small flight of stairs. It is the top 2 floors in an old house. We share bathroom with a business couple on the floor below. We are 5 minutes from Hampstead Heath, 5 minutes from Hampstead High St., 15 minutes from the school where the kids will be going. There is a Public Library just around the corner, and a Launderette only a block away. We couldn't be better situated. Landlady is orthodox Jewish rather garrulous and a bit schmaltzy, but *very* warm-hearted, and fond of kids.

In her autobiography, Margaret mentions that the Scots couple quarrelled constantly and that the smell of their kipper breakfasts filled her living quarters. Nevertheless, there seemed to be a certain romantic glow associated with the flat.

> I have just been interrupted for an hour in the writing of this letter by the fact that my flat was suddenly plunged into total darkness—the shillings had run out in the meter box, and when I put more in, there was a colourful blue flash which seemed to indicate that I'd blown every fuse in the house. I am having to re-learn the state of mind which regards electricity as a priceless treasure which more often than not exercises a stubborn will of its own and refuses to be exploited. Rhoda Levene, the landlady's daughter, came to the rescue with thousands of fuses and tools and a cheerful commentary.... At last, for no apparent reason, a kind of divine dispensation, the lights suddenly came on again, to the accompaniment of glad shouts of "Hallelujah" and "Mazeltov" from Rhoda and myself ... Like most flats here, it is an old house, and it is full of rather strange Victorian furniture, hatracks and such, which I prefer to the modern arborite and paper-covered monstrosities found in many rented apartments here. To me, it seems absolutely ideal.... Now all that remains is to put into effect your old slogan—"Back to your typewriter!"

A few days later, she assured Gordon Elliott of the delights inherent in her new situation and of her satisfaction in having fulfilled Virginia

Woolf's essential recipe for success for a woman writer: "Right now, I am so glad to be here that all I can do in the evenings is walk around the flat and gloat about it. A room of one's own. Am I selfish? Yes. But I needed this place so badly, and I found it—a kind of divine dispensation. We are going to be okay." The bravado has a touch of desperation in it. In Vancouver, she had shared her writing space with a television set in the den; in London, she wrote in her small cramped bedroom.

The "initial elation" had begun to disappear a month later and was followed by the "inevitable letdown." She now felt the "only kind of home" she valued was one associated with other writers, "members of my tribe." However, she soon realized, "I had had a kind of fantasy about taking part in the literary scene.... this did not happen." She did become friends with the novelist Alexander Baron and his wife, Delores, as well as the writer Jean Stubbs. Mordecai Richler, who had already published *Son of a Smaller Hero* and *The Apprenticeship of Duddy Kravitz*, was also living in London; he and his wife, Florence, were friendly. Although Margaret pointed out that Mordecai could act in the "brusque, understated style" for which he was well known, she also found in him a kindred spirit, a person of considerable warmth.

When her typescript arrived towards the end of November, she decided it did not read badly. "It may not be everyone's cup of tea, but it is what I want to say about these particular people." Despite rapid fluctuations between optimism and despair, she discovered, to her surprise, that she was at heart a survivor. "I do not despair. Also, I can't afford to drink a great deal, which is a good thing. I can't afford to smoke, but I do, anyway. I'm down to 25 Weights a day (they are those puny little half-size cigarettes) so I'm improving." At this time, "deep inhibitions" prevented her from going into pubs by herself.

A little more than two weeks later, her drinking almost got her into trouble at a party hosted by the Andrzejewskis:

> Yours truly quaffed too deeply and became overly friendly with a handsome Somali boy—I say "boy" advisedly, as when I thought of it afterwards I felt like his grandmother, to tell you the truth. Well,

> luckily before I had completely shattered my reputation, a sudden inner voice said very distinctly to me "Lady, what the hell do you think this is—the Roman Spring of Mrs. Stone?" When you find you're drinking, or etc, to drown your sorrows, it is time you quit. I quit. So it is tea for me, friend, just one gay round of tea and coffee after another. After a week of this strictly non-alcoholic regime, I can't say I feel any better, but I feel more reliable, as it were.... The day after that ill-starred party I was immersed in deep Celtic gloom and went around all day thinking "I am an old bitch, dying of dyspepsia and remorse". However, all these things pass. It hurts not to be able to have what you want, and it hurts perhaps even more not to be able to want wholeheartedly what you do have. But no doubt the fog will lift in time, and the way will become clear. At least, this is what I keep telling myself.

The path did not become clearer, however. Despite her earlier claim that she was inhibited from pub hopping, she went out many nights by herself to various places in search of George Lamming. In fact, one of the reasons she had been eager to settle in that section of London was because it was also the area where Lamming lived. When Margaret went out at night, she left Jocelyn (age ten) and David (age seven) by themselves with the assumption that Mrs. Levene or her daughter Rhoda would be nearby if the children needed help. She felt compelled to search out the person who, unbeknownst to himself, had become the focus of her existence.

Only five years later was she able to reflect on her attitude towards sex in that first year apart from her husband: "Sex ... is one aspect of my life which I have never experienced any guilt about, even including the really nutty series of brief encounters my first hellishly lonely year in London—I don't regret one minute of any of that. I had no sense of guilt at the time and I don't now—only gladness that I wasn't too affected by my Presbyterian background to take and give whatever warmth was there."

Nevertheless, by February 1963, she felt "lower than a snake's belly" and was filled with the "recurring anxiety" that she was "slightly insane."

> I think this is because I am at the moment trying to face up to, and assimilate, and do something about what I *really* think and feel, not what I am supposed to think and feel, and this is therefore a process which I have wanted and needed to undertake for some years, but it is also so much at variance with my "normal" life, in which one sought to do what everyone expected and thus not to alarm aunts, mother-in-law, etc. I keep getting letters from relatives, saying they *hope* the children are all right—clearly believing they are not all right at all.

Sometimes Margaret was so unconvinced of her own reality as a person that she took comfort in the existence of other Londoners, in the illusion "everything must be all right if it is moving along so normally on the surface." She took renewed encouragement from Elsie Laurence's letters of support but was disturbed by her mother-in-law's remark, "it is always easier to do what people expect of you, even in trivial things." The following sentence chilled her: "Also, as with suicide, one is afraid of failure."

In *Dance on the Earth*, Margaret refers to Sylvia Plath's suicide that same February 1963 in London. Like Plath, Margaret was an emigré woman writer separated from her husband, but there, she claimed, the resemblance ended: "But I knew in that instant, looking at the newspaper, that I was not within a million country miles of taking my own life. No thanks to me, and no blame to Sylvia Plath. I had been given, as a child, as a teenager, so much strength by my mothers." However, she was more intimidated by Plath's fate than she admitted in her autobiography. In April 1967, she told a friend:

> I don't think I ever felt that there would be some sudden revelation, or that everything would change, but I think I used to feel that one day I would achieve a kind of calm and would at last possess wisdom and would stop being afraid. As you say, it doesn't happen, and after a while you see that you've got the only self you're ever going

> to have, for life. I suppose if you realize that, and it really isn't bearable to you, then you do what Sylvia Plath did. I don't think I hate my own failings quite as much as I used to.

In August 1974, she returned to the topic of Plath's suicide in a letter to Ernest Buckler in which she tells him the parallels between herself and the American poet were obvious to her in 1963: "I mourned her as though it had been myself who died." In the winter of 1963, Margaret reached one of the lowest points of despair—a time when she indeed hated her own feelings—she was ever to experience. She seriously flirted with the idea of suicide but then turned her back resolutely against any such step. She felt driven, but she was not sure by what. Her search for Lamming took on the appearance of a quest for some sort of romantic hero to rescue her, but she had in some ways rejected the chivalrous side of her husband. Was her writing worth preserving at such enormous cost? Did she have the right to seek an independent existence? Why was she so driven? She could not sort out these burning issues and was left with a pervading sense of emptiness.

Soon after she arrived in London, she had a great deal of difficulty in coping with the amount of support money Jack had agreed to provide. Although she was desperate for Canada Council funding for which she had applied before she left Vancouver, she was not sanguine about her chances for success: "Probably they won't give me anything, as married women aren't supposed to need any money of their own, or something like that." Without such a subvention, she had to contemplate the possibility of taking on some sort of part-time work to make ends meet. Aunt Ruby, in particular, was opposed to any such course of action, feeling the children had been subjected to a great deal and would be further traumatized. The horrible paradox was that Aunt Ruby—the closest to an evil stepmother there was in Margaret's life—was also a professional woman, but one without dependents. Now, she was quite willing to criticize her niece for her pursuit of a career. The message seemed to be: women can only have careers if they completely sacrifice their personal lives. Otherwise, they should not even try.

That March, Margaret was not completely surprised when her request was turned down: "I am sure they did not really think I needed the money and of course in their terms I didn't, so I was not stunned or anything." A month later, rage had replaced resignation: "I do not feel brazenly brave about the Canada Council any longer. I hate the bastards. I have come to this feeling—I need that dough; they have it; they will not part with it, to me; so to hell with them. All I sincerely hope is this—that one of these years they will offer some of their cash to me, and that I will then be in a position to refuse, haughtily. What satisfaction! Well, almost the only times they give people money is when it is not really needed any longer. Nuts to them."

Much needed help and support came to the beleaguered author from her English publishers, Macmillan, and in particular from Rache Lovat Dickson, a transplanted Canadian who was the publisher of the trade list. For her, he was a "man in a million." One night when his wife was away in Yugoslavia, he invited her over to dinner. As Margaret recalled, "I got stoned and wept on his shoulder—how could I? I don't think he minded, in fact I think he was quite pleased in some odd way, so I don't feel too badly (is this an improvement? Yes, I really think it must be, as a few short months ago I would have spent days and days in guilty remorse over this kind of thing)." She was sufficiently trusting of Rache that she agreed at his insistence—despite her lifelong phobia about speaking in public or making public appearances—to be one of the speakers at the Canadian Universities Society Literary Supper in June 1963. She "sweated blood" but was otherwise okay. Earlier, on Valentine's Day, she accompanied him to the same group's Annual Ball, where she was afraid of "skidding on the floor and falling flat on my fanny, but God's grace was with me."

When Rache retired in 1964, Alan Maclean, who had been hired away from Collins by Maurice Macmillan in 1954, assumed his responsibilities. However, he had become actively engaged with Margaret's work well before that. John Gray at Macmillan in Toronto had recommended her as a short-story writer, and he published "The Rain Child" in the 1962 edition of *Winter's Tales.* In Alan—the son of Sir Donald Maclean, a Liberal cabinet minister knighted during the Great War, and the younger brother of Donald the spy—Margaret found a publisher who was, if anything, more keen on her work than Jack McClelland. She also made close friends of Alan and, later, his wife, Robin (they married in 1967). A reformed alcoholic two years older than Margaret, Alan possessed a warmth and wit that provided Margaret with much entertainment. Once, she accompanied the Dicksons to a wedding which Alan attended in the company of Muriel Spark, another of his authors. (Rebecca West and Lillian Hellman were also on his list.) Spark turned out to be "unexpectedly appealing—rather vixen, as you might expect, but not having in personal life (at least, to a casual view) the biting wit of her writing." The best part of the event was when the group from Macmillan was accused by an usher of not being guests but the singers paid to perform. "Later, Alan said what a fool he'd been—he ought to have said, 'Yes, we're the singers, and what's more, we haven't been paid yet.'"

Unlike many other publishers, he had a strong belief in the short story, even though he realized that this genre often presented serious financial risks in the market-place. For a number of years, he edited the annual collection of short stories, *Winter's Tales.* Although a great supporter of Margaret's, he was quite capable of rejecting work by her. On December 2, 1964, she wrote to him: "Re: my story, 'Horses of the Night,' I think it would be better, after all, if you returned it to me. Obviously, if I didn't get across the point to you, I didn't get it across, so never mind showing it to anyone else. In time, maybe, I'll see where it went wrong."

Right from the start of their relationship as publisher and author, Maclean—in stark contrast to Jack McClelland—told her he welcomed the idea of a collection of her West African stories. Knowing of her financial problems, he agreed immediately—soon after her arrival in England—to send her £100, the advance for *The Prophet's Camel Bell*;

later, he also sent her manuscripts to evaluate and paid her as a reader. (She also wrote scripts for the Hausa Section of the BBC African Service.) So trusting of Maclean did she become that she sent the typescript of *Hagar* to him in January 1963. She did this even though she was extremely unsure of the quality of the book; earlier, that autumn, she had even considered the radical step of changing the narrative from first to third person.

Meanwhile, later that January, she brought Jack McClelland up to date (without telling him the typescript was at Macmillan): "At the moment, I am typing out the novel which I told you about when I was in Toronto a year or so ago. I had put it away for a long time, as I was filled with terrible doubts about anything written with a Canadian setting. However, I got it out again when I arrived here, and I do not know why I was so fearful about it before. I've re-written parts of it, but the bones remain the same. For better or worse, this is the way I want to say it."

In his response, Jack told her he had reconsidered the short-story collection in light of Maclean's enthusiasm. This was welcome news, but nothing compared to the surprise phone call she received on February 14 from Maclean: "This book is going to make a difference to you, probably for the rest of your life." His words were prophetic, but in 1963 an ecstatic Margaret was more aware of the benefits she would receive in the short term.

> ALAN MACLEAN (MACMILLAN'S) LIKES *HAGAR*! HE LIKES IT! CAN IT BE TRUE? He has just phoned, and I am in something like a state of shock. He thinks it needs to be cut, somewhat, as it moves rather slowly in the beginning ... He also wonders about the title, thinking it makes it sound like an Old Testament tale, so I will give thought to that also ... He says he knows this kind of old lady very well, and that he finds her entire predicament and her death very moving. Adele, I feel as though my faith in life, in myself, in everything, has been miraculously restored to me. Of course, this novel meant a lot more than it should have done, to me, as in way it

> was (or became) a whole test of my own judgement—and luckily, I had got to the point where I knew that although it might not say anything to anyone else, it did say a lot to me, so perhaps really that was the true restoration of faith.... Nevertheless, in terms of novels, it meant the transition from writing about Africa to writing about my own people, the only ones I know from the inside, so on that level also it had almost too much significance for me.

In this wonderful, triumphant moment, she also realized she must in the end be her own judge and jury in assessing her literary career: "The real crux of the matter is that one must not be too dependent upon anyone else's point of view, and therefore I ought not to be moved too much either by acceptance or rejection." But her uncertainties about herself had been so great that she was filled with "enormous relief."

Four days later, to the elation of success was added a bittersweet note when Jack wrote from Pakistan, telling her how much he admired her bravery in carving out a career as a writer in isolation.

> Then I feel like bawling my eyes out, wondering about the irony of life, and how it can be possible that for so many years I wanted to communicate my feelings about many things to him, and now that he is finally interested in listening, I no longer care, and this seems so brutal on my part that I can't bear to think about it, but I can't deny it, either. One hopes, naturally, for some kind of change of heart which will make it possible for things to be resumed although on a different basis from before, as I can no longer live with too much of a disparity between the outer expression and the inner belief. I no longer think that I handled the whole business—coming here, etc—badly, however. I think now I did what was basically the right thing, out of pure instinct.... Jack ... still suffers from the same old feeling of purposelessness, or rather, lack of compelling purpose.

But Jack's sense of "compelling purpose" had been centred on his marriage, and it had been shattered, to a large degree, because of his wife's sense of a radically different "compelling purpose." No longer could she be the child-bride completely dependent on a "father-type husband"; no longer could she "go on being what amounted to some kind of projection of" Jack. Of one thing, Margaret was very sure: her name. In April, she reminded a recalcitrant Gordon: "P.S. I apologize, but only lightly, for the 'Margaret' ... do you think you could bring yourself to call me that? It is my name, actually, and I have to persevere with it." Even Adele had to toe the line: "Can you bear to refer to me as Margaret? This is becoming compulsive with me."

A mere two months after Macmillan had accepted the novel still provisionally entitled *Hagar*, the book was in page proofs, although Margaret had not heard from Jack McClelland about his reaction to the "old lady" novel. On June 29, 1963, she inquired if her agent in New York—John Cushman at the Willis Wing agency—had sent him the book. She could no longer figure out why she had had so many doubts about it:

> It seems to me to be the only really true thing I have ever written—this because it is the only thing written entirely from the inside, with the kind of knowledge that one can only have of one's own people, who are, as the Muslims say about Allah, as close to you as your own neck vein. I do not know why I had so many doubts about HAGAR, initially—possibly because I wasn't sure I could write about anything in which the theme was all inner, not outer.... Personally, I think she is a hell of an old lady! Of course, I may be prejudiced. Anyway, for better or worse, the voice in which she speaks is all her own, and I think now that I can't ever again be content to write in anything except this idiom, which is of course mine.

Margaret had discovered her own unique writing voice. As well, she would continue on another path initiated by her new book: she would create characters and situations which would allow her to exploit that special voice. In the future, she would not shirk from writing about a virgin spinster or a troubled, stir-crazy housewife, protagonists not calculated to shine in the public eye.

Before Jack McClelland could respond to Margaret's letter, he received an inquiry about her from Alfred Knopf, who remembered that his editors and Jack had once been at loggerheads about the quality of Leonard Cohen's writing. Jack had supported the Montreal poet and novelist enthusiastically, whereas the Knopf editors had seen little merit in him. Knopf had been told, erroneously, that McClelland & Stewart had agreed "in advance to publish anything that [Margaret Laurence] writes." On July 5, McClelland wrote Alfred Knopf: "While I could not confirm that we have agreed in advance to publish anything that Margaret Laurence writes, I would say that I don't anticipate that she will ever write anything that we shall not want to publish."

Although *This Side Jordan* had been offered to Knopf in 1959, they had rejected it. When Jack McClelland had offered the book to Knopf, he had done so in—for him—an extremely laidback way, disguising the fact that he was eager to place the book.

> This is simply a novel manuscript that has been recommended to us by a number of outside readers. It's had a cursory reading in our office and the feeling is that it may have some merit. I read the first two chapters only, and felt myself that it warranted a serious look, so I decided to leave it with you. I think the writer shows some promise. The background is interesting because it is possibly the first novel that has been set in Ghana. The writer is unknown to me. Whether it is publishable or not is anybody's guess. I would appreciate it if you would give it what attention you can and let us know whether or not you think it is something you want to publish.

In November 1959 an editor at Knopf told Alfred: "We have now had a report on the manuscript by Margaret Laurence that you left with us. Unfortunately I was unable to read it myself, but the report seems to confirm the impression you had, that this is not quite a successful book by a writer who shows considerable promise. Our reader felt that she had created an interesting situation and succeeded in creating the atmosphere of a place torn by racial conflict. But, I quote, 'the novel is not as tightly controlled as it should be, the author lapses into pages of rhetoric about the African "mystique," and the characters are often wooden. The writer should be watched; she can evoke a scene and a conflict, but is not yet master of her craft.'" In 1963, Knopf himself decided to review the entire matter when John Cushman offered three books as a package (*The Prophet's Camel Bell*, *The Tomorrow-Tamer* and *The Stone Angel*). Initially, Knopf was not enthusiastic about such a deal because "whoever takes her up will have quite a job on his hands."

Meanwhile, a very confused Jack McClelland wrote Margaret a no-nonsense letter telling her flatly that not only was her work being rushed into print but also that simultaneous publication of several works could prove disastrous:

> More often than not I find myself writing to you like a Dutch uncle.... What in hell goes on at Macmillan's? Have they gone completely berserk? They are rushing the short stories into print. They are rushing the novel into print ... Even if you were the second coming of Christ it would be foolish to publish three of your books in one season, or even three of your books between this fall and next spring.... please believe even though Macmillan is one of the great imprints in the publishing world that editorial policy in English publishing houses is inclined to be too damn lax.... It may be that you have rushed it too much. It may be that it has flaws. I know very well that you won't make changes unless you agree entirely with the suggestions that are made and I think this is the way it should be. But surely there is time to have HAGAR properly evaluated. This is going to be a key book in your writing career.

He strongly suggested she phone Alan Maclean and demand production of the Hagar novel cease immediately. Of course, she refused:

> I am sorry to be nasty about this matter, but I resented your remark about the second coming of Christ so much that it was very fortunate for both of us that you were not present at the time, otherwise I would have clobbered you with the nearest solid object available. I do not imagine that HAGAR is without flaws, nor am I so lacking in critical perception that I delude myself about the quality of my writing.... Please, Jack, do not ever imagine that I am at this point over-estimating my own abilities. My problem has always been the reverse—to have enough faith in my own writing capacities to be able to go on, in some fashion, because the alternative—not to go on—would mean that nothing at all was any good anywhere for me, since this kind of work appears to be a necessary condition of life.

Only five months earlier, in February 1963, Blanche Knopf had turned down *The Prophet's Camel Bell*, based on this chauvinistic reader's report by Patrick Gregory: "Mrs. Laurence spent a year or so in Somaliland with her engineer husband. Her narrative of this sojourn is lacking in any sort of distinction, for she brings to her work neither a gift for prose, nor a fund of erudition, nor a discriminating eye. At best, she provides us with an accurate picture of an average Canadian housewife's view of an exotic land. But this best is hardly worthy of serious attention."

However, it is not entirely surprising Alfred Knopf was willing to consider a change of opinion regarding Margaret Laurence. He respected Jack McClelland's instincts as a publisher and his own taste in books was almost diametrically opposed to his wife's—and to some of his editors. John Cushman, knowing very well the Knopfs often agreed to disagree—and in the process sometimes overruled each other—took pains to call Margaret Laurence to Alfred's attention.

Although they were both native New Yorkers, Blanche, who had been educated by French and German governesses, gravitated towards European writers (Gide, Mann and Sartre were great favourites) and refined English writers such as Elizabeth Bowen; in contrast, Alfred's taste led in the direction of books dealing with frontiers and the opening up of the American West. In particular, he was a great admirer of

Willa Cather, an author whose work bears many similarities to that of Margaret Laurence.

In 1963, the firm of Alfred A. Knopf had been in existence for forty-eight years and Alfred, one of the most renowned of American publishers, was seventy-one. Like his wife, he had a forceful personality and a passion for books of the highest quality. As a young man in the sales division of Doubleday, he enthusiastically and energetically promoted Conrad's *Chance* and, in the process, earned the author's undying gratitude. As a publisher, he believed high-quality typography should grace all the writings which bore his art decoish imprint, the borzoi. (In an article in *The New Yorker* in 1948, Geoffrey Hellman explained the origin of this logo: "Mrs. Knopf ... was crazy about Borzois in 1915, or thought she was, and suggested that they use a drawing of one as a trademark. 'I bought a couple of them later,' she says, 'and grew to despise them. One died and I gave the other to a kennel. I wished I'd picked a better dog for our imprint.'") In the sixties, Knopf's fiction list included Shirley Ann Grau, John Updike, Muriel Spark and Doris Lessing.

Knopf asked for three sets of reports on the three-book Laurence package. One reviewer—Henry Robbins—found *The Tomorrow-Tamer* a "collection of good but rather conventional stories ... I couldn't help but feel that I had gotten this message only too often before"; the same person could not understand "what all the excitement at Wing's office and Macmillan's is about, for [*Hagar*], evidently the prize in the three-book package, strikes me as an intelligently written but rather dreary tale.... The real failure for me comes, I suppose, in Mrs. Laurence's failure to make her pathetic matriarch into a really attractive character.... I certainly cannot see our taking her on at this point, and especially with *three* unsalable books." Another reader, "BWS," who compared Margaret Laurence to Daphne DuMaurier as a good "middle-brow writer," was much more favourably disposed, especially to the African books. However, his reaction to *Hagar* was diametrically opposed to his colleague's: "What makes this story strong is the author's refusal to let pathos obscure the harshness in Hagar's character." Leo Lemay, an editor in whose opinion Alfred Knopf had implicit trust, was even more enthusiastic than BWS:

> This novel, which I found unusually engrossing, will not appeal to everyone. It may not, as a matter of fact, appeal to very many readers, but it is the work of a good novelist, a writer who belongs on the Knopf list and a writer who will bring distinction and probably profit, someday, to the house.... I thought it quite remarkable that a woman in her middle thirties could so graphically project herself into the life of a woman over fifty years older. There is also, in this book, an unsparing honesty about the nature of the woman herself.... We should present this writer with a great deal of noise.

He concluded his report by mentioning he was not pleased with the title.

Suitable title or not, Alfred Knopf became sufficiently enthusiastic that he eventually decided to do something unique in the history of his firm: he would publish three new books (the American edition of *Prophet's* was entitled *New Wind in a Dry Land)* by the same author on the same day. "Well," he told Jack McClelland, "we are taking the plunge on Margaret Laurence, putting up no less than five thousand dollars for the three books." He was doing this because a "reasonable amount" of enthusiasm had been generated to offset "very negative reactions." He added: "I do want to say to you quite honestly that were it not for your enthusiasm for the lady and her work, we would not be taking her up."

Alfred Knopf was a careful reader. On January 29, 1964, he asked Margaret to explain the "geography" of *The Stone Angel*, which, as a non-Canadian, he found confusing. On February 1, she replied, providing her publisher with information on the various locales: "I don't think you are being dense in the slightest. For some reason, I was reluctant to explain anything more than was absolutely necessary, perhaps because I felt that the actual places were not the important thing. The names of the towns are fictitious, but Manawaka is meant to be located somewhere in southern Manitoba, like the town of Neepawa, where I grew up.... Hagar lived on the prairies for most of her life, but when she left her husband she went to the west coast of Canada, to a city which—although it is not named—is Vancouver.... When Hagar runs away from her son's house, in her last attempt at independence, she goes to a deserted fish cannery on the shore of the Pacific. When we lived in Vancouver, we had a summer cottage at a place called Point Roberts, which was actually in the State of Washington—a tiny point of land that had been cut off from the rest of America by the boundary between Canada and the U.S.A. We used to say that we owned part of the U.S.A. There was an old ramshackle fish cannery there, similar to the one in the story. A great deal of *The Stone Angel* was written at Point Roberts, so perhaps that is why it somehow found its way into the novel."

McClelland, who had been urging caution to Margaret, was thrilled, especially as he had finally had a chance to read *Hagar*: "I don't think it will be the easiest novel to sell that I have read recently, but I think it is a moving and a first-rate piece of writing.... I agree completely about the title. It is hopeless and I will take the matter up with the author right away." The title had also been a concern of Alan Maclean's. First of all, Margaret countered with "Rage Against the Dying" (the quote from Dylan Thomas is used as the book's epigraph); Maclean did not like this and made some suggestions, at which point she began rereading the Psalms for inspiration. Her new choice, "Sword in My Bones," displeased even her: "This title seemed to me to suggest either a who-dun-it by Mickey Spillane or some kind of blood-and-thunder story." In *Dance on the Earth*, Margaret states that the title of the book finally "stared out at me in the first sentence of the book itself" early in 1964; in fact, the dispute over the title was resolved by the end of September 1963.

Knopf's acceptance of her three books cheered Margaret, but, as she told Adele two months later, it also "frightened the hell out of" her. Why this was, she was uncertain. In large part, it was because she was afraid her literary career might be over just as it had begun. She was struggling with her new novel. She had "destroyed so many pages in the last six months" that she hated to think of the cost of the paper that had been trashed. Her new novel was about Stacey MacAindra and was the novel which eventually became *The Fire-Dwellers*, but in the autumn of

1963 her work on that book—probably because it was so close to her own recent experiences in Vancouver—became impossible.

She once told her friend Gordon Elliott: "One's writing is not meant to be bound up with one's life, but only jerks believe this." At times, when she valiantly attempted to work on that narrative, she became convinced she would be forced to return to Vancouver "to the same house and to the same groove, and then I get rather low in my mind and start hitting the bottle, which is very dangerous. I have been much better of late, however, having scared myself in this way so much that it provided the necessary shock or something. Anyway, I know now that I am not an alcoholic, which for a time I thought I must be, but I have to take care in this area and always will." At about the time she was wrestling with a novel that was completely resistant to her best efforts to bring it to life, Margaret had to cope with a miserable experience.

In mid-October 1963, Robert Weaver, who organized the CBC literary program "Anthology," was in London. He contacted Margaret and suggested they go to a party at Mordecai and Florence Richler's. Margaret must have been very surprised to see George Lamming there, accompanied by a woman named Ethel, a Jewish emigré from South Africa active in the anti-apartheid movement. The situation was awful enough for Margaret, but things became even worse when the playwright David Mercer began to pay court to Ethel and an enraged Lamming threatened to beat him up. Just as the two men were set to go at each other, Richler intervened (at some point, Lamming had complained to him about Mercer) and the threat of violence ended when Richler asked Mercer to leave. Margaret drank very heavily that evening and was beside herself with anguish when she and Weaver arrived back at Heath Hurst Road. As she stumbled up the stairs, she woke the children. Jocelyn, accustomed to looking after David, was frightened by the display of her out-of-control mother, but she had to stifle her own feelings in the wake of her small brother's tears. Weaver departed quickly and Jocelyn settled David. Margaret had passed out.

Margaret's behaviour on the evening she encountered Lamming was not typical of her response to excessive drinking. Usually, she would become maudlin and repetitive. Another hallmark of her drunken behaviour was that she would almost always speak of Neepawa, especially her grandfather Simpson. In drinking, she sought a state of consciousness that—if not true to the facts of her daily life—allowed her free access to her deepest feelings. She was also trying to exert some sort of control over reality by liberating herself from it and thus making it—for a short duration—less painful. The irony was that in returning to Neepawa when she drank, she probably made herself more unhappy in her daily life but, at the very same time, got in touch with the forces in her past out of which she constructed her greatest writings.

Earlier, in the summer of 1963, Frances Bolton, a twenty-one-year-old cousin of Jack Laurence's, had come over from Canada to live with Margaret and the children. She looked after the children while Margaret wrote; she also provided the exceedingly lonely writer with much needed companionship. In London, Margaret made friends with Alice Frick and Marjory Whitelaw, journalists associated with the CBC, and saw the Richlers occasionally, but otherwise knew very few people. Soon after she arrived in London, Margaret had joined the CND (Committee for Nuclear Disarmament) and even took part in the last day of the massive CND-organized Aldermaston March in the spring of 1963.

Without doubt, she felt close to despair, despite the incredible way her writing career was taking off. Late that autumn, she was delighted to take advantage of an offer made by Jack's firm to pay her way out to East Pakistan. She left the children with Nadine, who came down from Scotland, where she was now living, to look after them. Years later, Margaret wrote of an attempted seduction on the flight from London to Karachi. "The blankets were handed out by the stewardess, and the lights turned off for the night. There were three seats in the row, but only two were occupied. Me and the salesman. He began by expressing the opinion that we'd both be more comfortable if we removed the armrests between the seats. I, however, thought otherwise. After a weary night spent in fending off this clown, my inborn sense of tact and politeness was wearing decidedly thin. 'Well, at least it must be a change from the farmer's daughter,' I sourly commented."

When she arrived back that December, she sent Jack McClelland an enthusiastic report of her sojourn in the East:

> Having spent a month in the wilds of Pakistan I still have some feeling of unreality, although I am quickly being brought back to the realities of life by the English climate, which is pretty awful at the moment. I had a very good visit, during which my husband managed to take a week's local leave and we went to see a lot of ancient Hindu temples in India, which probably sounds rather deadly but was actually quite interesting, especially as they included the Black Pagoda at Konarak, famed for its pornographic carvings. I have personally unearthed (I think) the secret of the Black Pagoda—the reason why so many of the amorous postures look so uncomfortable is that owing to the rectangular shape of the building blocks all the couples had to be pictured in standing positions, and let's face it, the permutations and combinations are strictly limited to the human physique. With me, a little tourism goes a long way, but I must admit I found these temples quite beautiful, although the climate was extremely warm and there were odd moments when I would have traded every ancient temple in India for one very dry martini, well iced. We went swimming in the Bay of Bengal, which was marvellous, and I acquired a wonderful tan, which I am now unable to show off, as England is too cold to expose even an arm.

Eight days later, she sent an equally detailed description of the same trip to Adele, emphasizing, however, the ever-widening gulfs between her and her husband.

> It was strange to be called "Memsahib" again. I did not realize I had changed so much. I managed to act reasonably well, I think, although of course did become involved with arguments with other Europeans, as usual.... when all the old jazz about the useless natives

> comes up again, I react in all the expected ways.... I swore not to open my mouth, but of course I did, and this is embarrassing to Jack, as it always was. However, I must say he was very good about it, perhaps because I was less apologetic and maybe even less aggressive than before.... Anyway, domestically we got a lot of things settled, although for how long I would not like to say, as basically we simply do not want the same things. Jack, quite rightly, wants to go on working abroad and naturally needs a woman who will go with him, no questions asked. I can't do that, both for myself and on account of the kids, as I do not think they will get a good education if I teach them and even if he is in places where there are schools, I do not want to move them every year.... As it is my choice to stay here, however, it is also incumbent upon me to support myself, at least by 2/3, which is what it will be. J and I are in complete agreement upon this aspect. Let us only hope I can continue to make the odd shilling—I never believe that I will ever again earn anything, but we will be okay for about 2 years if I am very careful, I think ... Jack will be coming on leave in April, and will stay 2 months at that time.... Sometimes I feel so stricken with panic, Adele, when I think what I have done, which is to alter the whole course of my life.

During her first year in England, Margaret discovered—almost anew and in very painful ways—that all the "necessary conditions" of her writing life and of life itself often had to be paid for in exceedingly hard currency: emotional instability and recurring anxiety.

12

Happy, Unhappy or In-Between? (1964-1965)

"The day that changed my life and the lives of my children immeasurably for the better," Margaret recalled, "came in the late fall of 1963. Alan Maclean invited us to go along with him to Buckinghamshire, to see his family's old country house in Penn." Her first visit to Elm Cottage (often referred to by her by the nickname, Elmcot) was by luck rather than design. Convinced that Margaret and David would profit from a day in the country (Jocelyn was away on a school trip), Alan took them on an outing to Beaconsfield with the intention of looking over Elm Cottage in nearby Penn, which he and his brother in New Zealand had inherited when their mother, Lady Maclean, died in 1962. As the three of them walked through the house—somewhat messy and tattered because it had had a variety of tenants—Margaret was inspired to ask if she might rent the property. Alan suggested she think the matter over, but, after a sleepless night, Margaret called a startled Alan at the crack of dawn the next morning to confirm the arrangement.

In a letter to Jack McClelland, she mentioned her great joy in moving on December 30 to the cottage at Penn, a small village near High Wycombe. In fact "cottage" was not the right word: "It has five

Elm Cottage.

bedrooms, which is certainly not my idea of a cottage. It is furnished, and is old and rambling, just the kind of house I have always wanted. I can't afford to live in Hampstead, as rents are too high, and I think it will be better for my kids to be in the country, anyway, where they will have their own yard and can keep dogs, cats and goldfish, etc. The house will probably be cold as charity during the winter, but we are greatly looking forward to having our own house." Margaret needed a refuge to escape to after the fiery turbulence into which she had been thrown even while living in relatively pastoral Hampstead. Her stay in the East had had its traumatic side, as she confessed to Ethel Wilson: "Calcutta itself is bad enough, with more human suffering and despair than I had believed possible—crowds of maimed beggars, and countless people sleeping in the streets because they had no homes. Added to this, the shock of the news about [the] Kennedy [assassination]—that morning I felt as though everything were hopeless."

Two weeks after moving to the house, Margaret was in state of euphoria at the bold, decisive step she had taken in removing herself and the children from London.

Margaret Laurence walking on Beacon Hill in Penn, with Ringo, the family dog.

> What I appear to have taken on is this: an old and certainly uneconomical house, which I think is going to cost the earth to heat ... It is a house which people have loved and cared about.... It was rented to American service families for some time, and has been very much neglected, and now it really needs attention and work. The living room has lovely red tile floors, a bay window overlooking the garden, and a beautiful fireplace. There are 5 bedrooms, one of which I hope ultimately to be able to rent.... At the moment I am in the last stages of sheer physical exhaustion, having been working harder than I have ever done in my entire life, turfing out old junk, scrubbing floors and walls, painting woodwork and furniture, making curtains, re-finishing old oak tables etc.... The kids love the house, and are very pleased to be here, as they each have their own quite large room, and also a playroom downstairs ... and a large garden which promises to be a good thing in the warmer weather.

The three Laurences enjoyed the "moving parties" whereby they heaved furniture from one room to another. The children, desperate to escape the confines of their London flat, felt they had been given a wonderful gift. Nevertheless, they were uprooted yet again. Jocelyn, who was eleven when the move was announced, had formed a close friendship with a girl at school. David, three years younger, looked forward more eagerly to the move.

The house, which stood on two-thirds of an acre, had a huge lawn in the front, where there were two giant beech trees and the elm tree after which the house was named. "At one side there was a mulberry tree that produced quantities of red-purple berries, almost impossible to pick, for they were on the high and somewhat fragile branches, and all we could do was to shake the boughs and gather up the semi-squashed fruit from the grass. At the front of the house was a wisteria, so old and gnarled it was virtually a tree, and its vine branches climbed up as high as the children's bedrooms. The back garden had once grown vegetables, and for the most of our time there, it was a wild garden of nettles and dock-leaves." Margaret was not quite so rhapsodic about the various boarders she took in to make ends meet during her first three years at Elmcot. Her workspace at Elmcot was a dramatic improvement over her bedroom in London. She would write in longhand on the table in the living room with the bay window; her desk—where she typed—was in a small alcove off the living room.

Although Margaret spoke warmly of the house, its grounds and Alan's generosity in making the house available, she regarded her neighbours as merely an accumulation of snotty Tories. But her view of her new neighbours was a little misguided. Penn, she claimed, was a place inhabited by tradespeople, by wealthy families who had been there for generations and by the newly wealthy who wanted to be within easy commuting distance of London. This is true. In addition, the local MP may have been renowned as a caricature of extremely right-wing views, but the town was famous for its musical life. In Margaret's time, the inhabitants included Gerald Moore, the pianoforte accompanist and Myra Hess, the pianist.

The villagers of Penn tended to have negative views of Americans, but Margaret was quick to insist she was Canadian and thus infinitely different. For her, part of the charm of Penn was that there she could be a totally private person: "no one in this area knows me from a hole in the ground, and in fact among my County neighbours I am thought to be a pretty low-class North American gypsy or something, which is just great." In her own way, she tended to practise reverse snobbery about the landed gentry, but she had a deep affection for Lady Maclean, whose portrait (lent by Alan) hung in the downstairs hall. The young, long-haired woman, who wore a white dress which gave her the look of a pensive Alice in Wonderland, became the spirit of the house. Sometimes, a weary, discouraged Margaret would converse with "The Lady" whose benign presence provided her with comfort and inspiration.

For Margaret, the shops surrounding the village green were the centre of her new neighbourhood. Woodbridge's, a small family business, supplied most of her provisions. The nearby post office also housed a sweet shop and sold women's clothing. There were also a second-hand furniture shop, a second-hand bookshop, the butcher's shop and the Red Lion pub. Two cats—Calico and, later, Topaz—joined the household on a permanent basis. Babysitting was provided by Mr. and Mrs. Charlett who lived in the small brick and flint cottage on the grounds of The Beacon, on Beacon Hill opposite Elm Cottage. From Mr. Charlett, who was the head gardener at The Beacon, and Mrs. Charlett, Margaret acquired all kinds of lore about the countryside.

When describing her departure from London in *Dance*, Margaret does not mention she rented a *pied-à-terre* in Bayswater. This allowed her a spot in London she could call her own. Although loneliness was an inevitable part of her life, she escaped to London to keep in touch with Canadian friends and to keep her sex life segregated from her children:

> The presence of my children meant that, in the deepest sense, loneliness could never be a real threat. I severely missed having a mate, however, someone to talk things over with and to share worries with, but there were also times when I would have settled merely for a sexual relationship. I had one or two sexual liaisons, of such a brief span that they really don't deserve the term affairs, and I quickly realized

> that casual sex was not for me. It was a foregone conclusion, in my mind, that I would never take a man to Elm Cottage.... Anyway, living out in the wilds of Buckinghamshire, where was I going to meet anyone? I used to wonder if I had deliberately isolated myself so that a relationship with a man would be all but impossible.

A few years later, in a letter to Nadine Jones, she recalled an event from this time: "I feel somehow lonely for the sound of my own speech, and even for the puritanical responses which make a Canadian man long for passionate sex while at the same time worrying like mad about what the landlady will think (this actually happened to me once, in London, with a Canadian actor, and I was so delighted to find someone who worried more about the trivialities than I did!)." To Al Purdy, she made a facetious reference to an incident which may have involved the same man: "Once got laid on Hampstead Heath, but that was long ago and never again. (That was a Canadian, come to think of it—I seem to have some strange penchant for Canadians—how odd)."

According to Margaret, she had two careers at Elm Cottage: writing and parenting. "I would stop writing a few hours before the children arrived home from school, not only to make dinner and do the domestic stuff but also to be mentally and emotionally out of the fictional world and back in the world of my life. Heaven knows I was not Supermum. There were many times when I felt frazzled and worried by domestic crises...." In the children's memories, the demarcation in their mother's existence was not as clear-cut as she later claimed. A flicker of disappointment would cross her face if they arrived home early for lunch or if they announced a school holiday she had forgotten. In Vancouver and London, Margaret had often been short-tempered. On a day-to-day basis, the children now found that their mother's emotional outbursts occurred less frequently. But the children also had to deal with their mother on the nights when she had nightmares. She would moan so loudly, they would be awakened and rush into her bedroom. In such a state, since she was impossible to rouse, they would have to resort to squeezing a wet washcloth over her face. When awake, she could not recall the nightmares.

Margaret—the children found—could be implacable. The children were angry with her when she peremptorily had the family dog Ringo put to sleep: Margaret insisted that she could not manage him (Ringo would run away, dig up the gardens of various neighbours, and be returned by policemen), but Jocelyn and David were convinced that their mother could have salvaged the situation more effectively.

By the middle of March 1964, she had reached some semblance of tranquillity, although one tinged with melancholia: "Are you happy, unhappy or in-between?" she asked Adele. "Actually, I have come to the conclusion that it doesn't matter so much whether one is happy or not, as long as you aren't in despair. I am not in despair, but I seem to live in a state of more or less constant panic, and maybe I just have to accept that it won't ever be any different."

Margaret was certain she lacked one essential ingredient in her make-up: guts. However, she retained a semblance of faith in herself, even though her financial prospects looked grim. The advance of five thousand dollars from Knopf would last a year and then she would be "practically broke. When I realize this, I start feeling horrible, so I am trying not to think of it." She could not bear to apply once again to the Canada Council. Still, she could not prevent herself from feeling "absurdly optimistic, partly because I have now stopped keeping liquor in the house and I find I can get along without it after all."

In early June, Margaret met Jack in Greece, one of the many trips on which they attempted to resume conjugal life. They went on a four-day coach trip from Athens to Delphi, then to Patras, Olympia and Mycenae; they wound up their holiday by spending a few days at a beach near Athens. Their tour was the "Ultra Classical." "Why," Jack asked her, "be half-classical when the chance may never come again to be *ultra*-classical?" When she wrote of this trip in a travel piece for *Holiday* (published as "Sayonara, Agamemnon" in January 1966), she provided a humorous, probably fictionalized account of the hazards of international tourism. However, in a letter to Adele Wiseman, she emphasized the incompatibilities between herself and Jack:

> We decided we would have to compromise, as I prefer to go to one spot and stay there and look around rather slowly, and Jack likes to zoom around like lightning and see a million places in a week. So we spent half our time in going on a bus tour around various parts of Greece, and the other half in sun-bathing and swimming at a beach near Athens. It worked out very well, and we both enjoyed both halves of the trip, to our mutual surprise.

Jack, who was on long leave, spent a great deal of time at Elm Cottage that spring. Before he arrived, Margaret confided in Adele: "I don't want him to see [a copy of *The Stone Angel*], or say anything about it. There must be something very hard in my nature, and it has been a shock to find this out." At Penn, she felt saner and calmer than she had in a long time. By July, the Laurences had reached an understanding of sorts—regarding their house in Vancouver, which had been rented to a friend. According to Margaret, the decision to part with the house was Jack's—not hers: "He decided to sell the house. I would not ever live in it under any circumstances, but it was up to him to decide what to do with it, as it is his house, not mine, at least that was my feeling. I always hated it anyway, but was too much of a coward to say so for a long time."

Her view of her career in 1964 is best encapsulated in a letter to Jane Rule. In her letter to Margaret, Jane had obviously spoken of the high price she might have to pay for her honesty in describing lesbian experience. Jane's reflections prompted a similar burst of honesty in Margaret: "I was interested in what you said about not knowing yet, yourself, what special price you might have to pay for the particular kind of book you have written. My own feeling is that whatever kind of book, there is always some quite unexpected price and that one can never afford it, but you can pay it all the same, because what else can you do except pack up and die? I think the surprising thing is to find you can pay it, whatever it is, and that you are in some ways tougher than you ever imagined." By the middle of 1964, her "special price" included her marriage and her native land and, what is more, she was having an incredibly difficult time in trying to write a new novel.

Part of the problem was Jack, who having returned from Vancouver, was again staying with his family at Elm Cottage that August.

> Things are going along reasonably well, I guess. What I feel chiefly at the moment, I think, is that I may be doing my best (or am I? how does one know?) but my best is none too damned good. We are back now in the old groove of me trying to split myself three ways, and sometimes feeling that I'm doing a pretty rotten job on all three fronts as it were. I do not seem to have sufficient reserves of calm and affection and gentleness and I frequently feel like a mean old bitch who must be nearly impossible for anyone to get along with. However, I also feel that I must *not* begin basically doubting my own reality again, as if I do, I'm really lost. I have to keep to my own course, even if this often seems selfish or unjustified in some way, in terms of other people.

How, Margaret was asking herself, could she preserve her writing self when everything seemed to conspire to rob of her of that essential part of her being? She was upset when Fred Schulhof wrote to Jack, suggesting how various compromises might save the Laurence marriage. Gordon Elliott was another friend who, from his vantage point, thought the Laurence marriage should be made to work. Margaret was polite but firm: "We were fortunate in Vancouver to have good friends, but apart from that, many things were not going well—if it had been otherwise, we would have stayed [together], but it was not otherwise. I hope you can accept all this, because it is really all I feel I can say."

After Jack left on November 2, she was very depressed, having almost convinced herself she should have returned to his new post in Somaliland with him. She had a great affection for Jack; their relationship had been successful sexually; she may have had a lingering guilty feeling that a wife had a duty to accompany her husband. The simple truth was that she and Jack had been very good for each other. She was still in love with him. But she did not wish to go backwards. Her way of purging herself of such turbulent feelings was to write a short story. She so submerged herself in this task that she could imagine "the real world [was] fictional, and the inner world the real one." She described herself as inert, but she was preoccupied with a number of tasks. She did book reviews for the BBC, two articles for the *Women's Mirror*, three articles for *Holiday* and worked on a number of short stories.

If 1963 had been a landmark year in Margaret's career in terms of the sheer number of books accepted for publication, 1964 was the year that began her ascent to star status. Late in 1963, the historical novelist Mary Renault, a great admirer of *This Side Jordan*, was even more welcoming of *The Tomorrow-Tamer*: "Margaret Laurence's stature increases with each new book. She is now without equal as the novelist of Africa in transition.... These short stories with their compassion, dignity and humour, their brilliant evocations of character and scene, show her impressive gifts at their best." Notices the next year in *The Globe and Mail*, *The Tamarack Review*, and *The Canadian Forum* were enthusiastic; *The Prophet's Camel Bell* also received strong reviews. But it was *The Stone Angel* (published in England c. March 8, 1964, in Canada on May 23, and in the United States on June 15) that unveiled a major writer, even though the good notices were not enough to make it, as Jack McClelland told Margaret, "a major best-seller here, but it's had a truly fine reception and we are well satisfied with the sale at least."

The Stone Angel is now recognized as one of the greatest novels written by a Canadian. The reviewers in Canada—and elsewhere—did not sense they were reading a masterpiece, although most were polite in recognizing the technical brilliance Margaret Laurence had achieved. In fact, Hagar took a while to become an iconic figure in the history of Canadian literature, perhaps because Margaret's powerful old lady is far more crusty than she is endearing.

A year earlier, in January 1963, she confided to Adele that the character in *The Stone Angel* whose dilemma was closest to her own was

John, Hagar's second and favourite son: "He is the person whom I feel the most for." Hagar—despite strong, rebellious feelings, a person who lives her entire life by convention—abandons Manawaka and her husband, Bram, and takes John with her to the coast. She perceives John to be temperamentally her child (as opposed to her first-born, Marvin). As John later points out to her, she has reversed the truth of the situation. Like his father, John despises conventionality and is very much an outsider in his father's mould. Unlike his mother, John is not the kind of person who can repress turbulent emotions. John's death—caused by his heavy drinking—is attributable in part to Hagar's meddling.

During the writing of *The Stone Angel*, Margaret may have come to a knowledge of the Hagar-like side of her nature, but she also came to the realization that, like John, she had been the victim of a powerful parental figure not unlike Hagar. Part of the inner turbulence she was experiencing in the early sixties came from an increased awareness that her own nature was divided between such extremes of power and weakness.

The Hagar-like portion of Margaret's character is best captured in a portrait photograph of 1964. On the back of the copy she inserted in her own album, she wrote: "M—England—1964—photo used on *A Jest of God* 1966—I look like the Dragon Lady—I really *love* this pic—it doesn't look at all like me, but it looks good." She liked this image because it captured the ruthless streak in her character, that part of the self that could be both ambitious and, if necessary, selfish. The softer side of Margaret can be discerned in a snapshot from the same time in which she poses in front of Woodbridge's in the heart of Penn. She looks a bit expectantly at the camera, trying to assume a benign, motherly smile. The two photographs show vastly different but real sides of the sitter.

In the spring of 1964, Margaret's habitual shyness was in place when she was summoned to London to lunch with the formidable Blanche Knopf, who regularly visited England and Europe to meet authors. Knopf ordered a lunch comprised of vodka, olives and an egg dish.

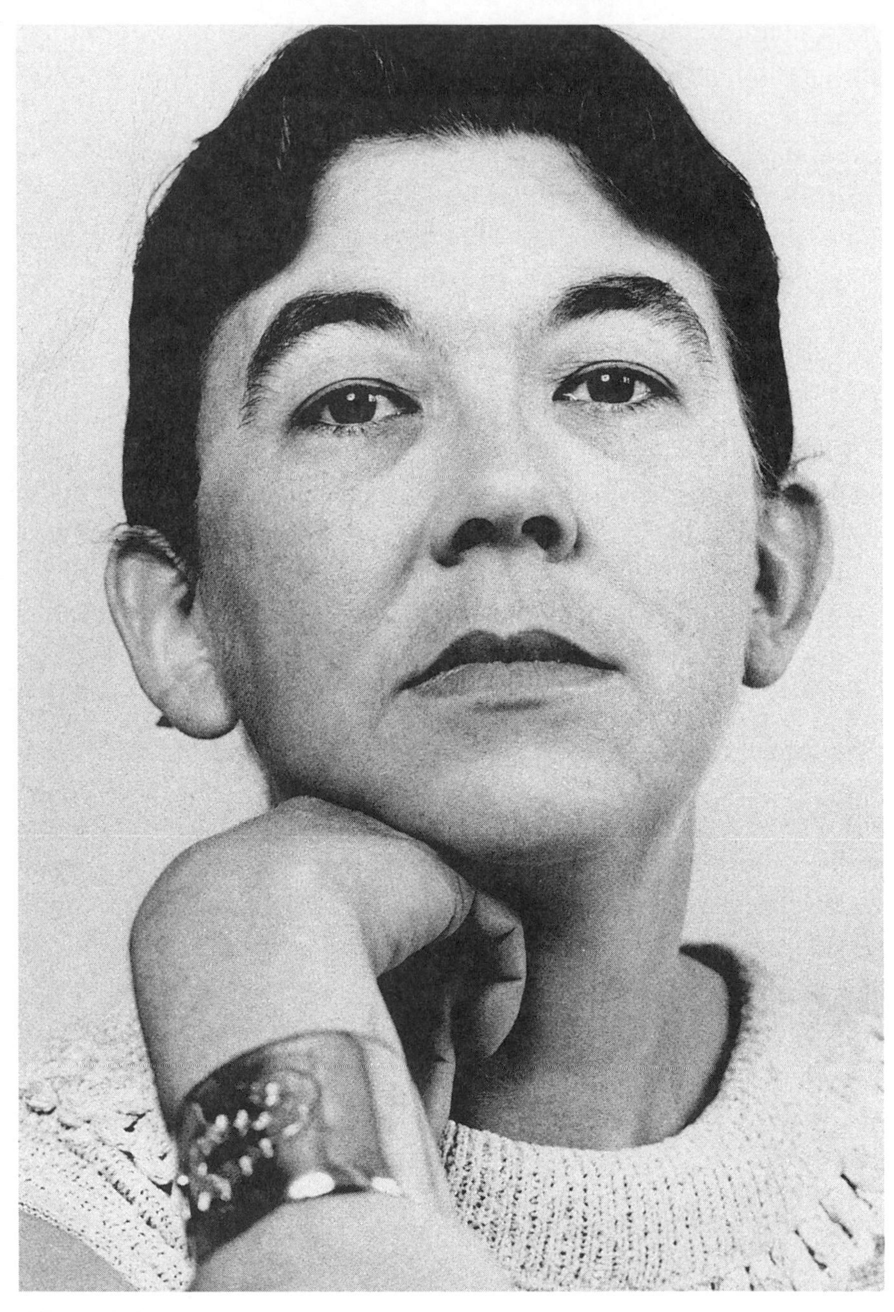

Margaret Laurence. 1964.

Margaret Laurence in Penn. c. 1964.

"Man, what sophistication it must take to do that! (I ordered steak)," a very impressed author informed Adele.

As 1964 drew to a close, Margaret, unable to work effectively on her next novel, was "as relaxed as a power drill." That week, she saw her *modus operandi* as futile: "I've been going in to London about once a week, and this takes up an effective 2 days, so I am quitting it, because it is too unsettling." Three weeks later, she could *feel* Rachel coming into being: "I know the character is there—I don't have any doubt at all about that—I've known her for too long to feel any doubt about her existence—but the problem of method continues to bug me."

> God damn it. I cannot stop attempting this novel, because I know it is there, but I have not yet found the way to it. This gives me the feeling that I am somehow choking. I have recently come to the conclusion that this one will have to be written with my head, I mean with me directing operations, and this is a responsibility which I can hardly bear, as previously I felt that the character was in charge and all I had to do was put it down. But this time the person is very

> evasive, and this is part of her, and very understandable, but she is damn well making life impossible for me. I think that the grace for which one hopes will not come, perhaps, this time. Lacking it, I don't see any way except to put down as simply and directly as possible the things that happen, and to try not to tell lies. I don't believe this is enough, but it appears to be all I have to handle at the moment. Perhaps it will change. I've made so many bad beginnings on this one that anyone in their right mind would give it up and do something else. But I can't.

Rachel had been haunting Margaret for six years, she claimed. But this did not seem to matter very much: "Now I know so much about her that the whole thing seems impossible ... and I do not have enough resources to do it. Well, never mind. We are not dead yet."

At times, Margaret the writer had the "kind of feeling a Catholic might have when excommunicated." At the very same time Rachel was resistant to her creator's wishes, the creator was unsure of form. In a letter to Robert Hallstead, a former teacher at United College, she claimed that the crux of the situation which confronted her had been summed up in a recent issue of *The Observer*: the problem with the traditional novel was that its forms no longer corresponded to the ways in which contemporary man perceived life, whereas most experimental novels were unreadable. The other problem that invaded Margaret was a sense of her own non-existence.

> I suppose I have a very shaky sense of my own reality and can only be certain (or reasonably so) when I've taken on another cloak or temporarily become someone else. I said to someone a long time ago that *The Stone Angel* was written in a way similar to the Stanislavsky Method—naturally, I was not speaking seriously, but now I wonder if maybe this wasn't true after all. I have this feeling which I've had for many years that I tell lies all the time except when I am speaking with the few members of my tribe whom I trust absolutely,

> and that in general I can't speak truthfully except through someone else's mouth.

In this extraordinary passage, she reveals the necessity of the writing life for her. If she cannot write, she has no identity.

At the same time she struggled with a resistant book, Margaret claimed that she had no guts, but it is a special kind of bravery that propels a writer to write a novel about a ninety-year-old woman and then to turn her attention to one centred on a virgin spinster. Later that year, the immensity of what she had done would overcome her:

> What scares the hell out of me with this present novel is that when I read it over, it seems to me that it might appear as though parts of it were written when I was stoned, and in fact they weren't—this makes me wonder if I am more crazy than I want to believe?... If anything, it is too far-in, being about (I honestly hate to say it) an unmarried schoolteacher in a prairie town. How corny can you get? She is, however, real, and although she is an anachronism, she knows it, which is the whole thing. I have the feeling that it will be awful if it turns out to be no good, because the people (her, especially) are there, and I really wanted to say to her, "I'm sorry, baby, maybe I haven't done so well by you."
>
> Have personal dilemmas any meaning any more? My most strong faith is that they have, and must. What, in a world sense, could matter less than the unhappiness of an unmarried woman teacher in a small town? But viewed in another way, what could matter more? I suppose it is a kind of study in ironies, and the ironies are those dealt by fate, but they can be liberating in the long run.

In *The Stone Angel*, Hagar finds a measure of redemption when she is able to talk frankly of John's death—and her hand in it; she also becomes more open and thus vulnerable to others. Margaret's new book was also dealing with redemption but in a fundamentally different way:

how can Rachel—against tremendous odds—discover and, in the process, transform herself? In a way, Margaret was trying to redeem herself from her own troubled past, but the process was arduous and, of course, fraught-filled.

Margaret was still trying to recover from Jack's stay at Elm Cottage. For her—despite some good times—this had been an "absolute nightmare." A year later, she told Nadine: "Last year at this time, I was almost ready to put my head in the oven. But I recovered..." The awful truth was that having Jack around re-created the conditions on which they had parted and the horrible dilemmas that had confronted her at that time. After he returned to Africa, she realized that "the pendulum-swings of feeling about my writing simply reflected a similar state of mind re: him—I fluctuated between feeling I *must* keep the marriage going somehow ... and feeling that I simply could not return to that relationship." Therefore, she was enormously relieved when Jack wrote to tell her he had fallen in love with a twenty-one-year-old Peace Corps volunteer: "I could not help feeling the (to me) irony of it—the old patterns repeat themselves. He does in fact need someone who is similar to what I was at 21, but I am not that way any longer, and at last he does realize I am not, but what can he do about it? He can't change, and I can't, either." (Jack's affair with this young woman was short-lived.)

At about the same time she tried to look realistically at her marriage, she was able to discard her previously rather conventional refusal to admit she sometimes drank too much: "Do you know that it is only within the last couple of years that I could ever openly admit that I ever got drunk? Strange. Especially as I had been doing so with monotonous regularity for many years. I am not keeping liquor in the house at the moment, and do not find this as difficult as I had anticipated, so maybe this will last for awhile too. I haven't gone on the wagon ... I buy a bottle or two of wine, one night a week, when I do not plan to do any work. It is ridiculous not to be able to keep it around, but if it is here, I just drink it, so I might as well face the realities of my character." Yet, Margaret was never really able to face such "realities." Like many alcoholics, she refused to admit to herself—or anyone—that she drank too much. She also did not like to confront another truth: alcohol provided her—on a daily basis—with liberation from many of the anxieties of daily life.

In the winter of 1965, however, Margaret was relieved when she discovered the right way to convey the flux of reality in her new novel and was thus able to be more realistic about herself, almost in proportion to her ability to speak truthfully through Rachel. She was never open about a possible "real-life" source for Rachel, but Catherine Simpson Milne—the cousin who looked after Margaret when Verna died—was convinced (and furious) that Margaret had plundered the plot line of her life for material. For many years as a young and middle-aged woman, Catherine—whose father, Stuart, had been an undertaker—was a schoolteacher in Neepawa, where she lived with her widowed, hypochondriacal mother, Bertha. Then, suddenly, she moved herself and her mother to British Columbia, where she married soon after.

Shaky feelings about her marriage still barraged Margaret. She was quite prepared to be extremely open to Gordon Elliott about her strong feelings for him as a friend, but, at the same time, she outlined her requirements for their relationship to endure: "I care a very great deal about you, and I hope that you do about me, I mean really myself, not Jack's wife. But when Jack returned here last summer, he told me that you had said you tended, emotionally, always to take the man's side of the situation. If that is so, then it cannot really be helped, can it? although this hurt me very much—I don't mean *you* hurt me very much, as this is obviously not your intention, but only that it is a kind of sad irony, and if it exists, then there is no point trying to alter it, because one can't."

Realizing she had not accomplished what she had intended by way of writing in the past two years, she informed Jack McClelland in March: "After about three years of agonizing indecision, my husband and I are finally going to separate, and this has been pretty unsettling all around, needless to say. It has been in the offing for some considerable time, but I guess it is always rather difficult to take the final step, inevitable though it may be." Her uncertainties in this instance were countered by McClelland's decisiveness:

> I don't really know what one wants to hear when they have just recently decided to separate. Probably they don't want to hear anything, but for what it is worth, let me say to you that you have something that is more important than any marriage I've ever heard about. By which I mean your career, which I say in all humility should make you one of the great international writers in the next decade or so. I don't think you can afford to concern yourself about the dissolution of a marriage no matter how serious a jolt it may seem at the time. So forget it. It's of relatively no importance.

McClelland's response—meant to be supportive—would have been helpful if it had been written to another man, one used to compartmentalizing his life. Margaret Laurence was not able to do this: "All the men I know are either married, homosexual, or in another country. Well, we can't force the wheel of fate, I feel bloody awful sometimes when I think that my dancing (etc) days are more than likely over, but what the hell?" In her bedroom, she had a paper rooster, and on more than one occasion quipped that this was the "only cock" who would henceforth grace that room.

She provided a clear description of the bleak emotional future that awaited her in a letter to Gordon of April 1965:

> Interesting that you should say the woman never seems to you to be quite so alone as the man. I, of course, would have said the opposite! The fact that a woman does have children to think of, and to consider, whatever move he makes, means that she is often unable to make any move at all because she has not got the financial means and the psychological ability to gamble, in case it endangers them. Once she has moved out of her previous life pattern, she is more hampered in making new friends because she is not very free to move

> about, on account of the children. Re-marriage is never very likely for a woman with children, as few men would want to take on anyone else's kids. Therefore she has to accept the fact that she is on her own, permanently, and I don't think this is so very easy to accept, at least not for me. However, one does not really act in this way unless one has to, so it can be borne. I don't think it would be possible for any man-type person to feel more alone than I have in the past 3 years.

Margaret disagreed with Gordon on the state of her marriage, but was infuriated by her journalist friend Marjory Whitelaw, who spent an evening telling Margaret, "she didn't see how I could want to separate from a man as handsome and intelligent as J., also how mad I was to be burying myself out here in the country where I would never meet anyone, etc. I felt I could have done without all this good advice. I got glummer and glummer, and drank more and more of her gin. Nuts to all that. It simply is a waste of time. I will not go to her place any more."

In the spring of 1965, her mother-in-law was very confused as to the status of the on-again, off-again Laurence marriage, as can be gleaned from Margaret's letter to her old friend Nadine Jones: "It has been a rather difficult period, as I've begun getting letters from my family and also from Jack's mother, and this is hard to deal with, as I can't really explain anything. J's mother, however, is apparently under the impression that I have never explained anything to him, either—that I've more or less just said all is over without ever giving him an inkling about why. I suppose he believes this is the case. But after all these *years* (literally 2-½) of detailed analysis, I do not intend to say any more."

There were a few light moments in 1965. When she chose her music for the CBC radio programme, "Hermit's Choice," Margaret selected bagpipe music and Beethoven's Ninth. That summer, she made it to Scotland, where she stayed with the novelist and children's writer Jane Duncan, who ran a teashop in Cromarty during the summer: "When I was in Scotland, I spent the greater part of my time either drinking whisky or eating hot buttered scones, and I now have to go on a diet.... Quite a few people come mainly to see Jane Duncan, novelist, and Jane simply cannot sit down and talk to them for hours, so while I was there, she sort of threw me into the situation as a substitute writer (what a letdown for the clients!) and I sat and talked and drank tea and ate one scone after another. I thoroughly enjoyed it, and returned feeling that I could grapple with life once more. But now it is lettuce, lettuce all the way."

From childhood, Margaret had seen her Scots inheritance as a glamorous, romantic appendage. In preparation for her first trip to Scotland, she read about the breakup of the Highland clans culminating in the battle of Culloden and the Clearances. She now realized that the Highlanders "had been in the deepest possible ways forsaken; in the truest sense their hearts had been broken. This, not the romantic swashbuckling figures in Sir Walter Scott's novels, was the reality of the Highlanders." During this trip she visited a landscape in which such fearful struggles had been enacted: "Scotland had become real to me, both in its past and in its present. For myself, however, I still did not feel any sense of connection with its history. The story of the Highland Clearances moved me as much as the story of the slave trade, but no more."

This is a strange statement in that Margaret had already written so eloquently of colonialism and the remnants of slavery in Africa. In 1965, although she was of Lowlands stock, she identified with the plight of the Highlanders. Later, in Morag Gunn who is from Highlands ancestry, she would blend her ancestry with that of her fictional heroine. Ultimately, for her, the banished Scots were outsiders, who had been treated in a harsh, punitive manner by their English overlords. From the time of childhood, she had seen herself as an orphan, another form of outsider. As she saw herself more and more as a loner, Margaret came to grips with her Scots ancestry—although she obviously would have preferred to be of Highlands stock—and then incorporated it into her fiction.

Nineteen sixty-five presented Margaret with many other challenges. Earlier, in June, Aunt Ruby visited. Her first, troubled reaction to the

Laurence separation had been to write her niece: "Have you seen a marriage counsellor, dear? Some women in their middle age begin to resent their *marital responsibilities.*" In a tactfully worded reply, she assured the older woman that sex was not the problem. Margaret also had to cope with a strange Dutch-Canadian woman who wanted her to ghost-write a novel. This person's "bull-dozing kind of intensity" intimidated even her.

> She kept saying "I must fly over and talk to you—shall we say next week?" And I, petrified, kept saying, "Don't come—write!" She asked me when I was born, and when I said middle of July, she said with gruesome glee, "CANCER! Splendid!" ... After I put the phone down, I knew this answer was absolutely no good, and I paced the floor for about an hour, thinking of all that money, which all at once seemed real to me, and then I phoned her (these trans-Atlantic calls really alarm me—all I can think of is the cost) and said I was sorry but it was no dice.

On a more sombre note, Margaret was touched by a letter from her old teacher Robert Hallstead in which he commented that he could see an extremely religious person in the author of *The Stone Angel.* During the writing of her third novel, she herself had been surprised, "as the writing went on, to discover how much of it was about God, without this having been my intention at all." Although she was not at this time much interested in institutional Christianity, *The Stone Angel* contains two important, interrelated strands of commentary on it: Margaret was intuitively suspicious of any form of evangelical Christianity, but she was receptive to more orthodox religious systems. Towards the conclusion of the book, Murray Lees describes how his son burnt to death while he and his wife were at an Evangelical service conducted by the Reverend Pulsifer. Earlier, throughout the book, Hagar has had an antagonistic relationship with her minister, Mr. Troy. At the end of the book (Margaret's favourite scene in the entire novel), Hagar cajoles Mr. Troy into singing and, in the process, sees a different side of him—

> Then he opens his mouth and sings, and I'm the one who's taken aback now. He should sing always, and never speak. He should chant his sermons. The fumbling of his speech is gone. His voice is firm and sure....

—and touches the deep well of love and warmth within herself from which she has been for so long alien.

> This knowing comes upon me so forcefully, so shatteringly, and with such a bitterness as I have never felt before. I must always, always, have wanted that—simply to rejoice. How is it I never could? I know, I know. How long have I known? Or have I always known, in some far crevice of my heart, some cave too deeply buried, too concealed? Every good joy I might have held, in my man or any child of mine or even the plain light of morning, of walking the earth, all were forced to a standstill by some brake of proper appearances—oh, proper to whom? When did I ever speak the heart's truth?

As her life draws to a close, Hagar wonders why she was never able to speak the truths of her own heart. In those final moments, she sees the tragedies she has visited upon others and herself, but she is given a wonderful epiphany when she realizes life is a commingling of contrary forces: holiness and terror, tenderness and anger, angel and stone. The spiritual dimension is vital to an understanding of Hagar's final acceptance of herself as a righteous person; in 1965, Margaret was struggling with the conflicting forces of light and dark in her own soul.

That summer, Alan Maclean, who had become Margaret's principal editor as well as her English publisher, instructed her that it would be a good idea for her to send the manuscript of *A Jest of God* to him, because, as she said to Adele, "otherwise I would only pick at it and worry about it uselessly, as I cannot see it clearly enough now to do anything. So I did, then paced the floor for 5 days, and then he phoned and said he liked it ... Alan feels that it gets off to a slow start, and that, as A says, in the first few chapters, I 'grind the reader,' which I think is true."

Once Maclean had intervened, she was able to return to the typescript buoyed up with his endorsement. In October, Margaret, weary from a steady stream of summer visitors, was delighted to hear Jack McClelland was ecstatic about *A Jest of God*: "HALLELUJAH!... My difficulty always seems to be that I know quite well what the characters are like, and what they mean to me, but I am in a state of terrible apprehension until I discover how they appear to a few other people whose opinions I trust."

At the end of the year, she was apprehensive because Jack was in England for the year, taking a course leading to his master's degree in civil engineering at Southampton University. Nevertheless, she was certain her marriage was over—and that, in the process, many of her conflicted feelings had abated. Still, as she told Nadine, some contradictions could not be overcome—much less be understood. In this bold passage, she cries from the innermost parts of her divided heart:

> I know what you mean about split personality. I am the same. Sometimes I think only the kids matter to me, and then I get frightfully in need of talking with someone adult who speaks my language. Most of the time I am quite happy here, working and slouching around in slacks and sweaters, and then I get a terrible urge to dress up to the nines and of course to have some man who wants me and whom I want (not at the moment possible, it seems, but I'm not yet reconciled to this state of affairs, unfortunately).... So—this conflict of desires produces some degree of tension, naturally. But I'm pretty lucky at the moment in being able to have something of both worlds, even though I apparently cannot belong totally to either.
>
> If only one could be one thing or another—either mother or woman, either woman or writer—but God damn, to be split so many ways is JUST NOT FAIR. Anyway, we stumble on from day to day, and manage to survive.

More than men—Margaret is implying—women are torn between gender roles and gender identity, between gender identity and professional roles. Those conflicts—which had helped to end her marriage—did not disappear after the separation, so powerful were her feelings of guilt and resentment. Margaret may have made a choice, but she never really forgave herself for making it.

13

Jests of God

(1966)

On some days, "managing to survive" was a difficult enterprise for Margaret. In January 1966, she was "trying to lose the same damn ten pounds" in a Sisyphus-like battle with herself. This was part of her new year's resolution to become a new woman. "I will become very slim, very efficient. I will cut drinking entirely. I will cut down on cigarettes. I will work harder, and soon." However, she had become lethargic and "limp": "I don't even sit and brood any more. I just sit! All I want to think about is NOTHING." Her somnolent state was partially relieved by a dream of making love with a man on a train: "He turned out to be the son of Gypsy Rose Lee, who in her old age was selling high-class cosmetics. He took me to visit her, and the old beauty queen said she would give me a sample of perfume. She had two—one was called 'Faithful' and the other was called 'Betrayal'. The symbolism is so obvious that I think I must have a pretty unstable mind!"

In her sleeping and awake existences, cosmetics were a contentious issue. Jocelyn, now a young teenager, informed her she would have to cease wearing extremely bright lipstick because it dated her. "So I got some with-it pale lipstick, and the first time I wore it, I went into the Red Lion to buy some booze, and I was wearing my black slacks and an

Italian silk shirt printed with scenes from Dante's underworld, and one of the old geezers in the pub said 'Hello, Aubrey,' and then did a double-take and said 'Oh—it's not Aubrey.' I gave him a frosty but feminine (I hope) smile, and when I saw Jocelyn I said 'That's what I get for trying to be with-it—I'm mistaken for a teenage boy!'"

On the surface, many of the domestic problems in the Laurence marriage had reached a comfortable stalemate. Jack would travel up from Southampton to look after the children and Elm Cottage, allowing Margaret the unusual stay of a week at her London "pad"; he even joined her in London one day and took her to two James Bond films and then to dinner. This was "very nice and also kind of a laugh for both of us, as the external interpretation would probably be that we were going to re-join forces but in fact the reverse is true and that is why we both enjoyed it so much." For Jocelyn and David, Elmcot remained a secure bastion.

Although her financial prospects were brighter and Jack was providing money for the children, she still needed to look for ways to augment her income. In 1965, she had taken on the "job of editing and re-writing a really awful book on Canada," but she discarded the project in January 1966. However, she had agreed to do four scripts for the BBC on West African/Nigerian literature. She finished them, only to discover the producer wanted an impression of that part of the continent as seen through the eyes of its contemporary writers. "It would have been helpful," Margaret told Nadine, "if he had given me some idea of what he wanted four months ago, but he didn't." So that January, she was still "slogging along" at a snail's pace on a project which really did not interest her.

One way of cutting her losses, she decided, was to write a book on the subject: "After about 4 months reading and thinking about Nigerian writing, traditional and contemporary, I feel I've taken a do-it-yourself course in contemporary African writing, and I have so much material it nearly breaks my heart, as there isn't anything I can do with it, but maybe I'll write a book, which would be no hell critically as I am no academic critic and don't even know the jargon, but it might be interesting in an amateur way. I don't know."

The resulting book—*Long Drums and Cannons: Nigerian Dramatists and Novelists 1952-1966* (1968)—is the most forced piece of writing in Margaret Laurence's career. As she was well aware, she did not find the profession of academic critic one which fitted her. Throughout this book, one theme emerges clearly: "Perhaps the most enduringly interesting aspect of Nigerian literature, however, as of literature everywhere, is the insight it gives not only into immediate local dilemmas but, through these, into the human dilemma as a whole." She then explains how it is possible—if a text is well-written—to capture the human experience and transcend national boundaries: "The best of these Nigerian plays and novels reveals something of ourselves to us, whoever and wherever we are." It is obvious that in the work of Wole Soyinka, Chinua Achebe, Amos Tutuola, Flora Nwapa and their contemporaries Margaret Laurence also saw reflected many of her own themes:

> Much as they are caught up in immediate happenings, however, Nigerian novelists and dramatists have constantly expressed in their work themes which are not confined to one place or one time—the individual's effort to define himself, his need to come to terms with his ancestors and his gods, his uncertainties in relation to others, his conflicts in the face of his own opposed loyalties, the dichotomy of his longing for both peace and war, his perpetual battle to free himself from the fetters of the past and the compulsions of the present.

In *Dance on the Earth*, she referred to *Long Drums* as "rather amateurish," but she was much too harsh on herself. *Long Drums* is a good critical book, especially if it is seen as the work of a professional writer of fiction passing judgment on the works of her peers and, in the process, revealing to herself and her readers some of the controlling ideas in her own writing.

In the early winter of 1966, Margaret decided—with some trepidation—to give up her London "pad":

> I'm giving up my bedsitter because it gives me the creeps. I realize now that I am too old for a bedsitter life, and also when I think of entertaining my friends there, I realize I don't want to.... I'm glad I had this bedsitter experience, though, because it's made me realize something I had almost forgotten—how many people, living in bedsitters in cities like London, lead lives of almost total withdrawal from others.... There are 2 other women living in rooms in the house where I have my pad, and it seems to me that their lives must be almost unbearably lonely.

(A year later, she mentioned to Adele: "I'm giving up my bedsitter in Hampstead." Almost a month later, she informed her: "I decided a week or so ago to give up my bedsitter in Hampstead, much as I hate to. But for me to pay 3 pounds per week for a room is nonsense—I just cannot afford it, especially as I only use it 1 night per week, and in the summer less than that. This kind of room is useful only if one is meeting one's lover there—and let's face it, for the few times this kind of thing happens to me, it isn't bloody well worth three quid a week." From this, it would seem Margaret gave up the Bayswater bedsitter and then, quite soon after, rented another in Hampstead—which in turn she eventually gave up.)

During the time she wrote of the heartbreaking loneliness of Rachel's existence, she was well aware of a similar kind of grim isolation. Having completed that book—which concludes with Rachel's triumphant emergence from self-confinement—Margaret could no longer bear to continue experiencing such loneliness.

She was about to turn forty. She now became obsessed with trying to assimilate the idea of death, her "own or someone else's whom we can't bear to think of as not being here any more." She also pondered the mystery of her own existence, of the changes she had wilfully brought into being:

> Of course, with me, the process of having to earn one's own living came rather late in life, and as I had never really been on my own

> until I was 35 years old, I guess it is no wonder that I have been rather prone to feelings of horrible anxiety and panic re: money. Now that I've been in this house for more than 2 years, I am just beginning to be able to feel that perhaps things may continue for awhile without falling apart. For the first 2 years, every time I walked back along the road and saw the house, I used to think—my God, all that is *my* responsibility.

Money problems continued to overwhelm her, but she had become sufficiently confident about her earning power that she decided to extend the horizon of the excursions on which she took the children.

Since the move to Elm Cottage in 1964, she had confined jaunts with the children to visits to London. "Okay, guys," she would tell them, "we're not rich, but today we feel rich." Each child would be given a pound and had two choices as to what do with it: to put it into a post-office savings account or to spend it on books. Wisely, the children always bought books. "Laden down with our treasure, we would proceed to the second part of the ritual—tea at Fortnum and Mason's." In a letter to Jack McClelland, she provided an account of the trip she and the children took that April to Greece. This time, the itinerary was much more relaxed than her visit there with Jack two years before: "We've just returned from Greece where I took my children for a two-week holiday. We spent two days in Athens, then went by boat to Crete, where we stayed at the most beautiful beach I've ever seen. We also went to look at the ancient Minoan ruins at Knossos, which I've wanted to see for years. We had a marvellous time and came back to find that England had had about a foot of snow in our absence, so I guess we picked the right moment to go away."

When Margaret returned that spring, she had to deal with her conflicted feelings about the visit of her beloved mother-in-law, Elsie, to Elm Cottage and the simultaneous nervous breakdown of a friend, Ann, who was also staying with her. Her only respite was her affair with the "old lion," Jamal, the ambassador from an African nation to the Court of St. James.

Adele, this week has been pure unadulterated Murder. No—I am wrong—one splendid evening (somewhat to my surprise) with the old lion did much to maintain my sanity and morale. But I'll come to that later. The chief thing is that the friend who was staying here and who was going to look after the kids in August and September, this week had a serious breakdown and is now in a mental hospital ... I now feel that anyone with any brains ought to have seen this coming, and that I oughtn't to have ever considered her looking after the kids.... Ann is a person whom I met through the house, as it were, because she had kept house here for Alan Maclean's mother at one time.... (I should add that this week Jack's mother has been here—you can imagine the degree of tension).... Next morning, a steady procession of doctors, psychiatrists, area welfare officers, etc etc etc. Finally got her into a mental hospital, where she now is.... So—I must get her out, but without her thinking that I am withdrawing entirely. However much it hurts (and it will) she has to be made to understand that she must make her own home and her own life, and although this seems like hitting a person when they're down, I know it is now or never, and for my own survival I just have to harden my heart and not be too upset by my damaged self-image!... But all this, plus the inevitable strain of J's mother (however much I care about her, and I do) has really been something, this past week.

This week, in the midst of all this to-ing and fro-ing on the part of doctors etc, I went into London to see the old lion. I was absolutely determined that I would not break the date, even if my entire household was in a shambles and I had to offend everyone from my mother-in-law to the cleaning woman. I became, suddenly, SAVAGELY selfish. And I'm glad I did. Thought I might find he was less appealing when I saw him again, but actually he is more so. Very nice to meet a man to whom sex isn't a battlefield in which he has to prove himself by a display of superior strength, as with so many North American men, but rather a matter of very accomplished pleasure. Don't think I will probably see him again—or, rather, don't know and am not terribly concerned one way or

> another.... One is grateful (and my God, I really mean this!) for grace received.

There is a touch of soap opera in her attempt to juggle her conflicted feelings about her mother-in-law, her worry about her friend, her determination to see Jamal and her insistence on recognizing that selfishness is sometimes a necessary vice. However, there is also a note of serenity here. She is going to do what is in her own best interests.

In another description of her affair with Jamal, there is a glimpse of that side of Margaret which took tremendous joy in sex, in the sheer physical pleasure of one body being completely open to another's. On June 18, she confided to Nadine the wonderful experience she had had in "a brief but extremely sanity-saving encounter with one of the nicest men I've ever met—he is (oddly enough) an ambassador for an African country (which shall be nameless, but isn't Ghana or Somalia!). Have only been out with him several times, but it was like rain in the desert, believe me. He is intelligent, charming, sexy, and the most accomplished diplomat I've ever met. Also, of course, married with seven kids. Naturally. Never mind. Nothing serious about it, but it was just marvellous not to have to be serious, for a change."

Her affair with Jamal may also have lessened the serious pull George Lamming evidently still exerted over her. That May—for unknown reasons—Adele had provided her with his address and encouraged her friend to get in touch with him. As far as Margaret was concerned, this would be turning the clock back: "I forgot, in the confusion of my last 2 letters, to mention about your sending George's address, etc. It wasn't tactless in the least, Adele. I can't get in touch with him, though, because I don't think he would want me to, and at this point it is better for me that I don't, too."

At the very same time she had to deal with a host of personal problems, Margaret had to cope with Jack McClelland's determination to make her name a household word in Canada. With considerable acumen, he had determined she had to promote *A Jest of God* in Canada, and he proposed a rigorous—by any standard—schedule of media events for his would-be reclusive author. To be fair to him, his inspiration for a media circus was inspired by Margaret's letter to him of May 11: "I am homesick. I am also fed up, bored, and temporarily in need of a spell away from the role of mother. I am sick of working. I want to see some of my tribe again. So I have decided that I will go back to Canada for a visit for August and September.... Do you think it would be possible for me to find a hotel or bedsitting room or something in Toronto for three or four weeks, which wouldn't cost me the earth?" (Through the intervention of Robert Weaver, she had received a Canada Council travel grant which allowed her to go to Canada that summer.)

In this instance, she was the author of her own misfortunes, since her simple request fuelled her publisher's imagination. Well before the trip, exhausted by his expectations, Margaret attempted to set limits:

> I am quite willing to go along with publicity matters, UP TO A POINT. I want to be in Montreal, Vancouver and Winnipeg, as well as Toronto and New York. But Jack, PLEASE do not insist on much more than that. It is all very well to make a publicity deal out of all this, but I am beginning to wish I had paid for it all myself and not told anyone I was coming home. Because, you see, the difficulty is that I REALLY DO NEED A HOLIDAY *DESPERATELY.* I am not trying to be temperamental or difficult, honestly. I *do* want to go along with what you have in mind. But I really must protect myself to some extent, because at this point I am dead beat and I just do not think I can possibly face a trip which includes stop-offs in every major Canadian city, with all the politeness involved in each. Jack, I'm truly sorry. But please try to understand. I've gone through an awful lot of personal crisis in the past few years and have also written two books and am really tired ... please, boss, have a heart. Don't press me too far or I will fold up. I do not speak in jest, believe me.... Honestly, I *will* try to co-operate. BUT WE MUST COMPROMISE. I stand firm on that. Of course, the

main trouble—as always with you and myself—is that in any crisis both get so worked up and verbose! I appreciate you—*so much*—maybe that is why from time to time I feel free enough to get furious at you. Anyway, don't be mad at me, please. I will do my best, but please don't expect some kind of super performance from me, because I'm not capable of that, at this point.

I do hope you don't think I'm being awkward, but right now I feel lousy about the whole trip, because what I desperately need is a little relaxation and gaiety, and your description of events sounds about as gay as a session of the Ladies' Aid. Please forgive me for bitching. It makes me feel like a heel ... Believe me, Jack, I *do* recognize that one has to accept change—and after all these years, I see finally that I am no longer a simple country girl, etc etc. Whatever kind of writer I am is not so important—the fact is that I know now I am a writer, and therefore committed to this. But one is essentially a private person. And sometimes you reach the limits of your endurance, and this is how I feel now—that I just need to talk to friends and to shed some responsibilities even if only for a while.

Margaret could only write to the "Boss" in this way because she trusted him so completely. Yet, she knew full well, a writer's agenda can be drastically different from a publisher's. In the writing of *A Jest of God*, she had also reached a new plateau in self-esteem. Her brutal honesty to McClelland and her openness about her affair with Jamal show just how completely she, like Rachel, had been transformed from a woman who was tentative about her rights to one who took what was rightfully hers.

The Stone Angel—in its brilliant interweaving of time present with time past—is a majestic tour de force, whereas *A Jest of God* is a classically conceived, beautifully proportioned novel. Hagar changes only at the very end of her life whereas Rachel's story is an acutely observed portrayal of the slow, gradual transformation of a young middle-aged woman. Hagar's story is about the self-imposed isolation of a powerful woman whereas Rachel slowly learns to seize power. Ultimately, *A Jest of God* is about a woman who lives in desperate loneliness and then discards that darkness.

Of all the Manawaka novels, *A Jest of God* and *A Bird in the House* are the ones most centred on the town and its environment (in *The Stone Angel*, the elderly Hagar lives on the west coast of Canada—as does Stacey in *The Fire-Dwellers*; Morag Gunn's life extends well beyond the town of her birth). Hagar's problems with self-identity stem largely from her loss of her mother, whereas Rachel Cameron's mother is both sickly and meddling, hardly a suitable role model for either her or her sister, Stacey. If *The Stone Angel* is about a woman who incorporates a surfeit of male power, *A Jest of God* is about a woman who has no sense of power and thus no self-identity.

In *A Jest of God*, Rachel constantly catches sight of herself in a mirror or window. She does not like what she sees; more importantly, she does not know *what* she sees: "I don't look old. I don't look more than thirty. Or do I see my face falsely? How do I know how it looks to anyone else.... Do I have good bones? I can't tell. I'm no judge." Her fragility and inability to see herself extend to her fantasies when masturbating and even include denial that she is touching herself to the point of orgasm:

> She sees only his body distinctly, his shoulders, and arms deeply tanned, his belly flat and hard. He is wearing tight-fitting jeans, and his swelling sex shows. She touches him there, and he trembles.... Then they are lying along one another, their skins slippery. His hands, his mouth are on the wet warm skin of her inner thighs. Now—
>
> I didn't. I didn't. It was only to be able to sleep. The shadow prince. Am I unbalanced? Or only laughable?

In order to dramatize—and show the extent of—Rachel's sexual repression—Margaret Laurence describes Rachel in a variety of situations in which she is rendered powerless or is made invisible by others. To such, the author seems to suggest, is what Manawaka has reduced Rachel.

Unlike Hagar—whose life is determined by the absence of her mother—Rachel's sense of profound loss centres on her dead father. In a very real sense, the first two Manawaka novels re-create, respectively, the effect of the deaths of Verna Wemyss and Robert Wemyss on young Peggy Wemyss.

Ultimately, Rachel gains freedom when she acknowledges her sexuality—on her own terms and not on those of her lover, Nick. She becomes aware of herself as a sexual person, someone of value. But it is not just sexual awakening that allows Rachel to overcome her mother's manipulation and to make plans for a better future for herself. Rather, it is the resolve she makes (believing herself pregnant) to live an independent life without the child's father. Even after she realizes she is not pregnant, Rachel decides to make her own destiny and, in the process, to throw over the shackles of loneliness.

Rachel's new sense of autonomy and self-sovereignty are confirmed when she promises herself: "I will be light and straight as any feather. The wind will bear me, and I will drift and settle, and drift and settle. Anything may happen, where I am going. I will be different. I will remain the same." In creating Hagar and Rachel, Margaret Laurence returned in part to the literature of childhood. Hagar appears to be a harsh crone but locked up within her is the beautiful woman who emerges at the conclusion of *The Stone Angel*; Rachel is a Sleeping Beauty who kisses herself back to life.

Deaths, betrayals and acts of thoughtless cruelty abound in the first two Manawaka novels, but they are books about redemption, books in which the protagonists rescue themselves from themselves on behalf of themselves. By 1966, Margaret, who had taken charge of her life but had paid a heavy price in self-imposed isolation, felt like a butterfly finally released from its chrysalis.

In 1966, Margaret was invited to attend a different kind of celebration of independence. Six years before, the British Protectorate Somaliland had combined with the southern region of Somaliland, previously under Italian rule, to form the Somali republic. At the same party where she had met Jamal, she had encountered the Somali Minister of Information, who, in recognition of her commitment to his nation as evidenced in *A Tree for Poverty*, asked: "Would you like to come to Mogadishu for July 1st?" Without thinking the invitation was a serious one, she responded "Certainly." On May 31, she told Adele she was glad the invitation had been a bonafide one: "The way I feel right now, I am not turning down any opportunities for enjoyment, as I have lived in a Celtic gloom for quite long enough."

As she reported to Jack McClelland, her trip from June 27 to July 4 to attend the independence celebration had been wonderful: "I was only there a week, but I managed to see a lot of old friends, some of whom I had not seen in 14 years." The most eventful part of the journey may have been on the "dinky" airplane between Aden and Somaliland, when Margaret managed to lock herself in the washroom. "I had visions of the plane landing at Hargeisa, the old Somali friends there to welcome us, and me locked in the john." She pleaded for assistance, but neither the steward nor the other passengers congregated outside the toilet could help. Finally, with great cost to the skin on her hands, she forced the bolt to give way and emerged triumphant to rousing cheers. During this ordeal, when she noticed that the sandwiches which the stewards were to serve were stored in a bin in that confined enclosure, she comforted herself with the realization she would not starve.

In comparison to her trip to Africa, the journey to Canada proved arduous in many ways. Before she set off, she had to contend with an extremely angry Jack McClelland, furious that Macmillan published *A Jest of God* during the week of July 9—more than a full two months before the release of the Canadian and American editions—leading to the very real worry that booksellers in Canada might import copies from England and so bypass the McClelland & Stewart edition. The author herself was more understandably concerned with the good reviews the book received in the *Manchester Guardian Weekly* and *The Spectator.*

Some idea of the rather hectic schedule planned for Margaret can be gleaned from her telegram to McClelland of June 14: "Please cable if following plan OK Toronto July 30 to August 20 New York August 21st to August 27th Montreal August 28th to September 10th Vancouver September 11th to September 24th Winnipeg September 25 to October 2nd Toronto October 3rd to October 15th."

She was not pleased when Jack informed her that her proposed schedule did not "suit HIS plans" and was in fact too modest. Shortly after her arrival back at Elm Cottage, Margaret ruefully recalled her ordeal to Adele:

> When McClelland said "a working trip", he sure wasn't kidding. In the two months, I did a total of 17 radio interviews, 15 newspaper interviews, 4 TV interviews, and gave 4 talks. How I ever survived is a mystery.... The awful thing is that I do not personally believe it will make one damn of difference to sales of the book.... all I could think about was mere *survival*— ... the best part of the trip was seeing just a few people like yourself, Bob and Anne Hallstead, Bob Weaver, and one or two people in Vancouver.

Margaret's horrified recollection only hints at the complexities of her North American sojourn. The first problem she faced with an extended stay away from England was to find someone suitable to look after the children. Her friend, Ann, obviously could not undertake this task. Eventually, her neighbours Mr. and Mrs. Charlett agreed to take charge, but Jack Laurence travelled up from Southampton on weekends to be with his children. The trip itself "began in nightmare fashion and continued that way, with small breaks for humour." The first casualty was her case containing an entirely new wardrobe. She first noticed the suitcase was missing when her plane landed in Montreal en route to Toronto. Margaret had a tendency to go into over-drive when distraught, and this is exactly what happened. The officials told her to calm down, assuring her the suitcase would turn up when she arrived in Toronto. It was not there, and an incoherent and inconsolable Margaret reduced to one item of clothing—the blue and white linen dress she was wearing—made her way, accompanied by a representative of McClelland & Stewart, to the apartment Jack McClelland had rented for her on Avenue Road.

The flat contained fresh flowers and a much-needed bottle of whisky. "I fell into bed in my underwear and thought, 'Sufficient unto the days are the troubles thereof.'" Margaret, who had arrived on a Saturday, had no Canadian money with her. She now reached a very low point, desperately wishing she had never undertaken the trip back to Canada. She felt like the biblical Ruth, "in tears amid the alien corn." However, the superintendent of the apartment lent her five dollars. "I sashayed down Avenue Road, walking miles, or so it seemed, until I finally found a café and had breakfast. I have seldom felt so lonely and so out of place." The next day, Air Canada was extremely unfriendly. They had no record of any such missing piece of luggage "but we will take all the particulars, madam." That night, she dined with Jack and Elizabeth McClelland and, immediately afterwards, Jack had to battle Air Canada's offer of $50 in compensation for $580 in missing clothing.

Margaret—who recalled she had five hundred dollars stashed away in a Royal Bank account in Toronto—called on John and Chris Marshall for assistance. John had been the best man at her wedding, and Margaret and Chris had been colleagues at the YWCA in Winnipeg. Chris was a take-charge person, someone used to managing crises. Margaret was very direct during that phone conversation: "Chris, it's me. My suitcase got lost. I have no clothes. I have to do all this publicity stuff and I have *no clothes*! I have some money. Help! I don't know where to shop." When Margaret and Chris went shopping the next morning, they acquired a wide range of clothing: a gold lamé cocktail dress, three summer dresses, a light wool suit, two pairs of dressy sandals, several handbags and a suitcase. Never before having purchased so much in so little time, Margaret enjoyed the experience completely.

During that trip, Toronto became for her the V.M.—the Vile Metropolis. She did not enjoy the process of becoming famous. She was especially put off by the scorching TV lights, camera and camera cables which filled Jack McClelland's house at the launch party. This is what she said in *Dance on the Earth*: "A reviewer who had slashed *A Jest of God* came up to me at the party, wanting my approval for the damning review. I had, thank God, the presence of mind to say, 'I am not a spiritual masochist. Write what you like about my books, but don't expect me to approve when you pan one of them.'" The reviewer was the biographer Phyllis ("Pat") Grosskurth in *The Globe and Mail* ("Pathos Not Quite Enough"). In a letter of March 24, 1967 to Adele, Margaret gives an account of the encounter which seems a bit more realistic than that provided in *Dance*: "She didn't like my novel and gave it a horrible review and then proceeded to apologize to me for this fact—I wanted to say to her, look, it doesn't matter that you didn't like it, but please don't expect me to reassure you about it."

While in Toronto, she received two important phone calls. The first was from John Cushman, her agent (he had left Willis Wing to start his own agency and Margaret went with him). *Holiday* wanted her to write two pieces on Egypt. Lawrence Durrell had been the travel magazine's first choice, but Margaret was happy to say yes. The next phone call was much more problematic. Alan Maclean informed her that since he and Robin Empson were to marry soon, he had to sell Elm Cottage in order to buy a house in Sussex: "Do you want Elm Cottage, Margaret?" His anxious question flummoxed her: "Of course I do, but I don't have any money. Could you possibly wait until I get back to England?" He agreed to this, but she had no solution in sight to this new dilemma.

In her account of her first visit back to Canada since 1962, she omits at least three crucial details. First, her friendship with Nadine Jones came grinding to a halt. Although Margaret claimed she hated any form of publicity, Nadine found this not to be the case in Vancouver in 1966. That summer, although she had a newborn baby, she invited Margaret to stay with her, but she became offended when her old friend allowed all sorts of journalists to enter the house and "grandstanded" while she had to deal with a baby who was disturbed by the resulting hoopla. Margaret responded uncomprehendingly to Nadine's complaints. Second, Margaret made a brief stop-over in Neepawa and offended Mildred Musgrove, who had arranged a small gathering in her honour. Margaret told her: "I can't bear to see any of my mother's old friends." Third, she informed a somewhat startled Jack McClelland that she intended to "fuck" her way from coast to coast during this book tour. Of course, he had no idea whether or not she fulfilled this ambition.

Margaret Laurence. 1966.

Although she was reluctant to discuss it, Margaret had a moment of heart-breaking intensity when, on a "crazy" impulse, she visited the cemetery in Neepawa that autumn, "and looked at my family's stone—my father and my mother being skeletons somewhere there, quite meaninglessly, for if they exist at all (and they do—all the ancestors do) it is not in crumbling calcium bone but in my head." The memory of lives stolen from her had vividly coloured her writing career and created a deep longing for ancestors to whom she could belong.

Another stop-over was in New York City, which included a weekend stay at Alfred Knopf's estate at Purchase on Long Island. During that visit, Alfred, who was a camera enthusiast, took some portrait photos of Margaret. Here is the professional woman of letters at the age of forty. She looks a bit severe in her business suit, but the deep sadness of much of Margaret's life is captured in the rendition of her eyes, eyes that look as if they have beheld many sorrows. A family snapshot from the same time shows her in a more relaxed mood, her lovely features shown to advantage.

Margaret Laurence in garden at Penn. c. 1966.

Upon arrival back in England, she received another important phone call from her agent. Paul Newman and Joanne Woodward—in the manner of *dei ex machina*—wanted to buy an option on the film rights to *A Jest of God*. "Woodward's agent had seen the review of the novel in *Life* and had thought it might be something Woodward would like to do. So there I was. I suddenly had enough money to make a down payment and get a mortgage on Elm Cottage." (The purchase price was £8,000. Margaret made a down payment of £3,000 and took a mortgage for the remainder. The sum paid by Newman was $30,000.)

Two months later she was in Egypt. Her fourth trip of 1966 would bring her, she was afraid, to a nervous collapse, but she felt she had no choice but to accept the offer from *Holiday*. However, she could not bear to be parted from the children yet again, so she took them along on a month-long holiday and research trip (mid-December to mid-January). She thought of getting in touch with the Egyptian ambassador but decided against this because Jamal was "undoubtedly a pal" of his, and her request for information might look "unethical" and lead her back to the "old lion," whose den she no longer wanted to enter.

Always an unsteady traveller, she made arrangements with the Egyptian press attaché regarding her proposed voyage through the Suez Canal (the focus of one her essays) and asked if her "little ones" would be allowed on such a trip. Nonchalantly he replied, "Oh, I don't see why not, unless there might be some difficulty getting them up the rope ladder." It was Margaret who was terrified: "ROPE LADDER ... ye gods! ... I can see it all now ... very small item in the *Guardian*—'Canadian woman writer falls to death from rope ladder on oil tanker...' etc." Despite moments of comic and genuine terror, 1966 was an *annus mirabilis* for Margaret, a time in which she came into her own as a writer and as an independent woman.

14

The Multiplicity of Everything

(1967-1968)

As her belated New Year letter to Jack McClelland makes clear, Margaret had a wonderful trip to Egypt, but it was the "little ones" (now fourteen and eleven) who, had, not unexpectedly, been the really intrepid travellers:

> We only got home from Egypt a few days ago. The whole trip went splendidly, and was one of the most terrific experiences of my life. My kids also enjoyed it thoroughly, and I was very glad I'd taken them along, as they were really good companions. We spent a few days in Cairo, then down to Luxor, where we spent 10 days looking at Karnak Temple, Luxor Temple, the temples and tombs of the pharaohs and queens and nobles (with tomb paintings that look as though they'd been done yesterday instead of 3 thousand years ago). Then took a Nile steamer to Aswan—a 2 day trip, and the most relaxing time I've spent in years, and at Aswan saw the High Dam, which is fabulous. Then back to Cairo and over to Ismailia, on the Suez Canal, where we boarded a British tanker and travelled on the canal to Port Said. That was the only really ghastly experience of the trip—disembarking with the pilot at Port Said harbour—the tanker was

> zooming along, and the small pilot launch had to come alongside, and we had to totter down a very narrow gangway and leap aboard the launch—I was absolutely terrified, but we all made it, thank God, with no casualties other than my shattered nerves. My kids said, "Don't be ridiculous—there was no danger at all." It must be lovely to be courageous. Spent a week in Port Said, then back to Cairo, where we dutifully crawled through the claustrophobic tunnels in the Great Pyramid in order to say we'd done it (I can't think of any other reason why anyone would want to go through that kind of ordeal).

Dutifully, Margaret wrote her two pieces for *Holiday* ("Good Morning to the Grandson of Ramesses the Second" and "Captain Pilot Shawkat and Kipling's Ghost"), but the intervention of the Seven Days' War later that year meant that Egypt was no longer a tourist attraction and thus no longer a suitable destination for the readers of *Holiday*, which never published these essays. She did receive payment in full, however, and was in the bathtub one evening, "more or less whistling a merry tune and thinking how well things were going, when Jocelyn came pounding up the stairs and knocked on the bathroom door. 'Mum! Egypt and Israel are at war.' The moment of truth is sometimes humiliating. My first thought was not for the young Israelis and the young Egyptians set to killing one another. My first thought was, 'Thank God I got paid.'"

That January, she was elated when the money for the film option arrived and the purchase of Elm Cottage could go ahead. Margaret and Jack celebrated by spending two weeks in southern Spain. This trip helped to change the circumstances of their tumultuous see-sawing marriage, as did Jack's new job. After completing his master's degree at Southampton, Jack landed a post as irrigation consultant for the Ministry of Overseas Development. He would be based in Surrey but would travel several months at a time to the various places where projects were being set up. He had even taken a flat in Surbiton, Surrey.

Unfortunately, Jack's new job was not as well-paying as his others. He had to cut down the allowance he paid for the children. According to Margaret, the new sum would be suitable if she lived in a coldwater flat in Camden Town. "I wouldn't have minded (I *don't* mind) but what rather bugged me was the fact that he believes quite honestly that I have no financial worries at all," she told Adele. Injury was added to insult when Jack assured her: "You can't be worried by money—look at the way you live—big house in the country."

Shortly after she arrived back in England, she was involved in another short-lived affair, the details of which she confided to Adele:

> The man with whom I had a brief but very nice encounter—whom I think I mentioned to you—turned out to be, as I really had known he would, very anxious about upsetting his established way of life. He is a hell of a nice man, but he is old enough and wise enough to know that few of us can have our cake and eat it too. He'd love to pursue some kind of relationship (horrible word ... contemporary cliché) with me, if only it didn't mean difficult arrangements re: his wife. Is he wrong? Of course not. I can understand perfectly well how he feels. For one thing, like me, he is too old and too damn tired to risk everything he's spent many years in trying to maintain. So what in fact happens is that he phones me and makes an arrangement to meet me in London, and several days before the time he comes down with 'flu. Of course. What else? I did see him, not so long ago, and I wanted to say, "Look, it's okay, I know you find it too upsetting, so let's be thankful for what we've had and not press our luck too far, and goodbye and God Bless You..." etc.

In the midst of these somewhat rueful reflections, Jamal called. "Why didn't you phone me when you got back from Egypt?" Truthfully, she replied that she did not relish the rigamarole of trying to reach him through secretaries. As she talked to him, she realized once again what an amazingly kind person he was. He was also very amusing. Margaret, who could not help laughing at his high spirits, asked how he was. "I've been working like a nigger," he replied. Then, "he at least had the grace to cough awkwardly! He's a marvellous man, if you like unscrupulous men—he'd stab his own grandmother if it forwarded his career."

Four days after writing to Adele, she had reached a resolution—sort of: "Jack and I have decided to get together again, as we have both learned a lot in these 5 years and can now accept one another better as we are." To the same correspondent—Gordon Elliott—she added two weeks later: Jack "comes here most weekends, and we get on very well indeed. Strange, really. I think we've both changed a lot." They may have changed, but they were nevertheless wary of each other. During Jack's visits, the Laurences tried to resume their married lives, but then the barriers between them would reassert themselves. She wanted the solidity of a real relationship with a man—rather than the fleeting pleasures of brief encounters—but she did not really wish to commit herself to her marriage in any realistic way that would involve the daily burdens of domestic life.

Jack had been at one time more supportive of her work than anyone; he had tried to accommodate his wife's powerful talent. But he was a man of his age, one who was not ashamed of demanding that his wife's life be centred on his. For Jack, this was the only type of marriage that was acceptable. He hoped Margaret would come round to his way of thinking, and she toyed with this notion because she did love him. But theirs had become a long-distance relationship, one that worked on its own idiosyncratic terms as long as they were not together for too long. The simple truth was that they were deeply fond of each other but now had vastly different notions of what they wanted in life.

In December 1966, Al Purdy—who had missed meeting Margaret when she had been in Canada that autumn—wrote to tell her he "was just another admirer, and you have those ad nauseam I suppose. Went so far as to buy your books tho, and that's going pretty far for me." That declaration led to one by Margaret: "Owing to one of those ironies of life, you were the person I most wanted to meet when I was in Canada this summer and the only person in the whole country (almost) whom I didn't meet." Quickly, the Laurence-Purdy friendship flourished in letters.

These are exchanges between professional writers whose lives were consumed with the glories and travails of subduing words onto paper. That February, Margaret, who knew that no amount of effort would turn her into a Northrop Frye, was struggling with the book that became *Long Drums and Cannons* while, at the same time, trying to envision her future as a creative writer. It is a measure of her trust in Purdy that she could summarize her various dilemmas to him on February 19:

Al Purdy.

> I'm still attempting to finish a book about contemporary Nigerian prose (novels and plays), and why I ever wrote it I can't think, as I am certainly not a literary critic, and the North-American scientific-academic school of literary criticism scares the hell out of me (they are all so bright, one feels gloomily). Anyway, I want to get this out of the way, because I got hooked on the whole subject sufficiently to make it impossible to proceed until this particular thing is done. The only thing I really care about is to try to write about three more novels, and writing a novel is what I am supposed to be doing at the moment, with the Canada Council's financial help, and I am not doing it. I worry greatly over what they will think if (God forbid) they discover this unfortunate fact. Will I be cut off with a shilling, etc? If the novel is really there, it will be written; if it isn't, it won't—it is as simple as that. But it isn't always possible to do things to schedule. It would be great not to have to worry about money.

Previously, Jack Laurence, Adele Wiseman, Jane Rule, Alan Maclean and Jack McClelland had been the only persons to whom she would confide details about her writing life.

In Al Purdy, she discovered a person to add to a small list of confidantes. Why him? She had been struck by these lines from *The Cariboo Horses*: "surrounded by nothing / but beautiful trees / & I hate beautiful trees" (1965) in which Purdy had, by implication, praised the turbulent, wind-swept, often unpicturesque Canadian landscape. She also liked the direct virility of the speaking voice in his verse. Margaret, who could be rivalrous with other writers of prose, did not feel she was in competition with Purdy.

Although eight years older than she, this large, sprawling man shared similar experiences with her of the Depression, the scarring left in the wake of World War II, and small Scots-Irish Canadian towns. Unlike Margaret, he had not attended university, came from Eastern Ontario and had tried his hand at a number of jobs, including cab driver and factory worker. In her first letter to Purdy, she told him that she loved Elm Cottage because "it staggers along somehow, with damp walls and other blemishes but it has elegance and warmth ... I find it reassuring." From the outset, Margaret and Al found something "reassuring" in each other, perhaps in the fact that from the outside they seemed such ordinary people but within were consumed with similar overpowering obsessions with the life of writing.

That spring, she could not get on with the writing of her new novel. "In the end," she told Adele, "the only real joy [in writing] is in the doing of it, and that is the state one longs to have happen again. Writing has always seemed very much like making love, to me." Margaret used a similar metaphor when describing her dissatisfaction with the short stories and travel pieces she had recently completed: "I suppose I feel I haven't done anything because none of those things really matter to me, not the way a novel does. It's like having a few casual affairs." That May, she asked Jack McClelland to light one or two (mental) candles for her: "It makes me laugh bitterly when I think that years ago I believed that one's second novel would be easier, and then that one's third would be easier, and so on. But no. They get more difficult all the time. This one is going to take longer than the last, I fear. The main thing, however, as I keep telling myself, is not to make a major production of it, mentally. It's only another novel, not the second coming of Christ." Nevertheless, she was so "tense that my guts," she wryly observed, "could be used for violin strings."

Two months earlier, in March, Margaret was delighted to learn she had won the Governor General's Award for fiction for *A Jest of God.* Although astounded, stunned and grateful for the "dough," a lot of her nervous energy in the following two months was drained away by planning the trip to Ottawa. She worked on her next novel but was reasonably content to write the book in her head. She did manage to finish *Long Drums and Cannons* before leaving for Canada on May 26, but she experienced the "psycho-somatic business" (acute anxiety, nausea, swollen glands, sore throat, fever) that accompanied the completion of every book. "It never fails," she lamented to Adele.

During her one-week stay in Canada to receive the Governor General's Award, she visited with Adele in Montreal and then went on to Ottawa before catching her return flight back to London in Montreal. This compressed stay was much more enjoyable than her two-and-a-half-month stay the year before. The reason was simple: no pressure. She and Adele visited Expo several times and, when in the evening Margaret's anxieties got the better of her, Adele reassured her: "The book is starting. Relax."

Margaret and Adele continued to take great comfort from each other in their personal and literary lives. In some ways, short, stocky and bubbly Adele was a "Jewish mother" to Margaret, always willing to bestow the unconditional love, support and encouragement Margaret needed in her sometimes topsy-turvy life. Before her marriage to Dmitry Stone in 1966, Adele's life—although she used Winnipeg as her home base—had been even more peripatetic than Margaret's: London in 1950-1, Rome 1951-2, New York, 1957-60, Montreal, 1964-66. Although she had mounds of energy and considerable talent as a writer, she never approached Margaret in either accomplishment or output. Bothered though she was by the lack of recognition accorded her, she never begrudged Margaret her success. In fact, she was very proud of Margaret the person and the creator.

During her brief visit to Montreal, Adele introduced Margaret to Sinclair ("Jim") Ross, then in his forty-third year of service with the Royal Bank. She sensed he felt that he had outlived his creative gifts. "Who can reassure him? Because actually it is true." Confronted with the presence of a writer who had inspired her own work and, at the same time, realizing that his creative gifts had indeed deserted him, she pondered her own uncertain future: "I've felt for some time that I've got maybe ten more years, if lucky, and maybe three more novels, and then time to start running a boarding-house or something. This is not an unbearable thought—more unbearable is the thought of going on writing after one hasn't got any more to say, in a language which isn't spoken any more." This is an important reflection, heralding her sense that her writing career might not outlive her. Margaret's unflinching honesty can also be glimpsed here: she would never write just for the sake of writing—she had to have something to say.

Margaret Atwood.

At the Governor General's residence, Margaret Laurence met tiny, intense and witty Margaret Atwood, who had won the prize for poetry for *The Circle Game.* Jane Rule, a teacher of Atwood's, had told Margaret Laurence of the younger woman's fondness for fortune-telling with the Tarot pack. This sent a "twinge of fear" through the sometimes superstitious Laurence, who felt such occult activities smacked of psychological warfare. "She was, I thought, very serious, slightly (to me) intimidating because so brainy, and then the next day she phoned me and said she'd been glad to find I wasn't as intimidating as she thought I was going to be, from my picture. How strange we all are, and how vulnerable. Naturally, I warmed to her enormously after that. The thought that anyone might think me formidable is bizarre in the extreme." The ceremony at Rideau Hall "was much better than I had thought it would be" she told Adele. Claire Martin, who won the fiction award in French, was "an absolute honey." Just before Roland Michener entered the room, she got out her compact and dabbed her face. Finally, she shrugged and announced: "Oh well, it's not a beauty contest." Then she whispered: "Do you intend to make a reverence?" Margaret assured her that she herself did not know how to curtsy and that, in any event, she had been told that this bit of protocol had been abolished.

Al Purdy put in an appearance at the pre-dinner drinks session at the Country Club. When this "enormous man shambled in, I thought 'My God, he looks like a cowboy.'" Later that evening—when both of them had a great deal to drink—they attempted to have sex, but they were both so drunk the effort proved futile. (Margaret told a number of female friends about this incident. When I asked Purdy about it, he told me that he had "absolutely no recollection" of this event but he then assured me that this did not mean that it did not take place.)

During her one-week stay in Canada, Margaret was brought into touch with the past, present and future of Canadian literature. In a wonderful aside to Jack McClelland, she observed: "I was surprised at how little strain there was in the Government House ceremony—the great thing was that the writers didn't have to do anything except keep their mouths shut and look (if possible) decorative and not too dim-witted."

Margaret had been glad to go away and "equally glad" to come home, even though Jocelyn and David were now old enough to voice their displeasure at a mother who lived with them but almost always seemed unavailable: "My kids hate it when I'm writing, as I'm often rather absent in every way that matters and then the little brutes tell me I'm neglecting them, thus loading me with guilt which they don't mean to do at all."

Upon her return to Elm Cottage, Margaret envisioned herself as "some female Jacob wrestling with an angel who is mighty difficult." The angel was Stacey and the novel, *The Fire-Dwellers*, devoted to her. "A lot of" the book was, she informed Adele, "sheer crap, but in the places where I wasn't being too evasive or too strained, the voice of the character does break through." She was trying to salvage the useful parts of her old typescript, but she realized all too well that the reason she had—years before—set this book aside was because:

> The character was beginning to talk too much in my voice. I recognize now that of course she is talking in my voice—but only in 1 of my voices, and baby, I've got DOZENS of voices!! So what does it matter? The only good bits of what I wrote before are the bits where I let her talk the way she wanted, and these are the parts I'm trying to save. The thing is, they contain genuine aspects of her, and it's a violation of some kind to throw them away. So I can't begin from the beginning, as I had hoped, but have to patiently sort out the wheat (?) from the chaff, pausing only to complain mournfully to such people as you. Also, I see now that the character's dilemma, although related in some undercurrent way to my own, is actually very far from my own—and indeed, my own dilemma is now utterly different anyway, so perhaps I had to gain this distance to be able to write it.

A week later, Margaret had become, as she put it, "a pyromaniac ... a firebug." She went out to the garden and burned the hundreds of pages of the early drafts of *The Fire-Dwellers* which she had written three years before and had been attempting to resuscitate. "How can I have ever thought I could sort out the good bits? It is the character who is there, not the individual words. And she is still there, but I can't seem to reach her, or not yet.... I've also destroyed all the plans for the novel—ie. the intricate setting-down of plot, etc etc, which was another evasion I've indulged in with this one for some six years now. All gone. Consumed in flames. I don't need a bloody plan—either it will come by itself or it won't, and I certainly ought to know the people, as I've lived with them trampling around inside my skull for so many years." Such precipitous behaviour was an aspect of her character the children found unsettling. When she was uncertain, Margaret would often steamroll over an issue, as if being noisily aggressive was a substitute for considered action.

Her difficulties with the novel led her to wonder about her mental stability: "But do you think it is possible to crack up without knowing it? I feel very strange, Adele. I think that if I can't write this one, I can't write. But sometimes I feel I just won't ever be able to get through to it. So help me, it isn't for lack of trying. I think it was at one time lack of comprehension. Now it is lack of faith. It isn't any hell of a great expedition, in external terms—just another novel. But for me, crucial."

Could this new novel rise from its own ashes? That was the question she was forced to ask herself. She had not been able to write the book three years before because the voice of Stacey was so much like her own during the Vancouver years. In 1967, she thought she had obtained the necessary distance. Yet, her new "understanding" with her husband had returned her squarely to many of the dilemmas she had faced in British Columbia. Despite the new direction her marriage was taking, her two trips back to Canada had kindled in her a desire to return home, a suggestion to which Jocelyn was indifferent but which frightened David, who, only twelve at the time, loved Elmcot and the stability it bestowed on him. Of course, Jack had recently found work in England in an attempt to make his needs and his wife's congruent.

As she had been several years before, Margaret was loath to discuss troublesome issues with her husband, describing herself as a daughter afraid of confronting a harsh father: "I am petrified about a face-to-face encounter with him over this basic problem. I really do not think I can face him, or bring it up. My tendency, in his presence, is to smooth everything over, because I am too damn cowardly to do otherwise.... I am still so bloody scared to encounter him, and feel I will be bulldozed and will not be able to maintain myself before him.... what is hard is to assail an authority which one subconsciously feels to be unassailable, at the same time consciously knowing it is as broken a reed as oneself."

By September, she had reached Chapter Two but was deeply uncertain of her future as a writer, a woman and a person: "Actually, I feel like hell. I feel as though I have been battling for 5 years, only to find myself now back in the same situation exactly, personally and in writing, as I was 5 years ago. Except then I had the nearly completed manuscript of *The Stone Angel.* Now what have I got?"

The Fire-Dwellers is an even more ambitious book than *The Stone Angel,* perhaps because in 1967, Margaret was trying, as she told Al Purdy, "to get across the multiplicity of everything." By that, she meant the deep conflicts and irresolutions which seem to be at the core of the human situation. As she got older, she saw the task of reconciling opposites as impossible and thus redundant. But, she also realized, society does not like to think of itself as possessing unsolvable problems. Nevertheless, this was the real task that faced mid-twentieth century authors: "The attempt to deal with the shifting and ambiguous nature of reality" seemed to her "the only important thing that's happened in the novel in the past decade." She also knew all of the problems with her new book but none of the solutions.

That October, she discovered a new way of writing, a complete "breakaway" from the old narrative style. Her theory was good, but the resulting prose was at first unfortunately unreadable: "Visualized the outer and inner taking place simultaneously, in two columns, rather like a newspaper—would have been a nice contrast, the relation between the two being nil. It would work fine if you had a two-foot wide page and a reader with four eyes."

She was doing something else equally arduous in the same book: challenging the prevalent, stereotypical views of women who worked as homemakers. Hagar is no one's idea of "a sweet old lady," and in Rachel's rejection of the confined and confining world of Manawaka Margaret had disputed conventional views of the "single woman." In her new book, she was taking even more on board because any questioning of the role of women as mothers, wives and homemakers challenges all of the assumptions upon which patriarchy is based. Before, she had examined isolated portions of the women-in-the-world question; in her new book, she was looking at—and ultimately attacking—many of the assumptions society ignores but upon which its precarious foundations rest.

Both *The Stone Angel* and *A Jest of God* are written in the voices of their protagonists. In order to demonstrate Stacey's attempts to connect to the madness of the world and, in the process, to feel insane, Margaret uses a combination of first- and third-person narration in *The Fire-Dwellers*, an apocalyptic metaphor for all human beings, all victims of a media-driven, violence-prone world.

> The buildings at the heart of the city are brash, flashing with colors, solid and self-confident. Stacey is reassured by them, until she looks again and sees them charred, open to the impersonal winds, glass and steel broken like vulnerable live bones, shadows of people frog-splayed on the stone.

Life is hell, the title suggests—or, at the very least, a purgatory.

In the above passage, Stacey first sees the city as "brash" and "confident," but on second glance she sees it as "charred" and "vulnerable." Depending on your point of view, both perceptions are accurate. The trouble, Margaret argues, is that people are programmed to think that what is "normal" is necessarily good. Stacey—who has the gift of second-sight—is incapable of seeing things this way and, as a result, constantly suspects herself of being some sort of deviant or misfit, which, of course, she is from the prevailing male-dominated vision of the world:

> Stacey looks at her underwear on the chair but makes no move towards it. Her eyes are drawn back to the mirror.
>
> —Everything would be all right if only I was better educated. I mean, if I were. Or if I were beautiful. Okay, that's asking too much. Let's say if I took off ten or so pounds. Listen, Stacey, at thirty-nine, after four kids, you can't expect to look like a sylph. Maybe not, but for hips like mine there's no excuse. I wished I lived in some country where broad-beamed women were fashionable. Everything will be all right when the kids are older. I'll be more free. Free for what? What in hell is the matter with you, anyway? Everything *is* all right. *Everything is all right.* Come on, flat slob, get up off your ass and get going. There's a sale on downtown, remember?

In the first paragraph, the omniscient narrator tells us that Stacey looks in the mirror whereas the second allows us to enter Stacey's mind. In rapid turn, Stacey wishes and then fantasizes; she then questions and admonishes herself. Finally, she offers self-assurance before insulting herself.

The use of voice in *The Fire-Dwellers* is the work of a masterful writer, but while writing the book—which is in every way a high-wire act—Margaret obviously did not see it this way. She could not validate her own technical brilliance because she was evoking the sense of loneliness and despair she had experienced in Vancouver, that side of herself only Nadine Jones had been allowed to witness.

Many of the ideas in *The Fire-Dwellers* anticipate or reflect the ground-breaking work of Betty Friedan in *The Feminine Mystique* (1963), a book which sought to explain how a certain gestalt—not in the best interest of any woman—had come into being in the postwar world, a mind-set that suggested fulfillment for women was only to be found in marriage and child-bearing. Friedan argued that society had bound women by subtly forcing them to internalize such mistaken notions. She asked: "How can any woman see the whole truth within the bounds of her own life? How can she believe that voice inside herself, when it denies the conventional, accepted truths by which she has been living?" As housewives began voicing their unease, society came up with ridiculous explanations, from over-education to insufficient training in washing-machine repair, without confronting the basic problem, which was that children, a husband and a home did not necessarily satisfy women's needs to grow and fully explore their potentials.

Another non-fiction writer who may have influenced Margaret's new book was the prairie-born Marshall McLuhan, whose seminal books *The Gutenberg Galaxy* (1962) and *Understanding Media* (1964) showed how television had become so much a part of North American existence that it was sometimes impossible to separate the two. This is a condition of life Stacey is painfully aware of:

> Come on, you kids. Aren't you ever coming for breakfast?
> THIS IS THE EIGHT-O'CLOCK NEWS BOMBING RAIDS LAST NIGHT DESTROYED FOUR VILLAGES IN
>
> Mum! Where's my social studies scribbler?
>
> I don't know, Ian. Have you looked for it? ...
>
> WORD FROM OUR SPONSOR IF YOU HAVEN'T SEEN TOOLEY'S NEW SHOWROOM YOU'RE IN FOR A REAL COOL SURPRISE
>
> Chatter buzz wail
>
> Okay, Jen, I'll be up in a sec. Are you finished? Don't try to get off by yourself—I'm coming.
>
> You going to get your hair done, Stacey?
>
> Yes, of course, whaddya think?
>
> I only asked, for heaven's sake. No need to
>
> I'm sorry, Mac....
>
> ROAD DEATHS UP TEN PER CENT MAKING THIS MONTH THE WORST IN
>
> I got to take fifty cents, Mum.
>
> Duncan! What for?
>
> Cripples or something....

> WHEN QUESTIONED THE BOY SAID HE HAD SEEN THE GIRL TAKING THE PILLS BUT HE HAD NOT KNOWN THEY WERE

For Margaret—and *The Fire-Dwellers* displays this—the "novel must be moving closer to the film, as a means of catching the human dilemma." Another aspect of the book is her overwhelming fear that the fire next time would be worldwide destruction by nuclear war. At the end of the book, Stacey asks herself: "Will the fires go on, inside and out? Until the moment when they go out for me, the end of the world. And then I'll never know what may happen in the next episode." She cannot answer that—or any of the questions which overwhelm her perceptive, incredibly fine-tuned mind, and the narrative concludes on a deliberately indeterminate note: "She feels the city receding as she slides into sleep. Will it return tomorrow?" There is a lack of closure because in Margaret Laurence's view uncertainty is a hallmark of twentieth-century man's experience.

At the very same time she was dealing with the various dilemmas of bringing Stacey forcefully to life, Margaret—as a respite—wrote her first children's book, a book which had an irritating autobiographical point of origin:

> Our lawn had been inhabited by moles for a long time. Each day in spring and summer molehills would appear, about two feet high. David would scoop up the earth and throw it into the bushes.... The next morning there would be more mole mountains. One day I felt the grass actually springing under my feet. I was convinced there was an entire city of moles there, but I wasn't about to sacrifice my entire lawn to them. I put up a sign in our local post office: "Are there no mole catchers left in England?" My sign was answered. A mole catcher, complete with explosives and gas, went to work and cleared our lawn of moles. I felt like a murderer. I had already begun

> writing the first draft of *Jason's Quest*, in which one of the heroes is a mole. Nevertheless, it was a relief to be rid of them.

In the tragi-comic world of her first children's book, not only are heroes and villains easily distinguished from each other but also goodness confronts and vanquishes evil. Jason, a young mole searching for a cure to the sickness destroying Molanium, travels to Londinium to discover a cure. On his way, he is joined by Oliver, a tawny owl, and two cats, Calico and Topaz. As in many quest stories, the hero learns that the real discoveries are internal ones: "wisdom must be learned from life itself." Margaret—despite her earlier claim of being no Northrop Frye—gave a reading of this text worthy of the categories established in *The Anatomy of Criticism*: "a frivolous retelling of ... the 'heroic monomyth': Departure—Initiation—Return."

The children's novel provided only a momentary distraction from the issues raised by *The Fire-Dwellers*. Each scene had to be lived through from the inside, and she found "this process of going inside the thing harder and harder to bear" as she got older. With this new book, she had to confront a potentially hazardous truth: "I don't write directly out of personal experience, but all the same I often wonder how much of myself I'm revealing in novels and stories—in fact, I'm revealing the whole thing, but I always fondly hope that this isn't obvious to everyone."

Another revelation—one to become of central importance—that came to her during the writing of her fourth novel was a renewed fascination with religious belief, one which was residual although not "in the greybearded gent of our childhood Sunday schools." When writing she could feel the presence of a "personal god" or guardian angel who oversaw her work. The Ibo, she remembered, called such a deity a "chi": the "god within, that part of a person's spirit which directs their destiny." Throughout her entire life Margaret was a committed Christian, but her sense in the late 1960s of the centrality of the importance of religious belief was heightened by her awareness of the meaningless of so much of contemporary life, meaninglessness she encountered each day in the newspapers, radio and TV.

During the winter of 1968, she felt more "settled" in her marriage; there was a "kind of renaissance of feeling" between herself and Jack: "I guess," she reflected, "we always did love one another, despite difficulties, but a lot of things had to be sorted out." She added: "Think those 5 years taught both of us a hell of a lot." Despite the breakthrough, Margaret had some lingering doubts which she tried to overcome: "The old anxieties simply take on new masks. I think I was very nervous about returning to the role of wife, probably more than I needed to be. Also, took me some years to think of myself as being absolutely on my own, and now I had to re-shape the self image all over again into something new—married but not dependent."

However, the relationship between Jack and Margaret was anything but trouble-free, as can be seen in a letter to Alan Maclean. She had, she realized, been naive to be overly optimistic about reconciling her differences with her husband, even on rather routine domestic matters:

> Got home this morning, however, to discover house in an absolute shambles (J having gone this morning before I got home). I know I am compulsively tidy, and I do deplore this, but my GOD, surely the newspapers didn't have to be strewn all over the house, and bed left unmade, and a large pile of dirty shirts left conveniently out, presumably for me to launder. This probably sounds mean as hell, but I am so furious at the moment that I had to write to get it all off my chest. Soon I will feel more calm, probably, and will think I'm being pretty trivial. However, I see now that the house rules *must* be explained, tactfully if possible, but firmly.... it has to be made clear that there is really only one house rule here, and that is that every person looks after themselves. The kids make their own beds, for heaven's sake, so why shouldn't he? I guess the trouble is that there has always been either a mother or a wife or a steward-boy

> to take care of all these unmanly details. I am a proper bitch, possibly, talking this way. But the difficulty is the same old one—how to establish a relationship in which he can come here and see the kids (also me) without strain, and without making this his base, and without my having to take on the extra load of housework, which I am certainly at this point not prepared to do.

Despite her outburst—and her need to give voice to these strong feelings—she was "not downcast or even especially discouraged, as I seem to be rather more convinced of my own reality than I used to be (hurrah)." She was no longer a victim of the pernicious feminine mystique.

At the very same time she was trying to come to some sort of understanding about herself and Jack, she completed the first draft of *The Fire-Dwellers*, although she warned Jack McClelland that even she was not sure what she had accomplished: "First draft of novel is completed, thank God. I do not know at all what it is like—it may be positively lousy. I have to go through and add bits which have been left out, and cut out all excess verbiage, then re-type. It is slightly a mess at the moment, but think it will be done, with luck, in 2 months. The tone is so different from anything I've written before that I think that anyone who liked previous novels will probably not care for this one." Two days later, Margaret tried in a letter to explain her fear of failure to fellow novelist Jane Rule, who, by writing about lesbian experience, was also trying in her own way to extend the frontiers of Canadian fiction: "The odd thing is that the most worrying aspect is the feeling that one may not have done at all well by the characters. I *know* them, and I know they are there. But I keep feeling that I haven't put them down as they deserved—I haven't caught *enough* of them. I guess every writer feels this way, though. But the tone of this one is so different from anything I've ever written. No symbol, no poetic prose, no fancy bits of any kind—just idiomatic speech. Also, the main character is a white, anglo-saxon, middleaged mum—who could pick anyone more unlikely than that?"

Of course, the "mum" was the closest approximation to herself she had ever offered in her fiction. No wonder her "post-novel depression" was this time of "an unusually bizarre nature" in which she "really outdid herself." There had been parts of Margaret's character in Hagar and Rachel, but Stacey was really a version of herself, as she admitted to Al Purdy that June: "It's not autobiographical, but I share many of the main character's outlooks, and so I guess I feel I've made myself more vulnerable in this novel than I ever did before. I guess in a sense I've tried to work out my own acceptance of middle age (I don't mean that to sound gloomy) through writing this novel." The dilemma was certainly one faced by women of her own age: "I didn't pick" the topic of the book, she claimed, because it would have a wide appeal—"I don't even know if it will, and I don't care. I wrote it because it was there to be written."

During the winter of 1968, Margaret had been discussing the possibility of becoming writer-in-residence at the University of Toronto with Malcolm Ross, who was teaching at Trinity College. Earlier, she had been convinced her husband would mount serious objections to such a scheme, especially given the fact he had recently settled in England. In fact, he was supportive, even offering to arrange his schedule to be in England and thus look after the children when she was away. Margaret was pleasantly astounded: "God, Adele—does that indicate anything to you? To me, it indicates just how much both Jack and I have changed. Five years ago I would have ben scared stiff to contemplate such a job, and if I had, Jack would certainly never have agreed to put himself out in any way to make it possible, as he then believed a woman's place was etc etc." Two months later, when Margaret had a "hell of a scare" when Jocelyn's appendix almost burst before she could be operated on, she reflected again on how her husband was "the only human being upon whom I can really call in crises affecting my children."

Contrary to her usual practice, Margaret typed *The Fire-Dwellers* soon after finishing it. (All of her books were first written in scribblers.

Then, she—or someone else—would type the resulting draft or drafts. Drafts of both *This Side Jordan* and *The Stone Angel* were typed by Margaret at least a year after being written. In the case of *This Side Jordan*, Gordon Elliott had prepared the typescript sent to Jack McClelland. Margaret hired a typist to do *A Jest of God*.) So, she suffered through "the whole damn thing all over again" and thus read her "godforsaken novel ALL OVER AGAIN AND AGAIN AND AGAIN." In a letter towards the end of the year, she drew a personality assessment of herself which is in large part accurate: "I guess I have a real, if despicable, streak of spiritual masochism in me. If there isn't much to agonize about, I can always invent something.... one part of me is very practical and sensible, the other part is black Celt."

Having convinced herself she might have to find new publishers for her new novel, she was relieved when Alan Maclean told her that her new book was better than *A Jest of God*. In late June, Jack McClelland cabled a ringing endorsement of the book. However, she was not pleased when her editor at Knopf, Judith Jones, wrote. Like her counterparts at Macmillan and McClelland & Stewart, she had some problems with matters of clarity and the then-long description of the science-fiction novel by Luke, Stacey's lover. Judith really offended Margaret when she told her she did not like the proposed title, *The Fire-Dwellers*. When she informed McClelland of Jones's objection, he backed the American editor. At this point, Margaret's "Celtic anger" was aroused, but Maclean convinced her the best strategy was diplomacy and stubbornness, a tactic she used effectively. When Jack McClelland later complained about the financial drubbing—an advance of $1,500—he had endured at the hands of her agent, she playfully assured him that when he was on the dole, she and other M&S writers would "chip in" for a few hamburgers.

Of paramount interest to her as 1968 drew to a close was her future as writer and wife. She told Adele she had said everything she wanted to say in "expressing things through my own generation's idiom" because "I don't think I have anything more to say in that genre." Therefore, her next novel—if there was one—would be "something quite different, and maybe the last one I have to write." Her use of "have" is interesting, implying as it does that her books were part of a compulsive drive which was coming to an end.

Of the future of her marriage, she was even more unsure. In August, the Laurences had gone on holiday to Lake Como (Margaret's choice), whereas Jack had wanted to go to Ireland:

> The main cry of the woman in THE FIRE-DWELLERS is always "Everything's all right," but of course she does not believe it, and I guess I don't, either. In some ways, all is well. We have just returned from a 12 day holiday in Italy—stayed in a super hotel on the shores of Lake Como; gorgeous scenery, marvellous food, good wine, swimming pool, the lot.... Problem was that we went there because I and the kids decided we wanted sunshine, instead of going to Ireland as first planned when Jack came back from Honduras—Ireland would've been much cheaper, needless to say, and I paid difference ... but—you know, this is very hard on him, really. How to cope? He keeps telling me I've made more than he has in the past several years and alas this is true. By a fluke, in my terms, but he doesn't necessarily see that. Maybe I should just have gone to Ireland. But I didn't want to go to Ireland. All really quite complex, I guess. He has decided, apparently, to opt out re: theories of kid-rearing, and says he leaves it all to me, which makes me feel about 2000% more responsible than I want to feel, although I know he is doing it with the right feelings, in his terms, as he thinks we disagree so he's given up, and where does that leave me? He is so terribly tolerant, and sometimes I am really bitchy to him, and I hate myself, and I honestly pray to be able to be more loving and gentle, but then I'm not. I guess I would find him easier if he made more mistakes, but he genuinely doesn't. He doesn't ever drink too much or get overly angry—if he's angry, it is all kept inside. He never wastes money, as I do. He's physically so fit, unlike me—I get diarrhea on the slightest provocation, when more than 200 yards away from the nearest john, and what an embarrassment this is to me and all, having to

> desperately seek the nearest facilities. He's strong and muscular and fit and hard-working and a really good person, doing a job that is worthwhile and needs to be done—and I am speaking truly seriously—and he makes me feel like a slob. He doesn't mean to—I know that. And I also know it is very very difficult for him to cope with my so-called success—none of this matters a bit to me, except for the money, and in a way he *sees* this, but in a way what he sees is the money, which confuses and bewilders me but has more meaning for him—how odd. I really do feel quite inadequate as a wife, but the alternative of opting out appears worse for all of us than trying to stay in, so what I really need is for some grace to be given, I guess.

Some of Margaret's gloom was relieved when she and Jack attended the London premiere of *Rachel, Rachel*—the title of the film of *A Jest of God.* (She was very pleased that the planned title of the film—*Now I Lay Me Down*—had been dropped. When the title was changed abruptly at the eleventh hour, Panther, the publisher of the paperback released to coincide with the opening of the film, was left with masses of wrongly titled books.) She especially enjoyed meeting Joanne Woodward. Margaret, always shy in any public gathering, was timid about seeing the film, but she found it a more than adequate rendition of her fictional world. "The oddest things to me, apart from seeing Rachel in some kind of flesh, were the signs in the town—MANAWAKA THEATRE, etc ... I felt very peculiar, because the town name Manawaka came first to my mind about 20 years ago, when I made my first abortive attempt to write a novel." That evening, when she beheld her novel transformed into cinematic flesh, she must have had an overwhelming sense of "some grace," of how she had been able to capture the world of her childhood and young adulthood in terms wide and deep enough to become a story about the struggle of individuals everywhere to define, extend and grasp their own humanities.

15

Fire-Dweller

(1969)

"HERE I AM WITH FIVE CATS, 25 GODDAMN FUSCHIA PLANTS AND NO BOOZE." Such was Margaret's New Year 1969 lament to Al Purdy. After the struggle of the previous year in completing two books, she was understandably exhausted. At first, Macmillan had objected to the depiction of London in her children's novel *Jason's Quest*; they had serious reservations about her somewhat satirical send-up of sixties London on the grounds it would date the book too easily. Once Margaret had introduced the necessary revisions, they decided to go ahead with the book, which was published the following year to negative reviews in Canada. The *Toronto Daily Star*, for instance, labelled the book a "tedious disappointment," one of those "English whimsical animal books where the characters say things like 'Do shut up' and 'Now, luv.'"

Although she joked to Purdy that she never thought she would be reduced to keeping a cathouse, behind the merriment was a new worry. With a great deal of prescience, she was certain about the future non-existence of her writing life:

> I've only got one more book to write. I know I sound too pessimistic, etc etc, but it is just that I *know.* It will (if I'm lucky and given the

> grace to do it at all) not be done for a few years yet. I've always known exactly what to tackle next, and I know now. At one time it seemed I would never get them done, but now I can see the end of it. I don't even feel badly—in some odd way, it is a kind of relief. I can't really explain. I have a strange feeling that some other kind of work will present itself when the time comes. At one time I felt horrible about all this, and thought it was like becoming middle-aged or old, something I couldn't accept—but it isn't that way at all, and actually, becoming middle-aged or old isn't that way, either—a lot of things have changed recently in my point of view, I guess. I just think I am undergoing some kind of metamorphosis, that's all, and I'm not sure what's going to emerge, but I'm curiously optimistic.

In part, her cautious optimism was fuelled by her certainty that after an agonizingly long spell, her marriage was back on track. On January 26, she wrote in painstaking detail about the accord she and Jack had *seemed* to reach:

> He is as real to me as I am to myself, which is why in the end we cannot part. Even the husband-wife relationship ceases to be the prime important fact. We are one another's family now, after 22 years, the only remaining family, in essence, that either of us possesses. We are, as it were, related by blood now. I could never change my name, or marry anyone else. I could live with someone else, possibly, but not as wife. I have borne this name for more than half my life. I understand things about this relationship now which I did now know even a year ago. Which is possibly the reason why I can now feel pretty okay about it, without expecting things from it which it cannot give. I also believe that Jack is possibly one of the bravest people I have ever met, although he does not know that he is brave. He has overcome a tremendously damaging childhood, an inshutting background all around, and it has left him shut in, but he has never ceased to cope with his life in the best possible ways he could. When he went back to university at the age of fifty, and got

> his Master's degree, I thought that was one of the most courageous things I had ever heard. He is very different from me. He turns his problems outwards, and copes with life by coping with external circumstances. He builds irrigation setups and deals with the dry lands of the earth, trying to make them fertile. This, I believe, expresses an inner need. I, on the other hand, am inner-directed and tend to look inside, trying to comprehend the inner geography and this is why I am a novelist. It is just doing the same thing in different terms, that is all.

This heart-felt tribute to Jack Laurence could only have been penned when Margaret foresaw the end of her career as a writer. She could envision the possibility of resuming married life once again only when she decided the other, more crucial aspect of her life was winding down.

Up to 1969, *The Fire-Dwellers* had been Margaret's most overtly autobiographical fiction. In this year—and perhaps motivated in part by the raw honesty of that novel—she decided to collect her Vanessa MacLeod stories (with one exception, written and published between 1962 and 1967) into a book. These are the most transparently autobiographical writings she ever cast into fiction.

Later, Margaret was to claim *A Bird in the House* was not unlike a novel. This observation is particularly true in the author's handling of multiple first-person narrative voices: Vanessa at various ages during her childhood and Vanessa the adult. Margaret was quite clear on this point: "The narrative is, of course, that of Vanessa herself, but an older Vanessa, herself grown up, remembering how it was when she was ten.... The narrative voice, therefore, had to speak as though from two points in time, simultaneously."

The stories that comprise *A Bird in the House* are connected by the menacing presence of Grandfather Connor, but they are even more unified in their description of *how* Vanessa becomes an adult and a writer and in *what* she remembers about both processes. Margaret's arrangement of the stories serves a symbolic function in the sense that the growing complexity of the stories reflects a corresponding complexity and maturity in Vanessa. Each of the stories culminates in some way with Vanessa's haunting recognition: "That house in Manawaka is the one which, more than any other, I carry with me."

The straight chronology of the narratives is shattered by the death of Vanessa's father in the fourth story—the title one. In this way, the reader is actually allowed to feel the disruptive presence of death in the young girl's life. The final story, "Jericho's Brick Battlements," contains the most extended time-frame of the stories, going back to when Vanessa is four years old and moving forward to when she is forty years old. In this story, a note of forgiveness towards Grandfather Connor surfaces when the mature Vanessa proclaims: "I had feared and fought the old man, yet he proclaimed himself in my veins." Identifying her fictional alter-ego with Grandfather Connor was the closest Margaret could bring herself to forgiving Grandfather Simpson, of perhaps coming to terms with the fact that his acerbic behaviour had masked many insecurities.

Margaret wrote this story at a time when some of her psychic wounds were on the verge of healing—she had written and published a magnificent novel about the possibility of spiritual transformation and rebirth; she had completed a novel of daring stylistic complexity in which she reflected back upon the years in which her marriage had fallen apart; and she was convinced her broken marriage had at last been mended on terms acceptable to her and her spouse. She had every reason to be generous to her old spiritual nemesis.

In January 1969, Jack travelled to his next assignment in Swaziland. In a description of their leave-taking, she makes it quite clear they will not see each other for nine months, at which point he will return to England in order to supervise the children while she goes to Canada for the academic year 1969-1970. Despite the extremely unconventional approach to marriage revealed in this arrangement, she had reached some sort of accord with herself about the stability of her relationship with Jack. Missing ingredients in these plans are the children, age sixteen and thirteen, who were expected to fit into the complicated lives of their parents. Moreover, Margaret knew her children should not be apart from her for such a long stretch of time, but her need to get away from Elmcot blinded her to their needs.

In June 1968, Margaret humorously reflected on how she once again had chosen the wrong subject for *The Fire-Dwellers*: "Instead of writing a novel about a negro homosexual heroin-addicted dwarf, I had written a novel about a white anglo saxon protestant middle-aged mum—ye gods." She thought she was as prepared as possible for bad notices.

The notice in *Time*, insisting in the real life behind the fiction, irritated her: "They got just about everything all screwed up. The way they try to make out that *The Fire-Dwellers* is almost bound to be autobiographical seems like a sneaky trick and is also untrue. I wouldn't have minded if they'd described me as being built similar to a Ukrainian peasant woman, but 'slightly mannish without being unmotherly'—ye gods! Now I wish I had let my 'short brown hair' down to where it really grows, namely my shoulders, and had posed in a black lace nightie."

The Canadian reviews were mixed, as Margaret mentioned to Gordon:

> Split right down the middle. Dave Legate in the *Montreal Star* doesn't like the book but likes me and *The Stone Angel*, so is as kind as he can bring himself to be, which is rather nice of him. Two good reviews, Bill French in *Globe Magazine* and Marian Engel in *Saturday Night*, both of whom actually saw what I was driving at and could perceive all the themes and knew why the form had to be as it was—so thank God for that.... Two other terrible and passionately hating reviews, one of them of course Barry Callaghan in the *Toronto Telegram*, who does the best hatchet job which has ever been done on me. Barry has never liked anything I've written except *The Stone Angel*, and maybe it is easier to look at your grandmother than your wife/sister/mother.

She also commented: "For this and other reasons, I am not in very cheery frame of mind right now, but it will pass. Things were going too good for awhile there. Maybe I needed a spell of adversity. It would just be nice if God didn't deliver the blows on all fronts simultaneously, but that—to coin a phrase—is life."

Although she recognized that some male reviewers (such as William French) were quite capable of appreciating her new book, she sensed a lot of "enormous male hostility" in the notices. "Jesus," she exclaimed somewhat ingenuously to Adele, "I never meant to threaten anybody!!!" What frightened Margaret was the number of reviewers who hated Stacey: "this is so astonishing. To see these reviews (all by middle-aged males who might have wives like Stacey, I think—I really do believe this) which indicate that whatever a woman like that thinks, they DO NOT WANT TO KNOW.... One cannot help but feel that the novel in some ways is being judged on grounds other than literary."

That spring, she had both the pleasure and the pain of having Al and Eurithe Purdy as house guests for a month. While the Purdys were in Greece, Eurithe had become ill. Soon afterwards they travelled to London, where Margaret recommended a doctor. After visiting the couple one day in their small, cramped room in Earl's Court, she insisted they stay with her at Elmcot, assuring the Purdys her back bedroom was the perfect setting in which Eurithe could recuperate. Al, an inveterate collector of Canadian imprints, found many bargains in the local bookshops and became the wonder of the Penn post office because no one before had ever mailed so many parcels anywhere. Margaret got precious little work done, but she did have the chance to talk books with Al. In particular, she found someone sympathetic to her anger with the reviewers of *The Fire-Dwellers.* Despite her affection for the Purdys, they exasperated Margaret, who moaned about the heating bills and the large cans of beer with which Al filled her small fridge.

While the Purdys were with her, Margaret had a new crisis on her hands. In fact, on May 23, six days after writing to Gordon about the hostile notices *The Fire-Dwellers* had attracted, she wrote him another letter, one which explained the other "blow" which she had suffered:

> Personal troubles. No doubt too soon to begin to mention the subject, but my natural inclination is not to keep things in (which is why I have found past 2 years so hard). Jack (in Swaziland) thinks now he may have found a woman with whom he really can relate—she sounds so goddamn nice and so right for him, that I am really PRAYING it works out. Gordon, I do value him so much and care about him, but cannot be the kind of wife I know he needs. And at this point, I feel it is idiotic for both of us to go on torturing ourselves because we are not different people. I won't ever cease to care about him or to be concerned about him, nor he about me—that almost goes without saying. But—Gord, I am just *not* a suitable wife. I really have tried. But it does not work. I really *do* want him to be happy, but I can't make him so. I am what I have to be, and I just cannot force myself to be otherwise. I do so very much hope he will go through with it, and have the courage to begin again—it isn't easy. But he is a courageous person, so I do hope that it will come to pass.

For Jack, Margaret's solution to their problems was not his. By his definition of matrimony, he did not have a marriage—and he obviously did not see the prospect of any genuine renewal in his relationship with Margaret. In recently divorced Esther Christiansen, Danish by birth and a cartographer by profession, Jack, at fifty-three, discovered a woman who shared many of his ideals about companionship and intimacy. He informed his wife it was time to part ways.

In her letter, Margaret completely ignores issues of major significance to her. She tries to see things too much from Jack's perspective. For the past year, she had been convinced her relationship with Jack was about to be renewed, not killed. She was ready to make a new commitment to her marriage (or imagined she was about to). Completely downplayed in the letter to Gordon is her sense of outrage, betrayal and abandonment. Years later, in her autobiography, when she mentions the attempts on her and Jack's part to reconcile, the matter is treated with great vagueness, as if it had been a minor issue, one not worthy of spending much time on. Years later, she told a friend that Jack had been so wounded by her leaving him that it was necessary for them to get back together so that he could leave her.

Even to close friends, she could not talk openly about the devastation which overwhelmed her that spring. To Adele Wiseman and Al Purdy, she gave the same information. In her letter to Purdy, in an attempt to disguise from him (and herself) her anguish, she glides over and even trivializes the situation:

> I'm in better shape than I was, having now figured out why J's news affected me so oddly. It took me a long time when I first came to England to build up a self-image of a person who was a professional writer, not a housewife, and who could (wonder of wonders) actually cope with things like getting a mortgage and earning a living etc. Then when we decided to try again, I had to try all over again to return to self-image of housewife, while actually the outer and inner were in considerable conflict (probably not a bad thing at the time, as I was writing the F-D). Then, last week, another psychic change necessary. Back to self-image of professional writer etc etc. Actually, that being, as they say, the Real Me. Which I always knew. All the other bit was suppression suppression all the way, which worked not too well, as you undoubtedly know. I see now that I have to stick with this present concept of myself, as it is simply folly to try to pretend to be something you're not.... So whether or not he decides to go through with it, as far as I am concerned, I will have to go through with it now. This decision fills me with panic and alarm, but it is 100% necessary....

INSTANT ANALYSIS
CONSULT GYPSY ROSE MARGARET
MIND-EXPANDING AND HEAD-SHRINKING

> Also, of course, one does feel slight terror at thought of advancing age etc and me without a penny of insurance and no intention of getting any. And can I keep on writing and earning money? Well, one has to have some faith.

Every claim made by Margaret in this letter is true, but these are rationalizations, attempts to come to terms with an awful emotional impasse by not dealing directly with the accompanying feelings of frustration and rage. In effect, she says the "Real Me" is the writing self which must live alone, any other alternative being a form of repression. One part of Margaret told her that she deserved what happened to her, another urged her to deny a significant portion of her feelings because this was the only way to exert control over a tragic situation.

That summer, Margaret also had to deal with some serious objections to *A Bird in the House* raised by Judith Jones, her editor at Knopf since the time of the publication of *A Jest of God*. Trim, sparrowlike Judith, who had worked for Doubleday and Dutton in Paris, was hired by Blanche Knopf in 1957 to be editor of the translations of French writers such as Camus and Sartre. By the time she took over as Margaret's editor, her other writers included John Updike and Anne Tyler. She liked "off-the-wall" experimental writers as long as their narratives were coherent. In 1969, she had to deal with the additional fact that Robert Gottlieb, who by now had assumed most of Alfred Knopf's responsibilities, was not a particularly great admirer of Margaret's work. Judith was thus in the uncomfortable position of having to plead Margaret's case and of wishing to do everything in her power to make her work accessible to as large a reading public as possible.

In her letter to Margaret that May, Judith criticized "the disturbing ... overlapping of the material" and the "bits of information given as though not introduced before that get in the way of its being read as a continuous thing, a semi-novel, semi-memoir." Judith was also of the opinion the "stories" should be converted into "chapters" that would provide "in chronological sequence a series of different views of one thing, centring on different moments and on different people, but all circling in on Vanessa and moving towards that really lovely postscript-view from the vantage point of twenty years later, which ties the whole book together and puts it into perspective." She did not like the title—she wanted one more suggestive of the Connors and the MacLeods; she also wanted the "rounding-out" of each narrative to be eliminated on the grounds that this was a technique appropriate to individual stories, not collected stories.

On May 20, Margaret responded in an extremely conciliatory manner: "Upon further reflection, I think you are quite right. It will make a stronger whole, if some of the repetitive material is taken out and we try to unify the stories, or as you say, de-story them to some extent. I am naturally a little nervous about my ability to do this, but I think it will be wise to try." Three days later, Margaret, having regained her original confidence in her material, wrote Judith a letter rejecting her earlier compromising stand: "I'm terribly sorry about my apparent reversal of opinion—it is just that I could so well see what you meant, but upon further consideration, I don't feel I can change the basic structure of the collection ... it just seems to me that these stories came in the form they did, and I believe this is the only form they can take.... I *know* volumes of stories don't sell well. I know all these stories are so connected as to form almost one story ... But—I'm afraid the basic fabric has been woven, and I'm not really willing to try to alter its patterns."

Alan Maclean fully supported Margaret's resolve, although he had earlier expressed similar reservations to her. On May 29, Judith wrote a conciliatory letter to Margaret in which, although she reiterated many of her earlier objections, she spoke of the issues from the author's point of view: "I have an awful feeling that I overstated the case, that I made it seem as if there were much more of an operation to be performed than I intended. The last thing in the world I would ever want to do is to try to force something into something that it is not."

After receiving this letter, Margaret complained to her agent, John Cushman, about the changes that were being imposed upon her. In

June, Judith wrote again to apologize for having upset her and to state categorically her admiration for the stories: "John Cushman and I have just had a long discussion about your letter to him and although I know he has phoned you to reassure you, let [me] try to put your mind at rest on two points. I don't think you are hopelessly neurotic in your vacillations about all this. I respect your integrity about it and can understand perfectly well how you can see my argument.... and at the same time have second thoughts about the advisability of altering the stories so that they become something you had not intended them to be." She did sound a warning, however: "We will not be able to promote the book in quite the same way and, probably, as a result, we won't get as good an audience for it." (Judith offered Cushman a $2,500 advance instead of the $4,000 which she and Gottlieb had earlier talked about between themselves.)

In an internal memorandum to Gottlieb, Judith, who was confused about Margaret's behaviour, made some crucial points: "So, except for mending repetitions, we're right back where we started. But she seems to have let herself get very upset about the whole thing, particularly about her own neurotic behavior, and the only thing I could do was to reassure John that of course we'll publish and to write her a comforting letter. I'm sorry because we won't have as strong a book, but you can only push someone like Margaret so far without doing real damage."

In June 1969, Judith Jones obviously did not know how far Margaret Laurence had been pushed in her personal life. She was particularly annoyed by Margaret's wavering stand and by the fact she attempted to use her agent in order to win a battle that she, as editor, was quite content to let the writer win. What Judith called "neurotic" was Margaret's incredible "indecisiveness," her inability at times to make firm resolutions about her marriage and even her books.

Margaret also had a tendency to hear what she wanted to hear. A good example of this can be found in her description of the children's reaction to the news of the impending divorce: "worked myself into state of semi-collapse, anticipating all kinds of terrible reactions. Joc just grinned when I started my speech to her, and said very gently 'It's okay—I know what you're trying to say.' Dave more uncertain and very hard to know how he is taking it." Her account sounds plausible, but it is not exactly what Jocelyn and David remember. For a long time, they had been victims of the topsy-turvy state of their parents' marriage. They wanted a resolution to be imposed on the fraught, confusing situation. When Margaret informed them of the impending divorce, a very relieved and yet annoyed Jocelyn told her: "We're glad you guys have decided to do something at last." The children wanted their mother's histrionics about her failed marriage to disappear.

When discussing this turning point with Adele, she sought to assure her friend everything would turn out all right, but the letter seems also to be a missive to herself, as if offering herself a very tenuous form of encouragement:

> It is quite simple when adultery is the grounds, and I expect Esther will agree to that. It is only just a question of all of us playing out our little roles for the sake of the legal rituals, to satisfy decent middle-class society—I as the injured wife is a pretty funny picture, when you think of it, but that is what the law demands... It's odd—we will remain friends, and won't cease to care about one another. The time when the relationship worked best, during these years in England, was really when we were nominally separated and considered that we were friends rather than married. As far as my temporary panic is concerned, I think now it will take a certain period of readjustment before I once again get used to thinking of myself as once and for all on my own. But it'll be okay, I know, because if there is a real me, it is the writer one, I guess, although I have strong matriarchal leanings as well.

That summer, en route to Toronto and her post as writer-in-residence at the University of Toronto, Margaret and the children travelled together to British Columbia to visit Jack's mother, to whom Margaret wanted to break the news of the impending divorce. In a letter to Al Purdy that August, she provided an extensive account of her "Freudian accident":

> It was High Noon in Victoria when I ran into a lamp post. How is that for an opener? It is also true. I guess hardly anyone would believe how I got the gorgeous black eye which I am now sporting, but I swear that the following story is God's truth. My mother-in-law was having some people in for lunch, to meet me, and of course the atmosphere being what it was, namely polite and careful but somewhat sorrowful (she just having had Jack's explanatory letter—what terrible timing, me in the bosom of his family at that moment in history!), I felt I had to be home at the right time that morn. I had promised to be back by 12.30. It was then 12.30. David and I had been to see the Undersea Gardens and got so interested we stayed too long. There was the bus—right in front of Woolworth's. The next one would be along in 20 minutes' time. I CANNOT CREATE ANY DIFFICULTIES WITH MY MAW-IN-LAW AT THIS POINT—such was my thought. I zoomed across the street, looking all of the time at the bus. There was a metal box which housed the controls of the traffic lights, and it was attached to a lamp post. When I saw it looming in front of my eyes, it was too late. KAPOWIE! There I was, my life's blood gently fountaining all over the sidewalk outside Woolworth's. A sharp blow to the eyebrow and side of the head. Within seconds, a police car drew up and hustled David and myself to St. Joseph's Emergency Ward, where a nice young doctor did a lot of fancy embroidery in black thread on my right eyebrow, while David waited in the waiting room wondering if his mum was on her way to the morgue.

The incident is recounted with real zest but missing is the sadness of the situation, in which a very distracted, nervous Margaret hurt herself quite badly. There is a haunting irony in the visit to Victoria because Margaret conducted herself as if she was Elsie's child. A touch of sibling rivalry can be seen in this action, as if she wishes to prove she is a better child to her mother-in-law than her own son is. In this situation, she wanted to retain the affection of her third mother while letting go of that woman's son.

Margaret was not looking forward to her stay in the Vile Metropolis, and she was beside herself with anguish when she said goodbye to Jocelyn and David at the airport in Montreal (Ian and Sandy Cameron, young, hippyish friends of Margaret's friend Professor Clara Thomas of York University, had agreed to look after Elm Cottage and the children in her absence). The one-hour wait for her flight to Toronto was one of the most gruesome episodes in all her remembrances, so intensely alone did she feel.

What Margaret did not speak or write about to her friends—but what was obvious to them—was the change her divorce introduced into her drinking pattern. Previously, she had been a binge drinker, one who would consume alcohol under stress and then have the wherewithal to stop. For years, she had used alcohol to escape under moments of great stress. Writing was the consistent way in which she had coped creatively with the losses she had endured as a young child—it allowed her to mother herself. She could not deal with the loss of her husband in the same way and, at this time in her life, when she was on the verge of becoming Margaret Laurence, one of the greatest and most beloved of Canadian writers, she sought the comforts of alcoholic oblivion on a daily basis. When drunk, in addition to speaking of John Simpson, she lamented her failures as a parent, her difficulties with writing, her loss of Jack, "the only man I ever loved" (the last now becoming the predominant refrain). For her, time had to have a stop, and alcohol became an increasingly necessary potion.

Margaret Laurence. 1984.

Her appearance began to change markedly. She gained a lot of weight and, as she began to fill out, she became the Margaret Laurence recognizable to most Canadians. Her beauty may have faded, but the intensity of the eyes always held the spectator's attention.

That autumn she drank heavily, and her life had a particularly eerie quality to it. She was trying to adjust to Canada whereas she had to prepare to return to England in December for the divorce. "Yes," she told Purdy, "I'll recover from the divorce bit—it is just that it hits sudden and unexpected.... Goddamn it, if only I did not react in the flesh to everything."

Later, Margaret would speak very reluctantly of the actual proceedings, which were held in Guildford. Alan Maclean telephoned a few days before and in his typically friendly and warm way informed her: "Macmillan, your publishers, do not wish you to take 15 buses and 4 trains." So a car picked up Margaret and Sandy Cameron—who had to be prepared to testify in the event the judge wanted to be reassured the children were being properly cared for—and they were driven, chauffeur and all, to Surrey. Margaret's account to Purdy of the proceedings themselves is a bit woolly:

> —so when chips are down, no way of doing it painlessly. We both know this is only way. We both want it. We both also care terribly about the other—how does one cope with that? I had to take the witness stand (and they mean stand; you don't sit; you stand there shaking like proverbial aspen leaf, at least I did.) Questions all meaningless, dreadful, without relation to people's lives. I have one advantage, Al. It has always stood me in good stead. I shake in my flesh, but my voice never shakes. I was so goddamn scared when J took the stand, because he has not had the practise I have had, public-wise, and also is not a believer in being emotional—here is this prairie man, forced to stand up and speak, and no one, not even GOD has the right to ask him to do that. But he has to do it. Maybe I've been more prepared by having to be a public person in ways I knew to be phoney. Even so, I shook like the small winds through

> the poplars. And yet it was tougher for him, even tho he had his woman to go to, to hold his hand, to marry (odd word) as soon as possible, and so on. I did not see her—she was there, but I did not see her. I will, I guess, but not just yet.

To Adele, she added an important detail: "focussed my mind on Hagar."

As she left the chambers, Sandy overheard Margaret's solicitor offering comfort: "Well, Mrs. Laurence, that wasn't so bad, was it?" She shot back: "Yes, it was!" Margaret was referring to the fact that the magistrate had called her an "unnatural mother," who had neglected her children by returning to the wilds of Canada. Jack had had to defend his about-to-be-ex-wife of the charge of being an unfit parent.

If Margaret was cryptic about the court proceedings, she was forever silent about another matter. To Adele, she confessed: "I took I don't know (I really don't know—that is probably frightening) how many tranquillizers and slept for 2 days almost unbroken. Then rose and resumed life." She omitted to tell Adele that on the very evening of that black day, she took the pills in a locked bathroom at Elmcot and then yelled out she was going to kill herself. Ian, Sandy and the children all gathered outside the locked room, not knowing what Margaret had ingested. They pleaded with her to unlock the door, which she was at first unwilling to do. Finally, she listened to their pleas when they threatened to either call the police or break the door down. When she emerged and they questioned her about what she had taken, it was obvious she had taken an unusually large number of tranquillizers. At that point, she retired to her room and the long sleep of two days.

PART THREE

MARGARET LAURENCE

"How far could anyone see into the river? Not far. Near shore, in the shallows, the water was clear, and there were the clean and broken clamshells of creatures now dead, and the wavering of the underwater weed-forests, and the flicker of small live fishes, and the undulating lines of gold as the sand ripples received the sun. Only slightly further out, the water deepened and kept its light from sight."

The Diviners

16

The Uncharted Sea (1969-1972)

By 1969, Margaret Laurence was a celebrity in Canada. In retrospect, this is surprising. She was a serious woman writer who had lived in England for almost a decade, returning to her native land only on brief visits. Five circumstances help to explain her fame. There was the extraordinary teamwork of her three publishers (McClelland & Stewart, Macmillan and Knopf) in promoting her work throughout the entire English-speaking world. In this regard, Jack McClelland's relentless, creative gift for publicity was the most vital element holding this consortium together. Second, there was a great deal of interest in her within the Canadian academy, exemplified in Clara Thomas's ground-breaking work on Margaret—the first full-length book devoted to her—published by McClelland & Stewart in 1969. Third, readers in Canada, their interest in her aroused by McClelland & Stewart, responded with great enthusiasm and devotion. They were the real judges of her standing in the marketplace, since, throughout her entire writing career, she was not taken up in any great way by reviewers in Canada (William French of *The Globe and Mail* was the exception), who often treated her dismissively. Although Canada had produced major women writers before her—Sara Jeannette Duncan,

/ Maud Montgomery and Ethel Wilson—Margaret was the first "big-time" professional woman writer and, in some ways, an affront to the then predominantly male literary establishment. Fourth, other Canadian writers not only recognized her extraordinary gifts but also realized that her success might lead them in similar directions. Her winning of the Governor General's Award obviously contributed to her "star" status in the eyes of other writers. Fifth, although she was an exceedingly shy person, her warmth and kindness were evident in any encounters she had with the public.

There was also something about her that was "ordinary" in the most positive sense of that word. Although much of her existence was consumed by the desire to write, she had an incredible sense of the fabric of daily life and this facility was evident in any conversation with her. In Margaret Laurence the writer and the person, readers saw many of their own deepest concerns mirrored. She was much beloved because she reflected and expressed the hopes and fears of Canadians from all strata of society.

Universality is often used as a criterion in talking about great writers. Of all Canadian writers, Margaret Laurence understood most intuitively the dilemmas of being Canadian—of being torn apart by language issues, of being part of a band of old and recent immigrants uneasily assimilated together, of being attached to a nation that wanted its own identity apart from the United States and Europe, of being connected to a culture which wanted to be part of the North American continent and yet had to be distinctly different.

Margaret Laurence was also a fundamentally decent person, a writer who challenged Canadians to think the best of each other and to conduct themselves likewise. For women readers, especially, she showed how the appropriation of power by women could be conducted according to principles of enlightened self-interest.

Her kindness, generosity and good heart are legendary. When Ken Roberts, a young writer she had encouraged, was leaving Ontario to take up a post in Alberta, he came to say goodbye to Margaret, who burst into copious tears. He asked her why she was so emotional. She told him that, although she recognized twentieth-century man was a creature trained not to form close attachments, she had never been able to get used to losing close friends, even though death and separation had been part of her life since childhood. This side of her can be seen in the letter of condolence she sent to Michelle Tisseyre, the translator of her novels into French, when her two-year-old daughter died.

> You will understand and forgive the clumsiness of my words. In the face of the deepest tragedy that can befall a human being, the loss of a child, there are no words. It is that possibility of loss that every loving parent dwells with, from the moment of a child's birth, right through until a child becomes an adult and even after that, for always. There is a profound sense in which nobody can understand your pain unless they have felt it in their own flesh and heart. And yet, because I have feared so often for my two children, and have so very often rejoiced simply in their being, and have prayed for them only that they may survive ... there is also a way in which I know your pain. I know also the terrible and almost, at the time, unbelievable finality of loss, for my mother died when I was four years old and my father when I was ten. Pain is not qualitative, and yet I know in the deepest parts of my spirit that the loss of a child is the worst.

This letter is profoundly moving. Margaret fully understands her words cannot remedy the grief felt by a grieving parent, but knowing, as deeply as she did, her own worst fears and tragic losses, she reaches out to connect to Michelle's sorrow.

Margaret Laurence the celebrity also had a wonderful sense of fun and could even be mischievous. In 1978, when she attended the Canadian Studies conference in Calgary, she was thrilled to meet Manitoba-born writer Gabrielle Roy for the first time. During a dinner at which the two women were seated together, a young man burst into the restaurant and strode determinedly towards their table, managing, in the process, to bump into Roy. Seeing how agitated the young man was,

Margaret suggested he and she have a brief conversation away from the table. During their tête-à-tête, the young man assured her that she and Gabrielle Roy were the greatest writers Canada had ever produced. With a malicious gleam in her eye, she interrupted him: "That was Gabrielle you just crashed into."

There is another crucial aspect to the legendary Margaret Laurence: her chronic shyness at public events. She was not merely nervous. Her hands would shake badly; later, she would find it difficult to control the quaver in her voice. Her close friend, Malcolm Ross—who knew her both as Peggy Wemyss and Margaret Laurence—felt that not only her habitual fear of being seen in public but also her inability to say no and her corresponding generosity to all manner of causes and writers might have come in part from her sense she was undeserving or unworthy of the success she had obtained. In particular, he felt, her celebrated generosity might have been an act of penance, a way of making up for the fame (she felt) she had somehow unworthily garnered. There is a great deal of truth in this observation. She was a powerful person, but she was a powerful person who was often out of touch with—or suspicious of—her own remarkable strengths. Margaret never tried to create a public image, but she was quite content to appear to be what she was not: an ordinary middle-class woman who just happened to have created Hagar, Rachel and Stacey.

A word that came into Margaret's vocabulary with increasing frequency was "tribe," a term she uses to describe fellow writers, especially Canadian writers. The word's obvious communal import was significant to her—writers had to stick together—but so was the word's association with primitive groups: writers were tribal in that they did not conform to society's regimented expectations and were therefore "wild." In her dealings with young writers, her generosity of soul was evident, but she received much in return: the companionship and love of people whose talents she very much valued.

In the autumn of 1969, when she returned to Canada, many of the elements in the making of Margaret Laurence the celebrity had jelled into place. Ironically, all this happened at one of the greatest crisis points in her personal life, at the time her own pursuit of personal power had backfired. Also, she was in the very uneasy position of being an outsider in the essentially male domain of the University of Toronto's prestigious graduate residence, Massey College, founded six years before in 1963 by Robertson Davies. That September, she considered it "humorous that I am the first woman ever to ever have an office there. Robertson Davies, the Master (!) of Massey, said, 'Don't believe the myths you hear about this college—you are WELCOME.'" Soon, she was taking great enjoyment in a perk provided by her new job: "I did one SENSATIONAL thing the other day—I dictated letters to a secretary! A new experience, and one which I took to immediately. What luxury!"

In 1969, The University of Toronto, like many North American campuses, was a hotbed of student protest. In response, Margaret thought of barricading herself in her office or putting up a large sign: "LEAVE ME ALONE: I WALK TO A DIFFERENT DRUM." She was delighted to learn from Phyllis Grosskurth, a member of the writer-in-residence committee, that she was not expected to do too much. And then there was the student, one Mr. Parker, who showed up at her door. When she started to quiz him about his writing, he informed her he was an engineering student. "Well, why did you come to see me?" He explained that he lived at Devonshire Place—just opposite Massey—and wondered if she would treat them to a "talk session" one night. Confused, Margaret responded: "Why, sure ... that is ... well ... um ... er ... I guess so ... I mean, are they interested in talking about writing?" It was the turn of Mr. Parker to be surprised and confused: "Oh, no, there's lots of women in your books, and the guys want to talk about women." Another male visitor, this one middle-aged, spooked her when, in response to her advice to "Listen to how people talk if you're going to write fiction," he replied: "I don't very often hear people talking." She then arranged for her next-door neighbour, Phil, to come to her office if summoned by a certain code-phrase on the phone. "This cloak-and-dagger stuff was silly, no doubt, but it was a reassurance I needed."

Although Margaret had asked a number of people about the seemingly mysterious duties of a writer-in-residence before she arrived at the University of Toronto, she soon settled into a routine of reading the work of would-be writers and commenting on it. As she told Al Purdy, "the kids who will be real writers don't need me or you or any bloody person; they will survive." However, with the really promising young writers—those who wanted and could cope with real criticism, she was "hard as nails and [tore] their work apart." One of her most promising students was twenty-seven-year-old Don Bailey, who had recently been released from Warkworth Penitentiary where he had served nine years for armed robbery. To a mutual friend—Jane Rule—she spoke not only of the work she was doing with him but also of her own vantage point as a writer of fiction: "He has begun to make himself more vulnerable in the writing, and that is necessary, as you know. I don't think it matters a damn whether the fiction is partly autobiographical or not—it is still necessary to lay one's life on the line more than one really feels inclined to do." Once, in the event the young man was tempted to falter in his vocation, she repeated some words of wisdom: "as Jack McClelland always says to me—'Back to your typewriter, slob!'"

One of Don Bailey's memories was of Margaret's office at Massey College, where she "created a small fortress area in one corner of the room. She had moved her desk as close to the wall as possible and it was stacked with numerous piles of manuscripts through which she could peek and not be observed. But I knew that she was there because of the cloud of smoke." In Bailey's recollections of his conversations with her, one can hear the bravado she sometimes assumed with male friends. (There is a substantial difference in tone between Margaret's letters to men and women; this distinction is particularly obvious when one compares her letters to Al Purdy to those to Adele Wiseman when she is dealing with an identical topic. With Adele, she is usually brutally frank, but she often adds a dash of swagger when relating the same information to Purdy.) Upon being introduced to her, he somewhat awkwardly began:

"I'm ... honoured. I can't tell you..." This declaration was quickly interrupted: "Can the honour bullshit.... We're just two writers, lucky to meet each other. All day I get these people who parade through my office. They want to be writers ... bless their souls, the poor buggers. But they ain't. And I doubt that any of them'll even get close." (Among those who did were Gary Geddes, Dennis Lee and Frank Paci.)

That autumn, Margaret, who had sprained her ankle, was in no mood for the CBC television crew which arrived to film her in real-life situations. She told the CBC, "I damn well wasn't going to do much walking." But she soon got into the swing of things: "and there we were, with some of the Massey fellows casually (about as casual and spontaneous as the Coronation) strolling across the courtyard and greeting me like the old Fellow of Massey which I am, ho, ho." She gave a talk to the "little old ladies" of the Canadian Literature Society, who thought Canadian poetry began and ended with Bliss Carman and that "novels were nicer fifty years ago." She chortled when the woman introducing her stated: "Mrs. Laurence has 2 children at present." Earlier, in September, the sometimes publicity-shy writer agreed to appear on a TV panel show called "Man at the Centre" in the company of two psychologists and an anthropologist: "The talk was mainly about personal relationships in an urban situation—love in the concrete jungle, as it were. Somewhat to my surprise, I quite enjoyed doing it and found I was not nervous in the slightest."

In November, however, she shook like a leaf in a storm and felt like a lamb being led to the slaughter when she gave a public lecture as part of her duties as writer-in-residence. Afterwards, she was a nervous wreck, one who consumed a great deal of Scotch. That February, she was moved by Hugh MacLennan's appearance at a lecture she gave at McGill. She was too shy to say very much but wrote him immediately upon her return to Toronto: "I really wanted to tell you, that day, that I feel very deeply that I owe you a debt of gratitude as a novelist. It was really only through your novels, and those of Ethel Wilson, and Sinclair Ross, and very few others, that I came to an understanding of the simple fact that novels could be written *here* out of one's own background, and that in fact this was the only true soil for me to write out of. I would think all novelists of my generation, and those younger than I, must feel the same toward you."

The august halls of Massey College provided another amusing interlude when Margaret ran into Earle Birney accompanied by an exceedingly young woman. When living in Vancouver, she had known Earle slightly but thought him a kind and generous person, the very opposite of the stuffy people who comprised most of the literary community there. She was also aware of Earle's reputation as a womanizer. In an attempt to make appropriate chit-chat with the "young chick," she complimented her on her fun-fur coat. Then, unthinkingly, she added: "My daughter would love one like that." Later, she was ashamed of herself: "it occurs to me how awful it must've sounded. Like, if the kid is young enough to be *my* daughter, where does that leave Earle? I could've bitten my tongue out, but there—I didn't mean to be mean, and intentions must count for something."

But Margaret had to do some fast talking herself when her appearance caused some questions to be raised by some of the fellows: "Came back today with scarred and bleeding chin and had to say—oh, a skin condition. Thought of saying I grazed it on a bearded man, which, being the truth, nobody would've believed, but in the end didn't have the nerve to try that line. Don't worry—was an old friend, who mostly lives in Toronto, so this was the New Year surprise. I am vulnerable, sure, at the moment, but not so vulnerable as to go berserk with a stranger on the Earls Court Rd or somewhere." A few days later, she offered Al Purdy some further observations on the aftermath of this brief liaison: "Learned that the brief encounter with someone who bores the hell out of you in the morn is not for me. Much as I am in favour of sex, I also like to talk and I feel very strange and disoriented with someone I can't talk to at all. But one has to watch this pattern thing—I think possibly everyone's tendency is to keep on repeating the patterns of one's life over and over, and I think this is one reason I'm not really keen about the idea of ever marrying again—would probably end up with someone exactly like J. No, dammit, I wouldn't!"

Gradually, she settled into Massey College, although Toronto remained the V.M. She certainly did not enjoy the house she moved into on Glencairn Avenue that autumn: "The owners are tiny little people about 4 feet tall or so it seems, and both of them are excessively nervous and agitated about leaving their priceless 16th-century Italian furniture in the care of someone else, and they keep phoning and pleading with me to come over, so I do, and we have yet another conducted tour through the house, with both of them pouring thousands of little details into my ear, and me nodding and saying yes yes." One great pleasure during this stay was the availability in Toronto of Adele Wiseman, her husband, Dmitry Stone, and their young daughter, Tamara, born in June 1969. Even though they lived nearby, Margaret and Adele continued their habit of writing letters. In those days, she did not like speaking on the phone ("a deadly instrument"), and Adele did not like to speak about personal matters within earshot of her husband's two sons from a previous marriage.

For years, Margaret had been hinting at a permanent return to her native land. Even before the calamity of 1969, she had a very precise idea of why returning to Canada was crucial. There were "2 reasons—a) if I don't, I can't go on writing, because I shall have forgotten how the voices sound; b) I feel at this point in life a strong desire to lessen my own isolation and to take some part in the general aspect of Canadian writing." Her divorce that December may have been the direct impetus behind her decision to purchase some land in Canada. Perhaps the acquisition of land was her way of clearing the slate, of doing something for herself that would give her pleasure and of giving herself her own space separate from everyone else.

Margaret Laurence knew that she was a writer whose audience was largely Canadian. Despite the best efforts of both Alan Maclean in England and Alfred Knopf in the United States, Margaret Laurence never achieved a substantial international reputation, one on a par with the fame later accorded Margaret Atwood and Alice Munro. Perhaps the time was not ripe for a Canadian writer to achieve international acclaim. Moreover, Margaret Laurence was a writer whose vision was tied to the landscapes of Manitoba, British Columbia and Ontario. Her stories are universal ones, but they do not detach easily from the locales they so evocatively depict. She did gain some excellent notices; for example, in the United States, Granville Hicks in the *Saturday Review* praised the fine craftsmanship of *The Stone Angel* and Honor Tracy, in a review in the *New Republic*, marvelled at the book's exactitude in giving the reader "a portrait of a remarkable character and at the same time the picture of old age itself." Similar, favourable reviews can be found in the American press of *A Jest of God*. Tracy was unstinting in lauding *The Fire-Dwellers* in the *New York Times Book Review*: the "excellent writing is an exhilaration in itself: otherwise *The Fire-Dwellers* would leave many of us in pretty low spirits." Ultimately, this was a book which created an "Everywoman of today." Ironically, Margaret's greatest success in being brought to the attention of the large American market was in Paul Newman's sensitive film adaptation of *A Jest of God*, *Rachel, Rachel*, in which Manawaka becomes a New England town.

In 1969, she was not ready to abandon Elmcot, so she toyed instead with the idea of purchasing a cottage or summer home to which she could return for two or three months each year. Her first impulse was to buy near the Purdys in Ameliasburg. She fell in love with the region but quickly had second thoughts when she realized she would be two hundred miles from Toronto and a long distance away from her friends there. "Maybe," she told Al, "I am going to have to settle for something not so beautiful but more accessible." That was on October 14. On November 5, a little more than three weeks later, came the "big news":

> I have bought a cedar shack and lot on the Otonabee river! Much needs to be done to cottage, but it is liveable about 8 months per year as it stands now. Want to do all sorts of things to it, but will see how finances stand in spring. There are some other cottages, and my lot is only 76 feet of river front, but if I'm there alone, I don't think I really want no neighbours.... Three small bedrooms (room

> for my friends and kids); huge front window going up to roof, with view of the river—trees etc; no building likely on other side of river, as it is low-lying ground; permanent farmer living about 300 yards up the hill, and he goes to Peterborough every day with the milk, so charming lady like me might con a lift; only 5 miles from Peterborough, so taxi would cost about four bucks, which would not be at all bad.

One of the chief joys of her land acquisition—seven miles south of Peterborough—was that it allowed her to buy a slew of items from one of her favourite pieces of reading matter—Eaton's mail-order catalogue: "Wow! What reading! I have ordered everything for my cottage from it, and get home every night to find lovely parcels to open, like Christmas, and now I'm going to have to rent a small truck to get all the stuff from Toronto to my shack." Two crucial elements in the cottage's interior decoration were the posters of two of her great heroes, Louis Riel and Norman Bethune. Many of her friends stayed at the cottage. One of the most wonderful moments was the evening Alice Munro visited. The two played some music, drank a little, and then spontaneously got up to dance, their bodies swaying to the rhythms that filled the room.

The cottage also inspired Margaret's last novel. As Margaret sat at her workspace, a large table by the huge window, she could see the Otonabee River "flowing" in two directions. She described this scene in the opening of *The Diviners*: "The river flowed both ways." An early glimpse of one of the central elements in the construction of her next novel can be glimpsed in an aside to Jack McClelland that January: "I had long passionate conversations on the phone with the well-digger, as I had been told terrible and alarming tales of other people's experiences with well-diggers. At this point, my relationship with the well-digger is far from happy—he thinks I'm not going to pay him for the work he does, and I think he's going to go down 20 feet and charge me for 500 feet." When he telephoned to tell her that he had found water, she was amazed he did not have to go more than fifty feet down: "Lord, woman," he shot back, "you got enough water there for haffa Toronto."

That year in Canada, Margaret became more and more aware of her place in the Canadian literary community, a place she had once been content to ignore: "So Canada is parochial in some ways," she told McClelland. "I hate the infighting that goes on in so-called literary circles; it's too enclosed and all that—but goddamn it, it's my home and my people. I have lived away too long. And yet when I think of how I felt in Vancouver those years ago—I felt as tho I were totally isolated (I didn't know any writers there then; how odd that seems now). I went to England partly in order to feel less isolated, and in a sense I did what I wanted to do and I think it was the best possible thing that could've happened. But as you know, I have really wanted to come back here for some time now. I'm gradually manipulating myself into the position of being able to come back." In this context, "coming back" does not mean simply a physical return to a point of origin—it refers to seeing oneself as a part of a community.

Before, Al Purdy, Adele Wiseman, Jack McClelland and Jane Rule had been Margaret's principal contacts in the Canadian literary scene. From 1969 onwards, the references to other Canadian writers in her letters increase at a quick pace. This sojourn in Canada—even though she was settling there only on a part-time basis—forced her to relate to her contemporaries in a new way. Nevertheless, for a long time, she was extremely careful not to take sides publicly in any dispute. Indeed, in 1969-70, she could, in large measure, take an almost voyeuristic pleasure in seeing other people expose themselves.

Margaret Atwood's opposition to the flamboyantly heterosexual poet Irving Layton's rampant sexism provided great amusement: too bad she "takes Irving seriously; I don't blame her, actually, as I'd probably do the same, but I think it's a mistake, nonetheless. If he ever says to me that women novelists are only good for fucking, I will respond thus ... 'It well may be that some male poets are good only for poetry ... shall we adjourn to your hotel room and see?' Well, no, I guess that would be hitting below the belt, well-aimed ... who could fail to be impotent under such circumstances?" When she met Irving at York University, she informed him that when living in Hampstead, she had taken offence at his line: "The orgasmless women of Hampstead." After they debated this issue for some time, they discovered they were talking at cross purposes: "He had meant Hampstead Montreal and I naturally had thought he meant Hampstead London England."

Margaret had known and liked Mordecai Richler socially in England; she also admired his writing "a hell of a lot, *except* when he begins sounding off about Canada, and then I think he is years out of date and I never agreed with him anyway." For her, Barry Callaghan remained the incarnate male enemy: "Callaghan Fils, whom, as you know, I love rather less than I would love an attack of bubonic plague. He *is* oriented to New York, but what the clod doesn't see is that he is trying to gain acceptance in a Club which will always despise him—too bad he wants it so much, or thinks it valuable." A few years later, she would become one of Rudy Wiebe's greatest admirers, but in 1971 she spent a day "in a state of great fragility, reading improving things like Rudy Wiebe's very Christian novel, *First and Vital Candle*, and thinking what a much nicer person Rudy is than I am. Not as good a writer, tho."

Without doubt, the writer who most intrigued—and frightened—Margaret Laurence was Margaret Atwood, one of the young Canadian writers—others included Myrna Kostash and Silver Donald Cameron—who had made Elmcot the "Unofficial Canada House" and Margaret herself the "Low Commissioner." When necessary, she could be brutally honest with fledgling writers: "Maybe fiction isn't for you."

In January 1970, she told Purdy: "Did I mention I'd read M. Atwood's novel THE EDIBLE WOMAN? Quite good, but much more superficial than her poetry, I thought. I think she is a poet." This brief sentence encapsulates all her feelings about the woman novelist who was—and remained—her biggest rival. The same sentiment is repeated in a letter of November 1971 to Purdy: "I admire her poetry more than I can say. I also love her as a human, and somehow, once we really talked, did not feel her frightening, as I thought I might. Instead, I felt I could level with her. And probably did." Residual admiration and fear of Atwood can be seen in this aside in a letter to Ernest Buckler of November 1974: "I was talking, in my fiction, about survivors, long before Peggy [Margaret] Atwood said this was one main theme of Canadian fiction." Her tone in a letter to Margaret Atwood of December 1972 was quite different: "By now you will have had my letter, full of astound, re: SURVIVAL."

There was security in keeping Atwood in a niche—one which did not allow her the opportunity to compete with Margaret. But the two Margarets often shared similar sentiments, as can be seen in Margaret Laurence's letter to Margaret Atwood in April 1973: "I am really fed up with Mordecai's moaning about the awfulness of Canadian writing. Maybe we need a devil's advocate, but it would be nice if he admitted that a sizeable number of good books do come out in Canada each year now. You know, though, Peggy, I do not believe he reads Canadian books—I really don't. I would really like to know how many Canadian novels and books of poetry he has read in the past year—I bet it would be about two. Trouble is, at this point, he's made a side-profession of knocking Canada, and it's become a habit. Guess it wouldn't annoy me so much if he weren't a good writer!" Missing from this account of Mordecai is Margaret's reliance on him. On a number of occasions during the Elmcot years—"pissed out of her mind"—she would phone him in the middle of the night to talk about her loneliness and sense of desolation.

Towards the end of her stay at the University of Toronto, Margaret had to have her head measured for the mortarboard required for her to be properly attired to receive her first honorary degree—from McMaster University—in the spring of 1970. This was an event which she treated with great playfulness:

> Guess what? McMaster wants to know my head size, for academic hat. HEAD SIZE? ACADEMIC HAT? Good grief! Can you see me in mortar-board? The audience will be in fits of uncontrollable laughter. I thought of replying that HEAD SIZE sometimes shrunken, sometimes swollen, depending on mood. But contented myself

> with measuring skull and telling them I wasn't sure quite where to measure (eyebrows? forehead? etc) so had done it around the place where I would wear a headband if I were an Indian in a western movie. Hope they don't think I'm being flippant, because I am.

All in all, this extended visit to Canada made her feel connected to her native land, but ultimately she did not really like the duties of a writer-in-residence, as she realized in February 1970: "I enjoy talking to the kids, although I think it is largely a waste of time. But I am beginning to feel lonely for the inner world, and do want to get back to writing, and there is no way I can, until I leave here. I begin to resent this, and to feel I want to take off NOW.... All this academic life, plus seeing too many people, plus not being alone enough, plus the feeling of pressure of trivial work, is not at all good. I have 2 more months to go, that's all, praise God." Nevertheless, once she had returned to England, she missed Canada: "Last weeks ... were lovely, out in shack on Otonabee river, but also more filled with events than one would have imagined possible. I always think I am about to lead the quiet country life, which always turns out about as quiet as a three-ring circus. However, I did have some time alone, to sit on my riverside deck and contemplate the wildlife, so that was good. Hope to be back next summer, God willing."

Back in England that July, everything was fine, "more or less." But Elmcot needed many repairs, so Margaret was "immersed in passionate converse with builders, painters and Rising-Damp Specialists." She asked Jack McClelland: "You don't know about Rising Damp and Dry Rot? Lucky you. Lots of things now being done to the old dump so we can keep in business awhile longer."

There were some difficulties at Elmcot to which she did not like to refer. Principally, she was disgusted by her ex-husband's dislike of the "scene" there. When Ian and Sandy Cameron allowed an unmarried couple to join them and the children, he called these people "freeloaders" and "hippies." To Al, Margaret observed: "he knows he ain't paying the bills, I am." Nevertheless, Jack did not feel he could visit Elmcot "while those people are there" since he found himself "shaking with rage" at what he observed. To another friend, she lamented: The children "see their dad sometimes, but he has kind of opted out of any relationship with them, out of bewilderment, I think." She could be dismissive of Jack Laurence, but she also found it difficult to relate to children who were fast becoming adults. When she spent part of the next summer of 1971 at the shack, she confessed she was not looking forward to returning "into the loony bin that Elmcot will be in the autumn when I arrive, the kids with enormous deep problems (Who Am I? Where Am I Going? etc) and me feeling Heavens, it is I who have handed on all those hangups to them, so what should I do?"

During her stays in Canada, she worried about the children. But a part of her did not wish to be around them—or to have to deal with teenage angst. She could be very fierce, however, when anyone criticized Jocelyn and David—or the babysitting arrangements she made. In 1970, she had reviewed Percy Janes's novel *House of Hate* for *The Globe and Mail.* In its depiction of Saul Stone, the cantankerous father, this book bears a strong resemblance to some of the themes in her own writing. Late in 1971, the peripatetic Newfoundlander boarded at Elmcot, as she told Adele that October: "He will be here until spring, likely, as he is finishing a novel. Nice guy, but has lived very solitary life for many years so there is some adjustment necessary to our somewhat chaotic lifestyle here. However, it seems to be working out okay. He works in the garden, which is a great blessing from my point of view, as I generally don't." In August 1972, Margaret, who was at the shack, received "a very disturbing letter from Percy Janes, saying Elmcot is not his scene and never has been, and he is departing mid-October.... I have to say here and now that any attack upon my house and my people makes me react like some kind of tigress. He offered to tell me, a list of things, why Elmcot is not at all his scene and never has been—am I wrong to feel somewhat saddened and hurt? Yeah, likely. I guess he just cannot find his way clear to relating to a whole lot of people who float in and out of a house, as we do. Maybe he disapproves of us for other reasons—I am known to drink too much from time to time; my kids and other young couples come in and out, and the marriage-church vows are not demanded in our house; some of my kids [and other young people at Elmcot] smoke pot—oh heavens, big deal. But I guess it is that, what else? I do feel somewhat sad when I think of Percy, but I also feel pretty angry that he should offer to tell me what is wrong with my house and my household—that, I guess, I don't need to know, from him or from anyone. I become somewhat like a tigress, when anyone attacks my fortress and my young." Since she did not really want to know what was going on in her absence, she takes the moral high ground of anger and resentment in dealing with Janes's complaint. By doing so, she does not have to be too concerned to examine her own reluctance to return to the "loony bin." (In recounting her outrage, she does not bother to mention that she herself had experimented with smoking marijuana.)

Margaret did not want to be involved on a daily basis with young people who were trying to discover their own individualities—and, who, in the process, were rebelling against her. She feared day-to-day intimacy, even with her own children. This is one of the darkest—and most oblique—sides of her character. As a child, she had endured the deaths of her birth parents and, in the process, internalized a great many negative feelings about herself. She may have felt responsible for what happened, in the way young children will blame themselves for events in which they have had no hand. She may have learned as a young child that it was better for her to be isolated from others; if she withdrew from others and into a secret world of writing, perhaps she could escape further catastrophes descending upon her.

The pattern that asserted itself in any close dealings Margaret had with her husband and children was one of retreat. At about this time, she began to lament to Jocelyn and David: "I've been a bad mother to you kids." The children, although they may have agreed in part with this assertion, would, in their turn, have to soothe her: "No, no, you're a great mother." The reassurance would then close off any possibility of a genuine discussion of her failings as a mother. Quite often, she would write notes to the children instead of confronting problems face to face—these notes were often apologetic, providing explanations for her often explosive behaviour. But she could not bear to admit, even to herself, that she did not fulfil her role as parent perfectly. In *Dance on the Earth*, Margaret continually mentions writing and parenting as the twin concerns to which she dedicated her life; she even insists parenting always took pride of place over writing.

When she returned to England in 1970, she began the process of detaching herself from Elmcot and the children in what would become preparatory steps for returning to Canada on a permanent basis. "I've decided," she told Al, "to pay off the mortgage on Elm Cottage (with my ill-gotten gains) so that in 3 years' time I can rent the place.... I'm nervous about material for future novels. Don't care in a sense, because I think something will turn up." In September 1970, she owed the Halifax Building Society £4,366 on her mortgage, but had £5,367 in investments. Since the interest earned was less than the principal paid down on the mortgage each month and was taxable, she decided, as she told Alan and Robin Maclean, to take the risk entailed in reducing her savings to a mere thousand pounds: "The only thing I stand to gain by keeping the bloody mortgage is that if I get run over by a bus tomorrow, my kids will get not only the house but also the money I have now with the Halifax as investment. So what? If I pay it off, there isn't any legal hassle if I drop dead tomorrow, and they get £4,350 less. My aim in life is *not* to leave money to my kids."

At the very same time Margaret was paying off the mortgage on Elmcot, she was unsure once again about her career as a writer of fiction. She had recently agreed to do an article for *Maclean's* and a series of light essays for the *Vancouver Sun*. But her real concern was her conviction that her new novel (if she managed to write it) would be her last: "It doesn't matter, in a sense. If only I could receive from somewhere the grace to do this one. Dunno if I will or not. Feel it is very far away at the moment, and this breaks me up every time I think of it, but maybe it will come. But I'm buggered if I'll ever write a mockup of a novel only in order to go on writing. If it isn't really there any more, at whatever point, may God give me the strength to quit without self-dramatization or malice. It'll be others' turn then."

Then, in a less heavy mood, her comic and self-ironic side would assert itself: "Feel depressed sometimes when I think this coming novel, if it ever gets written, will be my last. But there. Maybe I'm fated to end my days running some kind of lunatic hostel for young Canadian writers who need a decent meal from time to time. It's the matriarch in me." And with the "Boss" she could even turn a fraught situation into the semblance of comedy: "Have had a terrible bloody year here, with many problems re: my young, and have had to throw out 8 months' work and thought, re: the novel I was trying to do. No dice. But have begun writing again, just last week, something quite different, probably unpublishable but I do not care one damn. I want to write it; I couldn't care less if no one else is interested. I will earn my living by—ahem—book reviews, publishers' reading, and I'm a pretty good cook/cum/charlady. If need be."

In a letter that was to prove oddly prophetic, she told Jack McClelland what the next decade might offer her: "You know something? I think I want to write one more novel, and maybe 1 more kids' book (not so important) and then I want to quit being a writer. I really feel that I want to quit being a fighter, Jack, and become a coach. Not that I can teach kids how to write—it isn't like that. It's just that maybe I can do reviews, and publishers' readers' reports, and the like. But the time is rapidly approaching when I cannot any longer endure the almost impossible stresses of novel writing. Also, I feel that after I've done this one more novel, it is now really the turn of the younger writers."

The Diviners proved to be a book of "almost impossible stresses," one that called forth every bit of fighting instinct in its often beleaguered author: "I suppose the greatest thing about writing is that one can say—indeed, *must* say—what you really feel, not what you are supposed to feel." That is a good credo, as long as the writer knows what she really feels. Soon after starting her new novel, Margaret knew many things about it but could not really sort out the conflicting emotions that besieged her. This is why the form the book should take evaded her:

> Trouble is, I know in a vague way what I want to do and I know almost too many details about the characters, etc, but I don't yet see *how* to do it. I only know many ways how *not* to do it. Every form and voice I've used before are useless now. This has to be quite different, of course, because it wants to attempt something different. Form, naturally, can't be developed or thought out in the abstract, by itself, but only in connection with the characters and the whole thing, and maybe I'm beginning to see, a little, how it might work. But it is always an uncharted sea.

For the past seven years, the "fictional situation" had been in her head; her life—and that of several other major characters—had "followed a somewhat parallel line." This project unleashed her ambitious side, but she did not want to wind up with a novel nine hundred pages long. She had no interest in "detailed social realism, which now seems to me totally unviable in fiction."

If she found a solution to the problem of form, she would, she knew, uncover the right tone—and thus get the right feelings into the book. By October 1970, she simply knew she needed a radical solution, one which might be different to that she had employed in *The Fire-Dwellers* but equally experimental in challenging the conventions of novel writing. "If I don't get started soon," she told Al, "I will no doubt end up in a mental hospital."

Two months later, Margaret had a strong sense of the novel "*existing* out there in space somewhere. If only I could pierce through to it." But she had not "yet learned the new language which I feel will be necessary for this thing. Migawd, if only I could wave my magic wand!" Three months later, she had retained the "main character and dilemma" but had to discard much of the "whole original idea." That was all well and good, but she felt she had wasted eight crucial months. However, form and feeling slowly started to come together: "The [idea] I want to try is something that scares me, hence my elaborate evasions." But she was a fighter, even though she had been so low in spirits as to "feel really suicidal."

A little more than a month later, the new novel began to emerge from the shadows in which it had dwelt for a long time:

> Things are changing, maybe for the better. I seem to have begun writing again, and am still so bloody scared that it will all go away that I hardly dare mention it.... A quite different novel from the one I so carefully planned and then had to throw out. I dunno where this is going to go, except in a general way, but I don't *want* to know yet, either. I would like, if God is good, to find out as I go along. I do not think this is likely to have much appeal to anyone but myself, because the reasons I'm doing it are not valid, I suspect, for very many people. However, that is not important. Even if it is not published, I would like to set it down somehow. The one I threw out, you know, was really great as a theory; as a novel it was dead before it even began. So, who knows? All I know is that I feel better than I have since I finished *The Fire-Dwellers*, which was in 1968, and for the first time since then, I want to get up in the mornings.

As the year progressed, things began to go more smoothly, but Margaret could be overly self-critical as on September 3, when she thought what she had written so far was "shit" and asked herself: "why don't I throw it in the fire?" She was also bothered by the fact that her new heroine, Morag Gunn, was a form of herself, perhaps more so than Stacey and Vanessa had ever been. "You could make some shrewd guesses," she informed Al, "about the main character ... and you would be both right and not right. Well, we will see. The division between fiction and so-called reality in my life seems an awfully uncertain one."

By 1972, Margaret had established a routine whereby she spent a portion of each summer in Canada. *The Diviners* was thus only the second of the Manawaka novels to be composed partly in Canada. During the writing of that book, Margaret, even back in England, felt the tug of Canada, towards which she was drawn in a new, fundamentally different way.

This can be seen, for example, in her response to the separatist FLQ crisis in the autumn of 1970: "I am pretty disenchanted with Trudeau, but all the same, I felt very sorry for him having to decide which course to take. When I asked myself what I'd do in his situation, all the old ineffectual liberal in me rose to the surface, as expected. I think I probably would have gone along with the FLQ's requests and tried to get the 2 men back alive, while at the same time convinced with part of my mind that this was the wrong decision."

At a more personal level, she was discouraged by the potential failure of her financially pressed publishing house, McClelland & Stewart. To Al Purdy—never a great admirer of Jack, whose firm he nicknamed "McStew"—she was blunt: "Look, you're right about him and you know you are—I feel somewhat the same about him: there are many things about him which I don't like, and God knows I have had my difficulties with him, like every other writer he's ever published, but the fact remains that he has been until recently the *only* good publisher in Canada, the only one prepared to take any risks on new or different writers." She was relieved when Margaret Atwood phoned to tell her Jack McClelland was not pulling out. "Personally," she told Al, "I think that Jack is fed up with the stresses and strains, and in many ways would like to get out of publishing, and I can see his point." In the summer of 1971, Jack McClelland, who had received a substantial loan from the government of Ontario, had printed a poster for Margaret, complete "with a comic take-off of the Ontario coat-of-arms." It stated: "No visitors allowed between Monday and Friday. An important work is going on."

When she received word she had been elected to the Order of Canada, some of her ambivalent feelings surfaced. She would accept the honour, but she was not willing to travel to Canada in April 1972 to receive it: "Have had various hassles re: this whole idiotic bit about Companion, Order of Canada," she told Adele. Although they did not "post the pretty brooches," they were willing to arrange a private ceremony. The ceremony was held on June 27. When she called ahead to ask if she could dress informally, she was given a firm no. With considerable relish, she described how before the Governor General entered the reception room on the day of the investiture, "an aide fastened a hook on my dress so that Michener could avoid grappling with my matronly bosom." Two years later, she confessed the full extent of her mixed feelings to Ernest Buckler—who had just been elected: "it is likely a whole load of b.s." However, she did "wear the little pin with the snowflake and the maple leaf—I kind of like it, to tell you the truth. So I guess I feel ambiguous. But I feel if Orders are being passed out, a) better they should be Canadian ones, and b) better that a few people in the arts should get them."

During the writing of this book in which she had reached the nineteenth scribbler in March 1972, she came to a new understanding of what she considered feminism to be, insights which determined in part its form. When she wrote *The Fire-Dwellers*, she had constructed a brilliant commentary on the feminine mystique—of the various ways in which women are supposed to fit into a male-dominated society, a critique which complements Betty Friedan. Since she was connecting racial and political issues (through the Métis) to Morag's life in her new novel, she was attempting to think through for herself the often thorny connections between personal and political issues:

> Personally, I've always gone a long way with Women's Lib, having discovered many of the now common theories for myself many years ago. However, there is one thing that I can't go along with—the parallel between women and blacks simply is not an accurate one, because in (let us say) colonial Africa, the Africans began to know quite clearly that the colonialists were the enemy, an enemy whom they needed to expel from their country in order to repossess their own lands. With women, although our culture has indeed tended to make them 2nd class citizens, men are not the enemy—that is, men are our brothers, lovers, the fathers of our children. This makes it much more subtle and difficult, in some ways, because the efforts of women to respect and free themselves *must* be done

> without damaging men—to deball men is *not* the object of the exercise; in doing that, women will only damage themselves as well, and also their children. However, I think that in some cases, if women have been dreadfully unsure of their own selves, this can cause a kind of desperate reaction, which is mostly, in my experience, not really the fault of the individual man with whom they are related, but comes from the inside. Freedom, in the profoundest sense even in colonial situations, must ultimately be an inner thing. I think this theme has been an obsessive one, in my writing, and maybe in doing the writing I've discovered a lot about my own dilemmas. One is lucky to be a writer, I think sometimes. Whatever strength one finds, ultimately, must come from inside oneself, and in a literal sense, no one can save anyone else, although you can reach out to touch others.

The distinction between personal and political issues is not maintained in *The Diviners*, but Margaret's insistence that freedom—if it existed—was within the self was a crucial part of her system of values. She was deeply reluctant to blame others for her own failings as a woman and as a person.

As work on *The Diviners* progressed at a steady rate towards the end of 1972, she even wrote songs for some of the characters, including "Song for Piquette." According to her, that character's death "has to be the most repeated death in fiction—it is told in *The Fire-Dwellers*, *A Bird in the House*, and again in this novel." To Al Purdy, she mused: "I wonder why [this death] haunts my imagination so much?"

Piquette makes her first appearance in the story "Crying of the Loons," the version of "The Loons" first published in the *Atlantic Advocate* of March 1966. Most of the stories which comprise *A Bird in the House* have an originating point in Margaret's own life history. Although it is more difficult to document, this is also true of this narrative. The best evidence comes from an interview with Wes McAmmond, one of her primary-school teachers: "Neepawa didn't have any French or Métis. [However] there was a little girl ... who came from Sandy Bar Reserve up on the lake [Lake Manitoba, north of Langruth] and was brought there with tuberculosis of the bone or something. I remember the child used to come to school from the hospital. She was in the charge of the nurses. They looked after her and sent her to school. I think Margaret probably befriended her." In "The Loons" it is Vanessa's father, the doctor, who befriends the little girl. Fearing that Piquette will not have the opportunity to rest her leg if she is returned to her family, he asks his wife to allow Piquette to vacation with their family. That summer, Vanessa makes many unsuccessful overtures to a sullen, silently resistant Piquette. Years later, the two encounter each other at the Regal Café, where Piquette informs Vanessa she is engaged to an "'English fella ... got blond wavy hair.' ... As I mouthed the conventional phrases [of congratulation], I could only guess how great her need must have been, that she had been forced to seek the very things that she so bitterly rejected."

Earlier in the story, Piquette had been disdainful of Vanessa's fascination with the loons. "'Who gives a good goddamn?' she said. It became increasingly obvious that, as an Indian, Piquette was a dead loss." Instead of listening to the mysterious sounds of the birds in the dead of night with Piquette, Vanessa does so with her father. As the story comes to a conclusion, Vanessa recalls: "I remember how Piquette had scorned to come along, when my father and I sat there and listened to the lake birds. It seemed to me now that in some unconscious and totally unrecognised way, Piquette might have been the only one, after all, who had heard the crying of the loons." On the surface, Piquette might have wanted to assimilate but in another, more profound way she knew the sound of the birds was a lament for a world from which they were being ruthlessly eliminated in the name of progress, just as her ancestors, the Métis, had been exterminated years before.

In between these events are two deaths. In the title story in *A Bird in the House* Ewen MacLeod dies shortly after befriending Piquette. Years later when Piquette meets Vanessa MacLeod, she says: "'Listen, you wanna know something, Vanessa?... Your dad was the only person in Manawaka that ever done anything good to me.'" When she turns eighteen, Vanessa leaves town. Upon her return, her mother asks if she ever wrote her about the death of Piquette Tonnere.

> "Either her husband left her, or she left him," my mother said. "I don't know which. Anyway, she came back here with two youngsters, both only babies—they must have been born very close together. She kept house, I guess, for Lazarus [her father] and her brothers, down in the valley there, in the old Tonnere place. I used to see her on the street sometimes, but she never spoke to me. She'd put on an awful lot of weight, and she looked a mess, to tell you the truth, a real slattern, dressed any old how. She was up in court a couple of times—drunk and disorderly, of course. One Saturday night last winter, during the coldest weather, Piquette was alone in the shack with the children. The Tonneres made home brew all the time, so I've heard, and Lazarus said later she'd been drinking most of the day when he and the boys went out in the evening. They had an old woodstove there—you know the kind, with exposed pipes. The shack caught fire. Piquette didn't get out, and neither did the children."

In an extremely distorted way, some elements of Margaret's own life are reflected here, particularly her reliance on alcohol, her concern middle-age had left her no longer attractive, her loss of her husband and her worry she neglected her children. But the passage is also—and more significantly and chillingly—about the death of a mother. The horrific, painful end of Piquette's life might have been emblematic of the author's fears about herself, but she might also be connecting it to the deep wound inflicted on her as a young child. As a girl, Piquette had an external sign—the limp—of her psychological ailment; Peggy the girl had carried the interior mark of the orphan.

There is another force at work. All her life, Margaret empathized with outsiders, persons who in some ways had been deprived of their birthrights. In Africa, she had identified with the Somalis and the

Ghanaians. During the writing of *The Diviners*, she transferred those concerns to the Métis, her use of that group offering her a way to Canadianize some of the themes of her early work. (Despite her claim to the contrary, she did link the plight of the orphaned Morag to the deprivations suffered by the Métis.)

But much more than Piquette, Morag Gunn is the Margaret Laurence figure in *The Diviners*. As her work progressed on that book, she came to the realization that making Morag a writer was really her "means of getting at the ways in which our ancestors stalk through our lives, the ways we make myths of our parental figures and even of our own lives, the ways in which we see ourselves turning into ancestors and myths." Such a methodology had a psychic angle: an attempt to reach back, touch and thus reconstitute her own lost "parental figures."

17

Ambiguity Everywhere (1972-1974)

By the end of 1972, Margaret was planning to leave Elmcot, "Project Canada" now being the focus of much of her attention. This resolve took hold at the very same time she was desperately trying to make her "mess" of a novel into some sort of coherent form. It was almost as if she had to throw herself into chaos in order to rescue her new book from the same forces. When she returned to Elmcot that autumn, she saw her home in a new way:

> Good ... to see Elmcot again, although strangely sad this time, in a way, because I know I am going to have to leave it—I always knew this, but it's different when the time is nearer, and the strange thing is that I *want* to leave it; I want to be in Canada, not England, now. And yet the damn place is so beautiful and there is so much of myself here, and so much of the kids, over 10 years. I sometimes find myself feeling I can't part with it, and yet I know, I mean I *really* know, that to keep it on when both kids [will be] away from home and when I myself would much rather be living in Canada, with friends within reachable distance, would be a disaster, living in the past, and that one cannot do. I guess I look at the place with new

> eyes, wanting to see it really clearly so I will never forget it—as if I would, anyway. An odd experience.

The sentiment is especially "odd" because it seems at one level to be willed and, since it is being induced at a moment of crisis, self-defeating.

With the exception of *The Stone Angel* and *The Diviners*, Margaret Laurence's Manawaka novels had been created away from Canada; since she sensed her writing life was drawing to a close, she no longer required the strength the writer can draw from being absent from the landscape that inspires her and which can be the source of art only when one is removed from it. Moreover, in *The Diviners*, Morag lives in a cottage with just more than a passing resemblance to Margaret's cottage. In the secluded landscape of retreat, Morag recalls her past life, some of which is spent outside Canada. In this way, *The Diviners* mirrors some key events in Margaret's in the early 1970s. The new book ends in Canada, and in this instance life had to follow art. In a profound sense, writing about an exile's return aroused in Margaret the need to do the same.

The messiness of her new book worried her, but she also took great pleasure in the possibility it might turn out, "longer than *War and Peace*, although not to say, of comparable quality." She was afraid her publishers would reject the book because of its length, but she took great pleasure in yet again being a female Jacob wrestling a book into shape.

Despite a choking cough, bronchitis and a sore throat, Margaret—by the autumn of 1972—was confident she could whip her "hell of a mess" of a novel into shape. She sometimes felt bloodied, but she was unbowed. She told her friend Mary Adachi: "Do you know what I really need?... (a) a Secretary to handle all correspondence; (b) Cook-housekeeper; (c) Gardener; (d) Daily woman 2 times weekly to clean massive fortress; and (e) as in Lady Chatterley, a Gamekeeper." Since these needs could not be met, "we plod on, kid. Life may be Hell but Death is nothing; Onward is our motto."

Ultimately, fear of being rejected did not bother her, so great was her sense of her own prowess as a writer, one who could fuse seemingly disparate elements together: "narrative present; narrative past in form of refilming of events; old tales and legends told to the main character when she was young and invented by her stepfather; bits of history; plot summaries of novel; and—wait for it—Songs! Yep. I have just composed 2 long ballads, and have even got the tune for one. A dear friend [Ian Cameron] who composes songs brought his guitar over the other evening and I told him the tune, and he sang the thing, making it sound like a Real Song! I was ecstatic!" Part of Margaret's joy came from the fact she was liberated from some of her sense of the loneliness of the writer's life through her collaboration with Ian on the songs.

By January 1973, she felt she might have gone over the top in her new book, but she took pleasure in the sense of community that had been engendered: "I have, I think, got absolutely out of my head in my middle age. The damn novel is now in 2nd draft, i.e. I have finished the typescript from the 28 scribblers full of bezazz, and this was finished only 2 days ago, so tomorrow we are all (Elmcot Commune, my kids and various Can friends) going to open a bottle of champagne. However. It still needs a lot of work, general cutting of corny bits and putting things into reasonable shape and so on." By February 3, she was triumphant: "MY NOVEL IS FINISHED. NOT JUST THE SECOND DRAFT. I HAVE NOW GONE OVER IT AND DONE AS MUCH FURTHER REWRITE AS I CAN AT THE MOMENT. IT IS *DONE*!!... I am really exhausted, but damn glad to have it done, at least for now." "But now," she reminded Al, "I enter the worst stage—waiting until I hear what the publishers think of it. In my head I write terrible reviews of it."

She was also sad. Her "withdrawal symptoms" were especially awful this time since, she realized, "this is the end of a 12-year involvement with Manawaka and its inhabitants, and as the wheel comes full circle in this novel, it will be the last of those.... So I feel a bit odd, and empty, as though part of my inner dwelling place has now been removed from me." If an "inner dwelling place" has been removed, it might be necessary to find a new physical space in which to exist. Of course, a sense of community—perhaps more accurately, the hope that she would become part of a group of writers—was an added inducement to return to Canada.

Margaret's sense of community had broadened to include many more Canadian writers than ever before. For example, she confessed to Margaret Atwood her reservations about *The Diviners*, a novel still very much in progress. She had, as she put it, doubts—but not basic doubts. She knew *The Diviners* would not be the book which had been in her head, but she could be satisfied with the fact that this kind of shortfall was a dilemma faced by all writers. She realized she would be accused of being topical because she had dealt with issues such as Women, the Métis, New Pioneers, Legend, Myth, History, Fiction as History, History as Fiction. Such a charge would be rubbish: "I'm dealing with things close to my own psyche and heart, that is all."

She was also content with the fact that her novel—more than any other—showed the rich complexities of life: "Ambiguity is everywhere. But mainly, I get this sense of continuum—even in our chaos, there still seems to me to be a very real way in which the past is always the present, and the present is always both the past and the future." This book also dealt "not only with survival but freedom. By *freedom*, I do not mean any Garden of Eden, of course, which we must learn to relinquish along with our damaging innocence. My only regret (and it's an unreal one, I know, because all we can do is the best we can with what we have) is that I did not have more talent to convey the characters, to do justice them, to get them across in as real and living a way as I know them." To Jane Rule, she confessed it would be "ALL RIGHT" if *The Diviners* turned out to be her last book: "If it proves so, it won't be a tragic event; I really feel a kind of gladness at having brought that particular wheel full circle, and I am not in the least worried about what to do next." The sense of urgency had been vanquished. For a person as intense as Margaret, there was genuine relief in not feeling she had to "get it all down before I expire."

Her habitual sense of urgency was transferred to "Project Canada," an undertaking which presented a number of hurdles. The first was practical: her dubious, punishing tax status if she sold Elmcot and then left for Canada. That would make her subject to English taxes: Capital Gains (30% of sale price of house) and Emigrant (25% of all her assets). Her situation was complicated by the fact she planned to spend the 1973-1974 academic year as writer-in-residence in Canada, the first term at the University of Western Ontario, the second at Trent University.

The tax law also interfered with a cherished scheme: at the end 1973, having accrued much-needed additional cash from her job at the University of Western Ontario, she would purchase a house in or near Peterborough, not far from her cottage on the Otonabee; she would then sell Elmcot, and return permanently to Canada in 1974. In order, as she told Jane Rule, "to avoid handing over to the British government most of all I possess," she would have to modify her plans by selling Elmcot and moving to Canada in a single year, 1973.

A lucky break suddenly resolved this problem, as she excitedly told Adele the "GREAT NEWS" a little more than a month later on April 21, 1973:

> I have already sold ELMCOT. Wow. Never was a house sold so fast in this country. Adele, you won't believe it (yes, you will) because it is like A MIRACLE. I wrote a short note to the squire, my neighbour across the way in the great house, The Beacon, who actually is quite a good guy, telling him I had to sell this year, etc. Reason was—I thought he had a right to know, because he and I and various others here have been steadfastly against one neighbour who sold his 3-acre land to a developer who is trying to get building permission for 12 neo-Georgian houses (not, I may say, for the poor and needy, but for commuters and the like).... I wrote Mr. Wilson, just to inform him, as he and I had had some talks about the property next to mine and how to *not* have 12 neo-Georgian houses there, and I told him I planned to hold out (quite true) until end of June, and would try to sell to a private purchaser who would (a)

> want to occupy the house; and (b) would not cut down all the trees and sell the land to a developer. He responded thusly—would I be willing to sell it to *him*? He is quite wealthy, and would like this land simply so that the area does not become suburbia. I said YES.

As she revealed to Al, Margaret was quite pleased with the price of £25,000, although a developer would have paid £5,000 more: "Well, that is 3 times what I paid for the house; even reckoning the money I've put into it, it is twice the total amount of my investment in the place. Who needs more? More than that, and one is really getting greedy. I'll have had 10 good years here, very productive re: writing and a very good place for the kids to have grown up."

In making her plans to resettle in Canada, Margaret did not have to be particularly concerned about Jocelyn, who was to marry Peter Banks in May 1973. (The marriage lasted five months, although Peter and Jocelyn did not divorce until three years later.) In *Dance on the Earth*, she outlined her first plan regarding David: "I realized that once David graduated from secondary school the following spring [1973], I wanted to move back to Canada. I knew I'd have to sell Elm Cottage eventually, but I didn't want David to have to move out of his home the moment he left school. I arranged to rent the house to Ian and Sandy Cameron for a year, on the condition that David could live there, too, while I took up a one-term job at the University of Western Ontario and a spring term appointment at Trent." This scheme had to be abandoned when she became aware of her vulnerability to the two heavy taxes. However, Mr. Wilson wanted—having agreed to purchase Elmcot—to rent the house to a young married couple and asked if she knew anyone suitable. Thus, the Camerons rented from Mr. Wilson, and David retained his home at Elmcot.

Margaret's account is accurate—to a point. What she omits from her rendition was seventeen-year-old David's sense of outrage that his mother was casting him out. She was very blunt with him: he was old enough to be on his own, but, if he wished, he was welcome to live with her in Canada. In this instance, Margaret—who herself had undergone similar agonies, torments so excruciating that the memory of them led her to distance herself from others so that she would not re-experience them—was herself perceived as the abandoning mother.

On March 21, 1973, at the time she sold Elmcot, she regarded her recent luck as a personal triumph, as she boasted to Jack McClelland: "I may seem not too brilliant, finance-wise, but am in fact much brighter than most people realize." Any appearance that she was not a shrewd businesswoman was, according to her, truly deceptive. And she was also a person who got what she wanted: "I may be able to get to Canada sooner than expected; we'll see. I am the lady who gets to the airport not one but two hours before required." Significantly, she added, "I don't need advice—it's all going on fine."

Everything, however, did not go well in the late spring of 1973 with *The Diviners*. On June 7, Margaret gave this account to Adele:

> My American editor, Judith Jones, is in England now and came out on Monday. Knopf are enthusiastic about the novel (the title of which is THE DIVINERS), so that is good news. Judith and I had a five-hour nonstop session—she came out bearing Macmillan's criticisms as well as her own, as we've agreed I'll only have the one editor for this book. Nothing she said surprised me in the least. I knew what the areas of weakness were, but when I handed in the 2nd draft I just could not at that moment face trying to cope with more re-writing. However, Judith and I (and Macmillan's) are in total agreement this time re: what areas need to be revised or rewritten, and after our session I think I can see more or less how to tackle most of the problems. It will, I think, mean about 2 months of concentrated work, which is kind of awkward at this point, what with moving back to Canada.

In *Dance on the Earth*, Margaret, in discussing the short-story versus novel issue regarding *A Bird in the House*, makes this claim: "Judith Jones at Knopf, my editor of many years, had initially had a major disagreement with me for the first and only time." In fact, Judith's objections to *A Bird in the House* were trivial in comparison to her worries about *The Diviners.* As an editor, she liked experimental fiction which pushed the reader in new directions by the use of unorthodox narration. (Her favourite book by Margaret was *The Fire-Dwellers*; she especially admired the enormous technical risks the book took.) However, she was not willing to allow a writer to put into print material which was unfocused and undisciplined. When she read the typescript of *The Diviners*, she was convinced of two things: it bore the mark of genius and it was an utter mess. During that first reading, she was certain that within the chaos of an enormous typescript was a far more compact and coherent book waiting to be liberated.

Although she had acted as Margaret's American editor since *A Jest of God*, Judith's role in shaping her work had increased markedly in the following years. By the time of *A Bird in the House*, she had assumed principal responsibility for the Canadian writer within the Knopf–McClelland & Stewart–Macmillan consortium. In April 1973, she did not shirk that responsibility when she wrote Margaret requesting a meeting. Since no early draft of *The Diviners* survives, it is impossible to compare the completed novel to the material originally sent to the publishers. What is very clear is that all three houses wanted radical surgery performed before allowing the book to go into production and that Judith Jones had the full backing of Alan Maclean and Jack McClelland when she met with Margaret. Judith Jones's charm, diplomacy and intellectual rigour worked beautifully during their lengthy meeting because she was able to communicate her enthusiasm for the book at the very same time she laid down the law.

Judith and Margaret had met before in New York on least one occasion. They liked each other—Margaret feeling that Judith's childhood in rural Vermont gave her a decided edge in responding to the landscape of Manawaka. During their long meeting in 1973, Judith was startled by what she felt was a considerable deterioration in Margaret's mental state. More significantly, the novelist's demeanour that day completely surprised her. A few years before, Margaret had fought with her. On that day, she seemed overly compliant, her manner being that of an extremely young writer grateful for editorial strictures, even of the most radical kind. Judith's impression was that Margaret was befuddled by her own book and needed all the guidance that could be provided in order to put it into some sort of coherent shape.

This time round, Margaret did not complain to John Cushman. Her response to the critique she was offered can be seen in a six-page single-spaced letter she wrote to Judith less than a month later on July 2, two and a half pages of which are devoted to "MAJOR CHANGES." Most of these involve paring the narrative down so that subsidiary stories (by Skinner and Christie) do not interfere with plot coherence. On June 12, Jack McClelland wrote Margaret an uncharacteristically long (six-page) letter in which he expressed sentiments similar to those of Judith Jones:

> Let me start by saying that the manuscript contains some of the greatest writing that you have ever done. I have told you before that you are the only author that has improved every time out and I think you have kept your record intact. I read the manuscript in one sitting from about 9 o'clock at night until 4 in the morning. It's a very moving experience. I ended up in tears during the last half hour.... This is not to say that I think everything is right about the novel. I don't. I have your letter. I am totally in accord with its contents and most particularly the plan to work directly and solely with Judith Jones in bringing the script to its final form.

He went on to underscore the crucial point being made by Judith: "the problem with the novel is essentially that you have larded the script with material that impedes the flow and that really is unnecessary in terms of what you are trying to do. I read every page but I can be honest and tell you that it bugged me as a reader to have to do so because too often I was taken away from the narrative—from your own beautiful writing and characterization—and forced to read background material that I really didn't want or need." Her encounter with Judith, McClelland's letter and her moving plans galvanized Margaret, as can be seen in her letter to the "Boss" of July 4:

> I am enclosing a list of the revisions I've now made on THE DIVINERS. Yes, I think I have them all done—please do not shriek in horror; I can explain everything! I don't think I've rushed them. The truth is, Jack, that my well-known punctuality neurosis has become really bad, just lately. About three months ago, when I was fuming and carrying on about how difficult it would be for me to get the fourteen million tons of rubbish cleared out of this house, and actually get moved to Canada, my daughter said with admirable calm, "Ma, we all know what will really happen—you will have your suitcase packed and the house cleared and be ready to move on July 1st, and will be pacing the floor until July 22." And so it has proved. [After her meeting with Judith, she cleaned the house out and then spent 3-1/2 weeks working non-stop on the novel.] I feel kind of apologetic about getting it done now, because it may seem that I've rushed it. But I haven't.

"Clearing" Elmcot meant burning most of her correspondence and typescripts, the result being that Margaret Laurence's literary archive for most of her writing career is, unfortunately, scanty. The only furniture she kept from Elmcot were her desk and two chairs, a chest and a small table made by David.

Her last night at Elmcot was spent alone (David was visiting his sister and her new husband). She was not unhappy. She said goodbye to the Lady and walked through the rooms touching the bookshelves and the fireplaces, almost as if she wished to take with her the spirit of creativity the house had unleashed within her. "I went to bed and slept peacefully. The house, as always, protected me until the very end of our association."

Before her departure, Margaret announced that she did not wish to look for a house in the small, pretty town of Lakefield—close to the cottage—until she arrived in nearby Peterborough in January 1974 to be writer-in-residence at Trent University. She intended to be at the cottage at least a month before taking up her post at the University of Western Ontario but had no intention of house-hunting. With considerable knowledge of her mother's frequently precipitous behaviour, Jocelyn informed her: "Mum, I give you two weeks after you get to the shack."

Two weeks turned out to be two days. She telephoned a good number of realtors in Peterborough and environs. When these calls did not produce the desired results immediately, she phoned a firm in Lakefield with her list of specifications: "I want an old, two-storey, brick house with three bedrooms and a study. It has to be right in the village. I don't drive. I'm not a gardener, so I don't want a big lot. This is probably impossible, but it would also be marvellous to have a small, self-contained apartment that I could rent to a Trent student who could keep an eye on the place when I'm away." A somewhat startled voice at the other end of the line responded: "Mrs. Laurence, something like that has just come on the market and we haven't advertised it. Would you like to see it?" If she was taken aback, Margaret tried not to show it: "Yes, please drive out and pick me up this instant." A few minutes later, it was love at first sight: "There it was, just waiting for me, the very house I had described." Acting upon the principle that she who hesitates is forevermore lost, she bought the house that day.

In the cemetery of the village church is the grave of Major Samuel Strickland, a former British army officer, the founder of Lakefield. After establishing a farm in the wilderness there, he wrote of his adventures in *Twenty-seven Years in Canada West.* As Margaret well knew, his literary sisters, Susanna Moodie and Catharine Parr Traill, came to Upper Canada with their families in 1832, and at various times, lived near their brother. Both women were prolific writers before they emigrated to Canada, but they are best known for their accounts of their adventures in the Canadian wilderness, Susanna publishing *Roughing It in the Bush* in 1852, Catharine *The Backwoods of Canada* sixteen years earlier.

Catharine, who died in Lakefield in 1899 at the age of 97, was more enthusiastic about her experience in the New World, unlike her sister who, having survived a harrowing forest fire and being chased by a bear, wrote of her new life as being akin to that of a "condemned criminal." For Margaret, these two women were worthy role models, intrepid emigrant pioneers who responded with considerable dexterity and strength to the challenges that confronted them. In a very real sense, Margaret—born and brought up in the Prairies—saw herself as an outsider to small-town Ontario life and thus a spiritual descendant of the dauntless sisters.

In January 1974, she was not displeased to learn her Lakefield house "used to be a Funeral Home! I think this is hilarious, but the young tenants told me the fact very tentatively, perhaps thinking I would be horrified. The taxi lady, Mrs. Brethauer, whose husband Elwood owns Elwood's Taxi in Lakefield, said to me previously 'You've bought the old Anderson place', but did not say what Mr. Anderson's work had been." An elderly resident of Lakefield provided her with even more information: "'The Andersons kept it real nice,' he said. 'They used that big

8 Regent Street, Lakefield.

upstairs bedroom as a sitting room when the downstairs was ... um ... er ... busy.' The thought of the departed forefathers of the hamlet does not bother me at all. And seeing that the funeral home comes into all my Manawaka fiction, it seems kind of appropriate, somehow!"

Three months later, when Margaret got possession of the house, she described her supervision of the necessary renovations very much in the manner of a general summoning her various troops to their appointed rounds:

> 8 Regent Street, Lakefield, is coming along marvellously. I had it planned like a campaign—I got possession of it on March 17, and on March 18 the following were supposed to converge on house to begin work: Paperhanger/painter; carpenter; Bell Telephone; Kawartha Karpet Co (what a name) to measure for rugs in 2 rooms; window company to put on storms & screens, etc etc. And believe it or not, they all converged! I was there at 8.45 a.m. and it was really wild—people pouring in and out with ladders, paint, power-saws

The study at 8 Regent Street, Lakefield.

> and telephones. My deadline for all of them is April 15, and I think they're going to make it. The carpenter is a great guy—he is about 4 feet tall, but works with a speed and efficiency which is a joy to behold (especially if you're paying him by the hour). I'm having a hell of a lot of fun over this house. Max Doughty, the plumber, also bowled in to measure for downstairs john—he has done the plumbing for me for years at the shack, and is a really nice guy, darts around like a rather portly leprechaun with a pipe, making witty converse. I'd told him the place used to be a Funeral Home, so naturally he allowed as how I'd have to start writing ghost stories now.

She took great pleasure in her new home, especially with the various trips in search of antique pine furniture and in the arrival of a wide assortment of different-sized parcels filled with goods ordered from the Eaton's and Sears catalogues.

Immediately after Margaret moved to Regent Street, Evelyn Robinson, her next-door neighbour, called on her: "She was the first Lakefield person to visit me. The day I moved into my house, in May, 1974, she came to my door, bearing freshly baked cinnamon buns, and welcoming me to the village. Words really cannot express what this meant to me. I knew all at once that I was truly home." She took great pleasure in the quiet beauty of Lakefield. In particular, she loved the short walk to the post office to collect her mail (there is no postal delivery in Lakefield) and the easy stroll to the shops on the main street. Many residents remembered her ambling shuffle; some—taken aback by the fact she looked like a peasant woman—were startled to discover she was the famous writer.

The Margaret Laurence remembered by most Canadians was a portly woman with a slightly severe look. The severity gave way to benignity as soon as the observer's own eyes focused on her beautiful eyes, which radiated gentleness and compassion. Her lack of attention to some aspects of her appearance was a necessary by-product of getting older and not being able to do too much about it. Two other factors have to be considered, however. After the break-up of her marriage, she did not entertain any real hope of finding a permanent male companion. To a limited extent, she gave up on her sexuality and, as a result, did not care very much about her weight, once a source of considerable preoccupation. Second, as she got older, Margaret had the opportunity to say to hell with the conventions of what is or is not an attractive woman. In her writing life, she had put herself on the line in a series of ambitious books. What did she care what other people thought of her appearance?

The self-contained apartment was an added bonus, not because it generated income. The presence of a student or other tenant in that part of the house meant Margaret never felt completely isolated. She enjoyed the company of the young people who rented from her, often inviting them to use her washing machine and dryer. In turn, the tenants sometimes provided her with transportation by car, an important consideration in the life of a non-driver.

Although she gloated over the fact her new home had been a funeral parlour, she did not mention another obvious fact: 8 Regent Street and John Simpson's house bear an incredibly strong resemblance to each other; especially the interiors, almost as if Margaret could allow herself to return to Neepawa in place as well as in spirit once she had completed the Manawaka cycle. Had she in fact purged the ghosts of the past? Or was she still haunted by them? Could she only return to a small town in Canada once she had dealt some sort of *coup de grâce* to Neepawa and its inhabitants?

She certainly loved her new home:

> In all the years I visited Margaret in her Lakefield house [Don Bailey remembered] I think I sat in the living room three or four times. She was a kitchen person, preferring to reign in a kingdom that made her feel secure. It was a large room with an old [sideboard] near the window where she placed plants to catch the light.... The press-back chairs we sat in were from another time. The original wood flooring had been restored. Even the wallpaper was reminiscent of another era. So although it was a well-lit room with modern appliances, there was a sense of sitting in a farm kitchen from a long ago, safer, past.

The living room and dining room/kitchen were connected through a large archway, giving the first floor of the house the feel of one large room. Margaret often sat just inside the living room, where the telephone—no longer a vile instrument—was placed. The hallway to the house was spacious, the staircase there leading to one large and two small bedrooms and a large study on the second floor. In many ways, the move to Lakefield was a return home, to a version of Neepawa that was safe.

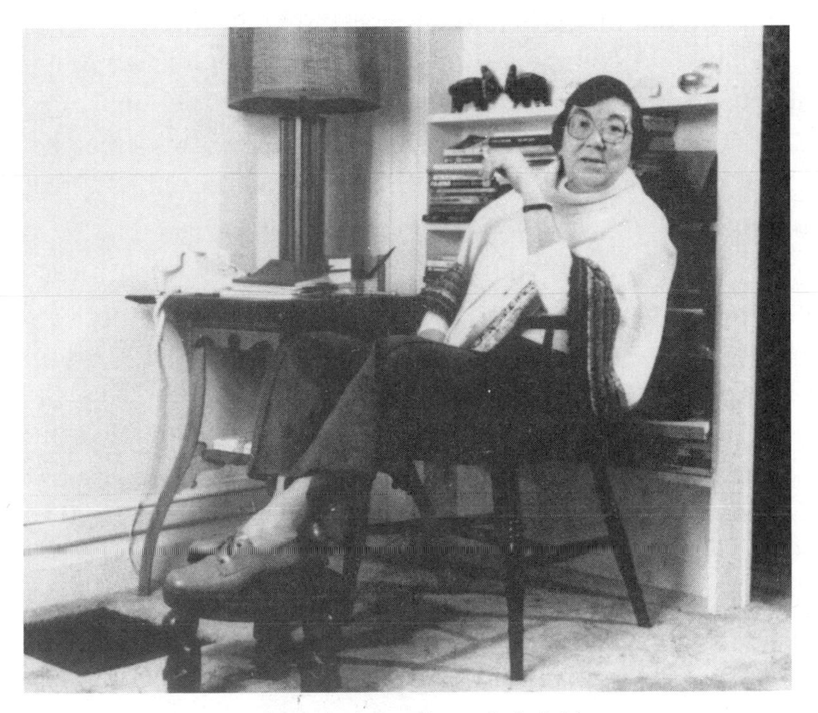

Margaret Laurence in her telephone alcove, Lakefield.

In the autumn of 1973, Margaret's energies were drawn to a series of new projects. One of these was a spin-off of *The Diviners.* She browbeat a very reluctant Jack McClelland into releasing a small 33-rpm record with the book: this recording—not really intended for sale to the public—was sent to all bookstores retailing the book and contained a recording of her songs. She also tried to induce him to publish Adele Wiseman's novel *Crackpot*, which had already been rejected by other houses. She began by explaining that Adele was the type of writer who was "very sensitive about editorial criticism and has never really had a first-rate editor whom she trusted.... I think she'd like to submit the novel to you, but is a bit shy owing to your not having published THE SACRIFICE. I told her (at no extra charge, Boss) that you might be a nut in some ways but you most definitely were not of an ungenerous spirit and would certainly not hold a grudge against her on account of her first novel. However, I think she'd rather you wrote to her about it, if you feel so inclined." Having attempted to arouse his interest, a somewhat embarrassed Margaret made it quite clear that Adele, unlike herself, would not tolerate major editorial intervention in the event he was inclined to publish: "The thing is this—as I understand the situation, she would *not* be willing to do major structural changes."

Late in 1972, Margaret Atwood had written to her about an issue of vital importance to them both: "We had a gathering of 18 people all the way from Alice Munro in the West to John Metcalf in New Brunswick and it went enormously better than anyone had any right to expect. No ranting and raving, no tantrums, sweet reason prevailed." Earlier, that spring, the first meeting Margaret could recall of the group that would become The Writers' Union of Canada had taken place in Atwood's office at Massey College: "No refreshments were served—we simply talked business." She was sarcastic because Barbara Amiel—a writer she loathed—had spoken in *Maclean's* of a meeting predating the Massey College one at which a "small group of Canada's literateurs, including Margaret Atwood and June Callwood, got together over beer and hot dogs at Toronto's Embassy tavern, and the Writers' Union of Canada was informally launched. This may well be so," Margaret told June, "[but] I was in England at the time."

The 1972 meeting was the prelude to the official formation of TWUC on November 3, 1973 at its first convention in Ottawa. Farley Mowat had been one of the first proponents of such an organization, which he felt should be formed to protect writers at a time when the Canadian book trade was expanding rapidly. Such an organization could have some clout because it represented a wide spectrum of authors, and it could offer professional advice on matters such as contracts.

Margaret, at a meeting in Toronto in the spring of 1973 (subsequent to the Massey College one), agreed to serve as interim president before the official founding of the group, but she told Jack McClelland—obviously not a great proponent of this banding together of writers—on October 7 that she had decided not to seek election to the presidency: "I've liked being interim President, but don't think my psychic energy will run to being President for the next year. I operate better in private situations, as you know, and am not very good at politicking—the strain is too great, and I absolutely hate hassles. I think it is all I can do to make myself do battle in my own life, when it has become necessary.... I've had another Freudian accident—this time I think I've busted a toe bone, opening a door sharply, right onto a foot. Those things [she had also sprained her back] are warnings to me to cut down on the areas of strain. I like it here at Western, but it's a psychic drain in odd ways that writing a novel is not—it is because I don't like being a public person, of course."

Quite eager to serve on committees and thus to be involved behind the scenes, she was willing to be a figurehead but not a "front person" who undertook a large number of public tasks. Early on, there was fighting between Pierre Berton and Farley Mowat, but this seemed to evaporate quickly. In his reply of October 12, Jack told her that, in his opinion, the objectives of the Writers' Union were confused and ultimately without purpose. He informed her she had much better ways of spending her time. A month later, a very stubborn Margaret wrote to McClelland again, outlining the splendid possibilities of the new organization: "The conference of the Writers' Union of Canada went really well over the weekend. I was there nearly 4 days, as I went in advance to help get things in order. We had 2 extremely intensive days, vetting the constitution, electing officers, setting up areas of action. I thought it was really great. Also, there was a very strong sense of solidarity ... —it was good to see everyone again. I'm on the Membership committee, which is okay, but otherwise no office. I feel optimistic about the union—I think it can really do some things." The "Boss" never changed his mind on this issue. For her, the sense of community engendered by the WU was crucial: "The thing that one *must* accept—or must agree to learn—is that we are all very lonely, isolated, etc, etc, and you cannot be a writer without being that, but you are also a human being, who wants most terribly to make contact." Among the writers Margaret met through TWUC—and formed friendships with—were: George Bowering, Graeme Gibson, Robert Kroetsch, Andreas Schroeder, Glen Sorestad, David Watmough and David Williams.

From the beginning, Margaret was aware standards of selection might prove a thorny issue since there was a general understanding among the fiction writers and poets that membership was for those in their ranks who had published at least one book. The creative writers also felt that the union should exist for them and not for journalists. Later, that would become part of a major quandary.

The spring of 1974—just as she completed her tours of duty at the University of Western Ontario and Trent University—provided Margaret with a new source of anxiety: reviews of *The Diviners.* This time, she was particularly stung by two notices, one by Phyllis Grosskurth in *The Globe and Mail,* the other by Robert Fulford in *The Toronto Star.*

The headline in the *Globe* of May 4, 1974 read: "A Looser, More Complex, More Sexually Uninhibited Laurence: and Never an Atwood Victim." For Margaret, this was dubious praise, as if she were being lauded for writing a sex manual. She poked a bit of fun at the reviewer in a letter to Purdy: "...said nothing about novel—talked about my other books, then said what a hell of a fine thing it was that I used so many 4-letter words in the novel, and how great I described sex." With Fulford, she was even angrier because he had interviewed her on the CBC on May 17, the day before his review was published and not voiced any of the objections which made their way into print: "He does not seem to understand or grasp the form of the damn thing at all. Well, the hell with it. Screw him. I like (liked?) the guy, too. I don't blame a person for giving a rotten review, but I do think it is dishonest to interview the writer on radio and not bring up a single criticism which will then appear in the written review.... Oh—he also quotes a bit re: Morag and sex, which is plainly romantic, and which in his context is awfully corny, but what he misses is that the interpretation of sex was for her when she was very young, with her newly married husband, and *of course* it was romantic."

The sexuality depicted in the book would be Margaret's nemesis for the remainder of her life; Fulford's criticism of the book's form made her blood boil—especially his claim, "no good editor had looked at it"—but the simple truth is that although Judith Jones had assisted her in reining in a great deal of extraneous material, the narrative is extraordinarily diffuse. However, it is no wonder Margaret could not combine all the elements that make up *The Diviners* because in that book she spoke of the deep contradictions in her own life—in any life—and of her inability to ever make a satisfactory resolution of them. The impossibilities of the book's form mirror the impossibilities of life.

The Diviners is Margaret Laurence's most ambitious book, the one into which she tried to squeeze her complex vision of life. It is also—in a profound way—her most autobiographical book. She explained it to Adele this way: "a character like Morag, just as with Stacey and even Rachel, is both me and not me ... but NOT me in the external sense at all. She is herself, of course.... (There are dozens of bits which are in some complex way based on your own experience)." In her writing career up to and including *A Jest of God*, Margaret had injected parts of herself into her heroines. In the second part of her career, she used her own life much more directly and openly. Stacey is Margaret's version of herself as a mad Vancouver housewife. Many of the episodes in *A Bird in the House* can be traced to real-life events. *The Diviners*—also a book about the growth and development of a writer—is a sequel to *A Bird in the House* but one whose stylistic experimentations (the Memorybank Movies, the interpolated tales, the deliberate grotesqueries, the Snapshots, the conversations between Morag and Catharine Parr Traill) owe much to *The Fire-Dwellers*.

Interestingly, Margaret deleted several telling self-reflections from the extant typescript: "I've been inventing myself all my life" and "Morag, looking in mirrors to see if she was really there (or here, as the case might be)." Like a mirror reflecting other mirrors, *The Diviners* reflects multiple images of the creator creating.

As autobiographical fiction, *The Diviners* is an extremely revealing work because it plunges its reader into Morag's—and Margaret's—inner world. It is also a novel that continually challenges the reader because it goes as far as it can in exploring the dark recesses of the protagonist's sensibility. In *A Bird in the House*, Vanessa loses only her father, not her mother. In *The Diviners*, Morag's parents die when she is five—

> *They remain shadows. Two sepia shadows on an old snapshot, two barely moving shadows in my head, shadows whose few remaining words and acts I have invented. Perhaps I only want their forgiveness for having forgotten them.*
>
> *I remember their deaths, but not their lives. Yet they're inside me, flowing unknown in my blood and moving unrecognized in my skull.*

—and she goes to live with Christie and Prin Logan, Manawaka's most celebrated eccentrics and outcasts.

> Christie is short, skinny, but actually quite strong. He looks *peculiar*. His head sort of comes forward when he walks, like he is in a hurry, but he isn't ever in a hurry. His hair, what's left of it, is sandy.... His teeth are bad and one is missing at the front but he never tries to hide it by putting his hand over or smiling with his mouth closed, oh no, not him. He always wears a blue heavy shirt, and overalls too big so they fall around him and make him look silly.
>
> That is the worst. How silly he looks. No. The worst is that he smells. He does wash. But he never gets rid of the smell. How much do other people notice? Plenty. You bet. Horseshit and garbage, putrid stuff, vegetables and that, rotten eggs and mouldy old clothes.

In giving Morag an outlandish childhood, Margaret finds an effective way to dramatize the incredible level of ostracization and loss endured by the young Morag—no such level of suffering is evoked in the more conventionally realistic storytelling of *A Bird in the House*.

The psychic level of autobiography captured in *The Diviners* can be glimpsed in a letter Margaret wrote to Adele Wiseman in 1980: "Although one does not keep on *mourning* for the rest of one's life, the real grief never ceases, and it is right that this should be so, I think. At least, this has been my own experience. As you know, my own mother died 50 years ago, when I was only 4, and yet there are times when I still grieve for her, as I do for my stepmother who died 22 years ago. I don't even think of them that often, but when I do, it is still with a sharp sense of loss." That "sharp sense of loss" was the emotional underpinning of her new book.

In *The Diviners*, she also looks at other elements in her life with a keenly focused eye. Jack Laurence was a civil engineer, not a Professor of English. Yet there can be no doubt that Brooke's condescending attitude towards his wife is meant to be a depiction of the Laurence marriage. Pique, the daughter of Morag and Jules Tonnere, is not based on Jocelyn Laurence; but in Morag's distanced relationship from her daughter, Margaret is evoking her sense of the loss of the childhood of her own children.

Margaret's last novel is a spiritual autobiography in which symbols and tropes are pushed to their farthest limits in order to recapture some very key, powerful experiences in the creator's life. In an important letter of January 13, 1972 to Adele, Margaret—in the midst of writing the book —provided an excellent guide to her methodology in mixing "real life" with fiction in the construction of the book; she is commenting on the similarities between Morag's friend Ella and the "real" Adele Wiseman:

> The thing is, people are going to call this novel highly autobiographical, and in some ways it *is*, although the main character's background is pretty different from my own (although Scots and in the same

> bloody town for heaven's sake!) But odd things are happening. The main character's best friend ... talks awfully like you, I regret to say. I mean, she does and she doesn't. She *isn't* you, I need hardly say—but any fool who knows both of us would never believe I didn't base the character on you. ADELE, I'M SORRY!!! I NEVER MEANT TO! It happened. What do I do?... Also has 2 sisters. And a great mama, ho ho.... The portrait of the friend isn't done in great depth, and is loving, of course, but ... some of the wisecrack talk between her and Morag could be you and me, when about 21, or even now for that matter. What shall I do? I didn't mean it to happen. No beastly secrets are revealed, I need hardly say. But it all bothers me, all the same. Also, it bothers me about the guy Morag married—I swear to God he is not Jack; he really is much different in every way, but of course some of the underneath emotional things are the same. I quite often think that although I have to write it, I may not want it published. On the other hand, how many people know me? I mean, would say—Aha! Not that many. Also, the main character, Morag, is not me, but alas is a writer about my age and certainly talks in one of my voices. Of course, I haven't had an illegitimate daughter by a Manitoba Métis whom I'd known since childhood, but let it pass.

In asserting that the "underneath emotional things are the same," she gives the essential clue to understanding that *The Diviners* is both a highly charged and a highly distilled portrait of the artist as girl and woman.

However, the distillation was far from perfect. Judith Jones may have assisted Margaret to rid *The Diviners* of extraneous material, but the book remains unfocused, teeming with too many digressive elements. These result in glaring faults, but the book has a compensating gloriousness of affect, in which the harmonious confusion of life is reflected. Put another way, *The Diviners* may be a failed masterpiece, but it could only have been written by a great writer.

Margaret Laurence, who knew at firsthand all the pains and pleasures of the writing-life, was well aware of the precarious but often very real connections between life and art. At the outset, Morag, worried about her daughter, reflects: "I've got my work to take my mind off my life. At forty-seven that's not such a terrible state of affairs. If I hadn't been a writer, I might've been a first-rate mess at this point." At the end of the novel, Morag, assessing her career as a writer, sees herself as a pseudo-diviner, a magician who pulls words out of hats. She has not come to a resolution to the complexities of her own existence, but she has a renewed sense of what is vital to her—her vocation.

> How far could anyone see into the river? Not far. Near shore, in the shallows, the water was clear, and there were the clean and broken clamshells of creatures now dead, and the wavering of the underwater weed-forests, and the flicker of small live fishes, and the undulating lines of gold as the sand ripples received the sun. Only slightly further out, the water deepened and kept its life from sight.
>
> Morag returned to the house, to write the remaining private and fictional words, and to set down her title.

In Margaret's own life, these were the last words she would put into print as a novelist. Even before she wrote *The Diviners*, she was aware her career as a writer of fiction was winding down. Rachel, Stacey and Vanessa wander in and out of Morag's story, giving *The Diviners* a finality lacking in the other Manawaka narratives. The suggestion is that the story of Morag is the summation of all that has gone before, the final instalment in a cycle concerned in large part with the various kinds of empowerment possible for women.

The Diviners is also the most socially relevant of the Manawaka books, returning the reader to many of the issues about racial differences in the African narratives. This is the portion of *The Diviners* that is most forced. The love story of Morag and Skinner—Piquette's brother—may be in part a fictional re-creation of Margaret's affair with George Lamming, but it is much more than that in its attempt to show the possibility of some sort of communication within the racial mix that is Canada. The writer's reach exceeds her grasp when she tries to link

Morag's dispossession by virtue of being an orphan to the racially motivated dispossession suffered by the Métis. On the other hand, she was convinced a writer had an obligation "to grapple with prime matters, good and evil" even though she might fail. After all, she recognized, no writer ever completely realized her vision. "Even Milton," she assured the novelist Timothy Findley, "didn't entirely succeed."

In her last novel, Margaret fused together the elements in her African and Manawakan narratives. *The Diviners* is also the most self-reflexive of her narratives: it is a novel about writing a novel, one which celebrates the extremes of joy and sorrow of the writing life. In *The Diviners*, she tells how—despite incredible emotional odds—she has survived to proclaim the truths of her heart and vibrantly relates the story of that broken and divided heart. In a sense, having completed *The Diviners*, she had had her say and had nothing more she desperately needed to say. She herself recognized this in August 1974 when she told Ernest Buckler: "I won't quit writing, but I won't, I think, enter another novel—not because I don't want to, but because it isn't there to be written. The ending of *The Diviners* pretty well sums up how I feel now, and I guess I worked out a lot of the inner terrors through that novel."

18

Christian Radical (1974-1976)

For Margaret, Lakefield provided a much-needed respite from places such as the Vile Metropolis, although she could get there easily in two and a half hours by bus. Throughout her life as a non-driver, she liked to be within striking distances of cities without actually having to put up with the inconvenience of living in them. In England, she had resided in a village with a rail station four to five miles away in High Wycombe.

Lakefield first proved its value as a refuge when, at exactly the same time she took possession of her new home, she had to be involved in some of the events surrounding the publication of *The Diviners*. Margaret was always resistant to the publicity stunts dreamed up by the "Boss," but even she could not resist the inspiration of the publicist to hold a launch in the form of a divining contest on the grounds of the Ontario Science Centre.

Before the event, a diviner found a place where two streams intersected and buried a marker there. Seven diviners showed up, all of whom got reasonably close to the marker, but only one person from the media —willow wands were available—had the gift. The crucial test was met: the reporters enjoyed themselves enormously. To Margaret, "it was just one more piece of magic associated with the novel."

Less pleasurable was the book signing at the Longhouse Book Shop in Toronto. She was stunned when she arrived to see people "lined up not only in the store but on the sidewalk for about a block. Many of them were carrying piles of my previous novels in both hardcover and paperback. I wanted to run." Clara Thomas saved the day when she arrived. "'Here's an aspirin,' she said loudly, rummaging in her handbag while muttering into my ear, 'It's a tranquillizer.' I gulped it down and said to her, 'Talk, just talk to me. I don't care a hoot what you say, just talk to me and keep on talking until I'm okay.'" The distraught author soon calmed down.

In Lakefield, Margaret's heavy drinking was known to only a few people. This was not a subject about which she encouraged conversation. In fact, like many heavy drinkers, she did not really like to admit that she was dependent on booze. Once, when Jocelyn and a friend from Toronto stayed overnight, the three drank until late at night. In the morning, the young man lamented his horrible hangover and inquired of Margaret if she was suffering a similar fate. She looked at him uncomprehendingly, as if he were speaking about something of which she had absolutely no knowledge. Some visitors to 8 Regent Street would assume she was drinking water—but she would be refilling her glass from the bottle of gin or Scotch kept in the laundry room near the kitchen. One friend recalled an evening when a drunken Margaret, having consumed all the liquor in her host's house and smoked all the cigarettes, scrounged the remaining butts and began to drain the contents of nearly empty bottles.

A good friend, the novelist Budge Wilson, who often went shopping with Margaret, was struck by the pleasure the famous writer took in ordinary things, such as towels from Sears. Margaret did not mind mixing brocaded sofas and chairs next to pine antiques. Tables with scratches were just fine with her because they showed a former owner or owners had used and therefore loved them. Her taste was extremely eclectic. She had a number of carvings and masks from Africa which were placed for the most part in her study. She loved these, but she also took special pleasure, for example, in the homey philosophy of Charles Schultz's Snoopy and Charlie Brown. Another great source of joy for her were mystery and detective novels, of which she had an enormous collection.

Another friend, the journalist Stevie Cameron, who was then teaching in the English department at Trent University, once took Margaret on a shopping jaunt to Pleasant Point. On the way there, Margaret was a "white-knuckle passenger" who would not allow the driver to take the highway. She also remembered the delight Margaret took in singing hymns at parties; she was also very proud of the fact that she knew every single verse of "The Maple Leaf Forever," which she would render with very little encouragement.

Her eyesight had begun to deteriorate slightly and she had also developed low-grade diabetes. She was no longer as strong as she looked. Many people thought her body matched her powerful intellect, but this was simply not true: "comes," she observed, "of having a 'carrying' voice and a build like a Russian peasant woman." Appearances were, she assured friends, deceiving. Nevertheless, the "old tobacco voice"—her nickname for the frequently rasping sound she produced—indicated to many that her health was not good.

Although Margaret no longer wore make-up and could joke about her appearance, she was extremely concerned with what she wore. Much of her clothing was acquired at Addition-Elle, in Peterborough, one of a chain of stores for full-figured women. There, she would buy gowns that hung loose. She also felt that her hair looked its best kept short and simple. Once, when Mona was visiting from British Columbia, she insisted on doing something with Margaret's coiffure. "You can do better," she assured Margaret, who nodded her head in assent. Later, somewhat apologetically, she brushed the "improvements" out because they were not her.

Gradually, Jocelyn and David gravitated back to Canada and to Toronto. Jocelyn became a journalist, David a photographer. Their relationship with their temperamental but loving mother was not always easy. Her drinking was an impediment, so were her easily hurt feelings. Margaret could not tolerate any criticism, for instance, of her ghastly cauliflower soup. The children grew tired of listening to their mother's laments about her loss of the capacity to write. But Margaret's fierce and abiding love for them was something they could count on. Jocelyn often mothered Margaret. For instance, she would buy dresses for her that might add a dash of style to her appearance.

Increasingly, Jocelyn found her mother's drinking hard to tolerate. She was aware that Margaret had lovingly prepared a bedroom for her at the Lakefield house (one for David also), and at first she enjoyed staying there. Then, Jocelyn's patience became stretched as her mother's drinking became heavier. After a while, she stopped staying overnight, although she visited on a regular basis.

Margaret had fought to survive as a writer at the very same time she was raising her children, and never squarely faced up to the fact that she had not been the mother she would have liked to have been. In their turn, the children were disappointed in the behaviour of their famous mother, feeling that they had paid an unfair price for her creativity. In relationships in which Margaret did not have to match the demands of motherhood with those of the writing life, she could be eminently successful.

Ken Adachi, the writer, journalist and book reviewer, and his wife, Mary, an editor, were good friends from Elmcot days. Margaret and Mary met at Canada House in London, where Mary was then employed and the friendship between the two women quickly deepened. After Margaret returned to Canada, Mary would frequently drive from Toronto to Lakefield to visit Margaret. Between Mary and Margaret, there were few barriers; they could air their deepest concerns to each other. One measure of the closeness between them was reflected in what Margaret called the "E.S.P. thing": when one friend was in crisis, the other would instantly be in touch. In Margaret, Mary found a kindred spirit, one who had bottomless reservoirs of compassion. Margaret knew of Mary's years as a child in an internment camp; she instinctively recognized that Mary's childhood suffering bore a remarkable similarity to her own. In a poem to commemorate Mary's birthday, Margaret penned words equally applicable to herself: "You've struggled your entire life/ Against the once-rejection." Mary never confronted Margaret about her drinking—people who did so were "harassing" her, Margaret claimed. She was deeply hostile to anyone who criticized her drinking. So Mary did what was the very best for her friend: she accepted her as she was.

However, Mary did find Margaret's drinking distressing. Once, Mary and Ken invited Margaret to dinner with others, where she consumed a lot of liquor and became boorish. After that, Mary never invited others in when Margaret was staying with her in Toronto. She felt the writer diminished herself when she imbibed too much, and did not want others to see Margaret in that state. Margaret herself recognized her drinking could be disconcerting, as she told Mary in an aside in a letter of April 21, 1973: "Please let us hope that I don't get to be too much of a bore for you, in the well known ways." When she stayed the night in Lakefield, Mary, a non-drinker, would go to bed early, in order to avoid seeing her friend totally inebriated. Sometimes Ken asked her: "Why do you put up with her?" The simple truth was that at the same time she experienced the "difficult" Margaret, Mary was in touch with an even greater force—the boundless love her friend bestowed upon her.

There was the Margaret who drank too much, but just as real was the woman who could be exceedingly attentive to the feelings of others. She instinctively knew, for example, that if you gave a birthday present to a small girl you should also buy a present for her even younger sister, whose feelings might otherwise be crushed.

Another constant in Margaret's life—and an important reason for being within striking distance of Toronto—was her friendship with Adele: she visited the Stones regularly, and the two families—when Jocelyn and David were back in Canada—often celebrated Thanksgiving, Christmas and Hanukkah together. These occasions—to which she looked forward eagerly—gave great pleasure to all the participants.

In Lakefield and Peterborough, Margaret had a good friend in Jean Murray Cole, whom she had known from Elmcot days when Jean had visited her there. At the time *The Diviners* was nearing completion, Jean was researching a book about her great-great-grandfather, Archibald MacDonald, who as a young man had led the first of the Selkirk settlers on the long march from York Factory to Churchill. In writing *The*

Diviners Margaret had given a similar Highland Scots ancestry to Morag and invented Piper Gunn, about whom Christie relates a number of stories. One day, Jean calmly informed an incredulous Margaret that there had been a real piper by the name of Gunn.

A few months after the publication of *The Diviners*, Margaret received a phone call from Alice Williams, who "lived at the Curve Lake Reserve near the village. Her mother was an Ojibway and her father a Norwegian. She said she had never called a writer before, but she wanted to let me know that I had got the Métis parts exactly right." Alice Williams claims that Margaret misunderstood what she said on the phone that day. As a child, Alice's experiences had been similar to Morag's, that being the portion of the book she praised during the conversation. It would seem, then, that the friendship began on a false assumption. (During the same call, Alice asked—based on the photo on the dust jacket—if she had native ancestry. She replied that she did not.)

Margaret's writing career may have been in abeyance, but it was a matter she could joke about in a letter to George Bowering of December 24, 1974: "My heavens, I'm not working on *anything*. It's all I can do to write my name on cheques, when necessary. I bat off the odd article and review, but they're far from deathless prose, although I sweat blood over the damn things, I must admit. I always tell people that I'm working on a kids' book, tho. They don't like to be told you're not working on anything. They think that's unbearably lazy, or immoral, or something of the sort." Many were the hours that she sat at her desk in her second-floor study trying to write; many were the anguished hours when nothing came.

Nineteen seventy-five became a banner year for the non-writing writer when she won both the Governor General's Award for fiction for the second time and the Molson Award. The latter gave her fifteen thousand tax-free dollars, but the most wonderful aspect of this largesse was meeting Jules Léger, the ailing Governor General who had suffered a serious stroke. She was moved by his courage in continuing public life.

A curious aspect of Margaret's resettlement in Canada is that it eventually brought her relationship with Al Purdy to an almost complete halt. To a certain extent, theirs was a friendship which found expression in letters crossing the Atlantic. Nevertheless, when they were together, they were perfectly amicable, or so it seemed. On March 9, 1973, she declared:

> I do not personally find myself worrying much over how long my own friendship with you will last; I have a kind of faith that it will, and I think you do, too, really. I imagine I know a fair amount about you, at this point, and you about me. If you can stand to see me drinking too much sometimes and talking rubbish or saying things I'd never say when sober, and still continue this by-now lengthy correspondence, then unless I suddenly decide that I'm pro-fascist or that what I want most in life is to get hitched to a Texas oil-magnate, I can't think you will feel you've been misjudging me all these years. Nor I you.

These strong sentiments began to be modified in August 1974 when she asked: "You've never said what you thought of *The Diviners*, which leads me to suspect you didn't like it. That's okay—you can tell me so. What is one more blow among the many? Seriously, I'd like to know what you thought, even if you hated it."

Not receiving any answer to this query, she summoned up the courage in December—in the midst of a night of drinking—to find out what was happening by phoning Purdy. The result was disastrous.

> I'm sorry. I really am. I was drunk when I phoned you, and I haven't the foggiest notion of what I said, but obviously it was stupid, thoughtless and hurtful. I don't have any excuse, so I won't try to make any. I'm not even really apologizing for my awful behaviour —I'm just saying I'm sorry, and I am, I am. It's awful that some of one's actions and words can't be undone or unsaid. I mean, if you put your hand through a windowpane in a spell of fury (as I did once; have also broken dishes), then you get another pane put in and

> no one is hurt except possibly your own hand and pocketbook. With words, no. There are times when I can bear to know that I sometimes talk like an idiot, but this isn't one of them. Please forgive me. It shall not happen again. As for that damn novel, in my saner moments, I cannot understand why I seem to need that kind of reassurance from you. God knows I'd feel much worse about it if you told me lies about your responses. You couldn't, tho, as I couldn't in that area, either. So—I really am sorry. I hate hurting my friends, but I do sometimes. Especially when my judgement is distorted and I go into my amateur headshrinker act, a truly repellent one.

She was not usually aggressive when she drank. She felt totally humiliated by her bad behaviour, but in reality she had simply asked Purdy for his reaction—any reaction—to the book. She was anxious for the simplest form of recognition and support. His inability to provide either and her corresponding inability to accept silence would fester, providing for the fuller break to come.

Another friend with whom Margaret had milder difficulties at about this time was the "Boss," with whom she disagreed on a number of issues: their differing stands on copyright regulations, her refusal to accept his invitation to write a short book on what it meant to be a Canadian, and his withholding of the Book-of-the-Month Club advance on *The Diviners* (he was doing so because this sum was being tallied against the advance initially paid by McClelland & Stewart).

The most serious misunderstanding involved the Canadian paperback rights to *The Diviners*, which were sold by McClelland & Stewart to Bantam (five years total but only two years exclusive rights). In November 1974, Margaret sought the assurance of Malcolm Ross, the editor of the New Canadian Library (NCL) that her last novel would ultimately join her other Canadian titles in that series. A year later, she became concerned when Dave Godfrey—whose novel *The New Ancestors* (1970), set in Ghana, she had enthusiastically puffed and reviewed—gave her "a certain amount of flack" about this agreement because another—Canadian—house had approached Jack McClelland to buy the rights.

The implication of Godfrey's complaint was that Margaret—through her publisher—was selling out to American interests. She was both annoyed and frightened at this request for information, as she told McClelland: "Then, (thus goes Godfrey's version), when Bantam said no dice in the USA unless they got the Canadian rights, you said Fine. He said in a rather sharp letter to me that he wanted the facts, because he didn't like to stab a friend without getting the facts." A very irritated McClelland explained to her that the offer from the other house must have been overlooked, but in any case he had accepted the Bantam deal only after they had agreed to stringent conditions. In any event, she had been blamed for a business arrangement over which she had no say.

The Diviners was a book which caused Margaret problems in every conceivable way. In February 1975, she participated on a "panel" at the Women's Art Association in Peterborough. The format was really a question and answer session wherein two people asked her questions, the predominant line of enquiry being "WHY HAD I USED ALL THOSE FOUR LETTER WORDS IN THE DIVINERS?" During what Margaret felt was a very assured reply on her part, she nervously fumbled on a cigarette, looked down to see the fringe of the tablecloth near her was on fire, and then heard her own voice yelling: "MY GOD! I've just set fire to the tablecloth!" A third of the ladies burst into laughter at this particular Freudian accident, and a friend, by way of assurance, told her: "Never mind, Margaret, at least it was only a 3-letter word." This was one of the last—and very few—occasions she was able to laugh at the controversy regarding the language in *The Diviners*, a book in which she attempted to present a complete picture of the interior and exterior worlds of Morag Gunn.

Two types of passages caused the controversy. There were those which use language deemed graphic, as in this reflective passage:

> Does that say anything about my parents, or only that I was born bloody-minded? I was born bloody-minded. It's cost me. I've paid

> through the nose. As they say. Also, one might add, through the head, heart and cunt.

And there were episodes which were considered pornographic because they describe love-making in a detailed way, in the process evoking the tumultuous pleasures of sex:

> "Let's sleep now," Jules says, "and after a while we'll wake up and fuck some more, eh?"
>
> In an hour or so, Morag wakens, and puts her head between his legs, sweeping her hair across his thighs. She takes his limp cock very gently in her mouth and caresses it with her tongue, and it lengthens and grows hard before he is even awake. Then he wakes and says *deeper*. After a while, she disentangles and he raises her until she is looking into his face in the grey-light of the room.
>
> "Ride my stallion, Morag."
>
> So she mounts him. He holds her shoulders and her long hair, penetrating up into her until she knows he has reached whatever core of being she has.

For Margaret Laurence, sex was an essential component in understanding any human being; in Morag, she created a heroine whose sexuality is very much a reflection of her own—a sexuality which has a strong mystical component to it, emphasizing as it does how the pleasures of the body can put individuals into contact with their essential humanity—and vulnerability. Another element in *The Diviners* also aroused a great deal of unspoken controversy: the trans-racial issue. Not only does Morag have a baby out of wedlock, but also Skinner Tonnere, Morag's lover and Pique's father, is a Métis. Margaret suspected, no doubt correctly, that objections to the sex in her book were inspired in large part by racist sentiments.

Because Margaret Laurence had put herself so fully into *The Diviners*, she made herself sensitive to any reading of the book which overemphasized one aspect of the book at the expense of the other. At the Women's Art Association, she had been nervous when interrogated about the book's "FOUR LETTER WORDS" but had—even though she almost managed to set fire to herself—defended the book and herself. She was not really prepared, however, for the banning controversy which erupted in the late winter of 1976.

In a letter to Malcolm Ross of February 14, 1976, she outlined the horrible situation which had confronted her:

> We are having a small storm in ye olde village teapot ... THE DIVINERS has apparently received some complaints from a few local parents and was then stricken from the Grade 13 course in Lakefield High—but not only did the local paper, the *Lakefield Leader*, and the Peterborough paper, the *Examiner*, take it up—it went out on the CP lines and has caused a kind of storm. The local English teachers, at all the county high schools (8) are united, apparently, in support of the novel, and there have been some incredible letters in support of the book, including some from local High School students and one (to the *Examiner*, a copy of which I received today) from the minister of the Lakefield United Church, so—Malcolm, maybe the Philistines won't win the day. Let us hope so. I think the local education authorities did not even suspect (because I guess they aren't readers) that a casual banning of the book might cause a wider uproar, but I'm glad that has happened. I think what probably happens is that the Board of Education gets 2 complaints from parents and then takes a book off course, hoping nobody will notice. Well, this time, they've noticed! It's a bit ironic that it should happen in my own village, eh? But that is Canadian life for you.

The Board's decision to remove *The Diviners* from the Grade 13 curriculum only at Lakefield High School was announced at a professional development day, whereupon the heads of several other English departments announced their revulsion at such an action. The irony was that Robert Buchanan, the head of the English department at Lakefield, was against the banning. A further irony was that the principal of the nearby

Kenner High School took it upon himself to ban Alice Munro's *Lives of Girls and Women* from the syllabus at his school.

One of Margaret's chief opponents was James Telford, a school trustee. In an interview, he claimed only Christians—by which Margaret thought he really meant "Pentecostals"—should be allowed to choose books for the curriculum; in his opinion, the high-school teachers had been infected with liberalism. However, the textbook review committee voted to restore *The Diviners* to the curriculum. Then the Board itself had to ratify this decision. After an open and extremely heated meeting, the Board voted 10 to 6 in favour of the book.

But the Committee of Citizens for Decency would not accept this decision, a very agitated Margaret informed Jane Rule: "They got up a petition vs the book, and the Rev Sam Buick opened his Dublin Street Pentecostal Church [in Peterborough] for 1 whole day so people could sign. He passed out handy xerox pages with the page references so people could look up and find the (marked) 'obscene' words and the sex scenes.... The novel was considered by his group to be unfit for kids of 18 to read under the guidance of a teacher in Grade 13, but it was quite okay for them to read the sex scenes totally out of context!" At a further meeting, the Board upheld its previous decision, but the book's enemies vowed to pack the School Board at the next municipal election. If they succeeded, Margaret told Jane, the Grade 13 students would be reading the Bobbsey Twins.

She tried to distance herself from the fundamentalists, who "damn near made a nervous wreck of me. I find it impossible to laugh at [them] —I think they are dangerous, bordering on fascist. I hope one of them doesn't hear a voice from God telling him to burn my house down." Some of their claims were ludicrous but alarming, one of her accusers going so far as to blame her for the existence of VD in Huron County. During this awful time, Adele Wiseman was unstinting in her support of her friend, as was Budge Wilson, who attended one of the open meetings to speak in support of Margaret. Ken and Mary Adachi were also unswerving in boosting their beleaguered friend. Joan Johnston, a colleague of Doug Williams, Alice's husband, in the probation service, became actively involved in the group that sprung to Margaret's side. Like Budge, Joan became Margaret's eyes and ears in the public arenas into which the distressed author did not dare venture. Joan, to use her own words, acted as a spy for her new friend, venturing one day to Sam Buick's church where she beheld twelve- and thirteen-year-old girls handing out sheets with page references to passages deemed salacious.

The opposition to her book paralysed Margaret, who always had a great deal of difficulty in any kind of public forum, much less one in which she was being attacked. Sometimes, she could joke about the matter, as in her letter to Jack McClelland, in the midst of a fight with him about her forthcoming collection of essays:

> My first reaction [to his suggested revisions] was one of incredulity and rage. However, my normally calm and indeed incredibly patient personality has once more re-asserted itself, and I am able to look at the situation with my usual tolerance and cool assessment. What a good idea about making the book a "great gift item"! Had you considered the vast possibilities of selling each copy individually wrapped in pink tissue paper, tied about with a wide pink ribbon? Or perhaps a tiny tasteful bunch of plastic forget-me-nots? This village, you know, has numerous gift shops—perhaps I might start one myself, handling only two items ... this book plus THE DIVINERS. I would, of course, call the shop ... PORN 'N CORN.

In his response, the "Boss" told her he was going to write the Peterborough *Examiner* "suggesting that they are on the right track; that all your books should be banned forthwith; that all your awards should be withdrawn because you are corrupting our children." Jokes aside, she became reluctant to be seen in Lakefield, becoming in the process extremely reclusive.

The controversy of 1976 helped to put even more nails into the coffin of the Laurence-Purdy friendship. During that time, she telephoned Purdy yet again, having summoned up the courage to do so only when inebriated. In August 1976, she offered yet another apology:

> I have angered and hurt you, and I am sorry.
>
> I do not recall what I said, as I was somewhat drunk at the time. My intention, as I dimly recall, was to phone to see if I could re-establish what has seemed for some time to me a slightly sagging friendship.
>
> What I accomplished, of course, was the reverse. I am sorry about this, too.
>
> Possibly I wanted subconsciously to wound you, as I myself still smart at the memory (I thought I didn't, but I do) of the way you shafted me re: *The Diviners*, first by silence and then when I asked your opinion of the book, finally, by saying this only: that I'd had enough feedback on that novel. If I did subconsciously wish to wound you, that is an unworthy thought and not one which I hold consciously.
>
> What with every fundamentalist in Peterborough County gunning for me (verbally, as yet) those six months, I may possibly be becoming a little paranoid. This is not a neurosis to which I ever laid claim, but who knows. Anyway, such is not an excuse or even an explanation.

Margaret was in a great deal of pain, and so unsure was she of herself that she acted as if she were completely at fault in the "sagging" of her friendship with Al.

The dispute between the two only got settled in a very uneven way during the winter of 1977, as can be glimpsed in this aside in a letter from Margaret: "Why didn't you tell me before that you had not previously read THE DIVINERS? If I'd known you hadn't read it before, I would not have taken on so, in bygone times. It's okay not to read a book, but to read it and not *say* anything.... well, let's not go into that again. That is over. But if you have all sorts of thoughts, whether positive or negative, I would like to hear an assortment of them." In the same letter, she made a heartfelt declaration, a real cry from the heart:

> Re: my writing. I wish people wouldn't think that I am in a state of despair, or am bowing out of life. Gee. It's not that way at all, Al. I hope I'll write another novel, and if I can get all these damn people who keep writing me letters of requests for interviews, etc, etc, off my back, I may even have some time to think. If another novel is given, I'll be grateful. If not, I won't be too upset. I don't think I'm useless in this life unless I'm writing—I would have thought that if I hadn't done the writing I was compelled to do, against great odds, then I would not have lived my life the way I was meant to live it. But I did my work, and I raised my kids and I kept a roof over the heads of us. If another true real novel comes along, and it may, then that will be a gift, a bonus. If not, then so be it, and I won't feel goddamn useless at all.

This letter—in which she talks about issues gnawing at her—has a powerful quality by virtue of its rawness, by the sender's incredible ability to talk about her feelings in such a naked way. After this, there are a handful of letters each way in the surviving Laurence-Purdy correspondence. The friendship was never terminated although there is a very discernible break. Too much had been requested by Margaret in the relationship and she must have felt not enough was given. In her life, this was a necessary loss, since her definition of friendship encompassed the ability to tell the other person her needs and to have those needs acknowledged. On Purdy's part, he felt perhaps that she had been too demanding, had asked for a commitment he was unwilling or unable to make.

At this time, Margaret had a quarrel with Jack McClelland about her forthcoming book—a collection of essays. He wanted to have some items deleted and objected to the various titles she proposed, including,

"Where the World Began." When she suggested *Heart of a Stranger*, he knew she had at last hit on the right title. The trouble with the book is not its contents—travel essays, journalistic pieces originally published in the *Vancouver Sun* and *Maclean's*, philosophical and autobiographical reflections—but with the expectation of a reading public that did not really want this kind of book from a writer from whom they expected "more." This situation distressed her: "what worries me is that I'm not supposed to have light words, or so some critics seem to think. When my essays ... came out, some reviewers said that it was pretty light stuff and not to be compared with a serious novel." In a slightly more jovial mood, she complained to Ernest Buckler: "AREN'T SERIOUS WRITERS PERMITTED A CHORTLE OR TWO, AN IRONIC TWIST OR TWO, SOME LIGHT VERSE, SOME LAUGHTER IN THE MIDST OF ALL OF LIFE?"

One boost of confidence in the autumn of 1976 came from Jack McClelland's invitation to join the Board of his publishing firm. When she accepted, she informed him that her agenda would be to get more books by young writers published. Earlier, in the summer, she had slipped on the dock at the shack and broken a rib; her condition was complicated by pleurisy, itself aggravated by chain-smoking. So she attempted to reduce her intake of the "filthy weed" from fifty to six a day.

Her fiftieth birthday party that August was, as she put it, "sensational." David, Jocelyn, Adele and her family, Don and Anne Bailey, Timothy Findley and Bill Whitehead were among the guests on the front lawn of the shack; another guest, Peter MacLachlan, became a hero when he jumped into the river to save a drowning man who was visiting a neighbour. The day had a bit of a sad ending when a drunken Margaret announced—yet again—that she had written her last novel. She added: "And the last man who will grace my bed has come and gone." Five years earlier—six months before she turned forty-five—she had told Margaret Atwood, "after I'd had a couple of books published, my relationships with men always fell into 1 of 2 categories ... those who saw me as a woman and would rather not know about my writing, and those who accepted me as a writer and equal (mostly writers these guys) but kind of a quasi-male figure or sort of neuter, and who would cringe slightly if I mentioned ... my children." To Donald Cameron, she mentioned the lack of men in her life but quipped that there were "not many men this middle-aged novelist would be interested in!"

However, if Margaret was celibate during these years, it was not for want of trying. She had a crush on a local undertaker—who had a reputation in the area as a virile lady's man. Once, when very drunk, she made advances to the husband of a friend. On that evening, she was so out of control that she had to be dragged out to his car in order to be driven home.

What all Margaret's friends noticed was the desperate loneliness which enveloped her. They could have the most pleasant and wonderful of conversations with her and share her joy in the ordinary things of life—but she dwelt in a solitary space into which no one else could enter. She now lived alone and—in the last decade of her life—she no longer wanted to live that way. In many ways, her solitude was self-imposed. A part of her hated herself for this state of affairs; another knew it was the price she had extracted from herself to pay for her art.

The most sustaining event of 1976 was perhaps ironical in view of the fact that the enemies of *The Diviners* had painted its author a modern day Jezebel: the accusation of irreligiousness forced her to take stock of her stand on that issue and in the process brought about an important change, best reflected in a letter to McMaster University's Will Ready: "I have begun to go back ... to the church of my people, which is the United Church (my folks long ago were of course Presbyterians, but joined church union with those parts of the Methodist church which went along with the concept). I wanted to do this for about two years here, and felt—it sounds odd, but it's true—shy. I finally did make it, and felt as though I had come back home again."

One part of her move back to the United Church comes from a renewed sense of herself as an extremely moral person, a side of herself she had to reaffirm in the light of the scathing attacks on her. She was also moved by the public support given to her by Jack Patterson, the minister of the Lakefield United Church in a letter to the Peterborough *Examiner*; through conversation with him, she found the path back. Margaret returned to church slowly, at first accompanied by the minister's wife. Later, although she even gave money for repairs to the church, she always left just before the service concluded—never staying for the lemonade and cookies that were available to members of the congregation directly after the service. Once, she attended church in the company of the Jewish artist Mendelson Joe, who was dressed in a Toronto Maple Leaf sweatshirt and blue jeans; she was deeply touched by the warm reception he was given despite his unconventional attire.

Her religious beliefs were most clearly stated in a letter to the elderly novelist Hubert Evans—who in his writings wrote with great sympathy of the plight of the natives: "I suppose that is one reason I feel so much connection with you and your writing, because we are both, in our different ways, Christian radicals. Would you agree? To me, it seems that good works without faith isn't enough, as we all stand so much in need of grace. But 'faith' without 'good works' ... ie a sense of social responsibility and the belief that the world around us *is* our responsibility, seems to me to be ... if not an empty faith, then at least a faith lacking in some kind of human dimension, the recognition of the reality of others and of others' pain."

Margaret's Christ was the social radical, the revolutionary who threw the money changers out of the temple and who hungered for social justice. In a letter to Evans of March 1982, she provided further details about her personal theology: "...a sense of grace. Yes. I think that's partly what I have indeed been writing about, all these years. A sense of the gift of God's grace, the sense of something *given*, not because deserved, of course, but because just given. That is how I have felt about my writing. Naturally, that does not mean mystical stuff and no work! God does not pick up the biro and write the words! But as I grow older, Hubert, says the young one of nearly 56 now, I come to feel more and more a sense of true gift and grace, as far as my work is concerned. It *is*, however, my own responsibility, as a human being with free will, to do with that as I can and as I choose. I think I've chosen to try to do whatever that gift of grace has made me think and write. As I grow older, which I seem to do daily (surprise surprise), it seems to me that I have to look at myself as a kind of very unorthodox Christian, but a Christian all the same. The social gospel is what seems to matter to me more and more. Why should any person say, as the fundamentalist born-again (?) Christians do, that saving *one's own* soul, by proclaiming Jesus as your spiritual saviour, is ALL that is necessary in this life? Hubert, I am astounded and downcast by those guys, I tell you straight. This seems to me to be a totally blinkered view of a gospel that I feel very greatly drawn to, and responsible to.... it seems to me that what still comes across, throughout those thousands of years of history, is a message by a young Jew who was educated probably by the Essenes, and whose new doctrine was simply another commandment, 'Thou shall love thy neighbour as thyself.'"

As a respite from all the troubles of the year, Margaret, Jocelyn and David spent Christmas 1976 in England. At a carol service given by the Royal Choral Society at the Royal Albert Hall she could feel the presence of the Christian dispensation as "the whole mighty audience, *thousands*, including me, rose and we sang our hearts out. It was magnificent. I could not see the printed words through my tears." In those wonderful moments, she returned in spirit to childhood Christmases and, in spite of the awfulness of the world and the rebuffs she had recently endured, she was filled with hope.

19

Lost Histories (1977-1985)

"I HAVE DONE nothing, it seems, for months (years!) except run around to seminars and conferences and so on." This was Margaret's complaint in June 1977. If her life continued to be dominated by such activities, the "one or two faint ideas" she had about a new novel would "never grow." She was, of course, paying the price for being Canada's most-beloved—and vilified—writer.

A part of her clearly recognized her writing career as a novelist might be over, but she also had the ambition to create new works of fiction. Mary Adachi was in charge of furnishing her with the scribblers in which she wrote. This was not an easy job because she knew Margaret was having difficulty writing and she wanted to encourage her by providing an ample supply of notebooks, while being careful not to exacerbate the problem by burdening her with too many.

Just as Margaret had earlier set fire to her literary archive before leaving Elmcot, she later destroyed virtually all the work on the two or three novels she worked on after her arrival back in Canada. Although the references in her letters to these various projects are vague and she never directly talked about these "lost" novels, it is possible to reconstruct some information about them. Her first ambition was to write a novel about the Old Left in Winnipeg, a group that had fascinated her many years before. She dropped this project in favour of a new Manawaka novel, but then realized she could not do this because those books formed a coherent whole. Such a project would be a "refuge," not a new creative beginning. One of the books she actually began can be glimpsed in a 1979 letter to Adele Wiseman: "I want to do something, sometime, with the evangelist thing, but I wonder if at this point in my life it would come out sounding like a desire for revenge." This novel would have been a kind of Elmer Gantry narrative, one which explored the inner workings of the fundamentalists who had so viciously attacked her.

At first glance, this seems an extraordinary project, given Margaret's other books. However, in *The Stone Angel* and *A Bird in the House*, the stern, authoritarian demeanour of her grandfather had served as inspiration. A book on the fundamentalists would have returned her to that domain. Her skills as a writer were not satirical, and a book about the fundamentalists would have required her to delve into the world of—and, in the process, perhaps write sympathetically about—her enemies. Her insecure side pulled her in the direction of a book in which to some extent she would have explained and justified the conduct of her opponents. The strong, resilient side of Margaret ultimately resisted any such impulse because it would have been a form of capitulation.

But she worked on various novel projects for long stretches of time. On September 5, 1981, she mentioned that after "thinking about a novel for about 3 years, I've finally got going ... (after 5 false starts ... rather depressing). It sure doesn't get easier." In 1980, she outlined the grim situation to Gabrielle Roy: "My writing goes so slowly and so badly, of late. I have three times made a false start on a novel, and so far have torn up about 50 pp of handwriting. However, my handwriting is somewhat large and scrawling, so it isn't as much as it sounds. I am pretty sure there is a novel there, somewhere, if only I can find it, or at least find my way into it." As never before, her confidence—difficult to muster—would suddenly flow away.

On September 14, 1981, she caught sight of the possibility of being at long last on to something:

> Work progressing very slowly, but oddly enough I feel a kind of confidence beginning to grow. What puts me off the track is when I get too upset about the state of the world and think—what am I *doing*, writing fiction, when the world is falling apart? Then again, I used to feel like that 25 years ago in Vancouver, and at many times since. We have to go on working.

Less than a week later, she had crashed:

> I hate everything I've written so far in this damn so-called novel. The problems are still there, namely that the forum is formulas and the writing is garbage. I am *not*—repeat, *not*—in despair, however, just feel very quiet and don't feel like talking very much. I will get over it. I have this persistent feeling that one day there will be some kind of revelation, and I will know pretty well how to go about telling the story.
>
> There is always the fear that perhaps the gift really *has* departed. If so, (and I don't say it *is* so) Morag never knew the half of how painful that would be.

By January 1982, she had to face the fact the "gift" might indeed have passed beyond her ability to reclaim it:

> Have stuck to my realistic schedule this week, and have re-written (for the 100th time) the first part of Chapter I. Now I'm stuck again. Have just sat at that damn desk for about 2 hours. Nothing. Zilch. I know what I want to do but am scared to begin. The next bit has to be totally re-shaped in every way from the first way I did it—I must not even look at the some 75 pp (handwritten) I did before. I think of a sign that used to be on a local shop (shoppe?) ... Antiques & Junque. Those 75 pp are Junque. But contain the thread of the narrative I want. I don't know why I experience more crises of confidence these past few years than I ever did before.

So many factors contributed to the "why": for the most part, she had written most effectively about Canada when away from it; she may well have said what she wanted to say in the Manawaka novels; she had always resisted "mockups" of novels, pieces of fiction written just to write something; she had been publicly branded as immoral and irreligious. And so unable to write and badly scarred by the attacks of the zealots, she began to take stock of her religious values.

Margaret's religious sensibility, reawakened following her brush with the fundamentalists, forced her to define her brand of Christianity in opposition to theirs. She thought of herself as a Christian, and the fundamentalists proclaimed themselves such. How was this possible?

In the winter of 1976, her old friends Lois and Roy Wilson, then United Church ministers in Hamilton, received a surprise phone call: "This is a friend out of your past. It's Margaret Laurence, and I'm here signing books and I'm bored to death. Can I come over?" At that meeting, Margaret renewed her friendship with her two friends from United College days.

Tiny, wiry and dynamic Lois quickly realized Margaret's religious convictions were in the process of being revitalized. So close did the two become that Margaret later agreed to participate in a dialogue sermon with Lois in Kingston in 1979. In 1982, shortly after Lois was elected Moderator of the United Church, she received a letter from Margaret which read in its entirety:

> Hallelujah, Hallelujah, Hallelujah, Hallelujah
> Hallelujah, Hallelujah, Hallelujah, Hallelujah.

The revitalized friendship between the two women cut two ways. Margaret prepared for Lois in about 1980 "A Selected and Highly Personal List of Canadian Novels in the Past Couple of Years," which includes Adele Wiseman's *Crackpot*, Alice Munro's *Who Do You Think You Are?*, Margaret Atwood's *Life Before Man*, Jane Rule's *The Young in*

One Another's Arms, Marian Engel's *The Glassy Sea*, Oonah McFee's *Sandbars*, Florence Evans' *A Man without Passion*, Timothy Findley's *The Wars*, Matt Cohen's *The Sweet Second Summer of Kitty Malone*, Rudy Wiebe's *The Scorched-Wood People*, Robertson Davies' Deptford trilogy, three novels by each of Jack Hodgins and Gabrielle Roy, and two by Don Bailey.

In turn, Lois provided her with a list of books by contemporary feminist theologians. The influence of such writers can be seen in one of the reflections Margaret offered at Kingston:

> I have a feeling that there has to be more recognition of the kind of female principle in God. I don't mean people going around with T-shirts saying: "Trust in the Lord; She will provide." That is a trivial way of looking at it. But after centuries of thinking of God in strictly male, rather authoritarian terms, it seems to me that there has to be some recognition of the female principle in God. We understand God, of course, very imperfectly. We really cannot define the informing spirit of the Universe because that is the mystery at the core of life.... I think many women nowadays, and many men, feel the need to incorporate that sense of both the motherhood and fatherhood in the Holy Spirit.

Rather than allowing herself to be spiritually browbeaten by the fundamentalists, Margaret used the experience to renew her faith and to achieve a new vision of the ineffable power of God, one that included at its centre the notion of female power. Of course, the acquisition of power by women is one of the central themes of her fiction. Late in life, she was able to blend that concern with her religious beliefs. Another important early relationship that was revived in the late 1970s was with her brother, Robert, his wife, Pat, and their two daughters. With Bob and Lois, in particular, she was retracing roots, trying to get in touch with the Peggy Wemyss of years before.

Even if she had been able to write on a consistent basis, Margaret Laurence the secluded public figure would have found it extremely difficult to find time in which to do so. She provided an excellent analysis of her situation to Frank Paci: "My problem is not *isolation*; it *is* not having enough time to contemplate, think, pace the floor, try to get into this damn novel that I feel is there somewhere. I have an unfortunate tendency to get myself involved in Good Causes." She was constantly besieged by writers and/or their publishers for blurbs for their books—"tender messages" or "TMs" she called them; from 1974, she published at least twenty-five essays, introductions and book reviews. She also intervened on behalf of other writers, usually without being asked and without informing the person she was attempting to assist. For example, she tried on several occasions to interest Judith Jones in Alice Munro well before Knopf became that writer's American publisher. Sometimes, Margaret lost patience with the trappings of fame, particularly when she felt someone was taking advantage of her. In a moment of uncharacteristic honesty on this sore point, she exploded in a letter to Andreas Schroeder: "I am not Mother Earth. In fact, I do not feel that at present I can call myself a writer, as I have been unable (not through lack of trying) to write what I would like to write, for some years now. For some time, if I am not mistaken, I did try to help other and younger writers. Now I need help. A shocking thought? Mum isn't strong?" She needed help, but her drinking was off-putting to even close friends, who were embarrassed by seeing someone of her stature reduced to speaking in childish babble. When they were with her, Jocelyn and David felt the same way.

In 1977, in an attempt to keep the plenitude of "Good Causes" at bay, she prepared a form letter listing twenty-two activities which she could not undertake (giving publishing advice, editing or reading manuscripts, giving interviews). In order to protect herself from the likes of the boorish woman who telephones Morag near the beginning of *The Diviners*, Margaret resorted to an unlisted phone number.

The "Good Causes" she did take on included membership on the board of directors of Energy Probe, writing campaign materials for the

NDP in 1980 and working on Lynn McDonald's election campaign in 1984, active involvement with Project Ploughshares and Operation Dismantle, and agreeing in 1981 to become Chancellor of Trent University.

Even good works could be hazardous. In April 1984, she allowed Freedom of Choice to send a letter out under her signature (with a photograph) and asked Leslie Paul, the national coordinator, to let her see some of the responses. She advised Margaret that this was not a good idea, but the president of Freedom of Choice overrode this decision when it became necessary to report some of the mail to the police. One of these stated: "I want to get you pregnant and then we'll kill him (or her) together. Fun? Wow! Afterwards we'll eat the child for dinner!" For a woman living alone and in an extremely accessible place in a small village, this would have been very frightening. She sent this material to Adele with a note attached: "I hate to send you this terrible stuff. But here it is—we have to know."

In the midst of the banning scandal in 1976, Margaret had agreed to join the Board of McClelland & Stewart, but she soon was at loggerheads with the "Boss." Certainly, she found herself in a distinct minority, feeling she did not have much in common with the captains of industry she met there. In March 1977, she voiced her strong disagreement to the publishing of a second Roloff Beny book on Iran, which she argued was an extremely repressive regime. In September 1977, she went behind McClelland's back and sent a letter to members of the Board concerning the Writers' Union. As her letter to Purdy of September 28 makes clear, she did not enjoy being part of a process which was meaningless and depressing:

> Every time I attend a board meeting I come away feeling so depressed I think I can't stand to remain on the Board. I don't think I will, either, after the year I promised is up, in the spring. What good do I do? None. The Board is only a figurehead ... Jack [has] already decided exactly what to do. Every time I raise my voice, or write long letters to Jack, he listens attentively or replies in an equally long letter, and pays not a scrap of heed. All the news seems bad,

> financially, which means they will take fewer and fewer risks with first novels, or with any thing remotely experimental or different. At times I just want only to stop thinking about it all. I get disrupted for days afterwards—emotional retrogression.

She stayed on for four years, not resigning until May 20, 1980, citing a potential conflict of interest: "As my whole professional life is tied up with McClelland & Stewart and as most of my income for some years now has come from royalties on books published by the firm, it is obviously in my interest that those books should remain in print."

Despite this desire, she did not like McClelland's publicity/fund-raising stunts, such as the Night of the 100 Authors wherein the chosen writers paraded into a large, glittering ballroom where they were to be joined by their host or hosts (wealthy sponsors). To her agent, John Cushman, she penned her reflections: "Thank God I had lunch with you that day ... that was the only good thing that happened.... After the authors' cocktail party, we, the authors, were led as lambs to the slaughter, into what was apparently a long basement corridor connecting one kitchen with another ... The corridor was airless ... My feet hurt. I got more and more irritated ... 'If this line does not move soon,' I proclaimed, 'I AM GOING HOME,' [whereupon her publicist offered to take her in before anyone else]. 'Are you out of your head? I'm a socialist!'" Finally, when they got to the dining room, Margaret's host for the evening was not there.

In 1982, an exhausted Jack McClelland decided to become Chairman of the Board and to leave the actual day-to-day running of his firm to Linda McKnight, who succeeded him as president. Margaret, who was also trying to simplify her life, told the "Boss" how much he had meant to her, despite the various scraps. These included the fight over the title of *The Fire-Dwellers*: "At the time I didn't realize that the firm was in dire straits financially and you had a lot more on your mind than the title of one author's book. I also recall the famous battle over the Writers' Union contract, when I angrily wrote to all the Board members. Ye gods, I now think the union contract is far too ambitious and complicated and needs to be simplified and made more realistic (I think this is being done). Also the fight re: the Iran book ... Well, we have disagreed a lot, throughout the years, Jack, but the main thing is that I have always felt I could express my views and that although you might disagree with them, you would always take them seriously."

She was an outspoken champion of social justice, one who never had patience with the polite mechanics of democracy. So when she felt McClelland was unwilling to listen to the concerns of the Writers' Union on the issue of contracts, she had taken action. Now her appointment as Chancellor of Trent quickly brought her into similar hot water. By definition, a Chancellor acts as a ceremonial figurehead, and, on paper, it seemed a brilliant stroke to invite one of Canada's most famous women to serve in that capacity at the nearby university. In the process, Margaret's passionate nature was overlooked.

Nine months after having been installed as Chancellor, she challenged the contents of a report which in her view would irrevocably and negatively transform the nature of the small university, the proposed changes being backed by Donald Theall, the president. For some reason, she did not receive the report until it had been in the hands of the other members of the Board for two weeks. Meanwhile, faculty members had appealed to her, providing her with their side of the story. After studying the report for two days, she sent a six-page single-spaced letter to the Board chairman, providing carbon copies to eight others. Her letter was later printed in full and thus available to all members of the Trent community. When a furious Theall telephoned, she invited him to lunch the next day. He berated her for forty-five minutes on her unseemly behaviour, not touching the meal she had prepared.

Margaret, meanwhile, remained a vehement supporter of the Writers' Union. Clear-eyed about its role, she offered the novelist and editor John Metcalf some frank advice: "But I really don't see how you can blame the union, John, just because someone who is a member gave you an unfavourable review. We stand together (hopefully) on matters concerning our common welfare and financial advancement (although goodness knows there are bound to be, always, many differences of opinion about how those issues should be approached, too) but not necessarily in terms of our views on anything else, whether political or the assessment or writing or whatever. I certainly don't expect the union to take responsibility for what I say."

In the late seventies, Margaret had many responsibilities which ate up her time. For example, she had to read a great deal of the work of others when she served as member of the jury for the Governor General's Award for fiction, reading an average of seventy books a year. She worried about the sale of her books, particularly the Manawaka novels, which were available from two paperback publishers, Bantam-Seal and the New Canadian Library. The price of the Seal mass-market edition was markedly lower than the quality paperback edition. She informed Jack McClelland in May 1978:

> As I mentioned to you on the phone, when I agreed to have all the Manawaka books brought out in Seal editions, just as when I agreed to have THE DIVINERS brought out in the Bantam Canada edition, I was concerned that the mass paperback edition would cut into the NCL sales. I thought this made sense at the time. Now, however, I learn that Bantam has sent out a catalogue including the Seal editions, making a big play of having all my Manawaka books in cheap paperback, and has circulated this catalogue throughout the academic world in this country. You said you couldn't prevent them from doing so. But I thought M & S owned a controlling share in Seal Books. In the catalogue, no mention is even made of Seal except the emblem at the end of the catalogue, in a very tiny reproduction. The Bantam and Seal editions of my books sell for $1.95. The NCL for prices ranging from about $2.25 to $3.95. No fanfare whatsoever was made of the fact that, with the publication of THE DIVINERS in the NCL, now *all* my fiction is available in

> that series. With Bantam giving lots of publicity to the Manawaka books in mass paperback editions, what will obviously happen is that these will supplant the NCL editions for use in school and university courses, thus cutting my income on these books approximately in half.

In the following year, her royalty payments took a sharp dip. From the time of the publication of *The Diviners* until 1979, as she told Hugh MacLennan—who taught at McGill—"my income was just about as much as a full professor of English—I thought, wow! And that really *was* something, Hugh, as you know. However, last year my income dropped by almost exactly 50%, a nasty shock that told me I had been living in a fool's paradise—taking my time getting into another novel, getting out to dozens of high schools and university classes in CanLit, mostly unpaid, spreading the good word."

That decline may have contributed to her resolve in 1980 to sell the cottage, where she continued to spend the summer months, although her explanation of her decision was somewhat different:

> It has been wonderful for 10 years, and I wrote most of THE DIVINERS there, but I think it has served its blessed purpose. I find it a bit of a hassle to have 2 places, and in 6 years I have come to love this village very much and to feel a part of this small community, so I don't need to get away. Also, the cottage was so much bound up in my mind with the writing of THE DIVINERS that I found I couldn't really write there any longer. This doesn't mean that if I manage to write another novel I'll have to sell up here in Lakefield! The cottage itself wasn't a part of the novel, but that particular view of the Otonabee river really was and that is the first time ever that the view I looked at, each time I raised my eyes from what I was writing, came into the writing naturally and as if meant to be. I think, too, I am trying to simplify my life in order to concentrate as much as I can on what is ahead, I hope.

"Simplify" was exactly what Margaret was not able to do, so demanding were the requests she received and so overly demanding were her expectations of herself.

One activity to which Margaret gave her left-over time from various causes and public appearances was children's literature. In 1979-80, she published three books for young readers: *The Olden Days Coat, Six Darn Cows* and *The Christmas Birthday Story.* Jack McClelland, the publisher of the first title, was not amused to learn in July 1979 that she had another "juvenile" coming out with James Lorimer in the same fall season. Why was this happening?, he asked Margaret's editor, Jennifer Glossop, who was also startled by the news. The "Boss" cannot have been thrilled by the rather nonchalant answer the phone call produced: "When I called her to ask about it," Glossop reported to McClelland, "she was very apologetic and said she should have told you about it earlier but she doesn't think it will be competition ... The book is part of a series for young readers (ages 5-6)."

Margaret was not quite as carefree about her Christmas book, published by McClelland & Stewart and Knopf, as she told McClelland on August 9, 1980: "the little book *may* be condemned by the same rednecks who condemned *The Diviners,* as blasphemous, because Mary and Joseph don't care whether their child turns out to be a girl or a boy. Actually, I hope that doesn't happen—what a hell of a way to sell books. I've had enough of being called nasty names."

This book, as she told Malcolm Ross, had an interesting genesis: it had been written twenty-one years earlier "when my kids (in Vancouver) were 4 and 7. I lost my only copy in 1962 when I moved to England with the kids, and only found it 3 years ago, when I discovered quite by accident that it was still being used in the Unitarian Church Sunday School in Vancouver. I got a copy, re-wrote it to some extent, and asked the Toronto artist Helen Lucas if she would do the pictures." The expected condemnation came from a different source, as can be seen in the wounded writer's letter to McClelland: "Wow! Was that ever a stinker of a review in *The Globe* last Saturday! That same babe, Jacquie Hunt, whoever she is, did a review last year of THE OLDEN DAYS COAT, and said substantially the same thing—text terrible, pics great."

The politics of the book world amused and frightened her. In May 1981, she was surprised and only limitedly pleased when the Canadian Booksellers' Association named her "Author of the Year": "Somewhat to my embarrassment, the CBA has apparently named me Author of the Year. I certainly don't know why, as I haven't published an adult novel in years, but I suppose it is the re-issuing of some of my books in paperback plus the kids' books." The one-thousand-dollar award was, in any event, "better than a slap across the face with a wet fish."

In the early eighties, Margaret became involved in literary power politics of a very different sort. For some years, she and Adele had kept an informal "Hit List," sometimes referred to as "The Shit List." Names entered there were those who had in some way offended either woman. Since the list was a conjoint one, an enemy of one woman was seen as the enemy of the other. In her career as a writer, Adele Wiseman—who had not published a great deal—had obviously not been as successful as Margaret, who gracefully maintained she wrote for her own time whereas Adele wrote for the ages. Much more interested than Margaret in the intrigues within the book world, Adele had also become increasingly bitter over time at the lack of recognition she had received. She would often become vituperative and, Margaret, out of a sense of loyalty, would join her lead. At the end of her life, Margaret made a critical reference to Adele in her journal: Adele "of course has been my dearest friend & colleague for so long. ~~But sometimes~~." In those crossed-out words, the reader can catch a glimpse of her feeling of exasperation at the relentlessness of Adele's rage.

Margaret may not have liked the rage, but she knew Adele had been unfailingly loyal. At some level, it must have been difficult for Adele to remain a close and uncritical friend to a writer of celebrity status. Adele's anger at the injustices she endured was never focused on Margaret. So close was she to her that she could forgive her for obtaining the fame that always eluded her. In fact, she continued to relish Margaret's success. The bitterness was only part of her character—she remained vibrant, warm and compulsively generous. As young women, the two had formed a bond based on the notion that they had to comfort each other in the face of life's numerous difficulties. That compact was never abandoned.

Although Margaret's interest in the Union had remained strong, she had never wanted any kind of limelight. She was willing to work on committees but otherwise did not take a strong daily interest in the politics of the organization. Adele acted otherwise. She was furious when more and more non-fiction writers (i.e. journalists) started to join the Union in increasing numbers; June Callwood's election as chairperson in 1979 was for her the nadir. As far as she was concerned, the Union was no longer going to be a band of essentially creative writers joined together (June Callwood, however, was a founding member of TWUC). Adele and three other writers (Peter Such, Joyce Marshall and Judith Merril)—known as "The Gang of Four"—resigned as a group in the wake of problems with office staff; at the time, accusations of financial irregularities were bandied back and forth. Margaret, obviously feeling under pressure to be loyal to Adele, resigned from the Union on October 8, 1982, citing, among other reasons, the Union's dismal relationship with the Canada Council, the "partying" fervour that had taken over recent AGMs, the Union's unwillingness to challenge the federal government on important political and social issues. "I do not resign in anger at all, but rather from a sense that I can no longer give anything to the union, nor the union to me.... I do feel that the union has departed from its original intentions."

At about this time, however, Margaret declined to join the "Club," Adele's attempt to form an alternative consortium to the Writers' Union. Moreover, none of her stated reasons for leaving the Union tie into Adele's. There is, perhaps, a more direct—although contorted—way to explain what happened in 1982, one which is hinted at in a letter to Marian Engel of January 31, 1983: "I would just like you to know that my letter of resignation from the union (which is not a confidential letter and can presumably be seen by anyone who wishes to check out my carefully considered reasons) was written *before* I discovered that my daughter had been subjected to the distressing phone calls of which you are aware. The two things were in no way connected."

Many members of the writing and publishing community in Canada were well aware that Margaret drank too much. Although no one broached the topic with her, many friends and acquaintances thought she was killing herself. Marian Engel—whose novel *Bear* had enjoyed a remarkable *succès de scandale* in 1976 and herself a heavy drinker—was concerned about Margaret. In her cryptic diary entries for October 26, and October 30, 1982, a few weeks after the resignation, Marian—who had discussed the matter in detail with her good friend, Peggy (Margaret) Atwood—mentions that Margaret had been outraged by Peggy's criticism of her drinking in a phone call to Jocelyn, then executive editor of *Toronto Life* magazine. She began by referring to the animosity that had been unleashed, placing herself and Peggy on one side, Margaret and Adele on the other.

> 26 October
> Now we are gossips, & traitors & very hurt. Letters, phone calls flying.
>
> She is quite right that she [Margaret] helped me more than I did her. Should rather die than take the lower position. The dreadful thing is that if she goes on drinking she will.
>
> She's written off the Union, most writer friends. Except of course Adele whose hate grows like a ball of butter, it seems.
>
> Well, too, if Adele forms her salon, it will get the Union back to being a Union not a club.
>
> I was hurt. Now I'm relieved. Something had to be done. Peg did it; we backed her. There's a crisis.
>
> Oh, I hope she doesn't withdraw entirely. I hope she SEES.
>
> It wasn't until Peg told me drinkers were boring that I saw.
>
> M's jealousy of P is on the surface now—surfacing for *Survival.*

Oct 30
... now I realize how few friends I have here & without *Margaret.* And will she savage me? Oh Margaret, Margaret I loved you, but *no one* is God & it is madness to believe lies.

* * *

Long talk with Peg about Margaret
She spoke to Joc
Joc told not Marg but Adele
Peg says that the old Marg doesn't exist any more.
Adele has a new patient
Marg's pretences are now out in the open
She has nowhere to go

Marian Engel's fragmentary entries seem to suggest that events had reached a crisis point, perhaps culminating in Margaret's resignation from the Union, and thus having "nowhere to go."

In the autumn of 1982, a visiting writer friend told Peggy Atwood that something had to be done about Margaret Laurence's excessive drinking. This friend insisted Peggy was the person to undertake the delicate task of confronting Margaret about her self-destructive behaviour. Peggy was not certain this was a good idea, presumably on the grounds that a person who drank excessively would not stop if ordered to do so. She decided to phone Jocelyn, who politely responded: "Mum may drink too much, it worries me too, but that's her business." Jocelyn decided not to tell her mother about the phone call but, obviously bothered by it, confided in Adele, who informed a furious and humiliated Margaret about it.

Since Margaret's return to Canada, her friendship with Margaret Atwood had undergone a curious metamorphosis. Although she was kind—sometimes excessively so—to other, especially younger, writers, she had always been a bit uneasy about Margaret Atwood, who she maintained was a gifted poet but not a great novelist. In Canada in the late seventies and early eighties, Margaret Atwood was the only other woman writer anywhere in the same league. Jealousy amongst writers is a dark, complex emotion—one difficult for Margaret to admit to or even think about. Once, she told a friend she had not become a writer in order to enter the "immortality stakes" but she did not completely (or realistically) believe that. And, in reality, she felt that Margaret Atwood was the only other woman in Canada who could surpass her.

In her turn, Atwood was no longer willing to play the role of acolyte. In her dealings with Laurence, she had found the older writer excessively self-centred, a relationship dictated on her terms being the only option. Friendship—which implies equality—was out of the question. And Atwood—who had a genuine affection and concern for Margaret—resented the older woman's behaviour, in part because of her legendary graciousness to other members of her "tribe." But Margaret Laurence, no longer able to write, was threatened by her and was, in turn, resentful. Atwood certainly had not enjoyed being around a drunken Margaret during her one visit to the cottage: she had been both bored and dismayed.

Under pressure, Peggy Atwood made a phone call that sadly led to nothing but trouble. Margaret was furious, but she never confronted Peggy, although she placed her at the top of the "shit list." She obviously felt that Peggy had wanted to humiliate, not assist her. In subsequent years, Peggy would hear nasty stories about herself disseminated by either Margaret or Adele. Margaret's departure from the Union—with which both Engel (as founding Chairperson) and Atwood (Chairperson 1981) were intimately involved—may well have been her public response to the phone call.

This story has a strange coda. Marian Engel had been a friend of Margaret's before the Atwood incident. When, two years later, Marian Engel was dying, that relationship was revived and intensified, leading to exchanges of letters in which Margaret attempted to define her own particular brand of feminism and to locate a new writing voice. The link forged between the two was one based on the fact they were professional women writers—both with broken marriages—who had tried to balance the rearing of children with the demands of their calling.

> Personally, I think that a lot of women writers in this country, whether with children or not, and whether with mates or not, have been HEROIC. But one thing we have NOT been is bloodless, and you know, Virginia [Woolf]'s writing, much of which I read long ago, never did strike a chord in my heart.... it always seemed so cerebral, so bloodless.... But she never chose to write about things closest to her own heart and spirit, and obviously I am not talking here about writing in any direct autobiographical way. I think a lot of Canadian women writers ... quite frankly ... have been braver.

If Virginia Woolf was not a suitable model, Jane Austen was:

> ...the more I read her and think about her, such a subtle and strong feminist! *In them days!* But those days, apparently so far back, are not so very different from our own. Is this not always the way? I think so. Strong women did always have the difficulties that Austen presents, and people like you and I have lived through that, too. With, I may say, tolerable success. We pass on a whole lot of things to the children, both female and male, or so I hope and pray and know.

Another woman writer Margaret greatly admired was Emily Brontë, whose *Wuthering Heights* she had often picked up on sleepless nights. At the very end of her life, she told herself: "I am in spirit like wild Emily, but in life more like Charlotte."

After she abandoned work on three projects for novels, Margaret became determined on one centred on mothers and daughters, obviously a book which could talk about "strong women" and the "passing on" of certain vital, often ignored issues, overlooked because they were part of female history. (The surviving fragments of the novel, *Dance on the Earth*, are described in the Appendix.) By May 1984, having determined to write such a book as non-fiction, she told Marian: "I find myself writing odd things, not a novel, more like things about my ancestral families, especially the women. History has been written, and lines of descent traced, through the male lines. More and more I want to speak about women (always have, of course, in my fiction, but now I want to get closer to my own experience.... not necessarily directly autobiographical, but close, I guess). We will see. What stuns me, looking at my own family, is how pitifully little I know about the women, even my grandmothers ... and how much about the men. Lost histories ... perhaps we must invent them in order to rediscover them." The act of "rediscovery" and "re-invention" of "lost histories" would be her last book, *Dance on the Earth*.

20

The Diviner

(1986-1987)

By the early 1980s, Margaret had made a good recovery from the banning controversy. She no longer felt like some sort of undesirable in Lakefield. In May 1981, she was even an enthusiastic participant in the Victoria Day celebrations.

> Craft displays, hot dog stands on main street, which is closed to cars, people wandering around in genuine and pseudo Victorian costumes! I have a long printed dress, slightly Victorian in appearance, on which last year, for the same event, I sewed a bunch of lace I once bought from an English gypsy, plus a long black cape lined with scarlet—a girl in England once made it for me, and I hardly ever wear it, but it's dandy for such an occasion as this.... Last evening I was one of the *five* judges in a Queen Victoria Look-Alike Contest. There were *three* contestants!!

At the same event, she was moved by the sight of a little boy in a fiddling contest: "I could hardly look at him, with his pants slipping a trifle and revealing his undershirt, and his face with snub nose and a small frown of total concentration—I thought I'd start weeping, as I remember always doing when my kids were little, at the Sunday school Christmas concerts."

Her lively sense of fun about her life in the village extended to this mock press release, written for Adele's delectation, concerning her Canadian answer to Paul Newman's Own salad dressings. Her riposte was called "Margaret of Blue Gables Own."

> Margaret Laurence fans, most of whom have already joined her for dinner or lunch in her quaint and picturesque village here, can now taste in the privacy of their own homes one of her mouth-watering delicacies.
>
> For years, the bleary-eyed writer and fanatical non-athlete has made a cauliflower soup from incredibly cheap ingredients, and has served it to her helpless family and such of her friends as could be unwittingly trapped into tasting the tasty repast. For years, her family and friends have suggested to her that the cheap concoction could be a way to beat inflation and relieve the ailment, from which she periodically suffers, known as Writers' Panic, believed by medical authorities to be caused by financial doubts.

After 1983, when Joan Johnston retired, she and Margaret were often together. Almost every day, Joan would pick up the phone to the announcement, "C'est moi." The two would go on shopping expeditions together, with the last "obligatory stop" (Margaret's phrase) at the LCBO at the edge of town to buy gin and whisky (usually Johnnie Walker Red but Glenfiddich when Margaret felt rich). They often went out for lunch, where Margaret would order a martini straight up.

There were more formal occasions in the early eighties. In March 1982, she was given an honorary degree (Doctor of Sacred Letters) from Emmanuel College, a part of Victoria University at the University of Toronto. This tribute, as Margaret knew, had been arranged specifically as a vote of confidence in the morality inherent in all her writings, especially *The Diviners*. Before the ceremony, she was at table with the slightly intimidating literary critic Northrop Frye ("many people," she asserted, "jovially refer to him as Norrie, but I am not one of them."). She thanked Frye: "This degree means a very great deal to me because it seems a vote of confidence from some of my own people." He replied, very gently: "I believe that was the intention."

Once Margaret caught the glimmer of a book she could actually write—her mothers and daughters project—she withdrew as much as possible from public life. In April 1983, she decided not to let her name stand for a further term as Chancellor of Trent. What she needed, she claimed, was a two-year sabbatical from public life, although she was willing to remain on the various boards of which she was a member. Another problem was one of "cash flow." She had to dip into her savings at a much faster clip than with which she was comfortable. For example, she had also been taking the bus to Toronto on an average of once a week: that too would have to cease.

In January 1985, Margaret wrote a letter of consolation to a friend: "Death is so strange. I aspire to be a Christian, yet I cannot say I feel certain of a life-after-death, or even if I think that it matters. I have a sense that *something* happens, but that it is not given to us to know, until the time. Possibly something so far beyond our present human minds that we cannot conceive of it." This moving, wistful reflection was in part inspired by a new controversy surrounding her books.

One of her first references to the new assault is in a letter to Budge Wilson: "This idiot lady. Mrs. Helen Trotter of the Burleigh-Anstruther TWP council, decided to go for the jugular. She says, as you have heard, that *The Stone Angel* shows 'disrespect for humanity.' How lunatic can a supposedly sane person get?" In a more reflective mood, she tried to see the matter from the viewpoint of her opponents:

> Of course, the opponents like Mrs. Trotter are sincere and well-meaning and mainly born-again fundamentalist Christians, who do not recognize that there are any other kinds of Christians, never mind any other religions. What they want to do is to dictate what all

> our children may or may not read or be taught in High Schools.... And when they rank me with the pornographers, I become very anguished and angry. They have been saying that my books are "dirty, disgusting and degrading" ... they have not read them, except perhaps in a few passages here and there, and they certainly have not read them with any understanding at all.... I can't tell them that ... they can't hear. They can't understand that an old garbageman in a little town [Christie in *The Diviners*] could be, indeed, a kind of Christ-like figure, a scapegoat for the town's self-righteous people, a man who knew about the importance of the ancestors and tried to give Morag this sense of the importance of the past and of her own people, a man who, really, was, in my view, gifted with God's grace. How can I explain to those who cannot see? Well, obviously I cannot. But when Mrs. Trotter said that THE STONE ANGEL shows "disrespect for humanity," I was really upset.... I vowed this time that it would not upset me, but of course it has. How can I explain to the fundamentalists, who would not recognize me as a Christian, how I feel and what things I have put into those books?

This time, Margaret was determined to battle her opponents. The passivity that had overwhelmed her before vanished. In part, this was because of the incredible support she had received during the first banning controversy. There were other factors at work. In the intervening years, Margaret, in redefining her Christianity, knew herself to be a truly moral person. In addition, in the wake of the controversies and in the aftermath of an exceedingly long writer's block, she now realized another book was within her grasp, one in which she could proclaim her religious beliefs.

Her self-confidence reasserted itself: "I decided [she informed Budge] to fight back this time, and have had interviews with the press, with radio and TV, phone interviews, you name it. Not only on my own behalf but on behalf of all other contemporary and also Canadian writers. I was on with Gzowski on 'Morningside' on December 31, and of course all these things also generate a lot of mail. I am daily getting lots of letters in support of my books. I do reply to as many as I can, but it does tend to swamp me. Anyway, the Peterborough Board of Education meets on Jan 24, so we will see. This time I don't feel so much hurt as angry and outraged." The normally shy Margaret was always comfortable with Peter Gzowski, whom she called the "best interviewer in the business" and "a really nice guy," but she even enjoyed her appearance as the "mystery guest" on "Front Page Challenge" on April 20, 1985 when she stumped the combined expertise of Pierre Berton, Betty Kennedy, Allan Fotheringham and Knowlton Nash.

In the midst of her gruelling schedule, Margaret was having trouble with her right eye, which had a cataract. Later, in the spring of 1985, she was diagnosed as having carpal tunnel syndrome in the right hand and wrist. She had other worries. Although she coped well with the new controversy, she was scared again that some zealot might attack her at home.

Shortly after the school board yet again refused to ban Margaret's books, she had to put up in June 1984 with a prank in the humour column ("The Mason Line") in the *Lakefield Chronicle*, wherein a new novel by her was announced.

> The first thing to say about Margaret Laurence's latest novel, *Singing Fire*, is that it is brilliant. The author of *The Stone Angel* and *The Diviners* is back with a vengeance, and there seems every reason to believe that this new book will swiftly establish itself as a contemporary classic of our young literature. This said, it should also be noted that *Fire* has a special significance for Lakefield residents. The novel is set in an Ontario village so transparently like her own that Ms. Laurence stuns with her audacity. Not only has she appropriated the geography of Lakefield, she has also borrowed its very streets and public buildings: and additionally—and most daringly—several Lakefield personalities are clearly recognizable among her characters, and two recent local scandals have been skilfully woven into the fabric of a compelling narrative.... Readers who objected to the celebration of Unnatural Sexual Practices in *The Diviners* will be relieved to learn that *Singing Fire* has only six, brief steamy passages. They

> are found on pages 6-9, 22-23, 42-49, 101-111, 152-154 and 206-53, and can be skipped over, if the reader is so inclined, without doing violence to the story's flow.

An outraged Margaret told Adele: "This bugger took on the wrong adversary! I am going to scare the shit out of him!!! (I hope)." She instructed her lawyer to write a letter informing Paul Mason and the newspaper that the piece was libellous, but she dropped the matter when the young journalist offered her a profuse apology.

Despite this and all other impediments, her social calendar was very full in the early eighties. In the middle of November 1985, she was again in Toronto—as she explained in a circular letter sent to friends at Christmas—"for a meeting with Energy Probe, on whose board I serve, and we had a two-hour meeting and then went to a three-hour meeting with the staff and board of Ontario Hydro. We are trying to persuade Ontario Hydro that it would be a bad thing for them to sell tritium and export it to the USA, because they would not have any control over how it is used and it would undoubtedly be used in the manufacture of yet more nuclear weapons. This is a very complex issue, but we have to keep on trying, our position being that Canada cannot have any credibility as a 'non-nuclear weapons' country if we are giving aid and support to such things as testing the cruise missile or making parts for nuclear arms or (Hydro's plan) selling tritium for 'civilian purposes' when those 'civilian' purposes cannot possibly be assured. Who knows what good we do?"

On January 10, 1986, she told Louise Kubik (formerly Louise Alguire) that she had, at long last, reached a firm resolve: "TO SAY A FIRM *NO* TO EVERYTHING AND TO TAKE AT LEAST ONE YEAR'S SABBATICAL, EVEN FROM THE MANY GOOD CAUSES I SUPPORT, IN ORDER TO CONTINUE WITH WHAT I REALLY WANT TO DO, AND HAVE BEGUN, NAMELY SELECTED MEMOIRS DEALING MAINLY WITH MY THREE MOTHERS."

Margaret's decision that January was determined by the realization it "was either IT or ME," the "IT" being public engagements. For the first time in a long while, she was eager to get at her scribblers. In her new project, Margaret attempted to rewrite and reinvent the past. Although she was not able to write the novel about mothers and daughters she had first envisioned, she used many of her skills as a novelist to imagine the past and in the process produce a non-fiction book about how women can have extremely strong views about all manner of issues and have the power—if they wish to seize it—to impose those views on society.

In many ways, *The Diviners*, in its depiction of the relationship between Morag and Pique, is a mother-daughter novel. Of course, all of her novels are about various kinds of power. In *Dance on the Earth*, she shows herself as a person who gained power as a woman through the agency of other women. This, the real agenda of Margaret's new book, results in a narrative that omits many pertinent biographical facts the reader might expect to find in an autobiography.

All autobiographies—largely because they are by definition subjective—tell lies in some way or other. *Dance on the Earth* was never intended to be autobiographical in any significant generic sense; it is—as the subtitle declares—a collection of "memoirs," a carefully selected recollection of the history of Margaret's womanhood. Some of the claims of the book—such as the assertion she had three mothers—may not be psychologically accurate, but they are the author's way of attempting to define her coming into being as a professional woman writer who was also a mother. This book contains a bit of wishful thinking in that Margaret asserts that in her life she had given equal emphasis to writing and child-rearing.

There are other problems. The book's central image is derived from the modern hymn, "Lord of the Dance," which allows Margaret to place herself in a position of power, as one who controls and ordains. Yet, in the foreword, she speaks at length of the bronze sculpture, "Crucified Woman," by Almuth Lutkenhaus: "To me, she represents the anguish of the ages, the repression, the injustice, the pain that has been inflicted upon women, both physically and emotionally." These two images clash. Were women victims or were they survivors? Were they weak or powerful? On one level, that of her writing career, Margaret Laurence knew the answer. She had chosen—as decisively as she could—her life as a writer. On a more personal level, she was not really sure. Since she never resolved this dilemma, the hymn and the sculpture reside uncomfortably side by side, metaphoric of the unease she herself had endured.

She might have asked herself the question: Did I win the battle to become a famous writer against tremendous odds but in the process lose my soul? She may never have been able to forgive herself for leaving her marriage, when a part of her felt that a woman did not have the right to make such a decision. At many turns in *Dance*, the reader can see the guilt that poisoned her existence.

That year there were major setbacks. A personal attack on her in *The Toronto Star* for her anti-nuclear stand upset her. She was deeply bothered by the death of Evelyn Robinson, her next-door neighbour for twelve years. Nevertheless, her good spirits remained fairly constant. She was tickled when she had the "enormous honour of having been named by *Chatelaine* as one of the Worst Dressed Canadians!" Her drinking continued unabated—by 1986, she usually had to go to bed extremely early, often by 7:30.

A mixture of the joys and sorrows of life overwhelmed her that July a week before her sixtieth birthday. She finished the first draft of *Dance* and four days later learned her brother, Bob, had terminal cancer. At once, she made plans to fly out to Alberta. The birthday celebration, with forty-two people in attendance at Joan and Glen Johnston's home on the Otonabee, was a great success, although friends noticed Margaret was more bothered by the heat than usual. When outside, she gasped for breath and often quickly retreated into the air-conditioned house.

Joan Johnston's birthday gift to Margaret were large, handsomely bound journals in which Margaret, having finished the first draft of *Dance on the Earth* in mid-July, confided even more memories. The first entry sets out the agenda for this new project:

> *July 18, 1986* — Today I am sixty years old. I have decided to keep a journal for this year, partly because a decade year seems a special one ... and partly because I think a lot of people in Canada might be interested to know how I spend my life in this quaint village.... I have not published an adult novel since 1974, & although I have since published a book of essays & 3 books for children, the worried ones either are not aware of this fact or point out that the last book was published in 1980. What has happened to Margaret Laurence? They tend to speculate, I gather. Has Margaret become a recluse, in the manner of J.D. Salinger? Has she suffered a series of nervous breakdowns? Is she an alcoholic or a drug addict? Well, *no*, actually. So I thought it might be of some general interest to keep a journal this year, at sixty, and set down some of the details of my daily life.

Although obviously intended as a more personal—and private—record than *Dance on the Earth*, she saw the resulting narrative as potentially publishable and decided therefore to conceal her drinking problem from the "people in Canada" who might be interested in her life. Much more than *Dance on the Earth*, the journal constantly veers between public and private reflections. Quite often, she stresses her love for her children and how that love has informed many of her actions. In particular, these statements seem to be made *to* the children and to any future readers. At other times, she seems to lose her reserve and to tell the diary her most intimate—unfiltered—thoughts.

During her visit with Bob, she instantly saw he did not wish to talk about either his illness or approaching death, so she played everything by ear. He enjoyed talking about their early lives together, about how he refused to be called "Bobby" after the age of seven, about John

Simpson. In some ways, they recognized, they had had happy childhoods. "I wish Bob had known our Dad. I was 9 when he died, but Bob was only 2. And he had to put up with Grandfather for many more years than I did, of course." Back from Alberta, Margaret decided to redecorate her house. Because the name appealed to her, she chose a white paint entitled "Free Spirit" for the interior. "My home," she realized, "is incredibly important to me, & always has been—all of them, throughout the years; I need it to *look* right, to look warm & calm & uncluttered & attractive ... possibly to stave off, or so I have often thought, the inner chaos."

The journal gave Margaret the opportunity to reflect on a number of issues, some of which had only been raised in passing in *Dance on the Earth*: "Got a letter from Mona today, my oldest friend. Among many other things she asked if I ever felt, at our age, sometimes totally alone. Yes, is the short answer. What worries me, however, is not the aloneness (of which I can bear & indeed need a great deal, even though the loneliness is sometimes hard) but the deterioration." She wondered about her status as a woman writer: had she been in her arduous and yet fulfilling life a "sort of half-assed pioneer" for other women?

She also pondered what the end of her life would bring, hoping especially that her children would not have to take care of her in her final years.

> I pray it will never be a task given to my children. I would much rather take my own life than have them saddled with the care of me when I am old &—heaven forbid—senile. I have never expected to live that long, but probably nobody expects it. The taking of one's own life I do *not* regard as a sin *ever*, but as a terrible, unthinkable & unbearable tragedy in the case of young people.... by the time one was either a) senile or b) terminally ill & in great pain, one probably would a) not know it or b) not be able to *do* anything. Also, what about the wherewithal, the means? How to suddenly get a huge supply of, e.g., barbiturates? Impossible. I've given thought to this, over the years, and it just seems too damn complex & difficult

> even to contemplate. Virginia Woolf drowned herself. I could never *never* do that. Hemingway shot himself. I've handled a gun only once in my life.... Forget suicide even if ever in dire straits. I will just have to shuffle on, & hope that a nifty heart attack seizes me before I become not myself any more. Do other people, still relatively healthy & so on, think about death as much as I do & have done for years? I don't know. And yet I don't feel morbid, & I love life very much. I guess it is just that I know it will end, possibly quite capriciously, & have known for really all my life, my mother having died when she was 34 & I was 4.

A week later, on August 21, she reflected again about her career, of what the future held for her, of her reputation as a refugee from the writing life: "I do not think I will write another novel—in fact, I know I won't. I did my books when I was given them to do, & 7 of the 14 turned out to be books of adult fiction ... I wish many people could understand this. Well, they don't & won't. I guess I seem some kind of strange person because I have not published an adult novel for 12 years. And won't & can't. Lord, don't they know how anguished that has been for me? No. Why should they?"

The next entry is dated "August 30—Saturday St Joseph's Hospital Peterborough" and begins abruptly: "A lifetime has happened since last I wrote in this Journal, just over a week ago. So much, indeed, that I don't know how I can put it all down. I can't put it all down, of course.... So much condensation will be necessary that I feel totally daunted because what I can write here will be so very little of what I have experienced & learned ... All this *sensible* kind of approach is garbage, actually. I am very frightened of dying quite soon, but I just can't give way to panic. I don't dare, or I really am finished."

The "lifetime" began on the morning of August 22 when Margaret was waiting for Joan to pick her up so they could go to their haidresser. Suddenly, she could not breathe and phoned her doctor, who summoned an ambulance. When Joan arrived at 8 Regent Street, an ambulance was just about to drive off with Margaret; the doctor explained the nature of the emergency. Joan followed the ambulance to St. Joseph's and remained with Margaret as she was admitted to Emergency and then Intensive Care. The first procedure was to drain her lungs, then to discover why they had filled up so quickly and dangerously.

Not unexpectedly, Margaret's novelist's eyes could not shut down, even though she was in the midst of acute anxiety as to her future:

> One thing ... has given me so much reassurance. I wrote *The Stone Angel* in the first draft in 1961. Twenty-five years ago ... I drew on some experience in hospital then, when I had my gall-bladder out, & there was indeed a very old woman *(not* Hagar) in the 4-bed ward where I was. Now so many years later, here in this hospital, with a great many very old & senile & semi-senile women, oh God, I know I did get it right. Amazing, I was 35 then, in hospital, & now I'm 60, & much closer to the really old people than I could ever have been then.

On August 31, Margaret wrote to Mona: "I have been in hospital a week, after a terrible attack on the 22nd—couldn't breathe. Thought it was heart, but it wasn't. Heart okay. They pumped about a quart of fluid out of my chest cavity. X-rays show nothing, but have to have more tests, biopsy, bronchoscopy, etc. It is pretty certain, they think, that I have lung cancer." "Pretty certain" became certain eight days later: "I am still in hospital but hope to be home sometime this week. Have had every test and x-ray known to man, some boring and some painful. Turns out I have cancer of kidney and lung, too advanced for treatment other than palliative. Prognosis is 6 months." Despite the crisis facing her, she had no doubt about what she was going to do with the time left to her: "I am DETERMINED to get first draft of these memoirs typed into 2nd draft, and will also use tape recorder, as I can read and dictate, even with editing, more quickly than I can type." She added: "Odd that I should have the same illness and in same places as my brother. Weird.

But I am so lucky that my kids are grown and that I have lived to do my lifework. No regrets." Her diagnosis having been confirmed and having determined treatment would be useless, she was released from hospital on September 9.

Joan Johnston typed the second draft of the typescript, incorporating corrections made on tape by Margaret. This typescript, begun on August 29 while Margaret was still in hospital, was completed on October 7. The third draft—made from her corrections dictated on to tape —was finished and typed by October 20.

Despite the rapid progress on revising the book, Margaret, who called herself a "dame demented," was deeply discouraged. That November, she asked Adele: "Please forgive me for the fairly miserable trip I put on you last evening, talking about my memoirs. It is just that I fluctuate in my feelings towards the manuscript. Sometimes I *do* feel it should be published, with *much editing*, and sometimes I feel the hell with it ... it shouldn't be published. Mostly I feel that it *should* be, but also that I really should be able to do more editing, and more importantly, more adding of anecdotes, myself, and I just do not think I can.... This 'passage' (my situation now) is a numbing experience, like writing, I guess ... one realizes that some things cannot be done by an act of will. Naturally, we have always known this, but it comes home more clearly to me right now. I was able to get to the third draft of those memoirs; I don't feel like continuing. If I felt okay, I would look forward to about a year of re-writing, editing, adding ... it actually would be pleasurable. But I don't feel like entering the manuscript again." When the second typed draft was completed, she placed the six huge notebooks in which she had written *Dance on the Earth* in the garbage. Adele objected but Margaret silenced her: "This isn't New York, & I'm not Norman Mailer. Nobody sifts through the green garbage bags in Lakefield!"

To the journal, Margaret confided her saddest feelings. On September 20, she made this entry: "5 p.m. I have spent 2 hours in bed, not sleeping, as I had hoped, but crying. I guess I am pretty sorry for myself." Three days later: "I feel so nauseated & can't stop shaking all over. I am so frightened. If I go back to hospital I will never get out alive." Five days after that, she made a resolve: "I would rather let go now, then go on to be one of those old old ladies in the hospital. I don't want to be Hagar."

"What," she asked herself, "shall I do if I keep on dying?" Everyone told her how sorry they were. "Frankly, I'm a bit sorry for myself." Her thoughts turned back to her "little mother's death" and to the fact she had "looked at death" since she was four. She was filled with self-recrimination:

> I really am an aberration. I was always a lonely child—(boo hoo—poor me) but I see suddenly that I *am* very strange & odd. How can one live for 60 years & feel fairly normal when one *isn't*?
>
> I wrote books & I did raise my kids. But mostly what I did was write books. *Why*? I no longer know. I always thought I *had* to do that—it was *important*. Why was it important?
>
> Most people believe it is important to love people, to have a mate.
>
> I believed it was important to love people, raise my beloved children, & *write books*.
>
> So here I am, at 60, dying. No mate for many years. Perhaps I was wrong.... I no longer know why I made the choice I did.... Are books worth it? I thought so. Now I do not know.——This last one, into which I have poured faith & energy seems now to be worth little. I don't know why I prayed & prayed, unconscionably, for a few more days, to complete a *book* that isn't worth anything.

On other days, she could summon up the reservoirs of self-esteem which were in her: "I am *not* a fatalist. But I know in my own heart, what I know. And what I know is *not* terrible."

Heartbroken by her brother's death on October 15, she prayed: "Please, God, help me, for I am in great distress." Three days later, she wrote: "I am just destroyed right now thinking of Bob. I can't stop crying, but *must.* I keep thinking of the hymn that Tommy Douglas requested for his funeral—the hymn that so long ago the Welsh coal-miners sang while they marched up Whitehall in 1929, to no avail:

'Guide me, O Thou great Jehovah.' I have to quit crying, & wash the dishes, I *have* to."

To friends, she showed her brave, resolute side. "I'm fine"—she said to those who inquired of her health not having heard the news of the cancer—"except I'm going to be dead soon." She was also deeply considerate of the feelings of those she was leaving behind. At the time Margaret was first diagnosed with cancer, Mary Adachi was in England, staying with a friend who worked at Canada House. In consultation with Ken, Margaret decided not to break the news to Mary until she returned: Margaret did not wish to "spoil" her friend's holiday. It "would serve no purpose" to distress someone thousands of miles away. At about the same time, Margaret wrote to Canada House where she was scheduled to give a reading the following May to mark the publication of the Virago editions of her books. In that letter, she bluntly stated that she had only six months to live and was therefore cancelling the engagement. Of course, Margaret had not considered Mary's connection to Canada House—and the fact that she might inadvertently hear the terrible news. When a distraught Mary telephoned, an equally distraught Margaret exclaimed: "Oh, kid, you weren't supposed to find out!"

Soon after Margaret called Lois Wilson to plan her funeral service. On the phone, Lois could hear the defiant and radiant Christianity of Margaret's last years but at the edge of the voice she could discern the deep sadness than engulfed her friend. Since Jocelyn was to marry Gary Michael Dault the following month, Margaret quipped: "My daughter is planning her wedding, & I am planning my funeral." Anticipation of the wedding provided Margaret with a much needed distraction—and filled her with a wonderful expectation: Jocelyn confided to her mother that she very much wanted to have a child.

Just after the phone call to Lois on October 23, Margaret made this entry:

> I do not know how many pills (taken perhaps with a *lot* of booze) would be enough to send me off forever. I have given much thought

> to this subject. A. I am very frightened of a lot of physical pain. B. I do NOT want my kids subjected to what Bob & I were, when our Mum was dying. C. If this goes on & on for months, [would try patience of friends] D. Once in hospital, forget it—one has no control over what will happen. E. I don't fear the Holy Spirit's wrath.... I fought the battle of the pills, but not, I am sure, for the last time! I may yield. [doesn't want to die before Jocelyn's wedding] Okay, God, we'll hang on for another month, eh?

Without doubt, there was a portion of Margaret Laurence that was pulled in the direction of death, the cancer making her poignantly aware of a wish for her life to be over. This is the real core issue behind the fear of being a nuisance: you can only be such if you feel you have nothing to offer in return for the care being provided. In a sense, she felt she had finished her life's work and had no reason to continue living. In such moments, she got in touch with her often exceedingly low self-image.

Adele Wiseman, Mary Adachi, Alice Williams, Jean Cole, Budge Wilson and Arlene Lampert visited on a regular basis, providing much appreciated help and support. These women pulled together, providing a strong bulwark against the fraught feelings that invaded their friend and her house. Joan Johnston was in constant attendance as was Jocelyn. David and his wife, Soña Holman, moved from San Francisco to Lakefield, where they occupied the apartment at the back of the house; they undertook the lion's share of the caretaking. In the midst of all this support, Margaret became bitterly angry at one friend—whose career she had helped advance—who treated her impending death as a sort of insult since it reminded her of her own mortality.

Margaret dreamed of Jocelyn and David as young children, of Marg, of herself and Jack when they were first in love "& taking off for yet another adventure." She remembered how the children had embarrassed her at the Old Winter Palace in Luxor by making the wine glasses sing; she recalled her engagement ring, which had once been Verna's.

Gradually, Margaret felt herself withdrawing from life, as if she had already entered a "different space"; this "strange sort of distancing" allowed her not to feel quite so badly about not being able to work further on *Dance on the Earth*. However, she did not like the uncertainty about her future: "Ambiguity is everywhere. I have always loved that ambiguity in relationship to language. It's not quite so loveable in relationship to my own life, at least not to me." She told herself: "I think I will be unable *truly* to accept my death until the *last moment*."

She was dismayed when she visited the doctor on November 26: "From all reports, it appears as though I may go for months & months & months. The cancer is building slowly, unlike what the doctors first thought. It may drag out for another *year*. I just *can't*.... I *have* explained to my dearest ones, that if I decide to take that final step it is or will be *only* because I need it for myself, *not* because I am fearful of being inconvenient." This fear began to dominate her. She worried that she had become a particularly heavy burden for David and Soña. She did not so much explain as hint that she might commit suicide.

Margaret was able to attend only Jocelyn's wedding ceremony, not the reception. In her journal, she expresses her delight in seeing Jack and Esther and mentions Soña drove her back to Lakefield immediately after the ceremony. These comments do not express the full range of feelings that were aroused. While milling about immediately after the ceremony, Margaret heard Jocelyn introduce Esther to someone as "my stepmother." On the grounds that Esther had never been any kind of mother to Jocelyn, Margaret took great offence, although she said nothing to Jocelyn. In an awful moment, she must have been brought back face to face with how central the loss of her husband had been to her. She felt humiliated, hurt and deeply alone. In many ways, she remained genuinely fond of Jack.

Shortly afterwards, Soña drove her mother-in-law back to the Adachis, where she had stayed the previous night. There, Margaret proceeded to become blindly drunk, giving full vent to her fury, a fury (directed mainly against Jack) which finds no expression in the journal since she realized it might become some day a public document.

What right did Esther have to the title of "stepmother"?: she had not reared Jocelyn and David. This was the gist of Margaret's complaint in response to her daughter's remark. She was dying and would, she realized, no longer be any kind of mother to Jocelyn. So unsure was she that she had indeed been a good parent, she was deeply wounded by a casual remark, almost as if she were on the lookout for an insult. Once again, her insecurities were triggered in an exceedingly painful way. Soña drove her back to Lakefield the following day.

On December 2, she reiterated to herself: "But I know I am on my last voyage, & if I cannot in myself bear all the storms of the humiliated & painful flesh I do not think the Holy Spirit will be anything except accepting.... *If* & *when* I make that decision, it will be mine & mine only, & no one else will know or be 'culpable' of even supporting. It will if it happens be between myself & God."

The decision to commit suicide became more real to Margaret when, on her way from her house to David and Soña's apartment on December 7, she slipped on some black ice and fractured her leg in two places. She returned to hospital for five days. For weeks, she had been certain she had planned for every eventuality, but now she was stymied. On December 12, the day before she returned home from hospital, she attempted to map her strategy:

> I should be feeling glad about going home tomorrow, & in a way I am. But this evening I feel very depressed. Once at home, I have to try to build up a supply of pills without appearing to do so, while recognizing that with this damn leg I am going to need to take more painkillers than I did before this accident. I not only can't talk about this to *anyone*—I have to try to make sure that no one suspects I have even contemplated self-deliverance. Timing, also, is all. I would have to be alone for two days...

> It would seem churlish in the extreme [to commit suicide so soon after returning from hospital] ... I wish You would just make this decision soon—I am ready for it.
>
> One always hears or reads that someone has "died peacefully". How can anyone except that person really know?
>
> This is an impossible situation. There is *no* way it can be worked out. There is no reason that I can see to drain & strain my children's and my friends' strength & lives, in order to maintain for me a "life".... My "life" revolves around a worn-out undependable body that is only a burden to me & others.... Sure I could have done much more with my life, but I have tried to do what was given me to do.
>
> God, please help me to relinquish my personal self in relinquishing my body which has been my dwelling place & is now crumbling.

The prospect of death terrified her, but she simply could not bear to subject herself to further humiliation. She had a huge twelve-pound cast from toes to thigh and, thus was no longer able to walk upstairs. Her living room became her bedroom. She slept in a hospital bed and had to use a walker to get around. However decrepit she felt, she knew she was not really like Hagar: "I have been able to give and receive love all my life." And yet she was not willing to go on with life at the price of pain, humiliation and complete self-abnegation. She felt powerless in the wake of the ravages that had overtaken her body and which were making it difficult for her to make any kind of rational decision. If she waited too long, she might be simply too weak to kill herself. At another level, she wanted time to finally have a stop.

Very much in the manner of her heroines, she discovered within herself the resolve to make an end to the body to which she was now unwillingly confined. She wanted—once again—to take charge of her own destiny, not fall victim to the whims of chance. Over the Christmas and New Year holidays, no opportunity presented itself. On January 3, she was by herself: "...today was to be the day I took the pills & got out. I arranged it all perfectly, Lord, & now *I can't do it.* I learned how much would be a lethal dose of Nembutol; I got that from one of my docs, by fibbing; I know how to do it, & the schedule, & how to try to prevent throwing up of the pills. I may yet have to try that but I *can't right now.*" (However, there was a dress rehearsal for the suicide a few days before she died: having heard that the biggest impediment to a successful suicide was the inability to dissolve the capsules, she opened a number of them and disintegrated them in boiling water.)

On the following day, she telephoned Jocelyn's new husband, Gary Michael, in Toronto with a message for Soña, who had gone to Toronto the day before and was due back later that day: No need to hurry back; I am feeling fine. Then, she followed the instructions she had read in a publication of the Hemlock Society.

> Later—Have made up my mind. God, please let this work. 6:45 pm —I took the toast & a glass of water an hour ago. Now is time to take the gravol so I won't throw up.
>
> Can you believe that I spent a long time searching for the damn tea kettle to get boiling water into which to dissolve the pills? Couldn't find it. Ever resourceful, I got hot water from the coffee maker by not putting in coffee.
>
> I spent an hour cracking open those damn capsules, with a knife, to get the powder. I have probably lost about ⅓ of the stuff.
>
> Clea the cat is racing around. I guess she knows something is going on.

There is a hiatus in the journal and then she made this final entry while waiting for death to arrive: "Please, my near & dear ones, forgive me & understand. I hope this potion works. My spirit is already in another country, & my body has become a damn nuisance. I have been so fortunate." This note was found by her body: "To my loved ones—I would like my funeral (open to all) announced in the Globe & Mail, & I would also like a memorial service in the L'field United Church."

In Margaret's existence, there had been a tumultuous struggle between self-imposed loneliness and the comforts of companionship and love. She often wanted to be alone, but she also hungered for the company of others. Nevertheless, she chose to face death by herself. As a close friend put it: "She dealt with herself harshly, with others gently. Also, she sought to serve." To the end she maintained her ability—in both good and bad times—to live life intensely. She really knew she was alive. She seized the days allotted to her, brief though they were.

In her writings, she wrote about a magnificent kind of courage, wherein an individual—against all the odds of self and society—attempts to define herself independently and creatively. For Margaret, this was a hard war, with many difficult battles—but she triumphed against the dark forces which beset her. From within herself, she found the power to divine the books and the friendships and the many acts of love and kindness which remain her enduring legacy.

BOOKS BY
MARGARET LAURENCE

A Tree for Poverty: Somali Poetry and Prose (1954)
This Side Jordan (1960)
The Prophet's Camel Bell (1963) published in the United States as *New Wind in a Dry Land* (Knopf, 1964)
The Tomorrow-Tamer (1963)
The Stone Angel (1964)
A Jest of God (1966)
Long Drums and Cannons: Nigerian Dramatists and Novelists 1952-1966 (1968)
The Fire-Dwellers (1969)
A Bird in the House (1970)
Jason's Quest (1970)
The Diviners (1974)
Heart of a Stranger (1976)
Six Darn Cows (1979)
The Olden Days Coat (1979)
The Christmas Birthday Story (1980)
Dance on the Earth: a Memoir (1989)

Appendix: Dance on the Earth (the novel)

The following notebooks and fragments (now at McMaster University Library) contain the only extant pieces of fiction in Margaret Laurence's handwriting, complementing the only extant typescripts of her novels which she sold to the same Library. This recently discovered material (which includes booklets, pamphlets, newspaper cuttings used in her research)—all dating from 1982-83—makes clear what the general themes and story line of this novel, centred on Allie Price Chorniuk, would have been.

This assortment of holograph material, all that remains of the mother and daughter novel which Margaret had hoped to write but which she abandoned at the time she began work on the book of memoirs that became *Dance on the Earth*, clearly demonstrates her intent to deal with the themes of other, abandoned novels: the origins and nature of fundamentalism and the historical significance of the Old Left in Winnipeg. In this novel, Margaret would also have been concerned with the Ukrainian immigration to Canada and the central importance of that group in the history of Manitoba; she intended to comment as well on the Scots migration and thus speak—directly and forcefully—of Canada as a blend of various ethnic groups. This narrative would also have highlighted women as shawomen, tribal magicians and healers who have mystical communion with the spirit world.

YELLOW UNDATED NOTEBOOK: *30 pages have entries*

This notebook contains a detailed chronology of a narrative centring on four characters:

1. Mairi McDuff, later Mary Price (an orphan born in Glasgow in 1900), emigrates to Canada at the age of fourteen and subsequently marries Albert (Bert) Pryce (Price), who is fifteen years older than she.
2. Alys (Allie) Price is born to Mairi and Bert in 1922; at the age of twenty, she marries Steve Chorniuk, a communist of Ukrainian descent who is ten years older than she.
3. Stephan (b. 1947), the son of Allie and Steve, marries Jen O'Brien (age 25) in 1975.
4. Mairi (b. 1977) is the daughter of Stephan and Jen.

As the chronology makes clear, this novel would have focused on Allie. Manawaka would be used as a setting for a significant portion of the narrative, although "time present" in the narrative would take place in 1982 and set—in a manner reminiscent of *The Diviners*—at Allie's home in Jordan's Landing, Ontario, and her cottage near Jordan's Landing. The lives of the characters would have been placed against key events in world and Canadian history from 1885 to 1982/3.

LIGHT GREEN FOLDER *into which miscellaneous papers have been inserted*

A. Recollections of Mairi: 10 pages long (dated by Margaret Laurence as having been written in 1982)

[1] *When I was a bairn, just a wee mite of a thing, at the Home, and before that, I used to try & try to bring to mind my mam's face. I never could, though. It seemed she must've been kind, & loved me real good, but I suppose most of us kids, them that didn't actually recall our mothers, must've dreamed them same dreams. How did I know? She might've been a whore who never gave a damn or a care about me ... But I never once believed my mother had been or mean—else, why would she have learned, I mean taught, me to write one name proper & I only four maybe, or five? I seemed, in them days, to recall very cloudy like, a woman, & me & her in a little grotty attic room somewhere in Glasgow.*

B. "One of the drafts of Mairi's early life in Canada—age 10 to 12": 66 pages long

Like Morag, Mairi is an orphan but one placed under the care of the sinister, brutal Sam Hogg. This material is reminiscent of some of the situations described in *Jane Eyre* and *Light in August*, e.g., the hair-cutting sequence owes a great deal to the same brutality inflicted upon Helen Burns at Lowood.

[54] *Snick-snick-snick. The scissors snip Mairi's hair away. All the thick black hair that at the Home she learned to wash & value, her pride, possibly her only one.*

C. "One of the drafts re: Allie's Milton Classes": twenty-six pages

In this piece of writing, Allie, who is trying to explain to her Grade XIII English class how Milton could have been partial to Satan as a character without being fully aware of the attraction, is challenged by a young male student who is disgusted with her tolerance of Satan's behaviour. (A two-page outline inserted into the folder indicates that this incident would mushroom into an attack on Allie by a group of fundamentalists, in a manner not dissimilar to the fate endured by Margaret.)

D. Reading notes on Milton

E. Various chronologies and notes

The form of the novel is indicated in this jotting: *"TO ALTERNATE—IN EACH CHAPTER. A. PRESENT—Present tense; third person; Allie's viewpoint; B. [Allie's] Journal for Mairi—(taped; the past histories)."*

DARK GREEN NOTEBOOK *dated Aug 3/82 on first page*: fourteen-page fragment from a narrative called *Dance on the Earth*. The time is autumn and Allie, with the assistance of her sister-in-law Stella, is closing her cottage near Jordan's Landing for the winter. Allie's difficulty in writing her recollections reflects the identical problems faced by her creator.

[1] *That day, Allie & Stella danced. Two old women, dancing on the earth, dancing their lives, dancing grief and blessings ... Allie thought of the Marys. That first Mairi, her mother ... the second Mary* [Allie's daughter who drowns at the age of two in the chronology], *always four, and the new Mairi.*

[11] *They danced on the grass, striking the earth firmly & strongly with their drumming bare feet, linking their hands, then drawing apart, alone, together, swaying & swirling.*

Here, each of them could be a shawoman, foremother, equal to shaman. Sha-womb-an. As it once was, perhaps, in the dawn of all the tribes. The women of the elders, dancing memory, dancing the dance of time, dancing because there were times when they chose to dance.

[12-13] *I don't know how to divide up these memories so they'll have some kind of form, Mairi. Form isn't the same as neatness. You understand. Neatness is optional, perhaps frivolous, even ridiculous, perhaps*

> *dangerous. Form is something else. Form is what I try to tell the kids about, in reading a novel or a poem or for God's sake Paradise Lost. Form is to try to give a shape to things so they'll be understood & felt.*

BLUE NOTEBOOK *dated 20 February 1983 on the first page:* ten-page fragment

The brief episode here depicts Allie thinking about her life and placing it in a book of memoirs for her young granddaughter. Allie's putative book, called *Dance on the Earth*, is giving her a great deal of difficulty, as in the dark green notebook of a year before.

> [1] *Mairi, this is for you, my grand-daughter, my only grandchild. Probably you will always be my only grandchild ...* [2] *I've tried so often to put all this down, & couldn't. I've started time & time again, in note-books, scrawling with a pen, or on a typewriter. Useless. Words wouldn't come.*

Although it is difficult—if not invalid—to explicate a novel that exists only in a series of work notes, chronologies and fragments, there can be little doubt that the novel *Dance on the Earth* would have been similar to *The Diviners* in form and in its depiction of the horrendous sense of abandonment felt by an orphan. However, Mairi would not have been the central character, that role being given to Mairi's daughter, Allie, a high-school teacher, whose remarks on Milton lead to a nasty confrontation with fundamentalist Christians.

Why did Margaret Laurence abandon a novel into which she placed much time and effort? She was always resistant to writing a "mockup" of a novel, by which she meant that a piece of fiction had to have its own purpose and life—she never wanted to retread old material. That is one reason why she could not bring this project to completion. There may be another important factor at work.

In many ways, *The Diviners* is the kind of novel that writers produce at the beginning of their careers, not the end. Margaret Laurence reversed the usual process. *The Diviners* is a *ßildungsroman,* a novel about the coming into being of a writer; it is also a book about the deprivations endured by Morag and her battle to find her spiritual centre and her writing voice.

Margaret Laurence barely managed to write *The Diviners,* so deep and vast were the struggles that went into the making of that book. The novel *Dance on the Earth,* in its re-creation of the condition of orphanage and the cruel indictment of the fundamentalists, was simply not a book that could be completed because in large part the process of writing it would have been too painful.

Sources

This biography has been largely written from primary sources of two kinds: 1) interviews with Margaret Laurence's children, relatives, close friends, writer-friends and acquaintances and 2) letters written by Margaret Laurence. In the Acknowledgements, I list all the people I have interviewed; in the endnotes I indicate when a specific person is the source of a piece of information or claim, and I give the month and year when I spoke with that person. In the same endnotes, I cite the archival source for all letters and manuscripts employed. Whether referring to typed or handwritten letters and manuscripts, all such references begin MS.

In recent years, knowledge of Margaret Laurence's life has been amplified by two excellent collections of her letters: John Lennox's *Margaret Laurence–Al Purdy, A Friendship in Letters: Selected Correspondence* and J.A. Wainwright's *A Very Large Soul: Selected Letters from Margaret Laurence to Canadian Writers*. These two books add immeasurably to our knowledge of Margaret Laurence's life, although there are a number of crucial omissions from both collections. In addition to her correspondence with Purdy, she wrote long and important letters to a number of friends, chief among whom are Adele Wiseman, Jack McClelland, Jane Rule and Gordon Elliott. Each of these four unpublished correspondences is extensive, and each contains crucial, new information. I have also gathered significant bits from other letters in smaller unpublished accumulations.

References to books, essays and archival material are incorporated into the endnotes. All references to Margaret Laurence's novels and stories are to the relevant volume in the New Canadian Library published by McClelland & Stewart. The exceptions are *A Tree for Poverty* (Toronto and Hamilton: ECW and McMaster University Library Press, 1993); *Long Drums and Cannons* (London: Macmillan, 1968); *Jason's Quest* (Toronto: McClelland

& Stewart, 1970); and *Heart of a Stranger* (Toronto: McClelland & Stewart, 1976).

For ease of reference, short titles are given for the two published collections of letters: Lennox for *Margaret Laurence–Al Purdy, A Friendship in Letters: Selected Correspondence* (Toronto: McClelland & Stewart, 1993), ed. John Lennox (when a letter or an excerpt from one is not in Lennox, the reference is to the appropriate document at Queen's University, the repository of the Laurence-Purdy letters); Wainwright for *A Very Large Soul: Selected Letters from Margaret Laurence to Canadian Writers*, ed. J.A. Wainwright (Dunvegan: Cormorant Books, 1995). In addition, I have shortened *Dance on the Earth* (Toronto: McClelland & Stewart, 1989) to *Dance.* Margaret Laurence is abbreviated to ML in all notes.

Margaret Laurence scholarship: A great deal has been written about Margaret Laurence's work, including collections of essays edited by Elizabeth Brady and Clara Thomas (1987), Greta Coger (1996), Kristjana Gunnars (1988), William H. New (1977), Colin Nicholson (1990), Michael Peterman (1978), John Sorfleet (1980), Christl Verduyn (1988) and George Woodcock (1983). There are also a number of interviews with her, including those with David Arnason and Dennis Cooley (1986), Viga Boland (1977), Donald Cameron (1973), Michel Fabre (1980, 1981), Graeme Gibson (1973) Hilda Kirkwood (1980), Robert Kroetsch (1970), Harriet Law (1977), Bernice Lever (1975), Rosemary Sullivan (1983), Clara Thomas (1972), Alan Twigg (1981) and Lois Wilson (1980). Full-length works devoted to Margaret Laurence include two books each by Clara Thomas (1969, 1976) and Patricia Morley (1981, 1991); there are also books by Helen Buss and Hildegard Kuester. The latter book—*The Crafting of Chaos* (Atlanta: Rodopi, 1994)—contains a useful bibliography. Susan J. Warwick's *Margaret Laurence: An Annotated Bibliography* (Toronto: ECW, 1979) is extremely helpful.

In preparing this book, I have read virtually all the critical essays devoted to Laurence and in many instances have indicated my indebtedness to various scholars in the endnotes. I should caution, however, that my readings of Margaret Laurence's writings are essentially my own and are influenced by the information I have gathered to write her life history.

Endnotes

Chapter One

3 "My mother": *Dance*, 24.

6 "I walk past": *A Jest of God*, 17.
"In summer": *The Stone Angel*, 4.

7 "plain as the winter turnips": *A Bird in the House*, 11.
Simpson house: In the registry of land titles, John Simpson is not listed as owner/occupant until 1903; the house may have been built as early as 1895.
"The works of her art": *Dance*, 12.
Stuart: He graduated from high school when he was fourteen, attended Wesley College in Winnipeg (later folded into United College) for two years, and then worked in a bank for two years. When he turned eighteen, he assisted his father in his various enterprises.

8 "I have a picture": *Dance*, 28.

9 "That year": *Dance*, 46-7.
"did not feel": Interview with Olive Pennie, May 1995.
"Verna is": *Dance*, 33.

10 "He was the only person": *Dance*, 29.
Scots ancestry: In a letter to Will Ready of 19 August 1979 (MS: McMaster), she provided this account: "I ... am a Celt of sorts, being Irish [County Tyrone] on my mother's side and Scots on my father's [the Wemyss family were sept of the Clan MacDuff of Burntisland, Fifeshire], with a slight admixture of Sassenach blood, through one of my grandmothers who came of U[nited] E[mpire] L[oyalist] stock.... my grandfather Wemyss, whose family came from Fifeshire in the Lowlands of Scotland, believed firmly that we were directly descended

from the Picts, the little people of Scotland, and always said ... that the name of Wemyss meant 'cave-dweller'. I have found in recent years that in the Gaelic the word 'weem' does indeed mean a Pictish earth-house."

"No one could ever": *Heart of a Stranger*, 146-7.

11 mini-play: MS: York.

"But I am not": MS: York.

12 "One family legend": *Dance*, 29-30.

"The only traces": *Dance*, 31.

13 Verna and Bob Wemyss's house: In *Dance* (33), ML claimed that her parents had to "wait for several years until they had some money saved and their future home (and my birth home) was built." However, ML's birth home at 265 Vivian Street, to which she refers as the "Little House" (as opposed to the "Big House," the Simpson home), was probably built around 1915. The original structure was a small cottage to which additions, including a dormer, were added.

14 "My mother's idealization": *Dance*, 38.

Mother's Record: Compiled by Mary A. Clarke Colquhoun; Illustrated by L. Patterson Marsh (Chicago: Volland, 1923).

16 "Peggy Noni": Interview with Catherine Simpson Milne, December 1994.

"I am back": *Dance*, 25.

17 "'blood' children": Afterword to *The Fire-Dwellers*, 286.

Chapter Two

18 "that some": *Dance*, 48.

"a man": *Dance*, 48.

19 "They joined": *Dance*, 50.

"Mum was never": *Dance*, 50.

"I can only guess": *Dance*, 49.

"She told me": *Dance*, 49.

20 "In those pictures": *Dance*, 51.

"The entries": *Dance*, 27-8.
"I was pretty annoyed": *Dance*, 52.
"Blue Sky" and the playhouse: Information from Catherine Milne.
"It wasn't": *Dance*, 63.

21 "Mum is holding": *Dance*, 51.

22 "He had found it": *Dance*, 55.
"He had taken" *Dance*, 61.
"after our dad": *Dance*, 52.

23 "What's the matter": *Dance*, 52-3.
"small creature": *A Bird in the House*, 58.
"stale and old-smelling": *A Bird in the House*, 47.

24 "We would play"; "We used to take": *Margaret Laurence Review* (1992-3), 2 and 3, 40.
"I really am": ML Journal, 6 October 1966. MS: McMaster.

25 "My father": *Dance*, 55. In Neepawa, a rumour persists that Bob and his brother-in-law Stuart, who died in the same month and in similar circumstances, had been out drinking on New Year's Eve at the Odd Fellows Hall and, later, at a hotel. According to this piece of gossip, they left the hotel on foot but were so drunk that they fell in a snow bank, where they were not discovered until the following day. Their deaths could thus be due to influenza activated by hypothermia. I have discovered no hard evidence to support this story.
"I remember": *Dance*, 56.
"After a while": *A Bird in the House*, 103.

Chapter Three

26 "We didn't stay": *Dance*, 56.
"Sometimes": *Dance*, 57.
"carrying voice": *Dance*, 59.

27 "burning fury"; "I had been afraid": *Dance*, 58.
hatred of peonies: Greta Coger interview with Catherine Milne. Typescript provided by interviewer.

"corner where": *Dance*, 58.
"We all had": *Dance*, 60.
28 "She'd painted": *Dance*, 60.
"Girls": *Dance*, 60.
"shape of a portly": *Dance*, 61.
"I was writing": *Dance*, 61.
"I was off": *Dance*, 61.
29 "only deaths": *Dance*, 62.
30 "The name": *A Bird in the House*, 63.
31 "Then, as I gazed": *A Bird in the House*, 79.
"Suppressed unhappiness"; "He'll outlive me": *Dance*, 69.
"the huge and lengthy": *Dance*, 64.
32 "changed its function": *Dance*, 64.
"The indomitable Pearl"; "Both Anne and Emily": "Books That Mattered to Me," *Margaret Laurence: An Appreciation*, ed. Christl Verduyn (Peterborough: Broadview Press, 1988), 241.
"ear-boggling"; "I hated that": *Dance*, 66.
"She had done her best": *Dance*, 67.
33 "There was an outside": *Dance*, 67.
"We naturally ignored": *Dance*, 68.
"He likes": Interview with Louise Kubik, May 1995.
"even at my"; "Fortunately for": *Dance*, 70.
"too proud and shy"; "could be said": *Dance*, 71.
34 "That summer": *Dance*, 71-2.
35 "Potato salad": *A Bird in the House*, 124.
"The method": *A Bird in the House*, 125-6.
36 "I could not speak": *A Bird in the House*, 141.
"He had been": *A Bird in the House*, 142.
"Have you ever": *A Bird in the House*, 128.
37 Bud: Information from Ruth Bailey Parent.
"could have loved": *Dance* , 257.

Chapter Four

38 "Once upon a time": ML to Adele Wiseman, 22 March 1984. MS: York.
"heroic": *Dance*, 79.
ML and Donald Strath: Interviews with Mona Meredith and Louise Kubik, May 1995.
39 "Johnnie": ML Diary 14 August 1986. MS: McMaster.
the bridge game: interview with Louise Kubik, May 1995.
40 "The Land of Our Fathers": When ML told of this story's composition in *Dance*, she gave it the fictional title—"The Pillars of the Nation"—from *A Bird in the House.*
"The only part"; "My aunt's secretary": *Dance*, 73.
"It was written": *Dance*, 73-4.
"as though": *Dance*, 77.
"fighting": Interview with Mildred Musgrove, June 1995.
"with pungent and gooey": *Dance*, 78.
41 "I remember practically": *Dance*, 76.
"I studied": *Dance*, 76-7. W.L. Morton's *Manitoba: A History* (first published in 1957) was the text that made her aware of the real history of her province. "When I first read Morton's *Manitoba*, it was with a tremendous sense of excitement, combined with an angry sense of having been deprived when young, of my own heritage. I have since done a great deal of reading of prairie history, but it was Morton who first gave me the sense of my place's long and dramatic past.": "Books That Mattered to Me" in *Margaret Laurence: An Appreciation*, 245.
"I would have": "Books That Mattered to Me," in *Margaret Laurence: An Appreciation*, 245.
42 "I was": *Dance*, 75.
"Girls were": *Dance*, 75.
"All of us girls": *Dance*, 76.
"If you were a girl": *Dance*, 78-9.
43 "My mother": *Dance*, 81.
44 "When I was": *Dance*, 84.

"never to be seen": *Dance*, 84-5.
"man from Miramichi": *Dance*, 85.

45 "I fell in love": *Dance*, 86.

46 "absolutely right"; "brash": *Dance*, 87.
"I had at last"; "In love though I was": *Dance*, 88.
"Like me": *A Bird in the House*, 181.

47 "You ought": *A Bird in the House*, 184.
John Simpson on Derek's marital status: Joan Hind-Smith, *Three Voices* (Toronto: Clarke, Irwin, 1975), 11.
"When I married": Unpublished excerpt from typescript of *Dance*, 122. MS: McMaster.
"What I could not": *A Bird in the House*, 186.

48 "Since I was of an age": *Dance*, 89.
"When I left my home": Rosemary Sullivan, "An Interview with Margaret Laurence," *A Place to Stand On: Essays by and about Margaret Laurence, ed. George Woodcock*, Western Canadian Literary Documents Series, 4 (Edmonton: NeWest Press, 1983), 62-3.

49 "That pic of the three": ML to Louise Kubik, 26 February 1983. MS: Louise Kubik.

Chapter Five

50 "Winter": *The Diviners*, 193-4.
"Oh many": ML to Don Bailey, 18 February 1973. MS: University of Toronto.

51 "I remember": Lois Wilson, *Turning the World Upside Down: A Memoir*, (Toronto: Doubleday, 1989), 229.

52 "only to receive": *Dance*, 92.
"nearby hamburger"; "we spent": *Dance*, 92.
"they were as": *Dance*, 93.
"You hoped: *Dance*, 93.

53 "principles": *Dance*, 94.
"Kids from": *Dance*, 91.

"either mediocre": *Dance*, 101.
"Obviously": *Dance*, 101.
"When Peggy": Lois Wilson, *Turning the World Upside Down*, 230.
"Right from": Wilson, 230.

54 "You are expected": *Dance*, 95.
"we couldn't afford": ML, "Books That Mattered to Me" in *Margaret Laurence: An Appreciation*, 242.
"profoundly": *Dance*, 95.
"Who would have": 10 June 1982. MS: University of Toronto.
"Frankly": 30 November 1983. MS: University of Toronto.

55 "eager awareness": Interview with Malcolm Ross, June 1995.
"when I first": *Dance*, 5.
"As a short": *Dance*, 96.
"proceeded to": *Dance*, 97.

56 excerpts from "Calliope" and "Tal des Walde": *Vox*, 18 and 19.

57 "When I was in third year": ML to Don Bailey, 18 February 1973. MS: University of Toronto.
"Margaret was a year": As quoted in Harry Gutkin, *The Worst of Times, The Best of Times* (Toronto: Fitzhenry & Whiteside, 1987), 202.

58 "short rather": *The Diviners*, 195.
"in-group"; "friend for life": *The Diviners*, 195, 197.
"I always knew": Gutkin, *The Worst of Times*, 201-2.

59 "There was one winter": Gutkin, 199.

60 "my brother": *Dance*, 101.
"seriously": *Dance*, 102.

Chapter Six

61 "handsome devil": *First Lady of Manawaka* (Toronto: NFB, 1978).
"One day": *Dance*, 102.

62 "When she was eighteen": *Dance*, 125-6.

63 "a woman with a vocation": *Dance*, 128.

"I remember": *The Prophet's Camel Bell*, 153.
"He served: *Dance*, 102.
Watson Thomson: His books included *Pioneer in Community: Henri Lasserre's Contribution to the Fully Cooperative Society* (1949) and *Turning into Tomorrow* (1966).

64 Alice: Interview with Alice Dahlquist, July 1995.
"He is way too much": Interview with Mona Meredith, May 1995.
"must have thought": *Dance*, 103.
"Just before": *Dance*, 105.

65 "Why was she": Unpublished excerpt from typescript of *Dance*, 121. MS: McMaster.
"Mum was not": *Dance*, 103.
"incredibly happy": *Dance*, 104.

66 "a navy-blue suit": *Dance*, 5.
"Sex was never": Unpublished excerpt, *Dance*, 122. MS: McMaster.
"I don't think": Unpublished excerpt, *Dance*, 122. MS: McMaster.
"Stranded": *Dance*, 105.

67 party allegiance: In a letter to Al Purdy (23 October 1967), ML refers to her job at *The Westerner* as her "second job after college." In *Dance*, she gives the impression this was her first job. Lennox, 61.
Bill Ross: A great deal of useful information is contained in Doug Smith's biography of Bill Ross's brother: *Joe Zuken: Citizen and Socialist* (Toronto: James Lorimer, 1990).
"when I began": ML to Al Purdy, 23 October 1967. Lennox, 61.

68 "Those old-time": *Dance*, 107.
"the only co-operative": *Dance*, 107.
"North Winnipeg": *Dance*, 108.

69 "It had a gas-fire": "The Wemyss and Simpson Families: Some Facts, Dates, Legends." Undated typescript by ML: York.

70 "The long-awaited": ML to Adele Wiseman, January 1950. MS: York.
"we were going": ML to Guś and Sheila Andrzejewski, 22 April 1952. MS: Sheila Andrzejewski.
"When Jack and I": ML Journal, undated. MS: McMaster.

71 "England by Me": All citations are from the typescript, now at McMaster. The letter is dated 24 November 1949. Adele returned the typescript to ML in 1968.

72 "was over at Adele's": ML to the Wisemans, 17 November 1950. MS: York.

the thirty dams: This project was in response to the recommendations made by John A. Hunt in *A General Survey of the Somaliland Protectorate, 1944-1950*, (Hargeisa: Printed in London for the Somaliland Government, 1951).

"The average"; "a need to work"; "typical": *The Prophet's Camel Bell*, 11.

73 "We went": ML to the Wisemans. MS: York.

Chapter Seven

All citations in this chapter, except where noted below, are from *The Prophet's Camel Bell.*

75 "I've been going ahead": MS: York.

89 "We were so glad": To Guś and Sheila Andrzejewski, 9 November 1951. MS: Sheila Andrzejewski.

excerpts from "Uncertain Flowering": *Story: The Magazine of the Short Story in Book Form*, 4, eds. Whit and Hallie Burnett (New York: Wyn, 1953), 33, 34.

91 "In a country": *A Tree for Poverty*, 47.

93 "I long for you": *A Tree for Poverty*, 48.

"Suppose I kill": *A Tree for Poverty*, 135.

Michael Wilson: In *The Prophet's Camel Bell* (243-4), ML talks about "Matthew's" life after he left Somaliland: "He was working in the resettlement of Arab refugees. Ultimately, he returned to Africa, as he was almost bound to do, and took a post with the Information Service in a country which has recently gained its Independence ... I believe he [now] works for the work's sake, and because he loves Africa. Occasionally he has tried to settle down in England, but he never stays for long." In about 1958—as ML's letters to Adele Wiseman of

28 February and 10 September 1959 (MS: York) make clear—he tried to place *This Side Jordan* with Macmillan.

94 "Still, it was interesting": ML to Adele Wiseman, 30 January 1952. MS: York.

"separate entities": *Margaret Laurence in Conversation with Clara Thomas.* Canadian Writers on Video Series. (Toronto: Mirus Films/ECW, 1985).

"for it really": "Half-War, Half-Peace." Unpublished paper: York, 5.

"I've been terribly": MS: York.

95 "The reason"; "a Steinbeck": MS: York.

only one surviving story set in Somaliland: However, ML may have adapted or integrated portions of her now-lost Somali stories into *The Tomorrow-Tamer*, all ten stories of which are set in the Gold Coast. There is a great deal of evidence to suggest that she worked on a variety of short stories while in Somaliland, although she does not mention them in *The Prophet's Camel Bell.* In December 1953, she sent a Somali short story entitled "Amiina" to Malcolm Ross for inclusion in *Queen's Quarterly* (ML to Adele Wiseman, 14 December 1953. MS: York). This narrative is about a "Somali girl and [a] European bloke" who shoots himself (ML to Adele Wiseman, 27 November 1953. MS: York). Ross rejected the story, but he later accepted another story set in Somaliland, although he told ML in September 1954 that he would prefer to publish a more recent piece of work set in the Gold Coast. In response, ML sent him in 1955 "The Drummer of All the World," published in the Winter 1956 issue of *Queen's Quarterly.* This was ML's second African short story to be published, but the first to be set in West Africa.

In the Macmillan archives (in a letter of 7 May 1964) is a reference to one other African story which was possibly set in Somaliland: "Mrs. Cathcart, In and Out of Purdah."

"I have been writing": MS: Sheila Andrzejewski.

96 "I've been trying"; "bread from a": ML to Adele Wiseman, 30 January 1952. MS: York.

"it would be a waste": 30 January 1952. MS: York.

97 "I nearly lost her": 16 January 1969. MS: York.

Chapter Eight

99 "excessively African": ML to Adele Wiseman, 7 August 1952. MS: York.
"the whole problem": ML to Adele Wiseman, 18 August 1952. MS: York.
"I was in labour": MS: York.
"The spirit is willing": *Dance*, 140.

100 "Did I have": *Dance*, 140.
"She is so sturdy": *Dance*, 138, 140.
"I was ecstatic": *Dance*, 109.
"I thought I could": *Dance*, 109.

101 "A lady gets dressed": *Dance*, 109.
"wished I would"; "lesser species"; "a tendency to convulsions": *Dance*, 141-2.
"when it is someone": ML to Al Purdy, 5 January 1968. Lennox, 81-2.
"After the first week": ML to Adele Wiseman, 1 December 1952. MS: York.

102 "architect-designed": *Dance*, 143.
"How the hell": *Dance*, 143.
"The country is": ML to Adele Wiseman, 1 December 1952. MS: York.

104 "We have been lucky": ML to Adele Wiseman, 1 December 1952. MS: York.
"When young African men": *Dance*, 17.
"proprietoress of"; "I lose all semblance": ML to Adele Wiseman, 22 December 1952. MS: York.

105 "You and Jack": ML to Adele Wiseman, 22 December 1952. MS: York.
"Uncertain Flowering": Later in life, ML *seems* to have forgotten about "Uncertain Flowering"; she never referred to it as part of her canon. The story was rediscovered by W.J. Keith in "'Uncertain Flowering': An Overlooked Short Story by Margaret Laurence," *Canadian Literature* 112 (1987), 202-5. The typescripts at Princeton were discovered by Donez Xiques. See "New Light on Margaret Laurence's First Short Story," *Canadian Notes and Queries* 42 (Spring 1990), 14-21.

106 "You asked": MS: Princeton.

"Books of short stories": Whit Burnett to ML, 4 February 1953. MS carbon: Princeton.

"I had not realized": ML to Whit Burnett, 12 February 1953. MS: Princeton.

107 "I keep telling": ML to Adele Wiseman, 20 July 1953. MS: York.

"naked and slippery": *Dance*, 143.

"Fortunately": 8 June 1953. MS: York.

"It happened": ML to Adele Wiseman, 27 November 1953. MS: York.

"When Mum went back": *Dance*, 109.

108 "You are the only person": ML to Adele Wiseman, 16 January 1953 [really 1954]. MS: York.

109 "I am doing": ML to Adele Wiseman, 16 January 1953 [really 1954]. MS: York. An earlier letter to Adele Wiseman of 27 November 1953 (MS: York) confirms this, showing that ML's third, unpublished novel was told, like *This Side Jordan*, from two perspectives, one black, the other white: "It's got two parts, really and within those parts it's made up of related but separated episodes—I don't know whether that's a bad thing or not, but I don't think it can be helped, because it takes place in two worlds, so to speak, the Somali and the European. I had hoped to have the first draft done by the time we go home on leave, but I won't even have part one done."

"Yet there was a weariness": *Dance*, 110.

110 "Now for the big news": MS: York.

Jack Laurence: Interview with him, December 1994.

111 "I suppose having": ML to Adele Wiseman, 10 March 1954. MS: York.

"Sometimes, I feel"; "Don't bother": *Dance*, 145-6.

"Well, sometimes": *Dance*, 147.

"I thought": *Dance*, 145.

112 "an African midwife": *Dance*, 151.

"When the final stage": *Dance*, 148-9.

113 "No, I want": *Dance*, 149-50.

"I began writing": *Dance*, 152.

writing of *This Side Jordan*: See ML to Adele Wiseman, 3 April 1956. MS: York.

"dark, dusty": *Dance*, 111.

114 "couldn't understand": *Dance*, 111.

"Just before the taxi": *Dance*, 112.

"I scribbled": *Dance*, 152.

115 "An odd thing"; "an intellectual desert": ML to Adele Wiseman, 3 April 1956. MS: York.

"There were times": *Dance*, 153.

Ofosu: I have not been able to uncover more documentary information about him than that given above. Ofosu is, however, "Mensah" in the essay "The Very Best Intentions," first published in 1964 and then reprinted in *Heart of a Stranger* (33-43), where ML provided an introduction to the piece: "This was the first article I ever had published. It appeared in 1964. I was nervous about it because the friend I was describing was still living in Ghana, a known opponent to the Nkrumah regime. I took pains to conceal his identity—his name isn't Mensah and he isn't a lawyer. He subsequently got out of Ghana, with his family, and lived in America for some years. After the fall of Nkrumah, he was able to return home." (33).

ML and Ofosu: *Heart of a Stranger*, 34ff.

121 "fairly intense": Interview with Cay, August 1995.

"except for Jack": ML to Adele Wiseman, 10 March 1954. MS: York.

122 "I can't talk": ML to Adele Wiseman, 23 July 1956. MS: York.

123 "I've finished": ML to Adele Wiseman, 28 May 1956. MS: York.

"Did you feel": ML to Adele Wiseman, 10 July 1956. MS: York.

124 "—Oh, River": *This Side Jordan*, 270.

an African voice: "Voice" and the appropriation of it are central issues in critical discussions of ML's African fiction. W.H. New in "The Other and I: Laurence's African Stories," in *A Place to Stand On: Essays by and about Margaret Laurence*, 113-34, maintains that the stories told by an African storyteller are flawed because ML does not sufficiently understand the perspective of such narrators. ML, however, was sympathetic to such figures, whereas she later felt that she had been much too distant and critical of Miranda's point of view in *This Side Jordan*. Chinua Achebe, in *Morning Yet on Creation Day: Essays*

(London: Heinemann, 1975), 12, maintains that ML had an excellent understanding of the writings discussed in *Long Drums and Cannons*; there can be no doubt that such a sensibility and sympathy can be found in the West African stories and *This Side Jordan*.

125 "Just before": *Dance*, 112.
"My aunt": MS: York.

Chapter Nine

126 "Great Air Disasters": *Heart of a Stranger*, 134.
"You're young": *Dance*, 113.

127 "I often felt": *Dance*, 113.
"She not only": *Dance*, 114-5.
"I have a room": ML to Adele Wiseman, 18 February 1957. MS: York.

128 "Every day"; "I decided": *Dance*, 115.
"I think": *Dance*, 116.
"Dear, I think": *Dance*, 117.
"Honestly": ML to Adele Wiseman, 1 December 1957. MS: York.

129 "Despite the fact": *Dance*, 117.
"I picture"; "because you"; "an overpowering urge": ML to Adele Wiseman, 17 March 1957. MS: York.

130 "it was a stinking place": ML to Adele Wiseman, 17 February 1958. MS: York.
"The nurses tied": *Dance*, 119.
"had turned very dark": *Dance*, 120.
"I've never liked": *Dance*, 120.

131 "God, please": ML Journal, 2 December 1986. MS: McMaster.
"good for laughs"; "When I saw": ML to Adele Wiseman, 12 June 1957. MS: York.

132 "When you have": MS: York.

133 "Now, Adele": ML to Adele Wiseman, 17 February 1958. MS: York.

135 "country people": ML to Adele Wiseman, 14 August 1958. MS: York.
"I am not much": ML to Adele Wiseman, 22 December 1958. MS: York.

"I really don't care": ML to Adele Wiseman, 13 May 1959. MS: York.
"however you cut"; "veritable babe": ML to Adele Wiseman, 28 February 1959. MS: York.

136 "Both, in their widely": ML to Adele Wiseman, 28 February 1959. MS: York.
"I have been hearing": Gordon Elliott to Jack McClelland, 1 March 1959. MS: McClelland & Stewart Archive, McMaster.

137 "I very much appreciate": Jack McClelland to Gordon Elliott, 5 March 1989. MS: McClelland & Stewart Archive, McMaster.

138 "purple prose": ML to Janis Rapoport, 5 February 1968; Wainwright, 156.
"Hurrah!": ML to Adele Wiseman, 1 December 1959. MS: York.
"Without periodic": ML to Adele Wiseman, 13 May 1959. MS: York.

139 "puerile outpourings": ML to Adele Wiseman, 15 May 1959. MS: York.
"if we did not": ML to Adele Wiseman, 21 July 1960. MS: York.
"bawled like": ML to Adele Wiseman, 6 May 1960. MS: York.
"Whoever heard": ML to Adele Wiseman, 16 January 1960. MS: York.

140 "It was fairly primitive": *Dance*, 157.
"everybody and his dog": ML to Adele Wiseman, 6 May 1960. MS: York.

142 "bashing away": ML to Adele Wiseman, 15 May 1959. MS: York.
"quite a number"; "about a dwarf"; "about an Italian-American"; "a man's reach": ML to Adele Wiseman, 30 October 1959. MS: York.

143 "She is so terrific": ML to Adele Wiseman, 13 June 1962. MS: York.
characterization of Nathaniel and Miranda: The West African stories and, in particular, *This Side Jordan*—in which a direct contrast/comparison between the white heroine and the black schoolmaster is the basis of the plot action—is in part indebted to ML's reading of Pamela Powesland's 1956 translation of O. Mannoni's *Prospero and Caliban: The Psychology of Colonization,* published in French in 1950. On 10 January 1971, ML told Margaret Atwood: "The whole colonial situation, of course (i.e. the woman as black) I not unnaturally figured out years ago when living in Africa, helped somewhat by the French psychologist Mannoni, whose book ... for a time was my bible." Wainwright, 2.

"I could have wept": ML to Adele Wiseman, 13 May 1959. MS: York. The best general treatment of ML's West African stories, *This Side Jordan* and *Long Drums and Cannons* can be found in Fiona Sparrow's excellent book, *Into Africa with Margaret Laurence* (Toronto: ECW Press, 1992). See also the helpful, discerning introduction by Donez Xiques to the 1993 edition of *A Tree for Poverty*, (Toronto: ECW Press and McMaster University Library Press, 1993), 7-17.

"I reviewed my life": ML to Adele Wiseman, 21 July 1960. MS: York.

144 "I presume"; "This particular": MS: McClelland and Stewart Archive. McMaster.

"I have just returned": Jack McClelland to Ian MacKenzie, 28 November 1960. MS: McClelland & Stewart Archive. McMaster.

145 "I've had": ML to Adele Wiseman, 3 December 1960. MS: York.

"I enclose": ML to Adele Wiseman, 5 September 1961. MS: York.

146 "I always felt": ML to Adele Wiseman, 5 September 1961. MS: York.

"Jack McC": MS: York.

147 "planned in rough": ML to Adele Wiseman, 29 October 1960. MS: York.

"Right now": ML to Adele Wiseman, 29 October 1960. MS: York.

"over, and I": ML to Adele Wiseman, 22 January 1961. MS: York.

148 "I've changed my name": MS: York.

Chapter Ten

151 "sick of Africa": ML to Adele Wiseman, 22 January 1961. MS: York.

152 "know enough": ML to Adele Wiseman, 22 January 1961. MS: York.

"Re: your suggestion": ML to Jack McClelland, 22 January 1961. MS: McMaster.

"My view hasn't changed": Jack McClelland to ML, 26 January 1961. MS copy: McMaster.

"were so permeated": ML to Adele Wiseman, 29 March 1961. MS: York.

153 "he is one": ML to Adele Wiseman, 29 March 1961. MS: York.

"Probably the publishers": ML to Adele Wiseman, 5 September 1961. MS: York.

154 "What amuses me": ML to Adele Wiseman, 5 September 1961. MS: York.

"we don't seem": MS: York.

"You're the first woman": Interview with June and Fred Schulhof, May 1995.

155 Girl Guide cookies: Interview with Gordon Elliott, December 1994.

Lino Magagna: Interview with him, October 1995.

Mona and Jack: Interview with Mona Meredith, May 1995.

156 the Laurence marriage: Interview with Nadine Jones, May 1995.

157 "the fact that I once": ML to Al Purdy, 2 July 1968. MS: Queen's.

158 "you said that it seemed": ML to Gordon Elliott, 12 March 1965. MS: Gordon Elliott.

Alice recalled: Wainwright, 142.

159 "I didn't so much mind": ML to Adele Wiseman, 5 September 1961. MS: York.

"I wrote to Mr. Buchholzer's publishers": 24 July 1962. MS: Macmillan Archive, Basingstoke.

"I wrote it": ML to Adele Wiseman, 8 October 1961. MS: York.

160 "I wrote *The Stone Angel*": ML Journal, 30 August 1986. MS: McMaster.

John Simpson and Hagar: Interview with Budge Wilson, April 1995.

Buckler: ML told Ernest Buckler on 30 August 1974 (Wainwright, 26): "My first novel had recently come out, and I was beginning to think seriously about how I could return ... to the background which was truly my own. Your novel both scared and heartened me—the power and scope of it."

161 Hagar and her father: In *The Crafting of Chaos* (Rodopi: Amsterdam and Atlanta, 1994), Hildegard Kuester argues: "In *The Stone Angel* male identity is synonymous with strength, whereas female identity embodies weakness. Since Hagar defines herself as strong and independent, the gap between her own ideas of herself and her female role seems to be insurmountable. Her difficulty in finding a fully fledged identity

originates in a manifest imbalance between traditionally male and female values" (43).

162 "I used to wonder"; "I can't": *The Stone Angel*, 59, 25.
"My feeling": Rosemary Sullivan, "An Interview with Margaret Laurence," *A Place to Stand On*, 68, 69.

163 "terrible mess": ML to Adele Wiseman, 17 March 1962. MS: York.
"the old-lady novel": ML to Adele Wiseman, 13 June 1962. MS: York.
"I often feel"; "kind of screen": ML to Adele Wiseman, 5 August 1962. MS: York.

164 "I always had the feeling": ML to Adele Wiseman, 13 January 1962. MS: York.
"How much of yourself": ML to Adele Wiseman, 13 June 1962. MS: York.
"I have far too much respect": MS: York.

165 "When I wrote": *Dance*, 158.

166 ML as essentially a short story writer: See ML to Adele Wiseman, 11 December 1962. MS: York.
"How can I": *The Fire-Dwellers*, 123.
"I am taking": ML to Adele Wiseman, 13 June 1962. MS: York.

167 "I am back": MS: McMaster.
"abroad again": ML to Adele Wiseman, 13 January 1962. MS: York.
"Jack and I have been trying": ML to Gordon Elliott, 17 August [1962]. MS: McMaster.
"It is still not quite certain": ML to Adele Wiseman, 29 August 1962. MS: York.

168 "I met the other day": MS: York.
ML's affair with Lamming: When I met with George Lamming in Barbados in June 1996, he told me he had met ML at a party given by Binky Marks, the proprietor of The Co-Op Bookstore on Pender Street, in Vancouver; he thought they had perhaps seen one another one further time. Their conversations had been political in nature, centring on their mutual interest in Ghana, which he had visited. He did not recall that their relationship had ever become intimate, but when I asked him to deny statements by ML to the contrary, he

refused to do so on the grounds that it was not his "style" to comment on such matters. I pressed him on this point several times, since, I pointed out, it should be relatively easy—despite his "style"—to state something that had not occurred had indeed not occurred. He refused to make any further statement. ML alleged to many women friends that she had slept with Lamming; shortly before she died, she mentioned her affair with Lamming to her daughter and named him as her lover.

"When I first found out": ML to Don Bailey, 12 February 1972. MS: University of Toronto.

"was a crucial": ML Journal, 27 October 1986. MS: McMaster.

170 "very revolutionary"; "although Jack": ML to Adele Wiseman, 5 August 1962. MS: York.

"I suppose I should say": *Dance*, 158.

Chapter Eleven

172 "My real concern": ML to Adele Wiseman, 5 August 1962. MS: York.

173 Mona and ML's affair: Interview with Mona Meredith, May 1995.

"Well, to begin": ML to Adele Wiseman, undated. MS: York.

"When I first came": ML to Adele Wiseman, 16 January 1969. MS: York.

174 "I almost seemed": *Dance*, 159-60.

"She told me": *Dance*, 129.

"We have landed": ML to Adele Wiseman, 28 October 1962. MS: York.

175 "I have just been": ML to Adele Wiseman, 29 October 1962. MS: York.

176 "Right now": ML to Gordon Elliott, 1 November 1962. MS: McMaster.

"initial elation": ML to Adele Wiseman, 25 November 1962. MS: York.

"It may not be everybody's"; "yours truly quaffed:" ML to Adele Wiseman, 11 December 1962. MS: York.

177 "Sex": ML to Al Purdy, 2 July 1968. MS: Queen's.

"lower than a snake's belly": ML to Adele Wiseman, 11 February 1963. MS: York.

178 "I think this is because"; "everything must be"; "Also, as with suicide": ML to Adele Wiseman, 11 February 1963. MS: York.
"But I knew": *Dance*, 162.
"I don't think I ever": ML to Al Purdy, 27 April 1967. Lennox, 21-22.
179 "I mourned her": ML to Ernest Buckler, 30 August 1974. Wainwright, 28.
"Probably they won't": ML to Gordon Elliott, 1 November 1962. MS: McMaster.
180 "I am sure": ML to Gordon Elliott, 10 March 1963. MS: McMaster.
"I do not feel": ML to Gordon Elliott, 29 April 1963. MS: McMaster.
"man in a million"; "sweated blood": ML to Adele Wiseman, 12 June 1963. MS: York.
"skidding": ML to Adele Wiseman, 18 February 1963. MS: York.
181 "unexpectedly appealing"; "Later, Alan": ML to Adele Wiseman, 18 February 1963. MS: York.
"Re: my story": 2 December 1964. MS: Macmillan Archive, Basingstoke. This story was published in *Chatelaine* in 1967.
182 "At the moment": ML to Jack McClelland, 17 January 1963. MS: McMaster.
Alan Maclean and Hagar: ML to Adele Wiseman, 14 February 1963. MS: York.
183 "Then I feel like": ML to Adele Wiseman, 18 February 1963. MS: York.
184 "father-type husband": ML to Adele Wiseman, 8 March 1965. MS: York.
"P.S. I apologize": ML to Gordon Elliott, 29 April 1963. MS: McMaster.
"Can you bear": ML to Adele Wiseman, 17 August 1963. MS: York.
"It seems to me": ML to Jack McClelland, 29 June 1963. MS: McMaster.
185 "in advance": Alfred A. Knopf to Jack McClelland, 3 July 1963. MS: McMaster.
"While I could not": Jack McClelland to Alfred A. Knopf, 5 July 1963. MS: Knopf Archive, University of Texas.

"This is simply": Jack McClelland to Herbert Weinstock, 10 April 1959. MS: McClelland & Stewart Archive, McMaster.

186 "whoever takes her up": Alfred Knopf to Jack McClelland, 3 July 1963. MS: McClelland & Stewart Archive, McMaster.

"More often than not": Jack McClelland to ML, 5 July 1963. MS copy: McMaster.

187 "I am sorry to be nasty": ML to Jack McClelland, 8 July 1963. MS: McMaster.

Blanche Knopf: Blanche Knopf to Josephine Rogers (Willis Wing Agency), 19 February 1963. MS: Texas. Patrick Gregory's comments are included in a letter from Alfred Knopf to Jack McClelland, 11 June 1963; MS: Texas.

188 Reports on ML: All these reports are in the Margaret Laurence folder in the Knopf Archive at the University of Texas.

189 "Well, we are taking": Alfred A. Knopf to Jack McClelland, 15 August 1963. MS: Texas.

Alfred Knopf and the geography of *The Stone Angel*: MS: Texas.

190 "I don't think": Jack McClelland to Alfred A. Knopf, 21 August 1963. MS: McMaster.

"This title": ML to Jack McClelland, 26 August 1963. MS: McMaster.

dispute over title: See ML to Jack McClelland, 27 September 1963. MS: McMaster.

"frightened the hell": ML to Adele Wiseman, 8 April 1963. MS: York.

abandons work on novel about Stacey: ML to George Woodcock, 11 April 1978 (MS: Queen's): "An odd thing—before I began writing *A Jest of God*, I started *The Fire-Dwellers* and got about 100 pp done and realized I had to write *A Jest of God* first—the other just wasn't happening the way it should, so I threw out what I'd done on *The Fire-Dwellers* and did *A Jest of God* first."

191 "One's writing": ML to Gordon Elliott, 29 April 1963. MS: McMaster.

"to the same house": ML to Adele Wiseman, 1 October 1963. MS: York.

the Richler party: Interview with Robert and Audrey Weaver, July 1995; information from Mordecai and Florence Richler.

192 "The blankets": "The Wild Blue Yonder," in *Heart of a Stranger*, 135.

193 "Having spent a month": ML to Jack McClelland, 10 December 1963. MS: McMaster.
"It was strange": ML to Adele Wiseman, 18 December 1963. MS: York.

Chapter Twelve

195 "The day": *Dance*, 167.
"it has five bedrooms": ML to Jack McClelland, 10 December 1963. MS: McMaster.
196 "Calcutta itself": ML to Ethel Wilson, 21 January 1964. MS: University of British Columbia.
197 "What I appear": ML to Adele Wiseman, 17 January 1964. MS: York.
198 "At one side": MS: McMaster.
199 "no one in this area": ML to Jack McClelland, 20 July 1970. MS: McMaster.
"The presence of my children": *Dance*, 170.
200 "I feel somehow lonely": ML to Nadine Jones, 29 May 1966. MS: Nadine Jones.
"Once got laid": ML to Al Purdy, 3 January 1970. MS: Queen's.
"I would stop writing": *Dance*, 170.
201 "Are you happy": ML to Adele Wiseman, 15 March 1964. MS: York.
"practically broke"; "absurdly optimistic": ML to Adele Wiseman, 10 April 1964. MS: York.
"Why be half-classical": *Heart of a Stranger*, 19.
202 "We decided": ML to Adele Wiseman, 25 June 1964. MS: York.
"I don't want him": ML to Adele Wiseman, 15 March 1964. MS: York.
"He decided to sell": ML to Adele Wiseman, 10 July 1964. MS: York.
"I was interested": ML to Jane Rule, 24 August 1964. MS: University of British Columbia.
203 "Things are going along": ML to Adele Wiseman, 24 August 1964. MS: York.
"We were fortunate": ML to Gordon Elliott, 17 June 1964. MS: McMaster.

204 "the real world": ML to Adele Wiseman, 19 November 1964. MS: York.
Mary Renault: ML file: McClelland & Stewart Archive. MS: McMaster.
"a major best-seller": Jack McClelland to ML, 9 November 1964. MS: McMaster.
205 "He is the person": ML to Adele Wiseman, 2 January 1963. MS: York.
extremes of power and weakness: Valuable comments on this aspect of *The Stone Angel* can be found in Helen Buss, "Margaret Laurence's Dark Lovers," *Atlantis* 11 (Spring 1986), 97-107; Joan Coldwell, "Hagar as Meg Merrilies, The Homeless Gypsy," *Journal of Canadian Fiction* 27 (Summer 1980), 92-100; Constance Rooke, "A Feminist Reading of *The Stone Angel*," *Canadian Literature* 93 (Summer 1982), 26-41.
207 "Man, what sophistication": ML to Adele Wiseman, 10 July 1964. MS: York.
"as relaxed"; "I've been going": ML to Adele Wiseman, 10 December 1964. MS: York.
"I know the character": ML to Adele Wiseman, 31 December 1964. MS: York.
"God damn it": ML to Adele Wiseman, 31 December 1964. MS: York.
208 "kind of feeling": ML to Jane Rule, 1 January 1965. MS: University of British Columbia.
contemporary man and the novel: ML to Robert Hallstead, 15 January 1965. MS: University of Winnipeg.
"I suppose": ML to Adele Wiseman, 24 January 1965. MS: York.
209 "What scares the hell": ML to Adele Wiseman, 17 August 1965. MS: York.
"Have personal dilemmas": ML to Adele Wiseman, 6 September 1965. MS: York.
210 "absolute nightmare"; "Last year" ML to Nadine Jones, 16 January 1966. MS: Nadine Jones.
"I could not help feeling": ML to Adele Wiseman, 8 March 1965. MS: York.
"Do you know": ML to Adele Wiseman, 7 February 1965. MS: York.

211 Catherine Milne: Interview with Pennie Jamieson, May 1995.
"I care a very great deal": ML to Gordon Elliott, 12 March 1965. MS: McMaster.
"After about three years": ML to Jack McClelland, 29 March 1965. MS: McMaster.
212 "I don't really know": Jack McClelland to ML, 29 March 1965. MS: McMaster.
"All the men": ML to Adele Wiseman, 5 April 1965. MS: York.
"Interesting that you": ML to Gordon Elliott, 12 April 1965. MS: McMaster.
213 "she didn't see": ML to Nadine Jones, 11 May 1965. MS: Nadine Jones.
"It has been a rather": ML to Nadine Jones, 11 May 1965. MS: Nadine Jones.
"When I was in Scotland": ML to Jack McClelland, 9 September 1965. MS: McMaster. In her letters from this time, ML states she was going to Scotland alone. However, Jocelyn and David did accompany her, a fact that can be ascertained by consulting the essay, "Road from the Isles," published in *Maclean's* on 2 May 1966 and reprinted in *Heart of a Stranger.*
214 "had been in the deepest possible": *Heart of a Stranger*, 148.
"Scotland had become": *Heart of a Stranger*, 155. During the Easter holiday of 1969, ML took David and a friend of his to Scotland. During that visit, they saw the battle-site of Culloden, "and I told the boys all about the '45 [Rebellion]—any tour with me is a tour of history, absolutely inaccurate but dramatic as hell!" ML to Don Cameron, 12 May 1969. Wainwright, 49.
215 "Have you seen": ML to Adele Wiseman, 17 May 1965. MS: York.
"bull-dozing kind": ML to Adele Wiseman, 27 June 1965. MS: York.
"She kept saying": ML to Robert Hallstead, 21 July 1965. MS: University of Winnipeg.
ML's favourite scene in *The Stone Angel*: See ML to Robert Hallstead, 26 April 1965. MS: University of Winnipeg.
216 "Then he opens"; "This knowing": *The Stone Angel*, 291-2.
"otherwise I would": ML to Adele Wiseman, 17 August 1965. MS: York.

217 "HALLELUJAH!": ML to Jack McClelland, 20 October 1965. MS: McMaster.
"I know what you mean": ML to Nadine Jones, 10 December 1965. MS: Nadine Jones.

Chapter Thirteen

219 "managing to survive"; "He turned out": ML to Nadine Jones, 16 January 1966. MS: Nadine Jones.
"So I got": ML to Gordon Elliott, 17 January 1966. MS: McMaster.
220 "very nice": ML to Gordon Elliott, 17 January 1966. MS: McMaster.
"job of editing"; "It would have been": ML to Nadine Jones, 16 January 1966. MS: Nadine Jones.
"slogging along": ML to Nadine Jones, 16 January 1966. MS: Nadine Jones.
"After about 4 months": ML to Adele Wiseman, 16 January 1966. MS: York.
221 "Perhaps the most": *Long Drums and Cannons*, 10.
"The best of these"; "Much as they": *Long Drums and Cannons*, 203.
"rather amateurish": *Dance*, 153.
222 "I'm giving up": ML to Adele Wiseman, 20 February 1966. MS: York.
"I'm giving up my bedsitter in Hampstead": ML to Adele Wiseman, 13 March 1967. MS: York.
"I decided": ML to Adele Wiseman, 11 April 1967. MS: York.
"own or someone"; "Of course, with me": ML to Adele Wiseman, 27 April 1966. MS: York.
223 "Okay, guys"; "laden down with": *Dance*, 175.
"We've just returned": ML to Jack McClelland, 27 April 1966. MS: McMaster.
224 "Adele, this week": ML to Adele Wiseman, 29 May 1966. MS: York.
225 "a brief but extremely": ML to Nadine Jones, 18 June 1966. MS: Nadine Jones.
"I forgot": ML to Adele Wiseman, 31 May 1966. MS: York.

226 "I am homesick": MS: McMaster.
"I am quite willing": ML to Jack McClelland, 17 June 1966. MS: McMaster.
228 "I don't look old": *A Jest of God*, 23.
"She sees only his body": *A Jest of God*, 25.
229 "I will be light": *A Jest of God*, 209.
Rachel as a Sleeping Beauty: ML's favourite critical piece on *A Jest of God* was George Bowering's "That Fool of a Fear: Notes on *A Jest of God*," *Canadian Literature* 50 (Autumn 1971), 41-56. Also excellent is Helen Buss's, *Mother and Daughter Relationships in the Manawaka World of Margaret Laurence*, *English Literary Studies* 34 (Victoria: University of Victoria Press, 1985).
230 "The way I feel": MS: York.
"I was only there a week": ML to Jack McClelland, 9 July 1966. MS: McMaster.
"I had visions": "The Wild Blue Yonder," in *Heart of a Stranger*, 137.
231 "Please cable": MS: McMaster.
"suit HIS plans": ML to Nadine Jones, 18 June 1966. MS: Nadine Jones.
"When McClelland": ML to Adele Wiseman, 23 October 1966. MS: York.
"began in nightmare fashion": *Dance*, 178.
232 "I fell"; "I sashayed": *Dance*, 179.
"Chris, it's me": *Dance*, 181.
233 "A reviewer": *Dance*, 181.
"She didn't": 24 March 1967. MS: York.
Holiday: She had previously published three pieces in that magazine: "The Very Best Intentions" (November 1964), "The Epic Love of Elmii Bonderii" (November 1965), and "Sayonara, Agamemnon" (January 1966).
Nadine's complaints: Interview with Nadine Jones, April 1995.
234 "I can't bear": Interview with Mildred Musgrove, June 1995.
"fuck": Interview with Jack McClelland, July 1995.
235 "crazy"; "and looked": ML to Al Purdy, 9 December 1968. Lennox, 108.
236 "Woodward's agent": *Dance*, 181.

Jamal: ML to Adele Wiseman, 23 October 1966. MS: York.
"Oh, I don't see": ML to Gordon Elliott, 15 November 1966. MS: McMaster.

Chapter Fourteen

237 "We only got home": ML to Jack McClelland, 18 January 1967. MS: McMaster.
238 "more or less": *Dance*, 183.
239 "I wouldn't have minded"; "You can't be worried": ML to Adele Wiseman, 13 March 1967. MS: York.
"The man with whom"; "Why didn't you"; "I've been working"; "he at least": ML to Adele Wiseman, 9 April 1967. MS: York.
240 "Jack and I have decided": ML to Gordon Elliott, 13 April 1967. MS: McMaster.
"comes here": ML to Gordon Elliott, 26 April 1967. MS: Gordon Elliott.
"was just another admirer": Al Purdy to ML, 10 December 1966. Lennox, 3.
"Owing to one of": ML to Al Purdy, 16 January 1967. Lennox, 4.
241 Northrop Frye: ML to Jane Rule, 20 January 1967. MS: University of British Columbia.
"I'm still attempting": ML to Al Purdy, 19 February 1967. Lennox, 11.
242 "it staggers along": ML to Al Purdy, 16 January 1967. Lennox, 4.
"In the end": ML to Adele Wiseman, 9 April 1967. MS: York.
"I suppose I feel": ML to Adele Wiseman, 9 April 1967. MS: York.
"It makes me laugh": ML to Jack McClelland, 5 May 1967. MS: McMaster.
243 "tense that my": ML to Adele Wiseman, 17 May 1967. MS: York.
"psycho-somatic business": ML to Adele Wiseman, 2 May 1967. MS: York.
"The book is": ML to Jane Rule, 6 June 1967. MS: University of British Columbia.

244 Sinclair Ross: Despite this reservation, ML outlined in a letter to Adele Wiseman of 11 September 1967 (MS: York) the enormous admiration she had for Jim Ross's achievements: "have just finished writing Introduction to Sinclair Ross's short stories, for New Canadian Library. The stories all hang together so much—and in the end they reveal a prairie ethic that is positively frightening—the man has to prove absolutely strong in his own eyes; the woman has to endure all, silently. Impossible standards, and so people break down. Reading the stories, I felt such a sense of connection with the characters, even though they were in an era slightly before my adulthood. But I know them pretty well. The men who can't turn to their wives for comfort, in time of disaster, and so turn—I joke not—to their horses. The stories are all of a piece, and thank goodness they are coming out as a collection at last. Don't suppose Jim intended it that way, but within the era and that idiom, he has portrayed an entire people, their spiritual goals, their vulnerabilities. He really doesn't have to worry about whether he ever does anything more. He's done it. Not possible to communicate this to him, though."

"I've felt": ML to Jane Rule, 6 June 1967. MS: University of British Columbia.

245 Margaret Atwood: ML to Jane Rule, 6 June 1967. MS: University of British Columbia.

"enormous man": ML to Adele Wiseman, 6 June 1967. MS: York.

"I was surprised": ML to Jack McClelland, 23 June 1967. MS: McMaster.

246 "My kids": ML to Al Purdy, 6 June 1967. Lennox, 28.

"some female Jacob"; "A lot of"; "The character was": ML to Adele Wiseman, 21 June 1967. MS: York.

"A pyromaniac": ML to Adele Wiseman, 29 June 1967. MS: York.

247 "How can I ever"; "But do you think": ML to Adele Wiseman, 29 June 1967. MS: York.

"I am petrified": ML to Adele Wiseman, 21 September 1967. MS: York.

248 "Actually, I feel like hell": ML to Adele Wiseman, 27 September 1967. MS: York.

"to get across"; "The attempt to deal": ML to Al Purdy, 6 June 1967. Lennox, 28.
"breakaway"; "Visualized the outer": ML to Marjory Whitelaw, 11 October 1967. MS: York.
249 "The buildings": *The Fire-Dwellers*, 14-15.
250 "Stacey looks at": *The Fire-Dwellers*, 8.
"How can any woman": Betty Friedan, "The Feminine Mystique," *Feminism in Our Time*, ed. Miriam Schneir. (New York: Vintage Books, 1994), 66.
Betty Friedan: On 10 January 1971, ML told Margaret Atwood: "I remember refusing to read *The Feminine Mystique* by Betty Friedan, some years ago, because I thought the novel which was brewing might be kind of related, and I thought the reading of a whole lot of stuff which might agree but was doing it from the journalistic angle, *not* fiction (which tries to approach by being, not talking) might screw me up." Wainwright, 3.
251 Marshall McLuhan: See ML's comment on McLuhan in her letter to the Camerons, 21 October 1967. Wainwright, 44.
"Come on": *The Fire-Dwellers*, 86-7.
252 "novel must": ML to the Camerons, 21 October 1967. Wainwright, 44.
"Will the fires": *The Fire-Dwellers*, 280.
"She feels the city": *The Fire-Dwellers*, 281.
lack of closure: Excellent evaluations of *The Fire-Dwellers* can be found in Mathew Martin, "Dramas of Desire in Margaret Laurence's *A Jest of God*, *The Fire-Dwellers*, and *The Diviners*," *Studies in Canadian Literature* 19, Volume 1 (1994), 58-71; Miriam Packer, "The Dance of Life: *The Fire-Dwellers*," *Journal of Canadian Fiction* 27 (1980), 124-31; and Jamie S. Scott, "Fantasy, Nostalgia and the Courage to Be in Margaret Laurence's *The Fire-Dwellers*," *Commonwealth Novel in English* 4, Volume 1 (spring 1991), 89-101.
"Our lawn": *Dance*, 188-9.
253 "wisdom must be": *Jason's Quest*, 155.
"a frivolous": ML to Adele Wiseman, 11 September 1967. MS: York.
"this process": ML to Al Purdy, 11 December 1967. Lennox, 75.

"I don't write": ML to Al Purdy, 5 January 1968. Lennox, 82.
"in the greybearded": ML to Al Purdy, 2 July 1968. MS: Queen's.
254 "settled"; "kind of renaissance": ML to Adele Wiseman, 19 February 1968. MS: York.
"Got home this morning": ML to Alan Maclean, undated. MS: James King.
255 "not downcast": ML to Alan Maclean, undated. MS: James King.
"First draft": ML to Jack McClelland, 12 March 1968. MS: McMaster.
"The odd thing": ML to Jane Rule, 14 March 1968. MS: University of British Columbia.
256 "post-novel depression": ML to Adele Wiseman, 16 April 1968. MS: York.
"It's not autobiographical": ML to Al Purdy, 24 June 1968. MS: Queen's.
"I didn't pick": ML to Adele Wiseman, 3 September 1968. MS: York.
"God, Adele": ML to Adele Wiseman, 16 April 1968. MS: York.
"hell of a scare": ML to Adele Wiseman, 30 June 1968. MS: York.
257 "the whole damn thing": ML to Adele Wiseman, 4 April 1968. MS: York.
"godforsaken novel": ML to Adele Wiseman, 29 May 1968. MS: York.
"I guess I have": ML to Adele Wiseman, 29 November 1968. MS: York.
"chip in": ML to Jack McClelland, 26 July 1968. MS: McMaster.
"expressing things": ML to Adele Wiseman, 3 September 1968. MS: York.
258 "the main cry": ML to Adele Wiseman, 3 September 1968. MS: York.
259 "The oddest things": ML to Adele Wiseman, 9 December 1968. MS: York. "Manawaka" made its first appearance in "The Land of Our Fathers." See p. 40.

Chapter Fifteen

260 "HERE I AM": ML to Al Purdy, 10 January 1969. Lennox, 120.
Toronto Daily Star: 20 June 1970. The reviewer was Diana Goldsborough.
"I've only got": ML to Adele Wiseman, 1 January 1969. MS: York.
261 "He is as real": ML to Adele Wiseman, 26 January 1969. MS: York.

262 Vanessa MacLeod stories: 1963: "The Sound of the Singing," *Winter's Tales* 9 (1963); 1964: "To Set Our House in Order," *Ladies Home Journal*; "A Bird in the House," *Atlantic Monthly*; 1965: "The Mask of the Bear," *Winter's Tales* 11; 1966: "The Loons" (first published as "The Crying of the Loons"), *Atlantic Advocate*; 1967: "Horses of the Night," *Chatelaine*; "Nanuk," *Argosy*. The eighth, concluding story, "Jericho's Brick Battlements" was the only narrative first published in *A Bird in the House*.

"The narrative is": "Time and the Narrative Voice," *Margaret Laurence: The Writer and Her Critics*, ed. W.H. New (Toronto: McGraw-Hill Ryerson, 1977), 158-9.

263 "That house": *A Bird in the House*, 11.

"I had feared": *A Bird in the House*, 191.

264 "Instead of writing": ML to Al Purdy, 6 June 1968. Lennox, 87.

"They got just about": ML to Jack McClelland, 6 April 1969. MS: McMaster.

The Canadian reviews: ML to Gordon Elliott, 17 May 1969. MS: McMaster.

265 "enormous male hostility"; "this is so astonishing": ML to Adele Wiseman, 15 May 1969. MS: York.

266 "Personal troubles": ML to Gordon Elliott, 23 May 1969. MS: McMaster.

267 Jack's wound: Silver Donald Cameron, phone interview. September 1996.

"I'm in better shape": ML to Al Purdy, 24 May 1969. Lennox, 138-9.

268 Judith Jones's comments: MS: Texas.

269 "Upon further reflection"; "I'm terribly sorry"; "I have an awful feeling": MS: Texas.

270 "John Cushman and I"; Jones to Gottlieb: MS: Texas.

"worked myself into": ML to Adele Wiseman, 12 July 1969. MS: York.

271 "It is quite simple": ML to Adele Wiseman, 27 May 1969. MS: York.

272 "Freudian accident": ML to Al Purdy, 19 August 1969. MS: Queen's.

274 "Yes, I'll recover"; "—so when chips": ML to Al Purdy, 20 December 1969. MS: Queen's.

275 "focussed my mind": ML to Adele Wiseman, 30 December 1969. MS: York.
ML as unfit parent: The magistrate's remark must have come after this exchange between him and ML: "Do you take care of [David] when he is not at school?" he asked. Her reply: "He does not go to boarding school. He goes to day school and lives at home and I take care of him all the time." Since ML had been in Canada during the autumn of 1969, her statement was not literally true. See ML to Al Purdy, 20 December 1969. MS: Queen's.
"I took": ML to Adele Wiseman, 30 December 1969. MS: York.
Information on ML's suicide attempt comes from Jocelyn Laurence and Sandy Cameron.

Chapter Sixteen

280 leave-taking: Phone conversation with Ken Roberts, May 1996.
281 "You will understand": ML to Michelle Tisseyre, 9 June 1977. MS: Michelle Tisseyre.
282 "That was Gabrielle": Phone conversation with Ken Roberts, May 1996.
283 "humorous that I am": ML to Al Purdy, September 1969. MS: Queen's.
"I did one": ML to Al Purdy, September 1969. MS: Queen's.
"LEAVE ME ALONE": ML to Al Purdy, 11 February 1970. MS: Queen's.
"Listen to how": *Dance*, 194.
284 "the kids": ML to Al Purdy, 11 February 1970. MS: Queen's.
"hard as nails": ML to Al Purdy, 11 February 1970. MS: Queen's.
Don Bailey: Any reader of Don Bailey, *Memories of Margaret: My Friendship with Margaret Laurence* (Toronto: Prentice-Hall, 1989), should take into account the caveats sounded by Donez Xiques in her excellent review of the book in *The American Review of Canadian Studies* 22 (Spring 1992), 113-7. She calls into account the reliability

of the information supplied in the book; she also notes that it is essentially autobiographical in nature and that ML is a minor character in the badly misnamed book.

"He has begun": ML to Jane Rule, 26 January 1970. MS: University of British Columbia.

"as Jack McClelland": ML to Don Bailey, 26 January 1970. MS: University of Toronto.

"created a small fortress": Don Bailey, *Memories of Margaret*, 124.

285 "I'm honoured": Don Bailey, *Memories of Margaret*, 57.

"I damn well": ML to Al Purdy, 24 November 1969. MS: Queen's.

"The talk": ML to the Camerons, 27 September 1969. Wainwright, 51.

"I really wanted": ML to Hugh MacLennan, 16 February 1970. MS: Queen's.

286 "My daughter": ML to Al Purdy, 1 February 1970. MS: Queen's.

"Came back today": ML to Al Purdy, 3 January 1970. MS: Queen's.

"Learned that the brief encounter": ML to Al Purdy, 21 January 1970. MS: Queen's.

287 "The owners": ML to Al Purdy, September 1969. MS: Queen's.

"2 reasons": ML to the Camerons, 11 October 1967. Wainwright, 43.

288 Granville Hicks: *Saturday Review*, 13 June 1964, 25-6.

Honor Tracy: *New Republic*, 20 June 1964, 19-20.

Honor Tracy: *The New York Times Book Review*, 3 August 1969, 30.

"Maybe, I am going": ML to Al Purdy, 14 October 1969. MS: Queen's.

"I have bought": ML to Al Purdy, 5 November 1969. MS: Queen's.

289 "Wow! What reading!": ML to Jack McClelland, 9 April 1970. MS: McMaster.

"I had long passionate": ML to Jack McClelland, 21 January 1970. MS: McMaster.

290 "So Canada": ML to Jack McClelland, 21 January 1970. MS: McMaster.

"takes Irving": ML to Al Purdy, 19 March 1970. MS: Queen's.

291 "He had meant": ML to Al Purdy, 19 March 1970. MS: Queen's.

"a hell of a lot": ML to Al Purdy, 5 December 1971. MS: Queen's.

"Callaghan Fils": ML to Al Purdy, 5 December 1971. MS: Queen's.

"in a state": ML to Al Purdy, 3 September 1971. Lennox, 226.
"Low Commissioner": See ML to Will Ready, 8 February 1973. Wainwright, 162.
"Did I mention"; "I admire her poetry": MS: Queen's.
"I was talking": ML to Ernest Buckler, 13 November 1974. Wainwright, 32.
292 "I am really": MS: University of Toronto.
"pissed": Interview with Mordecai Richler, September 1996.
first honourary degree: Three years earlier, she had been made a Honorary Fellow of United College, the first woman and the youngest person to be granted this distinction. Subsequent honorary degrees were given to ML by Trent (1972), Dalhousie (1972), University of Toronto (1972), Carleton (1974), Brandon (1975), University of Western Ontario (1975), Queen's (1975), Mount Allison (1975), Simon Fraser (1977), York (1980), Emmanuel College, Victoria University, University of Toronto (1982).
"Guess what?": ML to Al Purdy, 24 April 1970. MS: Queen's.
293 "I enjoy talking": ML to Al Purdy, 22 February 1970. MS: Queen's.
"Last weeks"; "more or less"; "immersed in passionate": ML to Jack McClelland, 20 July 1970. MS: McMaster.
"You don't know": ML to Jack McClelland, 20 July 1970. MS: McMaster.
"he knows": ML to Al Purdy, 5 March 1970. MS: Queen's.
294 "while those people"; "shaking with rage": ML to Al Purdy, 5 March 1970. MS: Queen's.
"see their dad": ML to Don Bailey, 12 August 1970. MS: University of Toronto.
"into the loony bin": ML to Al Purdy, 3 September 1971. Lennox, 228.
"He will be here": ML to Adele Wiseman, 14 October 1971. MS: York.
"a very disturbing": ML to Harold Horwood, 29 August 1972. MS: University of Calgary.
296 "I've decided": 4 September 1970. Lennox, 185.
"The only thing": ML to Alan and Robin Maclean, 3 September 1970. MS: James King.
"It doesn't matter": ML to Don Bailey, 12 August 1970. MS: University of Toronto.

297 "Feel depressed": ML to Al Purdy, 14 August 1970. Lennox, 178.
"Have had a terrible": ML to Jack McClelland, 3 May 1971. MS: McMaster.
"You know something?": ML to Jack McClelland, 6 April 1971. MS: McMaster.
"I suppose": ML to Don Bailey, 12 August 1970. MS: McMaster.
298 "Trouble is"; "fictional situation"; "followed a"; "detailed social"; "If I don't": ML to Al Purdy, 13 October 1970. Lennox, 194-6.
"*existing* out there" and all subsequent references on this page: ML to Al Purdy, 22 March 1971. MS: Queen's.
299 "Things are changing": ML to Adele Wiseman, 1 May 1971. MS: York.
"why don't I"; "You could make": ML to Al Purdy, 3 September 1971. MS: Queen's.
300 "I am pretty disenchanted": ML to Adele Wiseman, 28 October 1970. MS: York.
"Look, you're right"; "Personally, I think": ML to Al Purdy, 3 April 1971. MS: Queen's.
"No visitors": *Dance*, 199.
"Have had various hassles": ML to Adele Wiseman, 24 February 1972. MS: York.
301 "an aide": *Dance*, 200.
"it is likely": ML to Ernest Buckler, 23 December 1974. Wainwright, 33.
"Personally": ML to John Metcalf, 28 March 1972. MS: University of Calgary.
302 "has to be the most": ML to Adele Wiseman, 18 December 1972. MS: York.
"I wonder why": ML to Al Purdy, 30 December 1972. Lennox, 262.
303 Little girl from Sandy Bay reserve: Wes McAmmond in conversation with Greta Coger on 25 July 1984. Typescript provided by the interviewer.
Citations from *A Bird in the House*: 117, 114, 120, 116, 118-9.
305 "means of getting": ML to Harold Horwood, 14 November 1972. Wainwright, 96.

Chapter Seventeen

306 "Good ... to see Elmcot": ML to Adele Wiseman, 3 November 1972. MS: York.

307 "longer than": ML to Jane Rule, 12 December 1972. MS: University of British Columbia.

"Do you know": ML to Mary Adachi, 3 November 1972. MS: Mary Adachi.

"narrative present": ML to Jane Rule, 12 December 1972. MS: University of British Columbia.

308 "I have, I think": ML to John Metcalf, 26 January 1973. Wainwright, 132-3.

"MY NOVEL IS FINISHED": ML to Al Purdy, 3 February 1973. Lennox, 269.

"withdrawal symptoms"; "this is the end": ML to Al Purdy, 3 February 1973. Lennox, 270.

309 "I'm dealing": ML to Margaret Atwood, 18 February 1973. MS: University of Toronto.

"Ambiguity is everywhere": ML to Margaret Atwood, 18 February 1973. MS: University of Toronto.

"ALL RIGHT"; "get it all": ML to Jane Rule, 21 February 1973. MS: University of British Columbia.

310 "to avoid handing over": ML to Jane Rule, 12 March 1973. MS: University of British Columbia.

"I have already sold": ML to Adele Wiseman, 23 April 1973. MS: York.

311 "Well, that is 3 times": ML to Al Purdy, 21 April 1973. Lennox, 277. Margaret finally moved back to Canada in 1974, not 1973. She was able to avoid the nefarious taxes because the sale of Elmcot took place in 1973, allowing her to cease her legal residency in England at the end of the year. In 1973, she also purchased a house in Lakefield, near Peterborough, although she did not reside there until March 1974.

"I realized": *Dance*, 201-2.

312 "I may seem": ML to Jack McClelland, 21 March 1973. MS: McMaster.

"My American editor": ML to Adele Wiseman, 7 June 1973. MS: York.

"Judith Jones": *Dance*, 198.

313 Since no early draft: However, the letters from Jones and McClelland to ML do provide a great deal of information about the draft originally sent to the publishers. Further information can be reconstructed by consulting ML's working notes on *The Diviners* (York); these papers include ML's copy of Jones's list (made *after* her five-hour meeting with ML) of suggested changes.

314 "MAJOR CHANGES": In the Knopf Archive (University of Texas), there are four pages of further revisions subsequently made by ML and sent to Judith Jones.

"Let me start": Jack McClelland to ML, 12 June 1973. MS: McMaster. On 28 August 1973, Judith Jones told Jack McClelland (MS: Texas): "You will see that there has been some major surgery performed—all for the good, I'm convinced, and the fact that Margaret feels the novel is much the better for it reinforces the conviction.... Your long letter to Margaret was wonderful, Jack, and a great help to me because we saw eye to eye on just about everything.... I hope we can all get together some time to celebrate the launching of this book. I am very excited about its possibilities and I feel strongly that Margaret has brought together some very powerful elements here and created a tremendously moving and dramatic story."

315 "I am enclosing": ML to Jack McClelland, 4 July 1973. MS: McMaster.

"Clearing" Elmcot: The only extant typescripts of the novels are at McMaster because the University librarian Will Ready, a friend and admirer of ML, purchased them from her at the various times the novels were completed. ML, who much appreciated the cash each purchase generated, was nevertheless extremely uncomfortable with anyone seeing such material.

"I went to bed": *Dance*, 204.

316 "Mum, I give": *Dance*, 205.

"I want an old": *Dance*, 205-6.

317 "used to be": ML to Al Purdy, 19 January 1974. MS: Queen's.

318 "8 Regent Street": ML to Al Purdy, 22 March 1974. MS: Queen's.

319 "She was the first": *Lakefield Chronicle*, 13 March 1986.

320 "In all the years": Don Bailey, *Memories of Margaret* (Toronto: Prentice-Hall, 1989), 204.

322 "very sensitive": ML to Jack McClelland, 7 October 1973. MS: York.
"We had a gathering"; "No refreshments"; "small group": ML to June Callwood, 30 August 1979. MS: TWUC Archive, McMaster.

323 "I've liked being": ML to Jack McClelland, 7 October 1973. MS: McMaster.
"The conference": ML to Jack McClelland, 6 November 1973. MS: McMaster.

324 "The thing that one": ML to the Camerons, 22 November 1968. Wainwright, 47.
quandary: Inclusion and exclusion were certainly the big issues facing the Membership Committee, as can be seen in ML's letter to John Metcalf of 23 November 1973 (MS: University of Calgary): "Re: Membership Committee, how are we going to organize things? I guess if a member is suggested and wants to join, we communicate by mail, eh? I mean, to all members of the committee. It may be quite a lot of letters for awhile. Do you have any secretarial help? I don't. I don't imagine you do, either. Well, press on!

"Re: new members—there are some who occur to me as possibilities right away. Do you think we should contact them and suggest that they might like to be members? I think we should. But this needs some working out, I think, John. That is, according to the constitution, we accept or reject all members by majority vote, but of course it seems clear that if a person clearly satisfies the conditions of membership and is not a borderline case, we really don't have the right to say NO. On the other hand, we've all got to say Okay, even if it is really automatic. What, then, should the procedure be? Do we circulate a list of potential members to all the committee—just send out a copy and ask each member the names and then mail it to the next member of the Committee? It would be done on a kind of standard form, it seems to me.... Shouldn't be difficult to work out something that will entail a minimum of work for all of us."

"said nothing": ML to Al Purdy, 22 May 1974. Lennox, 306. Fulford's account confirms the substance of ML's story but makes some crucial points in opposition to her point of view: "I was asked to interview her for the CBC, not debate her. I wanted to get from her the best possible account I could of what, from her point of view, went into the book. To impose my own views, at that stage, would have been offensive (because listeners had not yet had a chance to read the book) and counter-productive. I am aware that she was annoyed with me. I heard about it the same week, from the McClelland & Stewart publicity representative, Patricia Bowles. Patricia told her that she thought my behaviour in the interview purely professional, but Margaret was not appeased. Later she told others she thought I was "duplicitous." Robert Fulford to James King, 18 July 1996.

325 Fulford's reservation about style: However, he does make the crucial point that "the putting-together process is both substance and theme."
The Diviners and autobiography: In a letter of 27 June 1977 to David Williams, ML mentions that *The Diviners* could properly been seen as a spiritual autobiography.
"a character like Morag": ML to Adele Wiseman, 25 January 1974. MS: York.

326 excised passages: Typescript pages 10 and 113. MS: McMaster.
"*They remain shadows*": *The Diviners*, 27.
"Christie is short": *The Diviners*, 44.

327 "Although one does": ML to Adele Wiseman, 10 February 1980. MS: York.
"The thing is": ML to Adele Wiseman, 13 January 1972. MS: York.

329 "I've got my work": *The Diviners*, 12.
"How far could anyone": *The Diviners*, 477.

330 racial mix: ML commented on this aspect of *The Diviners* in a letter to George Woodcock of 12 August 1975 (MS: Queen's). In that book, she told him, she attempted to give the reader a sense of the relationship between history's dispossessed and ancestral myths. She herself saw a clear link between the dispossession of the Scots who emigrated to

Canada and the dispossession of the Métis. "So many parallels, and in so many ways. If I had your grasp of history, and your ability to put down events both movingly and analytically, I'd write about it. As it is, I have to suggest some of these themes through my own medium, fiction."

"Even Milton": ML to Timothy Findley, 8 January 1982. Wainwright, 82.

"I won't quit writing": ML to Ernest Buckler, 30 August 1974. Wainwright, 27.

Chapter Eighteen

331 "it was just": *Dance*, 211.

332 "lined up": *Dance*, 211-2.

333 "comes of having": ML to Harold Horwood, 22 July 1974. Wainwright, 99.

334 "You've struggled": *Dance*, 255.

335 "Please let us hope": ML to Mary Adachi, 21 April 1973. MS: Mary Adachi.

336 "lived at": *Dance*, 213.

"My heavens": Wainwright, 21.

337 "I do not personally": MS: Queen's.

"You've never said": ML to Al Purdy, 29 August 1974. MS: Queen's.

"I'm sorry": ML to Al Purdy, 15 December 1974. MS: Queen's.

338 "a certain amount"; "Then thus goes": ML to Jack McClelland, 11 July 1975. MS: McMaster. Two years later, when Godfrey's new book was published, ML wrote to Purdy on 15 February 1977 (MS: Queen's): "Have you seen his I CHING KANADA? He takes it seriously, and tells people to tell the I Ching according to him. I think now that Dave thinks the truth comes not from God but from Godfrey. As you probably know, he was very nasty re: THE DIVINERS coming out in Bantam Canada edition, and wrote me a very prickly letter. When I replied, saying that I'd agreed only to 2 yrs exclusive rights and 5 yrs total right and that it would come out in 1978 in the NCL, he made no reply.

"About a year ago, I happened to run into him when I was at a meeting with what was then the IPA [Independent Publishers Association], with the union Contract committee, and he came in to the office, and I said to him 'Did you get my letter?' He said 'Yes, but the novel looks pretty funny there, Margaret, it looks *pretty funny*.' I said 'I have two kids to put through university and I do not have an academic salary.' The hell with him. He used me, at one time. Okay, live and learn."

339 "WHY HAD I": ML to Ernest Buckler, 15 February 1975. Wainwright, 33-34.
"Does that say": *The Diviners*, 21.

340 "Let's sleep now": *The Diviners*, 365.
racist sentiments: Bailey, *Memories of Margaret*, 207.

341 "We are having": ML to Malcolm Ross, 14 February 1977. MS: University of Toronto.

342 Alice Munro: She had an extremely different reaction to the situation: "I thought it was a huge joke. And I wrote [ML] a funny letter about it because I thought it was so funny. But she and I, who were both verging on—at least into—middle age, were both rather cautious writers who had difficulty with some scenes, and suddenly we were thought of as being dirty. I thought this was hilarious. It gave me a new lease on life, like being thought a scarlet woman. She was a more serious person than I was, in the sense of her life in the world.... She grew up in a small town. She should have known there's a lot of ill will." Wainwright, 143.
"They got up": ML to Jane Rule, 9 June 1976. MS: University of British Columbia.
"damn near": ML to Al Purdy, 23 August 1976. MS: Queen's.
Huron County: See ML to Hugh MacLennan, 29 January 1979. Wainwright, 116. In a meeting with the county's Board of Education, ML's opponents cited sexually explicit content in *The Diviners* as the primary reason for its removal from the Grade 11 teaching list. The Huron County branch of the Catholic Women's League took the charges against ML one step further calling for *The Diviners* to be

removed from the Grade 13 curriculum. Clarice Dalton, the league spokesperson, admitted to never having read the book, but claimed to have seen excerpts and considered them "dirty" (*The Toronto Star*, 25 April 1978). In August 1978, the Huron County school board voted 9 to 7 to remove *The Diviners* from the Grade 13 curriculum. In 1978, a bakery worker and a Baptist minister initiated a similar campaign against *The Diviners* in the Annapolis Valley; in April 1978, an Etobicoke school board trustee unsuccessfully attempted to have *A Jest of God* banned as a high-school text because of its "swear words" and sexual content (*The Toronto Star*, 28 April 1978).

343 "My first reaction": ML to Jack McClelland, 23 February 1976. MS: McMaster.
"suggesting that they": Jack McClelland to Margaret Laurence, 23 February 1976. MS: McMaster.

344 "I have angered": ML to Al Purdy, 10 August 1976. MS: Queen's.
"Why didn't": ML to Al Purdy, 15 February 1977. Lennox, 340.

345 "Re: my writing": ML to Al Purdy, 15 February 1977. Lennox, 340-1.
Purdy on cessation of friendship with ML: When I asked Purdy about the abrupt but largely unexplained cessation of his correspondence with ML, he told me that his memory of that time was not good and that he had not read—and did not intend to read—John Lennox's edition of his correspondence with ML. Later during our conversation, I suggested that some of the letters not printed by Lennox suggested that his friendship with ML had "trailed off" because of her anger and hurt about his conduct regarding *The Diviners*—and perhaps because he had felt that ML had been "too demanding." He told me that I might well be right in making such an assumption but that I should also emphasize that his friendship with her was never broken. He went on to observe that a great many friendships simply "peter out" over the course of time.

346 "what worries me": ML to John Metcalf, 30 August 1977. Wainwright, 137.
"AREN'T SERIOUS WRITERS": ML to Ernest Buckler, 5 January 1978. Wainwright, 42.

"sensational": ML to Margaret Laurence, 6 August 1976. MS: Budge Wilson.
"And the last man": Bailey, 223.
"after I'd had": ML to Margaret Atwood, 10 January 1971. Wainwright, 2.
347 "I have begun": ML to Will Ready, 17 March 1977. Wainwright, 164.
348 "I suppose": ML to Hubert Evans, 4 July 1980. Wainwright, 71.
"a sense of grace": ML to Hubert Evans, 19 March 1982. Wainwright, 73.
349 "the whole mighty audience": ML to Hubert Evans, 17 February 1977. Wainwright, 69.

CHAPTER NINETEEN

350 "I have done nothing": ML to Al Purdy, 27 June 1977. MS: Queen's.
351 "I want to do": ML to Adele Wiseman, 20 January, 1979. MS: York.
"thinking about": ML to Frank Paci, 5 September 1981. Wainwright, 149.
"My writing": ML to Gabrielle Roy, 3 March 1980. Wainwright, 186.
352 "Work progressing": ML to Adele Wiseman, 14 September 1981. MS: York.
"I hate everything": ML to Adele Wiseman, 20 September 1981. MS: York.
"Have stuck": ML to Adele Wiseman, 22 January 1982. MS: York.
355 "My problem": ML to Frank Paci, 11 February 1981. Wainwright, 147.
"I am not": ML to Andreas Schroeder, 2 February 1981. Wainwright, 193.
356 "I want": Adele Wiseman papers. MS: York.
"Every time": ML to Al Purdy, 28 September 1977. Lennox, 359-60.
357 "As my whole professional": ML to Jack McClelland, 20 May 1980. MS: McMaster.
"Thank God": ML to John Cushman, 2 October 1982. MS: McMaster.
"At the time": ML to Jack McClelland, 16 March 1982. MS: McMaster.
358 "But I really don't": ML to John Metcalf, 12 January 1978. MS: University of Calgary.

359 "As I mentioned": ML to Jack McClelland, 29 May 1978. MS: McMaster

360 "my income": ML to Hugh MacLennan, 4 June 1980. Wainwright, 119.
"It has been": ML to Hubert Evans, 4 July 1980. Wainwright, 71.

361 "When I called": Jennifer Glossop to Jack McClelland, 23 July 1979. MS: McMaster.
"the little book": ML to Jack McClelland, 9 August 1980. MS: McMaster.
"when my kids": ML to Malcolm Ross, 10 August 1980. MS: University of Toronto.

362 "Wow!": ML to Jack McClelland, 4 November 1980. MS: McMaster.
"Somewhat to my": ML to Jack McClelland, 21 May 1981. MS: McMaster. In 1977, she had been given the Periodical Distributors' Award for the mass paperback edition of *A Jest of God*; in 1980, *The Olden Days Coat* won second prize, Canadian Library Association's Best Children's Books of 1979.
"of course has been": undated entry. MS: McMaster.

363 "I do not": Copy in the Adele Wiseman papers. MS: York. On 18 April 1983, while reflecting on her decision to withdraw from public life, she told Malcolm Ross (MS: University of Toronto): "What with The Writers' Union (from which I have reluctantly resigned, mostly because it seemed to me that most union members did not have any sense of an 'independent' union that would pay its own way without government funding ... I have always said 'he who pays the piper calls the tune' and for a *union* that's got to be right, but I'm in a very small minority)."
"I would just": MS: McMaster.

364 "Now we are": MS: McMaster.

366 "immortality stakes": ML to David Williams, 1 June 1981. Wainwright, 211.
Atwood surpassing Laurence: In a talk ("Books That Mattered to Me") given at the Bata Library at Trent University in 1980, ML concluded with special praise for five Canadian novels, four of them published within ten years and by men: Gabrielle Roy's *Bonheur d'occasion*, translated into English as *The Tin Flute* (1947), Rudy

Wiebe's *The Temptations of Big Bear* (1973), Robertson Davies' *Fifth Business* (1970), Timothy Findley's *The Wars* (1977), and Hugh MacLennan's *Voices in Time* (1980).

Atwood and Laurence: When Margaret Atwood learned that ML was dying, she wrote her a much-appreciated letter. In her reply of 13 November 1986, ML told her that she had been "cheering madly for" Atwood and Robertson Davies when they were finalists that year for the Booker Prize. (Wainwright, 9.) To her journal, she had earlier confided her hope that Davies would win the Booker because Atwood, being younger, would have another chance.

367 "Personally, I think": ML to Marian Engel, 1 April 1984. MS: McMaster.

"... the more": ML to Marian Engel, 12 January 1985. MS: McMaster.

"I am in spirit": Journal, 6 October 1986. MS: McMaster.

368 "I find myself": MS: McMaster.

Chapter Twenty

369 "Craft displays": ML to Adele Wiseman, 17 May 1981. MS: York.

"I could hardly": ML to Adele Wiseman, 17 May 1981. MS: York.

370 "Margaret Laurence fans": Undated but 1985.

371 "Death is so strange": ML to Budge Wilson, 9 January 1985. MS: Budge Wilson.

"Of course": Circular letter to friends, 30 January 1985. MS: Louise Kubik.

372 "I decided": ML to Budge Wilson, 9 January 1985. MS: Budge Wilson.

373 "best interviewer": Circular letter to friends, 30 January 1985. MS: Louise Kubik.

"The first thing": Wednesday, June 27, 1984. *Lakefield Chronicle*, 9.

374 "This bugger": Undated. Written on a photocopy of the offending article ML sent to Adele Wiseman.

"for a meeting": ML to Malcolm Ross, 19 November 1985 (circular letter). MS: University of Toronto.

"TO SAY": ML to Louise Kubik, 10 January 1986. MS: Louise Kubik.

375 "was either IT or ME": ML to Louise Kubik, 10 January 1986. MS: Louise Kubik.

"To me": *Dance*, 16. ML had been a staunch supporter of Lutkenhaus in the uproar following the installation of her sculpture (made in 1975 for International Women's Year) at Bloor Street United Church for four weeks in April 1979. Of course, the disapproval heaped on Lutkenhaus reminded ML of her own difficulties with *The Diviners.*

376 guilt: Joan Givner has written a brilliant review-essay ("A Broken Read") stressing the contradictory nature of *Dance* in *Margaret Laurence Review* 2-3, (1992, 1993), 26-30.

"enormous honour": Circular letter, 21 March 1986. MS: University of British Columbia.

377 "Today I am sixty": MS: McMaster. I refer to this unpublished journal many times in the following pages. When an entry is dated, I incorporate this information in the text or in the citation.

378 "I wish Bob"; "My home": Entry for 14 August.

"I pray": Entry for 14 August.

379 "I do not think": Entry for 21 August.

"A lifetime": Entry for 30 August.

380 "One thing ...": Undated entry.

"I have been": MS: Mona Meredith.

"I am DETERMINED": ML to Mona Meredith, 8 September 1986. MS: Mona Meredith.

381 drafts of her memoir: All dates for the various drafts are ML's, as written out by her on the box containing the third draft. The box and typescript are now at McMaster.

"Please forgive me": ML to Adele Wiseman, 12 November 1986. MS: York.

383 "Oh, kid": Interview with Mary Adachi, February 1997.

385 "Ambiguity is": MS: McMaster.

"From all reports": MS: McMaster

389 "She dealt": Malcolm Ross to James King, 30 April 1996. MS: James King.

Index